Other Books by Ann Fagan Ginger

MINIMIZING RACISM IN JURY TRIALS

THE NEW DRAFT LAW:
A MANUAL FOR LAWYERS AND COUNSELORS

CIVIL LIBERTIES DOCKET

CIVIL RIGHTS & LIBERTIES HANDBOOK

HUMAN RIGHTS CASEFINDER:
THE WARREN COURT ERA

THE
RELEVANT
LAWYERS

*Conversations out of court
on their clients, their practice,
their politics, their life style*

EDITED BY

Ann Fagan Ginger

SIMON AND SCHUSTER
New York

All photos by Clarence Towers, San Francisco, except the following: photo of Malcolm Burnstein by Tudor Processing Ltd., London; photo of Allan Brotsky by Allen's Studio, Los Angeles; photo of Mary Kaufman by James Rutledge of the Dayton Journal Herald.

Acknowledgments

To the speakers who contributed their time and ideas to the Tom Paine Summer School of 1970, including several who held meaningful sessions with the students on topics too specialized or far-ranging to be included in this book: Loren Bashin on lay counseling of draft and military clients, Siegfried Hesse on appellate practice, Peter Hunt on being a law clerk, J. Myron Jacobstein on legal research, Donald Jelinek on representing the Alcatraz Indians, Norman Leonard on administrative law, Hal Lipset on private detective work for lawyers, Dennis Roberts on affirmative suits before three-judge federal courts, Barry Williams on workmen's compensation, Elaine Black Yoneda on the International Labor Defense, and Karl Yoneda on the Japanese Relocation Camp experience.

To the Lillian Boehm Foundation for a grant that helped make possible the Tom Paine School, and to the Louis M. Rabinowitz Foundation for a grant that helped in producing the book from the taped sessions.

To the inspired typists who transcribed the tapes and prepared the final copy from a heavily edited messy manuscript: Madeleine Bratt, Christi Fett, Sue Geick, Stephanie Graham, Jean Hom, Jeffrey Loo, Sylvia Paull, Linda Rageh, Linda Richter, Susan Rosen, and Ruth Suzuki.

To the lawyers, students, and critics who contributed ideas and insights to the school and the book: Paul Bates, Mary Lynn Buss, Curt Duerod, Daisy Goodman, Cal Grigsby, Mr. and Mrs. William Jones, Kathleen Kahn, Katharine Lester, Richard Lysle, Al McLeod, John Ratcliff, Al Richmond, Karen and Stefan Rosenzweig, Elizabeth Sklut, Howard Strange, Duke Williams, Jean Yellin, and Sandra Younghans.

To Zipporah Collins, who helped edit the tape transcripts into chapters without destroying the oral flavor, which requires the highest skill. And to Dan Green, of Simon and Schuster, who reminded me, at crucial moments, that this is my book.

Since this book was not so much written as lived, it seems appropriate to mention my husband, James F. Wood, his daughter, Nina Wood, and my sons, Tom and Jim Ginger, for accepting and helping to maintain a home whose cookie jar has usually been filled with ideas. Thanks

5

are also due to Mary Montgomery, who put my house back together every week.

The most basic acknowledgment is to my remarkable parents, Sarah Robinson Fagan and the late Peter Fagan, who taught me most of what I know about thinking, reporting, and asking difficult questions.

*To all the lawyers, clients, and friends who
have tried to teach me what questions to
ask,
   especially the late, great lawyer
      CAROL KING.*

*For all who work to make law relevant
to justice and social change.*

CONTENTS

9

PREFACE

Practicing lawyers do not write books about the law. Occasionally one writes a sort of autobiography that tells part of the truth about the cases he won, and perhaps a little about the cases he lost, but very little about the law itself, or about his life as a whole. Reporters who write best sellers about spectacular trials and charismatic lawyers can provide even less of the total picture of the law and the lawyers. Instead, most books about the law are written by scholars and judges who write "hornbooks" and "restatements" laying out what the law is and should be from their vantage points as salaried employees of educational corporations and government, with some leisure and detachment to ponder the fundamental concepts of our legal system. But they leave out the lawyers, and also the clients.

Political scientists and law professors tend to compile casebooks containing excerpts from United States Supreme Court opinions, stressing the legal principles that allegedly are the sole basis for decision and form a logically consistent system. These books are used to train the next generation of law professors and clerks in what to do if they become Supreme Court justices. They don't tell a lawyer who has just passed the bar examination what to advise his first client to do in municipal court.

This book is by practicing lawyers and was written the only way such a book could be written—from taped conversations. The lawyers were asked to speak to the Tom Paine Summer Law School about significant cases they have handled, emphasizing points that arise frequently in political lawsuits. I started the school to help students answer the practical questions I faced on admission to the bar. I decided to become a lawyer without knowing any lawyers or having any conception of how a lawyer spends his time or pays his bills. I had read books about Clarence Darrow

13

and his client Eugene V. Debs, and had heard my parents discuss grand juries, frame-ups, and injunctions against strikers. I had picked up their historical perspective, their rejection of property ownership as the measure of a person's worth, their disapproval of people seeking to control their relatives through provisions in wills, their belief in buying and selling ideas as well as land and goods.

With this cultural heritage, I entered the pre-law program of the University of Michigan with the idea of learning how to represent unions and the movement for social change. To support myself, I got a part-time job in a typical small-town commercial law firm. As I typed wills and contracts, I quickly concluded that the law as practiced is a dirty business, without the clear-cut victories and villains I had dreamed of.

During this period I read about a famous immigration lawyer, Carol King of New York, and I wrote to her concerning my prospects for becoming a principled woman lawyer. She replied:

> It is hard for anyone to make a living at the law—and even more difficult for a woman. I had an easy time making out because I had enough money to carry me over, so I could do pretty much what I pleased, but if you are going to make a living practicing law, it is going to be dirty, and you can make up your mind to it. I can't quite figure out why that is so dreadful as you seem to think it is. When a picket knocks out a scab on the picket line, it isn't so pretty either; sometimes it is effective, sometimes it isn't.

She added, "If you want to practice law, go ahead and practice law, but if you are going to be fastidious, you had better get a job teaching economics in some workers' school and starve to death." She sent her best wishes along with this advice.

Law school proved to be an unexpected and traumatic experience. It was my first encounter with professors and students who openly accepted and acted on the theory that women are inferior to men.

But more than that, it was my first real encounter with the principles of feudalism and capitalism used as rules of law and public policy to decide disputes between human beings. The few students like myself who wanted to become people's lawyers were put off by the basic courses in Property and Contracts that set forth the law as it slowly evolved from feudalism to laissez-faire capitalism in England and early America through the rule against perpetuities and later the ingenious midwifery that brought forth corporations as citizens having rights under the Constitution. The books and the professors provided no real perspective on the short court opinions; they gave too little historical, economic, and social setting for the continual sale and devise of Blackacre, no explanation of its relevance to the tumultuous strike at Ford Motor Company a few miles away.

We couldn't sign up for a course on Employment Law, although the meaningful property rights and investments of the clients we wanted to serve were all related to their jobs. The complex legal problems of the person who would work for wages all his life (except when unemployed, ill, or retired) were not considered worthy of the minute analysis devoted to the control, sale, and exchange of land and goods covered in Real Property, Corporations, Wills and Trusts, Future Interests, Taxation, and Sales.

Years later, in the 1970s, when conflicts over the methods of law practice sharpened, I remembered Carol King's advice, as well as her remarkable warmth and personal concern for movement lawyers, combined with hard-hitting effectiveness against her opponent in court. The Tom Paine School was my contribution to the debate about law practice. The students were mostly law students, but some were undergraduates and others worked in law offices or in the community.

I asked the lawyers who spoke to emphasize the duality in practicing law: to discuss objective legal questions on which they are experts, and subjective questions on how they run their offices, and how their families fit in with their law practice. Sometimes we didn't get around to the subjective questions at all, and we never did justice to the family. We had some sharp exchanges on income and life style, wondering whether a four-day week is possible for movement lawyers and how they can spend some prime time with their families. We tangled on racism in unions and what is impossible when practicing law from the black perspective. We asked each other: What is a movement lawyer? What is he really after? Fame? Fortune? To make the society work a little better for his clients? Or to change the system in a fundamental sense?

We looked at many sides of each of these questions as the speakers described their experiences to illustrate their views. They talked about themselves and their clients—where they came from, what they believe, their roles and relationships. Since the best place to win a case is the first place, they emphasized their strategy and tactics in the trial court and only occasionally discussed appeals to the Supreme Court. (For citations to cases discussed, see the Index of Cases and Statutes.)

We didn't come up with any single set of answers, and since these sessions several of the lawyers have changed their jobs or partnerships or some of their ideas. Still the sessions were so rich in practical information and analysis of political litigation that the tapes were edited into this book, which can be read as autobiography, philosophy, jurisprudence, or practice manual.

Sessions of the Tom Paine Summer Law School in the garden outside the Meiklejohn Civil Liberties Library, Berkeley (with a tape recorder whirring discreetly in the background).

CAST OF CHARACTERS
[in order of appearance]

AFG Ann Fagan Ginger, lawyer acting as moderator, but occasionally tangling with **Speakers.**

Speakers Lawyers and a client, describing their positions at one moment in time and recounting their past experiences (not always verbatim).

Students Black and white men and women
attending colleges and law schools
working in law offices and as community organizers
asking questions and occasionally engaging in sharp exchanges with **Speakers.**

[in the wings]

Clients
Families
Friendly Lawyers
Opposition Lawyers
Witnesses
The Press
The Police
The Community
The Disciplinary Committee of the Bar Association
The Judges
The Law (both fixed and changing)

TIME

Summer 1970.

17

THE RELEVANT LAWYERS,
THE LAW, AND THE PRACTICE
Ann Fagan Ginger

I

Everyone seems to want a lawyer these days, to defend him against criminal charges or to file suit against the establishment. Everyone wants a lawyer who cares about people and who has seen enough of the existing institutions to believe that basic social change is necessary.

The lawyers in this book all fit this description. All are relevant to the movement for social change. Each lawyer thinks of himself as unique and makes use of his unique talents to win cases, but actually the careers of relevant lawyers throughout the country are remarkably similar. After working in Detroit, Cleveland, Washington, Boston, New York and Berkeley, I would say that the speakers in this book are representative movement lawyers. They started practicing law at different times, but since then have handled pretty much the same kinds of cases. They graduated from law school between 1935 and 1969, spanning several historical eras. During the New Deal, these lawyers and their colleagues represented tenants' unions and unemployed councils, new CIO unions, new government labor boards, and congressional committees (investigating World War I war profits and the labor spy racket). Many served in the Army in the war against fascism; others went with wartime government boards to curb profits and prices and to get wage increases. Right after World War II, they joined returning veterans, blacks, and unions to demand full employment, fair employment practices, a meaningful United Nations. (This period passed so quickly it is often forgotten.)

Around 1948 most of these lawyers lost their union clients due to the Cold War; others left the government service. They ended up in general practice, often specializing in automobile personal-injury work, and defending clients victimized during the Joe McCarthy era of the 1950s. These are the lawyers who went to Mississippi in the summers of 1964 and 1965 with the National Lawyers Guild Committee to Assist Southern Lawyers. The older law firms began to represent the growing people's movements, while some black lawyers and some new lawyers went to work in government poverty programs and civil-rights agencies. The end of the Warren Court saw many relevant lawyers concentrating on consumerism, draft, and drugs, peace, Panthers, and personal injury.

Of course, there are regional differences that determine the specific references to local cases. The lawyers in this book are mostly from the West Coast; they mention the Free Speech Movement and deportation cases against Harry Bridges, president of the International Longshoremen's and Warehousemen's Union, rather than Columbia University busts and the sit-down strikes in Michigan. The totality of the special Southern experience is not discussed here, although Ed Dawley talks as a black lawyer who left Virginia and Paul Harris as a white Los Angelino who worked briefly in Georgia (the contradictory sides of the civil-rights lawyers' migration).

The sixteen lawyers here represent a very small percentage of the lawyers in the country. Of the 350,000 American lawyers today, probably fewer than 10,000 share the views or participate in the kinds of law practice discussed here. But these relevant lawyers have had a tremendous impact on the law. They handle far more than their share of headline cases and those ultimately decided by the United States Supreme Court.

These lawyers are certainly not representative of the bar as a whole. The majority are members of some minority group in the society or in the profession. Only 4,000 lawyers in this country are black or Third World, 8,000 are women, and 4,000 work in poverty law offices or as public defenders. Our selection, like Noah's Ark, contains two lawyers from each of these groups, because they have been more active in the movement for social change than their numbers would suggest, and because their numbers are growing.

Employment opportunities have opened up since some of these lawyers graduated, but anti-Semitism is still practiced in some downtown firms in every major city. Independent-minded blacks and women still cannot get decent jobs as lawyers at equal wages in establishment firms, while independent-minded white males are often considered promising material. On this point, John George gives an accurate group portrait of the Northern black lawyer's experience in his description of his own practice. Ed Dawley starts with his role as a Southern black lawyer and then moves into his present job in a Western ghetto with the Office of Economic Opportunity legal-services program. Others refer specifically to their Jewish background and how it affected them in trying Nazi war criminals and in understanding union problems. Mary Kaufman mentions her initial difficulties in being accepted as a woman trial lawyer and in providing care for her son during long trials. Fay Stender discusses the question of self-identity, and her husband, Marvin, describes the role of women as legal secretaries in large law firms. Paul Harris debates with an experienced legal secretary about the role planned for women legal workers in his new community law office.

You can find counterparts of these lawyers in every metropolitan area and some rural regions. They practice in downtown and ghetto San Francisco and Oakland, in small-town Marin County, in Berkeley's middle-class foothills, and in the agricultural valley. One lawyer's firm has labor-law offices throughout the state, another visits clients in the Antilles, and the one New Yorker describes trials in Nuremberg, St. Louis, and Denver.

Most experienced lawyers take a somewhat pragmatic approach to their work. Trial and error appears to be the only way to make progress in a particular case. However, a few attorneys in this book seem to have worked out a conscious ideological approach to their cases and their lives. And all the lawyers here sound like philosophers. They have given some thought to their role in their profession in their country in this era. They have tried to see themselves in relation to the other citizens of the world and to make decisions on the basis of this perspective at least some of the time.

II

Everyone wants a lawyer today, and a lot of people want to become lawyers. They see the law as an effective means of helping individuals and of bringing about social change. They point to the series of people's victories in the courts and want to add to the list.

The lawyers in this book and their colleagues have won an impressive number of political cases recently, including defense of Black Panthers, draft refusers, and alleged conspirators, and affirmative suits for poor people, consumers, prisoners, and students. If there is any chance of continuing this string of victories in the present period, it will probably be the result of careful analysis of how these victories came about. Since it is more fun to analyze victories than defeats, this may be the right moment to make that study.

It is generally agreed that these victories were not solely the result of top-notch legal work by a few trial lawyers supported by research lawyers, other experts, and legal workers. Nor were they solely the result of filling the courtrooms, collecting funds for defense, and conducting mass campaigns to educate the communities on the social questions underlying the lawsuits. All of this work was done in the winning cases. But there was also something in the law for the lawyers to bring to the attention of the judge and the jury, to insist on, despite government objections.

The socially conscious lawyer in this country can find legal principles and court decisions to support his client's rights. Instead of damning the system as a whole, which has become popular recently, or praising the system as a whole, which has always been popular in some circles, the lawyers in this book try to analyze the specific features of the present system that they can use to defend their clients and to improve society. And they watch every development in the general law to see how it can be used to assist their clients.

Lawyers recognize that legal principles are not self-executing. It is a herculean task to get judges, prosecutors, and jurors to abide by certain legal principles when one party has challenged the economic-political power of the other party. But many lawyers for the movement also recognize that the establishment can be forced to obey its own rules under certain circumstances. At this point, they see their role as one of struggle for enforcement of these basic rules. They do not see any realistic alternative to that role.

No lawyer can believe in lawyers as magicians, or that movement clients and trial jurors can accomplish the miracle of justice by themselves. They need the assistance of legal tools. Movement lawyers constantly refer to the First, Fifth, and Fourteenth Amendments to buttress their legal arguments. They don't have time to study history for its own sake. They go back to the records of the periods when the people were on the move, in order to find precedents to help the people in motion today. And they have been successful in their search quite often because the principles of the American Revolution and the Reconstruction Period cut a wide swath.

The First and Fifth Amendments are part of the Bill of Rights adopted after the Revolutionary War. They express the spirit of the men who fought that war and won it and then found that they still owed rent to the patroon and still couldn't vote. Before Valley Forge they were indentured servants—virtual serfs for seven years —or apprentices, free laborers, mechanics, small farmers, or shopkeepers. They didn't become lawyers, merchants, shippers, or big landowners after the victory at Yorktown. Many had left England to better their lot in the new country, promised the chance to earn quick money and to buy thousand-acre lots without feudal fetters. But they discovered that a little feudalism came over on the *Mayflower,* and a lot of greed. For almost two hundred years they watched the land-grabbing by the king's favorites in the New World, and watched the establishment of semifeudal landed estates in the North and a slave-labor system in the South. They saw the foundations being built for the great American fortunes in real estate, shipping, manufacturing, and agriculture.

At the same time, the American merchant capitalists were discovering that the English restrictions on trade and industry hampered their growth. They finally became convinced that they could never build an independent American economic system unless they built an independent American governmental system as well. Their colleagues, the gentlemen theorists, and an occasional agitator like Tom Paine, were busy during this period studying the democratic theories of the French Encyclopedists and the Miltons, Lockes, and Levellers of England. When it was time to declare the United

States an independent government, Thomas Jefferson had the concepts handy: all men are created equal and are endowed with certain rights regardless of status.

Some economists call it the bourgeois-democratic revolution against feudalism and English imperialism; political scientists often call it the birth of modern democratic government. By whatever label, the American Revolution overthrew the system by force and violence. Then the founding fathers, many from the wealthy and professional classes, wrote a Constitution. They wanted to protect their new position, but they realized they had to permit some increase in the political power of the common people, who had just laid down their arms. Daniel Shays and other veterans of the Revolution were not ready to accept a return to pre-Revolutionary status. Many people threatened to reject the new Constitution unless it was amended to provide more guarantees of personal rights against the new federal government.

What the young American citizens wanted for themselves were the rights the upper classes had secured in England through hundreds of years of struggles against the crown. The contests among the king, the church, the landed gentry, and the merchant-capitalists had led to the development of legal principles to insure fairness in deciding disputes. These were, of course, disputes among parties of more or less equal power and influence, with all sides represented by lawyers. But the procedures established in their litigation could also be used in disputes between the establishment and the outsiders, in litigation between unequal parties. These principles might not fit neatly the problems of poor litigants, but they would help. They must be made universally applicable in the new Constitution—that was the demand in 1787.

At the same time, the competing economic groupings—the Northern mercantile capitalists, the Southern slave interests, the farmers who opposed industrialization—feared consolidated power in any of their adversaries. "Free competition" in business was essential for each group, and they could see that some "free competition" in the political sphere would serve their interests best.

The first ten amendments were the responses to all of these demands. They were approved by practical men of affairs who needed a strong central government in order to encourage and protect their property. They recognized a basic political principle: that no government can long endure without the consent of the governed, by whatever means that consent is obtained. As a result, the Constitution and the Bill of Rights not only protect the property rights of those with economic power, but also define and protect some of the human rights of the people who work for a living and have a vote in selecting government officials. First Amendment scholar Alexander Meiklejohn saw the Constitution as the expression of a sovereign people proudly and unequivocally declaring that the people shall have active supremacy over the subordinate agencies they create to serve their purposes; that the legislative, executive, and judicial agencies are merely creatures of the people and not themselves the government of the United States.

Adoption of the Bill of Rights didn't settle everything, of course. It opened up new struggles. Workingmen said that a trade union was not a criminal conspiracy. Runaway slaves and abolitionists said slavery was an abomination; slaves staged revolts. Indian tribes sued to get their land back. After seventy-five years, Northern industry decided to call a halt to the expansion of Southern slavery; it was competing with the Northern wage system and it required frequent wars with Mexico to gain new land, which did not interest the North. The Southern slave system was virtually outlawed in the Emancipation Proclamation and defeated on the battlefields of the Civil War. This change in the relations between the owners of property in slaves and the black people who worked to produce wealth was recorded in additional amendments to the Constitution—the Thirteenth, Fourteenth, and Fifteenth.* The sometimes violent and sometimes subtle efforts to destroy the meaning of these amendments and to end Reconstruction of the South fill volumes of the United States Supreme Court reports.†

In the short two hundred years since the United States established a sovereign government, its people have abolished two kinds of economic relationships, between masters and servants and between slaveowners and slaves. After these changes were won on the battlefields, lawyers were asked to put them into writing as permanent guides to behavior and to enforce them in the courts.

The resulting political documents were distributed around the

* Jacobus tenBroek's *Antislavery Origins of the Fourteenth Amendment* (1951) spells this out.
† See the telling history lesson in *Jones v. Alfred H. Mayer Co.,* 392 U.S. 409 (1968).

world (along with assurances that American streets were paved with gold). They brought to our shores millions of working people looking for jobs and expecting to find equal treatment for rich and poor. Their children studied the Bill of Rights and the Reconstruction Amendments in the public schools. These documents helped form the moral basis for the Niagara movement of black people, for the woman suffrage movement, and for the long battle (1900–1913) for a progressive tax on the income of the rich (Sixteenth Amendment).

The Great Depression, stretching from the end of the 1920s all the way to World War II, brought further changes in the American constitutional system. The New Deal grafted legislative limits onto the common law of capitalism. The establishment finally accepted government responsibility for the poor and the unemployed when the economic system does not function adequately. These changes did not take the form of constitutional amendments. Instead, there was an astronomical expansion of government functions through establishment of administrative agencies. (Of course, the lawyers in Congress who created the agencies felt the need to hire thousands of lawyers to write regulations and operate the new system.)

Since the founding of the United States, most lawyers have been retained by establishment forces in government and industry to represent them in the legislature, in the executive branch, and as judges and lawyers in court. But, at the same time, the canon of ethics for lawyers has required each lawyer to play a second role: "to undertake the defense of a person accused of crime, regardless of his personal opinion as to the guilt of the accused, . . . [and] to present every defense that the law of the land permits." Each lawyer is told to follow the principle that "no fear of judicial disfavor or public unpopularity should restrain him from the full discharge of his duty."

Lawyers who seek to be relevant to their clients' needs and to the need for social change must work within this contradiction. There is no other place to go. They are officers of the court and of the system, and they are simultaneously defenders of the victims and opponents of the system. The lawyer who succumbs to his economic need for a secure income, his social need for respectability and status, and his ego need for power fails to practice his profession according to these canons of ethics. But the lawyer who thinks first of his client and of the social problems in the system, the lawyer who obeys these canons to the full, frequently faces the obloquy and scorn of his colleagues and judges, and occasionally faces disciplinary proceedings or disbarment.

Lawyers are often criticized by laymen for mystifying the law, for speaking in riddles, for being incapable of making a simple direct statement of the law. The fault is not with the lawyers. Their work is based on contradictions at every turn in a society in which there is a conflict in the stated rules. The economic system says each man shall take what profit he can from the natural resources and from the work of others; the governmental system says all men are created equal, have equal political rights, and the right to use and protect the natural resources from individual greed.

We are witnessing a barrage of attacks on certain legal principles. They come from eminent lawyers and judges, from Nixon, Reagan, Burger, and the FBI, from committees of Congress and of the American Bar Association. Anyone reading these attacks can surmise which legal principles movement lawyers have found most effective, which ones the speakers in this book rely on most often.

First, we have an adversary system of law. It is assumed that the truth is most likely to be discovered when two sides appear in a formal hearing, with a representative for each side presenting evidence for his client and cross-examining witnesses for his opponent. In theory, the two sides are equal and are required to follow the same rules; there is no divine right of kings, no presumption that the government is right.

Second, in order to carry out this theory of equal justice under law, there must always be lawyers to advocate the viewpoint of people not in power and even of people contesting those in power. A well-to-do defendant in a criminal case has long had the right to an attorney to represent him against the power of the state, represented by a state's attorney; a solvent tenant has had the right to counsel when sued by his landlord. Recently the people's demands have led to a great expansion of this right to counsel so that now it often includes the right to have a lawyer paid by the government if the client has no funds.

Third, an attorney has a duty to his client, and must not refuse to take a case because of the unpopularity of the client or his cause. Although this canon has been honored more in the breach than in the observance during many periods, it has been of some help to lawyers for radicals even in the worst times. In times like the present, it has encouraged many young people to become lawyers so that they can represent movement clients.

Fourth, our system provides for trials by jury in many kinds of cases. A jury of twelve should contain many working people, citizens of all colors, and adults of all ages and both sexes, if it is drawn from a representative list. This means that citizens can exercise some governmental power directly, without intermediaries, and makes jury duty significant participatory democracy. In some courts, lawyers can question prospective jurors to eliminate those who are biased. This system of jury selection, when operated according to law, helps attorneys for underprivileged clients. They can appeal to the jurors' basic instincts of fairness and humanity, to their intelligence, their social convictions. If one or more come from the defendant's cultural group, they may understand his language and motivations. When a jury acquits a defendant, the verdict cannot be reversed even if it was based on conscience rather than on the law given by the judge. In addition, jury verdicts must be unanimous in criminal cases, which means that one juror voting to acquit can prevent conviction and require a new trial or dismissal of charges. These jury rules can lead to defeats for members of the establishment and the government. That may explain why they are followed so loosely and are now under serious attack.

Fifth, all criminal defendants are entitled to speedy and public trials. They cannot be held without bail before trial for extended periods, and the public must be permitted to attend their trials. (The authors of this principle surely never envisioned body searches of spectators, lawyers, and witnesses entering garrisoned courtrooms.)

Sixth, our system provides for an independent judiciary, with elective judges in many courts. The judges are subjected to pressures from many sides, not just one. Some pressures come from the common people, from their lawyers, and from the recognition that a judge sits in the spotlight of national and occasionally world opinion.

Seventh, our law is based on precedent. This means that a decision today should be based on a previous court decision on a similar problem, or on custom. In this country there is history on the side of the radical lawyer, but he will have to dig for it.*

Eighth, under our system of checks and balances, lawyers for the people can plead their clients' cause in court when there is a Warren heading up the Supreme Court, can shift to the legislative branch when voter registration drives are in full swing, and can push for administrative action when a Franklin Roosevelt is elected to the White House.

Lastly, lawyers representing movement clients today can turn to our basic governmental compact for their best arguments in most cases. The First Amendment guarantees the right of *freedom of expression* without prior restraint by the government. Fairness in criminal and civil cases (state and federal) is guaranteed in *due-process* provisions of the Constitution (habeas corpus and ex post facto clauses), in the Fourth, Fifth, Sixth, Seventh, and Eighth Amendments, and in the Fourteenth Amendment. The Fourteenth Amendment also adds the guarantee of *equal protection* of the laws regardless of previous economic condition, race, or nationality. The woman suffrage movement technically gave women only the right to vote (Nineteenth Amendment), but its social effect was to add women to the list of groups that must be treated equally under the Fourteenth Amendment. The long struggle to abolish poll taxes (Twenty-fourth Amendment) served as the background for the so-called war on poverty and added poor people to the list entitled to equal protection. The youth movement has now added young people to this list (Twenty-sixth Amendment).

To a practicing constitutional lawyer, the First Amendment is as clearly defined and permanent as the Empire State Building. It is both an inspiration to clients and a tool for lawyers. It is as intriguing as the *Mona Lisa* and as real as pi to a mathematician.

The same is true of the equal-protection clause of the Fourteenth Amendment. It seems to be as much a material object as a rapid transit system and can be extended with equal propriety and flexibility.

* Gustavus Meyers' *History of the Supreme Court* (1912) and Charles Beard's *Economic Interpretation of the Constitution* (1912) provide a starting point. Zechariah Chafee's books include the basic documents and describe the development of constitutional protections in the United States, as do Professor Mitchell Franklin's articles.

Due process is something else. It is an essential ingredient of the bricks used to build a convincing case. In a criminal case, its absence means there is a fundamental flaw in the whole structure and the case will not stand up against the attack of a good defense lawyer.

In this panoply of legal weapons available to the movement client and his lawyer, are some better than others? Can a principled person use them all with equally good conscience, or are some the shields of a coward?

Senator Joe McCarthy's snarling about "Fifth Amendment Communists" in the 1950s has led to the downgrading of procedural protections. They are often considered by progressives as tactics used only by Philadelphia lawyers. This view upset many activist clients and lawyers appearing before the House Un-American Activities Committee and other investigating bodies. In the 1960s and 1970s, it has plagued opponents of the Vietnam War and the draft. They have been told that it is more principled to be a conscientious objector because of religious belief than to fight the draft system on procedural grounds. Some of them feel that the exercise of religious convictions comes under the First Amendment while procedural fairness is just a superficial technicality.

This is a rather purist view on the choice of weapons. When we have to fight in their arena under their rules before their judges according to their timetable, why should we hobble ourselves by rejecting good strong peaceful weapons our ancestors forged for us to use in just such cases?

Since the 1930s lawyers representing people's movements have been bringing lawless government agencies to heel by attacking their denials of due process in cases in which they also trampled on civil liberties. Osmond K. Fraenkel, dean of American civil-liberties lawyers, first pointed this out to me, and it has been extremely helpful in practice. When Carol King and others started winning deportation and naturalization cases in the 1940s, it was usually because the Immigration Service had not followed its own rules or because its procedures shocked the conscience of a court committed to the preservation of bourgeois-democratic rights. In the 1950s and 1960s, the Subversive Activities Control Board threatened to send Communist Party leaders and members to jail for the rest of their lives for refusal to register under a law defining Communists as vicious subversives and permitting severe criminal and civil penalties against them. This attack was defeated in the Supreme Court because the statute required a person to incriminate himself in violation of the Fifth Amendment, not because freedom of expression was attacked in violation of the First Amendment.

Ten years later, lawyers schooled to think about due process found new holes in draft-board proceedings that were not as apparent to lawyers coming straight out of the religious and peace movements. Many of the victories in conscientious-objector and other draft cases have been won on just such procedural grounds. Several lawyers in this book describe current efforts to secure due process in all juvenile-court and prison proceedings.

There is clearly a great deal a socially conscious lawyer can do with the law in this country. One of the recurring questions in this book is: What are the limits on the power of a lawyer, as a lawyer. The speakers give examples of lawyers who think they are the prime movers and tend to use the wrong tactics, doing damage to their clients and occasionally to themselves. (Lawyers who seek to wear activist and legal hats simultaneously may suffer the same fate.)

Perhaps this is why Charles Garry emphasizes that the Sixth Amendment does not guarantee the right to counsel. The language says, rather: "In all criminal prosecutions, the accused shall enjoy the right . . . to have the *Assistance* of Counsel for his defence." This role of assistant to the client is interpreted differently by different lawyers in this collection, but they all agree that the lawyer loses when he gains complete control of a case, because he makes decisions that his client should make and that the client will have to live with.

Lawyers can sometimes play a very important role in airing social questions; they can play a decisive role in getting their clients out of jail and in keeping them out (or, in Nuremberg, in sending their opponents to jail). But lawyers, as lawyers, are not the key figures in constitutional law, in the struggle to preserve and extend the Bill of Rights, or in efforts to reorder the priorities and curb the power of the military-industrial complex.

Without a lawyer, a client can exercise his liberties and do his thing. Without a client, a lawyer cannot exercise his trade in court.

Of course, it is not one-sided. The activist client without a lawyer has a much greater chance of going to jail, and he may end up dead in a gas chamber. Still, the client takes the first step. If he hires a lawyer, it is as accompanist. The lawyer rarely gets the first move in the chess game of the law. Usually the government or business can make the first move, while the disadvantaged client can only respond.

Limitations on lawyers go even deeper than that. Law does not determine what the rules of society will be. As the Revolutionary and Civil War amendments to the Constitution indicate, law is only a method of recording rules society has adopted after bitter struggles, so that they can be referred to from time to time when there is a less basic dispute. Lawyers trained in the law, with words as tools, have the function of writing down clearly any agreements reached about what the law shall be. They do not have the power, and it is not their function, to determine what the relationships among people, or between people and property, will be. This is the limit of their trade, no matter how qualified or committed they are or how skillfully they use all of their tools.

III

While everyone wants a lawyer, and many want to become lawyers, almost nobody in the movement for social change is prepared to pay the full cost of legal representation.

When a client walks in to discuss a political case, many experienced political lawyers sift the situation through a screen of concerns about material and developmental problems. They listen to the facts with one part of their minds while another part is almost instinctively asking a series of questions: Can we possibly win? How serious will it be if we lose—for the client and for me? If we lose, will this case set a bad precedent for other cases? Should that be an important consideration?

They face other practical questions: How much time will it take to handle this case properly? Can I get along with this client in moments of tension and crisis for several years? Will I lose any paying clients if I take this case and get the publicity the case requires? What are the chances I will get cited for contempt or disbarred if I represent this client as vigorously as will be necessary? What if the client insists on determining his or her own courtroom behavior?

The fact is that most of the lawyers speaking here, and the majority of other American lawyers, are in private practice, rather than salaried employees of government, business concerns, large commercial law firms, or funded public-interest firms. The history of revelant lawyers in this country shows pretty clearly that only lawyers in private practice are able to handle movement cases on a continuing basis, giving them the attention they require. The common pattern is for a medium-sized law firm, financed by general practice, to provide an experienced lawyer and a novice to handle a major political case from beginning to end. The lawyers draw around them a group of legal workers, secretaries, investigators, volunteer lawyers, and experts from other fields, while the client and his friends develop a defense committee.

There is a reason why these lawyers have rejected the greater economic security and higher class status of some salaried positions. Several started on that path, but when the political climate changed they found they couldn't represent their political clients, so they left or were fired.

A small number of lawyers have worked on salary for the American Civil Liberties Union, NAACP Legal Defense and Educational Fund, National Association for the Advancement of Colored People, American Jewish Congress, Nader's Raiders, Center for Constitutional Rights, and similar groups handling public-law cases. The number has grown, but probably does not exceed 250 in the country. The significance of their work has obviously been disproportionate to their numbers. They have been joined by many lawyers in private practice who write amicus briefs and try cases periodically, with or without fee. A few hundred other lawyers work on salary for equal employment opportunity agencies in government, or for single-purpose legal-defense organizations.

Periodically movement groups and progressive local unions are organized on a stable basis and financed well enough to hire lawyers as house counsel to handle their work. The number of such organizations is usually quite small. If more jobs as house counsel become available, lawyers will have to weigh the greater political continuity and economic security against some loss of independence, recognizing that the lawyer who disagrees with his only client gives up his sole source of income.

Another method of handling public-law cases has been well publicized recently as large establishment firms have permitted some juniors to participate in some cases on a *pro bono publico* (no-fee) basis. When such work openly conflicts with the interests of major business clients of such firms, it seems unlikely that the *pro bono* work will be able to continue undisturbed, although there may be occasional exceptions.

Private practitioners are the only significant group of lawyers with an economic base that leaves room for movement cases. It is true that the lawyer in private practice who takes political cases occasionally loses a partner or a major client, but he has some independence and some protection from bankruptcy. If he has practiced awhile, many of his paying clients will stick with him even when he takes political cases of which they disapprove.

But the people's lawyer walks a never-ending tightrope, as several Tom Paine School lawyers attest. They have seen competent colleagues lose their footing and leave the law or drop their principles in the face of political, economic, and resultant marital problems. The remaining lawyers have learned to weigh the costs in representing movement clients. The costs and the time are obviously greater when it is necessary to establish a new legal principle in order to win, but the costs are high even when the lawyer is simply vindicating a right that has already been clearly defined.

Lawyers in private practice are in business, and for most progressive lawyers it is small-scale business with many pseudo supervisors. The clients are customers or consumers who provide the fees that cover the overhead, that pay salaries of employed lawyers, law clerks, legal workers, secretaries, and investigators, and that pay shares to the partners. Clients can fire a lawyer, and several speakers mention this in passing, indicating that it is often on their minds. Trial judges and jurors play a significant role in the life of a trial lawyer, since they are able to destroy his ability to earn a living, through contempt citations and jury defeats. Bar-association grievance committees hold a life-and-death power over the lawyer through threats of disciplinary and disbarment proceedings for alleged ambulance chasing or contemptuous behavior. The media have tremendous power over a lawyer's success. Archie

Brown, the only client with a chapter in this book, describes the results of no newspaper coverage; Carl Shapiro tells how the press can keep the judges honest.

In the face of all of these groups with a kind of supervisory power over the lawyer, how can he provide service to clients, especially those clients seeking to improve society? What should the relationship be between a movement client and a lawyer who takes movement cases and wants to be relevant to the people's cause? Every lawyer and client in the book discusses this question one way or another.

Movement clients expect dedicated, inspired, creative, unlimited, demystified—and successful—legal representation in political cases, free or at low cost. They expect their lawyers to have offices and staffs that can handle the paperwork on major cases and some of the public relations.

Movement people also expect competent representation at a reasonable fee in individual cases in which there is no overt political issue.

These are some standards! Should a lawyer even try to meet them?

In answering that question, the lawyers here analyze the clients they actually represent, not the perfect movement client they dream of. The descriptions range from George's candid snapshots of his criminal-law clients to McTernan's warm portrait of his martyred labor client and Brown's sketch of himself as a client.

Several lawyers express their respect and admiration for some of their clients, and many colleagues around the country would echo this emotion. Relevant lawyers could not continue the hard work of representing relevant clients unless many of these relationships became personally satisfying.* Of course, political lawyers do not necessarily, or often, agree with or join the organizations of their political clients. In a repressive period, an acute problem sometimes develops when liberal lawyers represent political clients but dissociate themselves from their clients' views in front of the judge and the jury. Garry speaks sharply against this practice.

The next series of questions for the relevant lawyer touches the

* The classic example of a political client's impact on a lawyer's life is told by Attorney Benjamin Davis in *Communist Councilman from Harlem: Autobiographical Notes Written in a Federal Penitentiary* (1969).

kind of structure he needs in order to survive and function. What kind of community should he create in his law office? How should the people in that community be expected to relate to one another?

In the traditional radical law office, lawyer partners are employers, and workers are employees who join a trade union. The employees negotiate a contract with the bosses concerning wages, hours, and working conditions (although such contracts are almost nonexistent in other kinds of law offices). Van Bourg and others assume this is the best system for protecting the interests of the legal workers, which are in fact contradictory to the interests of the lawyers as bosses. They favor collective bargaining to solve specific problems. Their politically conscious employees seek to avoid futile appeals to political comradeship with their bosses.

What about the new commune approach? It includes greater equality among all staff members, with legal workers and lawyers sometimes getting equal pay and sharing in decision-making on questions of office management, what nonpaying clients to represent, and sometimes on political-legal tactics. The pros and cons are hotly debated in this book.

Certainly a traditional office will be less effective if the relationships are exploitative and dishonest. But neat relationships among lawyers, legal workers, and clients do not ensure adequate legal representation. The ability to hold a good office discussion on repression does not necessarily carry with it the ability to prepare a convincing memo of law on a change of venue and file it in the proper court in sufficient copies by tomorrow morning.

Are the new communes utopian colonies operating in the belly of the beast?* What is the economic basis for their survival in this period? Will they be staffed to handle big movement cases? The commune models in Manhattan and Berkeley that have been described most often in national publications expired before their third anniversaries. Others continue to function and may supply some answers over the years.

The requirements are clear: a model that will provide a staff with as much continuity as possible, with the ability to handle last-minute emergencies, in an atmosphere conducive to sound lawyer-client relationships. The office must bring in fees to pay the staff regularly at salaries they can accept. It must find clients with

* See V. F. Calverton's *Where Angels Dared to Tread* (1941).

problems that are not too broad to make research difficult and not too narrow to limit staff relationships with other firms and movements. The office must handle cases that help build the reputation of the staff among judges and lawyers on both sides—the kind of reputation that is tremendously helpful in political cases.

If clients want law communes to continue, or any kind of relevant lawyers to be available, some may have to rethink their part of the bargain. A client is a client for a limited period of time, but a lawyer is a lawyer for life. Clients who think raising money for legal defense is really a diversion from political work may find their favorite lawyers going into cases to earn fees to pay their debts just when they are needed in the next mass bust. The Southern Conference Educational Fund, for example, has always taken the other position, considering the raising of legal-defense money an additional way to get people involved in the movement for social change, if only on a minimal basis at first.

Because the supply of political lawyers is always smaller than the demand, every method of getting lawyers involved in political cases is important. Any lawyer with a few hours every week can probably find a meaningful way to contribute to relevant cases, even if his regular work does not permit more time. Marvin Stender shows the kinds of political-legal work a busy partner in a commercial firm can do (although he may strain office relationships). The OEO lawyers describe the situation in legal-service offices, including the problems of practical politics when a Reagan can veto a program. Mary Kaufman and Fay Stender suggest another pattern. They handle one case or area of law at a time, obtaining financial support from the movement around that issue and not engaging in general practice.

However, no one has demonstrated that any particular life style ensures that a relevant lawyer will continue to be relevant and a good lawyer throughout his or her professional career. Some good radical lawyers have lived quite fat and fancy in the affluent years and have continued to handle some hard political cases and to train new lawyers. Others now reject clients they once courted. Some radical lawyers have lived on minimal income and been extremely devoted to the movement for a period, and then have started to make lots of money on nonmovement cases or have quit the profession. Others live on low incomes and do fine work all of their lives. A select few have been elected or appointed to office and have fought cleanly for social change from within the establishment.

This is a complex and contradictory society, and no one knows what objective conditions will trigger the best subjective responses from lawyers or how to ensure lifelong devotion to the cause of the common man. Yet it takes many years to create a great people's lawyer. There seems to be no substitute for the slow accretion of experience. How can we encourage good people to stay in the movement and in the practice, and discourage flashy representation that will not stand up over time?

The truth of the matter is that law is not a good occupation in which to develop an egalitarian, cooperative style of life. Van Bourg says the lawyer for the underdog must be able to dominate the courtroom, and many incidents in this book illustrate this point.

Can you deliberately set your course for the hurricane and expect to have a relaxed and loving life?

This puzzle has led many of the lawyers in this book to threaten to quit the practice at some point. It's just not worth the hassle. But they seem to give up practice pretty much the way Mark Twain gave up smoking.

These lawyers, and their colleagues around the country, are obviously fascinated with lawyering and dedicated to mastering their craft. The minute one of them decides he won't leave the law, he starts looking for more bodies to stand up in court as new clients line up at the door. Each lawyer recognizes that the law is jealous of his time, but no one seems able to leave work behind after office hours. Each is burdened to some degree by the confidential relationship with his client, and each carries his client's concerns with him until he comes up with some kind of solution to the immediate problem.

For long-range answers for individual clients, and society as a whole, look for clues in these chapters, and then see what lies ahead.

POLITICS
IN
THE
COURTROOM

FROM ARREST TO VERDICT
Malcolm Burnstein

AFG: Mal Burnstein is a trial attorney. He has participated in many of the major political cases in this area in the past ten years, including the University of California Free Speech Movement mass trial and the Oakland Seven antiwar "conspiracy" case.

I thought, Mal, that you could give us something of a guided tour through the stages of a political trial.

Burnstein: Sure. One definition I have of a political trial is any trial in which social attitudes that are not relevant to the subject matter of the suit are going to affect the result. The most obvious example is the question of racism. In American society a white man charged with committing a crime is not faced with the same problems that a black man faces. When a black man is charged with a crime in almost every place except Detroit now, he's facing white justice. Where a white jury is judging a black defendant, racism simply cannot help but affect the result.

Do you know what's happening now in Detroit?

AFG: The lawyers are asking prospective jurors dozens of questions, to uncover their racist attitudes and bias.

Burnstein: A recent trial in Detroit had twelve jurors plus two alternates, and twelve of the fourteen were black! But here we have so few black jurors on the panel that the prosecutor can get rid of most or all of them if he wants to.

41

So, a trial that, on its face, might simply be a straight criminal case has got an obvious political dimension to it if the defendant is black, and a defense lawyer who does not realize that fact ought to stay out of such a case. White jurors simply don't know what it means to be a black man, what a black man's life style is like, or what the words he uses mean. Unless the lawyer realizes the racism that is involved, he simply is not going to do a competent job for his client. Unless he recognizes that it is a political problem and treats it like other political cases, his client starts out at a disadvantage.

For years, during the Joe McCarthy era of repression and afterward, some people had the notion that you could "sanitize" trials, that you could excise the political elements. If you had a case of a political activist, you could sanitize the trial by strictly requiring the prosecution not to mention the guy's politics. It may be possible to get some judges and some prosecutors to cooperate in that sense, but if you think the Huey Newton trial would have had no political overtones as long as the prosecutor never once mentioned the Black Panthers, you just don't understand where society is at, as far as I'm concerned.

My attitude is that you don't fight like hell to keep all politics out of the trial, because that's impossible. What you have to do is meet it head on. And the way you do that is by starting to talk about the political questions as soon as you get into the courtroom. Do not sit back and let things seep in under the surface, because the jurors have read the newspapers and watched television. Meet the politics head on, and deal with it on a level that the jury and the judge can understand. Try to bring out from their own subconscious their political attitudes on the issues involved in the courtroom. Try to make them recognize the fairness or unfairness of those attitudes.

Since your client is going to get damned for political reasons anyway, bringing the stuff out in the open, it seems to me, will minimize the damage. We tried to do that in the Oakland Seven case. The seven defendants were charged with conspiracy to plan the Stop-the-Draft Week demonstrations in Oakland, back in October 1967. We were quite successful, I thought. We went into every aspect of the illegality and immorality of the war in Vietnam.

AFG: Did the district attorney object?

Burnstein: Sure. But the judge ruled in our favor. Almost any judge (anyone to the left of Julius Hoffman) would have had to let us find out whether the subject matter of the demonstration—opposition to the war—infuriated prospective jurors. A juror might support the war so strongly that he wouldn't be able to judge fairly whether the demonstration against the war had been conducted legally.

AFG: Could you have won that case if you had not been permitted to discuss the war?

Burnstein: Actually the jury decided the Oakland Seven case on First Amendment grounds. That's what they told the press afterward. Three or four of the jurors understood the right to freedom of expression, and they convinced all the others. I don't know if they would have been willing to go on First Amendment grounds if we hadn't gotten them to oppose the war. By the end of that trial every one of the jurors opposed the war in Vietnam. They sure as hell hadn't when they started. So how can we say?

AFG: We did figure it out statistically in the sit-in cases on Auto Row back in 1964. There were thirty-eight trials of ten defendants each, so we had a big sample to study. When the judges permitted lawyers to raise First Amendment questions and to discuss why the people were sitting in, and when there were blacks on the jury, those cases were won or got hung juries. When there were no blacks on the jury and/or they could not discuss why the people sat in, the defendants lost. So *that,* at least, seems fairly clear.

Burnstein: Yes. You see, it's psychological. In the abstract, the jury hears conflicting testimony and is supposed to decide what the facts actually are. But jurors are just like anybody else. They want to know *why* somebody does something. If they don't understand the defendant as a human being, he's going to get a lot worse shake from them.

I'm trying an interesting case right now that might be instructive for a number of reasons. One is that it is actually quite political but not overtly so. I'll change the names and switch some of the facts around, but basically it involves two young black men accused of killing a white policeman.

My client, I'll call him Johnson, was celebrating his twentieth birthday with his friend Williams, who is twenty-nine or thirty. They had been drinking at Johnson's sister's house. Around midnight, they got a ride to Market Street. They were probably too drunk to know exactly what they were doing, but one of them wanted to go visit a girl who lives in the area.

They were walking down Market Street, and they came to the window of a run-down little pawnshop. They stood there for a few minutes, and the window broke. The prosecutor's theory is that they jointly were attempting to burglarize the store, although nothing is missing from the window, with the possible exception of a ring worth about seventy-five cents.

Anyway, people in the bar and restaurant next door heard the sound of breaking glass, and two or three of them walked outside to see what was happening. They looked toward the pawnshop and saw one or two men in the alcove. Two policemen had gone into the restaurant half an hour before, on a meal break. So these people went in and got one of the policemen, I'll call him Officer Grey, and said, "Something's happening outside; you'd better go see." So Grey put on his helmet, picked up his billy club, and went out.

There are six eyewitnesses to what happened next, and each one tells a different story. But the upshot of it was that Officer Grey ended up on the ground, dead, shot with his own gun. The two young men ran away. According to the prosecution they got on a streetcar, rode for a couple of blocks, got off, and disappeared.

Police cars were cruising all over the neighborhood. They had a description from witnesses that one of the men was wearing green pants. The witnesses conflict, but most of them agree on green pants.

A few minutes later, a police car comes roaring up to a corner about three quarters of a mile away from the restaurant, where two young men are standing, one of them wearing green pants. The policemen jump out with their guns out, and the guy in green pants, Williams, whirls and starts shooting at them. They return the fire, and he disappears.

Two police cars chase him. They finally get him two or three blocks away, slumped down in a pool of his own blood. The gun they find on him turns out to be Officer Grey's gun, his second gun.

Grey had an official gun, but he had decided that wasn't enough firepower, so he had bought himself another one.

Meanwhile my client is still standing at the corner, where he is arrested five minutes later.

Williams has a prior felony record, unfortunately for him. Johnson, my client, has no record except for drunk driving.

There are no overt political overtones in the case. Neither defendant is involved in any political organization or operation. This is no Huey Newton case. But when you have two young black defendants in any criminal case, let alone when they're charged with killing a white cop, you simply can't ignore the political questions that necessarily come in.

So one of the first things I did was to challenge the jury-selection system. Out of 181 jurors questioned, only 6 were black. The population of San Francisco is 13.5 percent black (as of 1968). The percentage of prospective jurors who were black was 3.3 percent. I, of course, got nowhere with that challenge, but the foundation is laid for an appeal.

Student: Why do you say "of course"?

Burnstein: Because no superior-court judge in San Francisco would grant a motion for a mistrial on that basis. Either they don't believe in throwing the jury-selection system out or they don't have the guts to throw it out.

AFG: How does the system work?

Burnstein: It's pretty much the same everywhere. In northern California, twice a year the county jury commissioner makes up a list of prospective jurors. In San Francisco it's a list of 2,500 for every six-month period. Then the jury commissioner picks actual jury panels, actual venires, from that larger list. The list is picked geographically, from the voter registration lists. The presiding judge picks a number, say seventeen, and they feed that into a computer, which then spits out every seventeenth registered voter, by precinct. Then the jury commissioner calls up these people, and he asks, "Are you going to be available now, or in two months?" At that point he makes no effort to get geographic uniformity. So, when he calls forty people for jury duty in a particular trial, a bunch of them may even live on the same street. Also, the number of Third World people in the entire 2,500 is going to turn out to be less than their percentage in the population, because we know that Third World people are underrepresented as registered voters, for a number of reasons.

So a black man facing a criminal charge in northern California is facing white justice. It's not colorless justice; it's white justice.

AFG: This search for a fair representation of all groups on a jury is part of the struggle for equal protection of the law, regardless of race, creed, color, or previous condition of servitude, which was written into the Constitution in the Fourteenth Amendment after the Civil War. Now, of course, we all benefit from the idea, because it has been expanded to include equal protection regardless of sex, age, or economic status.

Burnstein: Equal protection is a key problem.

In this Johnson-Williams case, I've been pushing to get to trial, because my client is being held in jail without bail, and every day he serves now is dead time. If this were a case where I thought he might be convicted of first-degree murder, I would be in no rush. But here he could very well get a not-guilty verdict. It's a rough kind of case to try, because he could be acquitted of everything or he could be convicted of first-degree murder.

Student: How did they come up with a first-degree charge against your client?

Burnstein: They say he was an accomplice of Williams'. Williams is charged under the felony-murder rule: If in the course of committing a felony, such as armed robbery, a man shoots someone, he can be charged with first-degree murder even though he never intended to shoot anyone. The prosecutor could not conceivably prove that either defendant shot this poor cop with premeditation. They had never seen him until thirty seconds before he was dead. The only way the prosecutor could get first-degree murder out of this case is the felony-murder rule. And the felony would have to be attempted burglary.

Student: What's the possibility of having the two defendants tried separately?

Burnstein: I made two separate motions for severance. They were both denied.

Student: Does the prosecution always want to try them together?

Burnstein: Sure. Why the hell should the DA have to go through two trials? The important thing in the administration of justice in this country is the amount of money spent, not the people's rights. The object is to save the state money, right?

Student: What grounds are considered strong enough to grant severance?

Burnstein: You seldom get a severance unless the prosecutor consents.

AFG: Since you knew pretty early that the two cases would be tried together, did you try to talk to the lawyer for the other defendant or to get the two lawyers and the two clients together?

Burnstein: In any trial where you have another lawyer involved you try to work together as much as possible, as long as it is not detrimental to your client's interests. If you and your co-counsel are fighting all the time you are just doing the DA's work for him. Hell, the DA can sit back and let one of you guys convict the other one. So you try to avoid any gratuitous attacks on the other guy.

Sometimes it's not possible. Sometimes your client just wants to get himself off and to hell with the other guy. Sometimes the other lawyer won't cooperate. Sometimes you try to work together but it simply doesn't appear possible when you're actually in the case. Most often, though, if you set your mind to it you can keep the two guys away from each other's throats.

AFG: Who is the other lawyer in this case and what are his views?

Burnstein: He's Clinton White and his views are quite different from mine as far as politics go. But Clint's politics are changing. So are mine. Everyone's politics change.

AFG: How about your views on race?

Burnstein: Oh, our views are very close on race. I should explain that Clinton White is a black lawyer from this area. This is the first case that Clint and I have tried together, although we've watched each other work before.

AFG: Do you think there is a difference between a white lawyer trying a case for a black client and a black lawyer trying a case for a black client?

Burnstein: That's a difficult question. I don't know any way to successfully answer it. I mean, if a client is political himself, the lawyer has to relate to him on a conscious political basis, and the client will be judging him not only on the basis that he's white and the client is black but also on the basis of his politics versus the client's politics. If the client isn't political he's going to be judging the lawyer on a different basis.

AFG: You're talking about the client judging the attorney. Do you think that's important?

Burnstein: Of course it is. Unless you relate to your client you have a difficult time. Any trial is tough. If you're fighting with your client all the time, it's going to be a lot tougher. But I don't know of any general rule about how to relate to your client in the white–black situation. You play it like it comes.

In the case that I have now, my client doesn't have any of those hangups. He's young and not terribly sophisticated, and he just doesn't want to go to prison. I can hardly blame him.

AFG: Do you tell your client what to do or what you're going to do? Or do you ask him?

Burnstein: I let him decide whether I should tell him or ask him. Some clients say, "You're the lawyer. Get me off, and don't bother me with the details." Now, in an overtly political case the defendant is not going to take that approach. He's going to say, "I want to be involved in all the decision-making." I think that's great. I mean, in the final analysis it's the client who's going to go to jail for life or be executed, not me.

In the Oakland Seven trial, by God, we didn't make a single important decision, except to object to a particular question at trial. You can hardly consult with your clients while the questions and answers are going, you know; you jump up and object. But the clients were involved in all the real decisions in the case to the same extent as the lawyers.

AFG: How often do you talk to your client before the trial?

Burnstein: As often as is necessary, both to do your job right and to keep his spirits up. If your guy's out of custody, he can pick up the phone and call you if he has any questions, but when he's in that goddam jail someone has got to go see him fairly often to assure him that the world hasn't forgotten him. You have to keep up his morale. If your client falls apart, you're obviously not going to be in good shape to carry on the trial. Unfortunately or fortunately, human beings adjust very well to a lot of things. If you've read anything about the Nazi concentration camps, you understand that people can adjust to all kinds of unpleasant, difficult things, both psychologically and physically. The human being is a very strange animal with a very strong survival urge.

Student: How do you gather the facts from your client in jail?

Burnstein: Well, in a capital case I have to talk to him right there in the jail. In this case there's absolutely no possibility of getting my client out. I made four motions for bail. They were all denied, because it's a capital case.

Student: Did you expect to get bail?

Burnstein: Well, I didn't *expect* to, but I *should* have gotten it. My client is twenty years old, he has no criminal record (except drunk driving). He didn't have a gun. He never shot anybody. No jury is going to send this kid to the gas chamber; that's just ridiculous.

The prosecutor wouldn't have the gall to ask for the death penalty for him.

Student: How much privacy do you have in talking to your client in jail? Do you suspect that the rooms are bugged?

Burnstein: If it's a case where bail is possible, I never talk about the facts of the case. I tell my clients, "I'm not going to talk about the offense with you until you're out of jail." Exactly for that problem.

AFG: Hal Lipset, the private investigator, told us the other day you should just assume that everything you say is going to be overheard. And not just in a conference room in jail, or on the phone. He says the sophistication of recording techniques is so great that there's no problem, if someone has time and funds. And certainly the government has both—they can eavesdrop on anybody, and they say the Safe Streets Act of 1968 gives them the authority to do so.

Student: When you're investigating a case, whom do you talk to besides the client? What investigation do you do before trial?

Burnstein: Well, if you're lucky you get a case right after it breaks. That's when you can do the most effective investigation. Fortunately I was in on this case two days after the thing happened. I went to the restaurant and bar right away, and got one of the prosecution's prospective witnesses to tell me what happened. They just couldn't use him after that.

Student: I assume he hadn't yet been informed by the prosecution not to relate any evidence to anyone.

Burnstein: Right. I went to the restaurant, then I sent investigators out to all the prosecution witnesses whose names and addresses I could dredge up. You never know whether you're going to have the cooperation of the prosecution, especially in a cop-killing case. In this case, I made my formal discovery motion, and they made all the police reports and everything available.

Student: What is discovery?

Burnstein: It's a fairly new procedure to take some of the guess-work out of trying cases and to save time in court. Before trial in a criminal case, the defense can ask the prosecutor for the names of prospective witnesses and copies of documents and so forth. In the federal courts there is broad discovery, and also in some states, like California and New Jersey. It isn't settled how much discovery the DA can get out of the defense in a criminal case. In civil practice, like auto accident cases, there's broad discovery on both sides.

In the Johnson case, the DA didn't hold back on anything. But you don't know whether that will happen. Sometimes a lawyer may find it worthwhile to try to get the police report in advance. The defendant has almost always made a statement or "confession" to the police, and you need to see that. I've heard that some defense counsel will have an investigator bribe someone in the police department to get it.

Student: That's very interesting. It implies that there are occasionally illicit practices on the part of the police.

Burnstein: Sure there are. It's a straight financial transaction. Some guy who has access to the records department makes himself fifty bucks or something. Happens all the time.

AFG: Getting back to your case, you used professional investigators?

Burnstein: Yes. I used Hal Lipset until my client's money ran out, which was very soon. Then I used law students.

Generally, when there isn't a lot of money you should get the client to do a lot of the investigation work, unless he's in the bucket, like mine is. If it's a political case, he and his friends should be as interested in it as you are. Have them do your investigation, jury checking, and everything possible.

AFG: Do you ever do it yourself?

Burnstein: If you want the investigator to testify, you simply can't do the investigation yourself. Once you testify, you're forgoing your right to argue to the jury, you see?

Now, if you're investigating the facts you've got to act fast before people split and before their memories start flagging. When you find a witness, have him write out a statement and sign it. Or if he won't, you write it out and have him read it over, initial every page, and sign it. You pin the prosecution witnesses down in writing as soon as you can, whatever they're going to say. It doesn't matter what it is as long as you *know* what it is.

The minute the trial begins, you start talking about politics, and that means during jury selection. In federal courts, the judges question the jurors. In California and many other state courts, the lawyers do most of the jury questioning. The judge will acquaint the jurors with the nature of the charge, and he'll ask the jurors if they know any of the lawyers or the parties to the case. But basically the lawyers do the questioning.

I know that in some states the jurors are questioned individually —just one juror in the room at a time. But in most California courts all the jurors are sitting in the courtroom and hear the questions asked of the other jurors. That can save time, because you can ask, "Mrs. Smith, did you hear all the questions I asked Mr. Jones?" She says, "Yes." "Would you have answered them any differently?" Of course, if you asked Mr. Jones eighty-two questions, that's really a stupid question to ask Mrs. Smith.

The bad aspect of having all the jurors in the room is that the others soon learn what answers to give. In our current trial, we asked, "What's your attitude toward capital punishment?" One of the early jurors decided it would be nice to say he was "neutral." From then on just about every one of the 181 jurors questioned took the position that he or she was neutral on capital punishment. I don't even understand what being neutral about capital punishment means.

By the way, you all should know that jurors who support capital punishment are more likely to vote for guilt than jurors who oppose capital punishment. That's true in any kind of criminal case. It doesn't matter what the charge is—even drunk driving. So, if jurors who oppose capital punishment are excluded from criminal juries, the defendant no longer has a cross section of the community on the question of guilt or innocence; he's got prosecution-minded jurors.

The whole concept of jurors has turned exactly 180 degrees around now. The juries in ancient tradition were chosen precisely because they knew the parties and had been witnesses to the incident. The theory today is to try to find jurors who are presumably fresh out of an egg somewhere, who don't know anything. They then supposedly have an open mind to everything you're talking about. Of course that doesn't work any more than the earlier system did.

AFG: One of the problems is that liberals and radicals who are called for jury duty say constantly that they are prejudiced against the prosecution or the insurance company, or that they are absolutely against the death penalty. I think there are ways of answering the questions honestly that will still keep good people on the jury so that the defendants can really get a cross section of the community.

Burnstein: Now, technically the prospective jurors are questioned to determine whether there are grounds for disqualifying them for cause—bias and prejudice against the parties or on the issues of the case. There are two other purposes of voir dire that are more important, as far as I'm concerned. One is to try to find out whether you want to knock a juror off with a peremptory challenge—that is, without giving any reason. And the other, perhaps most important of all, is to try to establish some rapport with the jury and to educate them on the facts and issues in the case.

You have five or ten minutes at the most to talk to a prospective juror and try to develop some kind of personal relationship. The prosecutor almost invariably asks every juror the same questions. I always try to find some little personal comment or joke with each juror, about where they work or where they were born or something. You've got to be different with each one, to get a personal relationship going. It's just crucial.

Now, if the lawyer does his jury questioning correctly he never has to make an opening statement. Everything that he would say in his opening statement he's said in his voir dire of the jury. He's told what kind of evidence is going to come in, what his client's position is, and what the political and other issues in the case are.

AFG: Could you give us an example in your present case?

Burnstein: Sure. One of the points that we want the jury to keep in mind is the fact that Officer Grey didn't think one gun was enough for him; he had two. So we asked the jurors, "Would it disturb you in any way if you learned that the dead police officer was carrying a second gun?" We're asking the jurors whether they can be fair to the prosecution, right? That's essentially how the question sounded, but we're really telling the jurors that here's the kind of a cop who doesn't think that a single gun is enough for him. And, of course, the irony is that it was the second one that killed him.

We also talked about the fact that the defendants had been drinking. We asked, "If you learn during the course of the trial that the defendants had been drinking, would that prejudice you in any way? Do you take a drink yourself, Mr. Smith, every once in a while?"

And we talked about racism. We asked, "Do you think you can fairly judge a young black defendant? You're white; do you think that my client's going to get a fair trial with an all-white jury?" If you want to learn how to question jurors on racism, read Charlie Garry's voir dire in *Minimizing Racism in Jury Trials*. It's beautiful.

Then there's the presumption of innocence. We ask the jurors, "Do you really believe that the defendant is presumed innocent?" They answer, "Of course," "Sure," "Naturally." Then we go to another point and come back to it later: "Now, would you be surprised if, after this trial is over, my client is acquitted of all charges?" And if you get them to answer that fast enough, they say, "Yes." Essentially they feel, "What the hell are we doing here if he's not guilty of something?" So what does the presumption of innocence mean?

Student: Did the DA block the questions often?

Burnstein: In this trial we got very few objections during the jury questioning. That's strategy on the part of the DA, too. Whenever you make objections, you have to keep in mind not only whether your objection is legally relevant and proper but also what the jury is going to think of you for objecting. Sometimes you decide not to object, because the answer isn't terribly harmful and you don't want the jury to get the idea that you're trying to keep them from finding out what happened. Sometimes the jury understands why a lawyer has to object, but often they just get impatient.

Student: It seems like antagonizing the jury might be a problem in voir-dire questioning, too. Is it?

Burnstein: Did you watch Garry questioning the jury in the Los Siete de la Raza case? He's very hard-nosed and antagonistic toward the jurors, right? Charlie does that in every trial. The first time I watched him I was horrified. I thought, "How can this son of a bitch ever win a trial? Those jurors are going to hate his guts!"

Student: That's exactly the impression I got.

Burnstein: Well, it doesn't work that way. The prospective jurors who really flip out with that approach will show their hostility so blatantly that Garry can knock them off for cause or with a peremptory challenge. And the rest of the jurors soon begin to understand that he's doing it for a reason. Then, during the trial his tactics change. So the jury's final impression of Charlie is not that hard-nosed approach. And, third, especially in a long and tough trial, the jurors see the results of Charlie's approach and respect him for it. They see he's no sycophant; he's not going to lick their boots—he's a man. That's very important.

I've learned an awful lot from watching and trying cases with Charlie.

AFG: But that doesn't mean that everyone should do what he does.

Burnstein: No. Whatever else you do in court, be yourself. You simply cannot emulate another lawyer's style successfully. You've got to use your own style.

My own style is to try to be as relaxed and informal as possible, within the confines of the trial. You have to adjust that to the particular trial judge and kind of case. But even in this murder case—and you can't get anything more serious than a first-degree murder case—we crack jokes and try to keep the atmosphere in the courtroom informal so that we can develop a relationship with the jury. There are ways of doing that without detracting from the seriousness of the case.

Student: Do you explain that to your client, so he won't be offended?

Burnstein: Yes. You've got to make sure your client understands.

AFG: Do you like having spectators at a trial?

Burnstein: I usually don't pay much attention to spectators when I'm in court. But it makes me feel better for my client. I mean, I don't want the jury to feel that my client is isolated. I always like to have people in the courtroom who the jury knows are sympathetic to the defendant. In any kind of case, if the judge or jury gets the idea that nobody cares what they do to either side, they're going to feel free to act more arbitrary. There is an awful lot of psychology in law practice, whether it's political or any other kind.

Now, after jury selection, the next time you get to talk politics is during your opening statement. In criminal cases the prosecutor makes his opening statement first. In California, the defense can make its opening statement either immediately following the prosecution's or after the prosecution's case and at the beginning of the defense case. In a political case I often want to make an opening statement right after the prosecution's statement, to lay out as much of the politics as I can right away. But in this case I'm trying now, I did not make an opening statement right away, because I didn't want to reveal to the prosecutor what our major defense is.

Then comes the prosecution's case. In a political case, just like any other criminal case, you try to do two things in the course of the prosecutor's case. One is to use the prosecutor's witnesses to prove your own case in cross-examination. If you know your case well, by asking a prosecution witness the right questions on cross-examination you can often make him prove some part of your case. For example, in pretrial discovery, you examine all statements the prosecution's witnesses have given to the police before the trial. Those statements usually are taken before the police and prosecutor have a clear outline of their own case. So the witnesses say a lot of things in those statements that the prosecutor is not going to ask about at the trial, because they contradict what his other witnesses will say. But on cross-examination you can ask what the prosecutor left out, to impeach another prosecution witness or to bring out things that are helpful to the defense case.

Student: Does the prosecutor ever try to dummy up those statements?

Burnstein: I would not put it past some of them. But they would have a little problem doing that. They have witnesses who've just come in off the street, and a prosecutor doesn't know that he can trust them, you see? If he dummies up a statement, one of them is liable to scream bloody murder.

Student: How about a statement by a cop?

Burnstein: Well, a cop's statement is another story. But there again there's a little psychological factor. Policemen generally think they know how to write statements. It turns out that they really screw them up. But they get pretty mad if the prosecutor tries to tell them what to do. Our society has this strange notion that the prosecutor tells the police how to act. Usually it's the police who tell the prosecutor what to do.

Now, the second thing in cross-examination is to try to shake any testimony that was very damaging to your client, if you can. It's very hard to talk about cross-examination. You have to sit in courtrooms and watch it. But let me make a few general comments:

Whatever else you do, don't just go over the direct testimony! If there are harmful parts that you can't shake, just ignore them. If you do attack a witness's harmful testimony, don't go over it in the same order that the prosecution did; jump around. That gives you the best chance of showing up a phony statement. Remember that if you just get a witness to repeat the story he told on direct examination, you've let him stick the knife into your client twice instead of only once.

In this Johnson case, the prosecution's witnesses are so funny—they each have a different story about everything. In the first place, none of the witnesses from the restaurant can identify either defendant in lineups or in the courtroom. And then they conflict on all the details. When Officer Grey was outside getting himself into trouble, he shouted, "Go and get my partner." The guys trot back into the restaurant, and their testimony about where they found the other policeman you just wouldn't believe. Some witnesses found him in the bathroom. Others along the passage going back to it. And another witness said, "No, he was in this other room, standing under a chandelier looking at murals."

Student: Can you show that some of the witnesses are lying?

Burnstein: Usually even where you get a lot of conflicting statements by witnesses, you're not going to get anywhere telling the jury they are consciously lying. These witnesses are not involved with the police. They were just there in the restaurant. Most of them testified that they had been drinking. If they were consciously lying you'd think the DA would have gotten them to tell approximately the same story. You have to explain to the jury that they all *thought* they saw what they testified to but obviously some or all are mistaken about some or all of what they said. Perhaps nobody will ever really know what actually happened.

Okay. The prosecution's case is over; here comes the defense case. Again, trial work, criminal work, political work is like any other kind of law or aspect of life: You're only going to be as effective as the time you put in. If you've done your job correctly, you'll know all the prosecutor's possible witnesses and legal arguments—every case he's going to cite, every motion you will have to make, every piece of evidence he is going to try to introduce, and every argument you can make to keep that evidence out.

If you've done your work right, there should be damn few surprises. But there always *are* some. If you've asked one of your witnesses a question fifty times and got the same answer fifty times, when he actually comes up on the witness stand he's going to answer it a different way. It never fails; every witness is going to answer at least one question in a different way than you expect him to. And you have to learn not to react. Your face can't show anything at all. That kind of surprise you simply have to expect to happen.

Student: You go over and over a witness's testimony?

Burnstein: That depends. You have to avoid making the witness sound like he's been coached. He shouldn't give the same answers in exactly the same words on cross-examination that he gives on direct examination. That's one of the key indications that a witness was coached. So, tell your witnesses, "I'm not trying to get you to memorize any particular answers. What I want is that the subject matter of your answers always be the same when I ask you this question, not any particular words in the answer."

To prepare my own witnesses, I start by asking them what happened. Then I sit down with the story and put it into some kind of order that will make a good direct examination. Then I question my witness just as if he were on the witness stand, and we discuss his answers until he sees what I'm getting at with each question. I do that a couple of times. Then I cross-examine him. To do this you have to ask yourself what the hell a competent DA could ask your witness that might trick him up or hurt him or confuse him. You ask him precisely those questions. You fire them at him, and you insist on an answer. Then, after he has answered, you discuss his answers.

Now, I don't tell my witnesses what to wear, but I do tell them, "Whatever you wear, the jury is going to react better to you if you look neat and clean." I don't tell them to cut their hair or shave off their beards and any of that. To some extent it's taking on the life-style battle at the same time you're fighting the rest of the issues in the case. But I have found that if the witness at least looks neat and clean, even if he has long hair or whatever, the jury can accept him. I just don't think it's my business to make my witnesses or my clients change their life style. I try to tell them, "Look, the jury is square and middle-class. You would probably impress them more if you were to put on a suit and tie, but if not we can overcome that particular little handicap."

Each time you put a witness on the stand, you should ask enough preliminary questions so that the jury gets some notion of who that witness is. Ask him, "How old are you?" "Where do you live?" "What do you do?" "Have you got a family?" If you want the jury to believe what that witness says, you have to give them some appreciation of him as a person.

One stupid problem comes up all the time, especially with witnesses who have never been involved in a trial before. The prosecutor will ask, "Have you discussed your testimony with anybody before coming to court?"

The witness's first thought is to say, "No."

Then the DA says, "Well, you've discussed it with Mr. Burnstein, haven't you?"

"Well, yes, I guess I have."

"You've discussed it with your wife, haven't you?"

"Well, I guess I have." Pretty soon the witness looks like a fool. So you have to tell your witnesses that the prosecutor may ask that question and that the answer is "Of course I've discussed the case."

Another trick to warn your witnesses about is that the cross-examiner will try to make them mad, because when a witness gets mad he forgets what he was going to say and he's liable to say anything. Even if he doesn't say anything damaging, it makes a bad impression on the jury when a witness blows up. The witness is for one side or the other, but the jurors aren't, so they don't react as hostilely to the DA. You have to warn your witness, "Don't play into the prosecutor's hands. You're a friend of Joe's, right? That's why you want to be a witness. So don't blow up. Keep your cool."

You have to try to assess whether each person is going to be a good witness or a bad witness. If he's going to be a bad witness, but he's got some crucial testimony, keep the direct examination as short as possible and hope for the best on cross-examination. If you think a witness will respond well to questions, then you can have a much longer direct examination to bring out more things.

Frequently you need testimony by experts in a criminal case or in a personal-injury case—chemists or psychiatrists or whatever. I try to get people who can adjust to the judicial format and still be able to tell a story. A lot of guys may be really good shrinks or chemists but they freeze up when they get into court with all the restrictions as to the form of the question, relevancy, scope, and so forth.

AFG: Some people seem to feel there is something wrong or wasteful about taking personal-injury cases—that a lawyer should just take political cases.

Burnstein: The people who tell me it's wrong to take a P-I case had better find some other way for me to make a living while I'm trying these other cases. P-I cases pay the office expenses, and most political and criminal cases don't.

The only way you can make a living practicing straight criminal law is by having a volume practice and not trying your cases. You get fifty or sixty new cases a month, and you plead just about every goddam one guilty to something or other. You work out your arrangements with the district attorney's office and with the judges so that you can get more pleas than a private lawyer who doesn't specialize in criminal cases. You would be doing a good service for a lot of your clients. In point of fact, most people who are arrested can probably be proved guilty of something or other if the DA takes it to trial. That may be a hard line but it's probably true. So, by working out some kind of better plea and sentence, you may be doing your client a very good service.

But obviously if you do that exclusively your bargaining power in a tough case is reduced almost to zero, because the DA knows that you won't go to trial. That's why I would never do only criminal law. I want to be free to try every case that I feel ought to be tried.

Student: Do your political clients bring their paying cases to you?

Burnstein: That's one of several ironies in doing political work. The five of us who tried the Berkeley Free Speech Movement case in 1965 spent eleven weeks in the trial plus all the time in preparation and pretrial motions and the appeal and God knows what else. None of us got a single nickel out of that.

Later on some of the defendants in that case (and there were almost 800 defendants) had other legal matters—divorces, arrests for grass, auto accidents, all kinds of stuff—and they would not come to us. Some of them thought we were too busy, which I'm sorry about, but some of them said, "You're okay in a political case, but for this real criminal case we want to go to a regular lawyer who's got a fix in with the DA, see?" You know, you just want to strangle people sometimes.

Now let me move on to two final points in a trial: the closing argument and the instructions or charge to the jury.

Some lawyers take the position that instructions aren't very important; the jury doesn't pay much attention to them anyway, because they're long and confusing. These lawyers don't spend much time preparing proposed instructions to submit to the judge. I used to think along those lines, but I've changed my opinion in the last couple of years. I now think it's one of the most important parts of most trials, particularly political trials, and especially if there's a First Amendment question of some kind.

In California, the judge must disclose to counsel, before their closing arguments, what instructions he's going to give to the jury. The purpose of closing argument is to argue the facts *and the law*. It's to show how the testimony that the jury has heard fits into the law of the case. So you can't argue the law of the case until the judge tells you what it is.

Some lawyers like to talk just about facts or broad theories and strategies. I suppose it's a question of style. I think of myself as more of a book lawyer than a trial lawyer—as a constitutional scholar. So I take a book approach, and I like to talk law to the jury if at all possible.

You know the old line: If the law's on your side you pound the law, and if the facts are on your side you pound the facts, and if neither is on your side you pound the table. Well, if there's anything in the law that's on my side, I want to talk about it.

I like to read to the jury the very instructions that the judge is going to give them on any point I think is important. That serves several purposes. It enables me to relate the facts to the exact language the judge will use. And psychologically I've found that juries are very impressed with that. Later they hear the judge read the same thing, and they think, "Aha, that Mr. Burnstein's a smart guy. He knew what the judge was going to tell us. He was right about what the law of the case is."

So, if an instruction is at all helpful, use it. And if one is very harmful, I think you have to use *it* too. The jury's going to hear it anyway from the judge, and the prosecutor's going to talk to them about it. You might as well deal with it head on: read it to the jury, and show how the facts of the case don't fit into it.

Student: But I wonder sometimes if jurors really understand the instructions, because they are usually in legal jargon.

Burnstein: You've got twelve people, none of whom have ever been to law school. Most of them have never served on a jury before. And the judge reads them three quarters of an hour of legal garbage, right? It's all technical and complicated and he jumps from one place to the other. I've never yet been in a courtroom where the twelve jurors understood everything the judge said. But each juror understands or thinks he understands a portion of it. And I am convinced that most often the jurors make a conscientious effort to listen to what the judge is telling them and to apply it. So, if you want an acquittal you have to get a number of jurors to find something in the judge's instructions that convinces them, based on your closing argument, that the defendant is not guilty. You have to give the sympathetic jurors a handle to argue with the others in the jury room.

Student: Do the jurors get a copy of the instructions?

Burnstein: Some places they do; in California they don't. But they can come back and ask that the instructions be reread.

Now, often when a case is over and you talk to the jurors to find out why they did what they did, you find that they have very strange notions of what the judge told them. Sometimes it bears very little relationship to what he actually said. But I'm pretty well convinced that most jurors do try to follow the instructions. That's why I really think it's important to give friendly jurors something in those instructions that they can use to support your client.

The longer the instructions as a whole, the more important it is to stress the good ones in your argument. The jury can't remember a forty-five-minute legal lecture. They'll remember only the instructions that they've heard most and that make the most sense.

AFG: Do you think it's helpful to tell the jurors that they have the right to do what they think is right regardless of the instructions?

Burnstein: I usually say, "You know, I'm not sure of the jury as an institution anymore. I'm not sure it's workable or fair or just, as an institution. There used to be a time when jurors remembered and understood that they could simply ignore the judge's instructions in order to do justice." And then I pass on to something else quickly.

The law of the United States is probably clear that jurors do *not* have to follow the judge's instructions. In other words, if the jurors want to vote the defendant not guilty simply because they like the color of his shirt, there's nothing that the judge or the state or the prosecutor can do. They have that right. The U.S. Court of Appeals for the First Circuit recognized it explicitly in the case of Dr. Spock.

You may not be allowed to argue to the jury that they ought to ignore the judge's instructions—judges naturally get rather uptight about that. But there's no reason why you can't slip it in a little. It's the old saying: You can't unring a bell. That's why a political trial is a political trial, because outside the courtroom a lot of bells have been rung and the jurors' heads are ringing with political prejudice. So, as far as I'm concerned, you've not doing your client a service to simply not let any *new* bells be rung in the courtroom, even assuming that's possible.

Student: Suppose your client wants you to keep the politics out of it, like in the Spock situation, where some of the lawyers tried the case like a straight case?

Burnstein: That's one of the reasons they lost that case at the trial level, I think. Well, obviously your client has the final decision. If he wants to keep politics out, either you don't take the case or you do your best to keep politics out. You can present your arguments to him, but if he decides the other way, it's his case. In the final analysis, you're not the one going to jail.

In the Spock case, it seems to me, from what Jessica Mitford reported in her book on that trial, it wasn't so much the defendants who wanted to keep the politics out, it was some of their lawyers. The lawyers have got to realize what their role is. It seems to me that the lawyer's role is not to decide the political questions for his clients but to advise his clients as to the legal consequences. After all, a client doesn't have to go to law school to decide what's right or wrong with the American government, for instance. He's just as hip politically as the lawyer is.

Things seem to go full circle. We used to argue in the 1960s that the older lawyers were making political decisions for their clients when they should have let their clients make those decisions. Now the younger lawyers in the early 1970s are arguing that they should make the decisions for their clients because their clients are not as sophisticated and don't know as much about politics. That's very dangerous.

AFG: Mal, do you always use a jury in a criminal case?

Burnstein: In most criminal cases you *must* have a jury trial because the judge simply is not able to disbelieve police. If the witnesses against you are policemen, it's just axiomatic to have a jury trial.

In one case that I had, an old drunken bum of a cop took a statement from my client. This cop lied like a drunken sailor on the witness stand about whether the statement was voluntary, and we proved he perjured himself three ways at least. But when he walks up to testify, he and the judge nod to each other, you know? They've known each other for years. During my cross-examination, everyone in the courtroom could see what a liar this guy was. Then I move to exclude the statement on the grounds that it was not voluntary, based on the inspector's testimony and cross-examination, and the judge says, "No."

Another way to define a political trial is that it's the kind of a case where the judge throws out all theories of law and evidence and where he rules against you when you know damn well he can't. In a political trial you have to put out of your vocabulary the phrase "They can't do that to us"—because they will.

AFG: You sound like you get quite involved in a case. Can you do only one at a time?

Burnstein: You can do only one *trial* at a time. I have a hell of a lot—sixty, seventy cases—going at one time. While I'm in that courtroom I don't think of anything but that one trial. But life doesn't stop for my other clients while I'm trying that case. I call my office two or three times a day to give my secretary and the other lawyers instructions about my other cases, and I go to the office weekends and nights and mornings.

AFG: Changing the subject, could you talk about your proposal to amend the statute about the use of weapons by police?

Burnstein: Well, California law allows the police to shoot suspected felons in the course of apprehending them. It means that if a guy is really joyriding but appears at worst to be stealing a car and he runs away from the policeman, the policeman can take his gun and kill him. Now, that's absolute rot. Any society that institutionalizes that kind of reverence for property over life obviously has got its head up its ass.

We've been trying to get the California statute changed for two years now, to allow killing only for the protection of human safety, not for the protection of property—so that they can't shoot some guy who's running away with a television set in order to save the television set. It's just so obviously needed, if for no other reason than that a whole lot of innocent people get killed. If you've ever shot a handgun you know it's not the most accurate of weapons. When you hit your target it's usually through pure luck, not through any skill. Even in this Johnson case, there were supposedly a whole lot of shots fired at close range and the bullets went all over the place.

Student: You've been talking pretty freely about this pending case. How does that square with this gag rule that they're pushing right now?

Burnstein: There are many cases that hold that you can't take away a lawyer's and a defendant's right to freedom of speech under the guise of giving him a fair trial. First Amendment rights are not suspended before or during the trial. And, as I told you, I've changed the names and the details around.

AFG: Somebody was saying that if no publicity was allowed, the prosecution couldn't make any hay, either. But the *only* hope the defense has of getting popular support is by publicity. Otherwise most people will just say, "If the guy's a defendant he must be guilty of something."

Student: I've heard that one of the main things the left-wing lawyer has going for him is that the prosecutor is not as sharp, doesn't do his homework, and so on. Have you found that's true?

Burnstein: I think that's true to some extent. But you'd better not go home before a case and say, "I don't have to do much, because the DA's not going to do much and he's stupid besides."

You have to look at who becomes a prosecutor. It's a civil-service job with a steady salary coming in. Most bright lawyers don't want to be confined in that bag. I think it's pretty true that not all but a lot of the good young lawyers *are* left-wing by nature and inclination. The prosecutor, on the other hand, generally has one advantage: he's much more used to the courtroom and trial work and rules of evidence in criminal trials than most young left-wing lawyers. And he knows the judges and the court attachés.

AFG: He also has the whole government investigation network to draw on. The one thing he may *not* have is passion. In a particular case he might. Often he just wants to make a record for himself. But *you* may really care about your client, and also care very deeply that justice is done.

Burnstein: Not only for purposes of protecting your client, but also for purposes of doing your own job to your own satisfaction. You've got to take that into account, too.

POLITICAL LAWYERS AND
THEIR CLIENTS
Charles Garry

AFG: Charles Garry is a lawyer with over thirty years of experience in handling trial work, both civil and criminal. Before he became known nationally for representing Huey Newton, Bobby Seale, and Los Siete de la Raza, he represented union members during strikes in the 1930s and 1940s, victims of McCarthyism in the 1950s, and poor black people throughout his career. He has also done personal-injury, domestic-relations, and nonpolitical criminal trial work. He is a past president of the National Lawyers Guild San Francisco chapter, and a partner in the firm of Garry, Dreyfus, McTernan, and Brotsky.

Charles, how do you gather evidence and prepare for the defense of a political client? Maybe you can give us some specific examples from the first Huey Newton trial.

Garry: The first thing you do when you have a client in a serious case, or even a minor case, is to get to know something about him. It's fundamental—if you don't know your client, you're not going to be able to represent him. You've got to know what makes that client of yours tick, what makes him be like he is, what direction he comes from, and what direction he's going. If you don't, then you are failing in your basic responsibility as a trial counsel—your responsibility to marshal the facts.

You have to evaluate the kind of person you're dealing with. If

68

you have a responsive relationship with your client, you'll be able to project that feeling of confidence and security to others.

You've got to know your client's family, schooling, religious background—if he has any. If he's an atheist, you've got to know that, and you've got to know why. You've got to know your client's political views, his thoughts toward life itself. Of course you've got to know his marital status and, if he's not married, whether he's got a girl friend. If your client happens to be a homosexual, you should know that, and you should know the extent of the relationship. The sooner you find these things out, the better.

In the Huey Newton case, the alleged incident took place on October 28, 1967, and he was charged with murdering one policeman, assaulting another, and kidnapping someone else. I was contacted on November first, and I saw Huey on that same day. I felt right away that this man was totally and completely innocent. Huey was the kind of a person I immediately felt a warmth and friendship with; his charisma and his openness and frankness just came right through, even while he was lying in a hospital bed with a tube through his nose. He was in obvious pain from being shot, and the police were all around.

AFG: Even while you were talking to him?

Garry: Yes, the police were all over the place. They'd been kicking his hospital bed and calling him a "goddam dirty nigger son of a bitch," saying they were "going to cut off that tube in your nose so that you'll choke to death, so that the state won't have to bother trying you or gassing you," and things of that kind, right while he was in the hospital.

I immediately suggested that we get a twenty-four-hour nursing service that we would pay for ourselves, so that there would be some protection for him, and that was done.

The first thing I told Huey Newton was to keep his mouth shut. I tell this to every single client: "Don't talk to anybody"—especially if the client is in jail. What the authorities do is to put an agent or an informer or just another prisoner in with him, and they tell that prisoner, "Now, you get some information out of this bloke here, and in exchange we'll see that you're properly taken care of." For instance, in the case of Los Siete de la Raza, the Chicanos charged with the murder of one police officer and assault on another, they had four different people in the cell with the defendants. One of the four was a murderer who testified for the prosecution that one of Los Siete had made certain statements to him; the result is that this prisoner got a year in the county jail on a first-degree-murder charge, and he's out of jail now.

So you've got to warn your client, make him aware that he has no friends he can talk to. Let's assume his cellmate is a good guy. He tells this guy a lot of things. Well, the guy's not a stool pigeon. He's not going to tell anybody. But they can force him to give that information, because there's no confidential relationship between him and your client, as there is between you and your client. Unless there is an attorney–client relationship or clergyman–parishioner relationship, a person who refuses to testify can be held in contempt of court.

Just tell him to say, "My attorney has admonished me not to discuss this case at all with anyone." Don't let him discuss it with friends or relatives, even his parents, because if he's told the story to one person, that one person always has another confidential friend that he can tell it to, in absolute assurance that it will not be relayed, and it becomes a chain reaction. He might as well put it on television and get it over with.

Huey Newton's family is a very close-knit one. Huey being the baby, they just idolized him, not *because* he was the baby, but because he was a very humane, selfless person and very considerate of other people's feelings. I saw this immediately. And I began to study his background, and what the Black Panther Party was about.

This was all part of gathering the evidence. I had never heard of the Black Panther Party or of Huey Newton before this. I had been busy trying other kinds of cases, and when I'm working on a personal-injury case or a straight murder case that's what I concentrate on. So I had to find out what made the Black Panther Party and what made Huey Newton the type of person he was.

Ordinarily when you've got a case, you try to evaluate what the law is in relation to your client's problem. I did not have to do that. I knew what the law was from past experience. What I had to find out was what made my client have the outlook he had.

After all, under the Sixth Amendment of the United States Constitution, the client is entitled to *assistance* of counsel—the lawyer is only an assistant to the person who is defending himself. You can't be a good assistant unless you know who the principal is, what his weaknesses are and what his strengths are.

AFG: What if he doesn't tell you the truth or you don't think he's telling you the truth?

Garry: Well, Ann, telling the truth is irrelevant at this point, because you're finding out about his life, not about what happened in the case. You don't go into the facts of the case with him until such time as you get to know him.

In Huey Newton's case, my investigation of the facts was studying black history, the Black Panther Party, and Huey Newton.

AFG: What if he had come to a straight criminal lawyer who had no political background? Do you think the lawyer could have defended Newton without doing that?

Garry: No, he couldn't have. You see, there was a whole body of materials in existence that had a bearing on the case. For instance, there was an essay by Huey Newton in the Black Panther Party paper of July 17, 1967, in which he had made some very inflammatory statements. If someone read that without understanding its political context or the language of the ghetto, without understanding black history, he might find enough in there to show intent to commit first-degree murder by Huey Newton. If we hadn't understood the political concepts and complexities in Huey Newton's case, I believe he would have been convicted of murder.

AFG: In other words, you cannot have a successful nonpolitical defense for a political defendant?

Garry: It's impossible, just impossible.

AFG: And I think it also takes a long history of handling political and labor cases, and being friends with other lawyers who have handled them, to know how to proceed in a major political trial like this.

Student: Can you expand a little bit about the lawyer as an assistant to the defendant in his defense? How do you allow the defendant to express his political stance in the courtroom?

Garry: Well, let's take the Newton case as a classic example. His position was well known. He had written articles, he had spoken about his party's ten-point program. Since the Black Panther Party was formed to fill a need in the black community, in giving his views Huey was also giving the cry of the community. The black community itself was on trial.

So, before the trial even started, when I was questioning the prospective jurors in voir-dire examination, to decide which ones I wanted to strike from the jury, I went into my client's political views, his opposition to the war in Vietnam, his correlation of the war in Vietnam and the bombing of Hiroshima and the Korean War and all of the other things that were going on, as genocide against people of color. (This voir-dire examination is the subject of a book, *Minimizing Racism in Jury Trials*.) In my opening statement to the jury, I gave the ten-point program of the Black Panther Party. I told them that Huey Newton was a militant who believed that revolutionary change was necessary; I explained that revolutionary change meant abrupt change. When Huey took the stand, he spent two days talking about his philosophy and the Black Panther Party's political outlook. Because you can't duck it. It's there. There's no way of hiding it; what you have to do is project it.

Let me give you an example of the consequences when you try to hide it. Around March 1970, a Black Panther was tried in Los Angeles for alleged murder. The whole case, from picking the jury to the verdict, was done in four days; that includes sentencing the defendant to death! The lawyer who defended him had said, "Let's not talk about the fact that you're a member of the Black Panther Party. Let's not arouse that form of bias and prejudgment in the jury." Well, you can't duck it. You've got to tell the jury, "This is exactly what my client believes. Do you have any prejudgments about it?" Don't let the prosecution sneak it in by innuendo, by saying, "Now, we're not trying the Black Panther Party here, ladies and gentlemen of the jury, we're not trying the revolution; we're trying this man because he did something wrong: he killed a human being." Don't let him get you in that box. Make it very clear that this man is being tried because of his beliefs.

AFG: Could you successfully represent somebody you hated or didn't like or had no empathy for? Have you ever done it?

Garry: In an ordinary criminal case, with no political or racial overtones, I don't have to like my client or dislike him. Remember this: A person who has psychiatric problems, who is emotionally sick, is usually not a person you will like. In many instances the client is suspicious of you, he's paranoid, and you just can't get to like him. You've got to have empathy for him, though; you have to understand him, so that you can start relating to and explaining him.

I've defended some sixty-five first-degree-murder cases, and in some of these cases it wasn't until I began to know something about my client's background that I began to feel sympathetic toward him. But even then these clients will say and do things that rouse your antagonism. That's part of the illness they have. You've got to learn to handle that; you've got to be able to understand it, and when you're picking the jury you've got to tell the jury, "My client is emotionally upset; he's not well. Will you take that into account in evaluating this testimony?"

So, it's not a question of whether you like your client. I think a more germane question would be whether I'd be willing to represent a fascist or a Nazi. The answer is, I will not. Not that I don't think that person should have representation, but he's not going to have *my* representation. I don't know what I would do if there were no other lawyer but me. I hope I don't have to decide that question.

AFG: Do you think a lawyer should say, "I'm a lawyer and an officer of the court, and this person came to me and is my client; I may not agree with what he says or believes, but I think he has a right to representation"?

Garry: I would not be in the same courtroom with that kind of a lawyer. As a matter of fact, back in '68 there was a meeting of movement people and middle-class lawyers in Texas, and I was asked to speak to them. There were about 125 lawyers, establishment lawyers, who committed themselves to take movement cases, and I got them to agree that they would never at any time make a disclaimer of the type you mentioned. I said to them, "When you represent General Motors, you don't say to the judge, 'Now, I don't believe in General Motors' point of view, but they have the right to representation and I'm willing to represent them.' So why in hell do you say it when you're representing some man in a political case?"

In the Newton case, we not only had to bring the ideas into the courtroom, but we also had to project an image back to the community, let them know what the facts were. The first facts we became aware of were that Huey had been shot and that he was being mistreated in the hospital. He was lying on a gurney, one of those cots with wheels, and the police were all around, poking and abusing him while he lay there. Not only that, but he had been placed flat on his back with his arms stretched out, which we later learned was a very harmful position for someone who has had a bullet go through his abdomen. A white woman doctor saw a picture of this on the front page of the San Francisco *Sun Reporter,* a black-owned newspaper, and she got so incensed at what she saw that she wrote a letter apologizing as a medical doctor for the fact that there was a doctor standing there permitting the stretching of the abdomen like that.

So, as part of the factual presentation to the public and to the courtroom, we filed an independent lawsuit against the doctor and the hospital, charging them with malpractice. We felt that this was part and parcel of what had to be done. In filing the suit we were able to project a sympathetic image at a time when the general community was against Huey Newton. The Black Panther Party was looked down upon, and the small handful of friends that Newton had were confused and bewildered and lacking in support. They wanted me to issue a statement saying I had conclusive proof that Huey Newton was innocent. I was not in a position to make such a statement. It would have been premature. But they needed a rallying point, and this suit became the rallying point. The news of the police and the hospital ganging up on Huey Newton, harassing him and damaging his health, made tremendous public relations. And the tide began to turn; soon thereafter we were able to start a community movement demanding "Free Huey Now," to free Huey Newton without having to go to court.

The suit had other values, too: it smoked out some of the enemies in the criminal lawsuit. The minute we filed the civil law-suit and served the papers on the hospital and the doctor, the hospital lawyers wanted to take Huey Newton's deposition, to ask him a whole series of questions that he would have to answer under oath. Well, here I am, in the case less than thirty days; I haven't discussed any of the facts with my client, and he is now going to have his testimony taken under oath. You can well imagine that created a lot of strategic and practical problems. But I was right there with Huey, and I had him answer all the ques-tions that were asked except a few about where he had been and what had happened. And from the questions that were asked I could see that the hospital was working hand in hand with the district attorney and the police. Then from the questions that they asked after the replies by Huey I was able to infer that there were certain areas that they weren't sure about, certain blank areas.

AFG: Is this fairly common—that an affirmative suit, on the civil side, is helpful soon after a criminal case has been started?

Garry: Well, it depends on the circumstances of each case, Ann. There are cases where I would not file an affirmative suit.

In this instance we not only filed the malpractice suit, but we also filed an affirmative suit in the federal court, under Title 42 of the United States Code, Section 1983, which is the original civil-rights act passed during Reconstruction. This statute is the basic law that says you can sue someone, like a police officer, for depriv-ing you of your rights under the Constitution. We filed a suit against the mayor and police chief of Oakland for harassment and intimidation of the Black Panther Party and Huey Newton by arresting him and other Panthers with no probable cause, and for committing other illegal acts. That suit was very productive, and in fact it is still pending, all these many months. It has acted as a kind of tranquilizer on the establishment, discouraging them from more flagrant abuses against the black community.

Student: What was the resolution of the suit against the hospital?

Garry: The judge ruled that the case would be on ice until Huey *did* answer those questions that I hadn't allowed him to answer, so that ended that lawsuit. It served its purpose.

Student: You didn't want to let him answer the questions so that you could pursue that case?

Garry: No. You see, this deposition was being taken before the time when the grand jury indicted Huey, so I didn't have the benefit of the grand-jury testimony at that point. In California state courts, when a grand jury indicts you the proceedings are recorded and you get them in transcript form. So you learn an awful lot about what the prosecution has in its case. The transcript of the grand-jury indictment, when we got it, showed, for example, that the police officer who had allegedly been assaulted by Huey Newton could not testify that Huey had a gun in his hands.

A man named Dell Ross also testified to the grand jury. His story is very interesting. He said he was driving in his car with another man near the scene when he heard shots and heard two men running. The two men came up to his car. They opened the door, his passenger slipped out of the car and ran away, and the two men jumped in. He testified that one had a gun in his hand and told him, "Keep moving. I just shot a couple of dudes and I'll shoot you if you don't move." He testified that this man was the one who was wounded; so they construed that it was Huey Newton. Ross said that they forced him to drive a couple of miles, and then they both got out of the car and disappeared. So they charged Huey with one count of kidnapping, in addition to one count of assaulting a police officer with a deadly weapon, and one count for the murder of Officer Frey.

You can see that Ross gave a very important piece of testimony before the grand jury, and I would have to talk to Mr. Ross at one time or another. I did that about two weeks before the trial began.

AFG: Why did you wait so long?

Garry: For one thing, I couldn't find him. He was a migratory worker, illiterate. And then the opportunity wasn't proper. You know, you've got to talk to a witness in the proper atmosphere. He finally came to my office, and I taped him. Then two or three weeks later he was on the witness stand in Huey's trial.

AFG: You had called him?

Garry: No. He was the only witness related to the kidnapping charge—I wouldn't call him. It was up to the prosecution to present evidence to substantiate that charge. So the prosecution called him, but he said something like "I won't talk, Fifth Amendment." Then the prosecution offered him immunity from prosecution if he testified. But he still wouldn't testify. The judge said, "If you don't testify, I can put you in jail."

"All right, put me in jail."

Then the judge said, "Now, if you don't remember . . ."

"All right, I don't remember."

And from then on he couldn't remember a goddam thing. Well, the district attorney proceeded, with the concurrence of the judge, to refresh his memory by reading the entire testimony that he had given at the grand-jury hearing—over my vehement objection, of course. You see, a decision had just come down, about a week before Ross took the stand, which said that in a criminal case, if the defendant was not a party to the former proceeding, the statement made then can't be used in the case against that defendant. I called that to the judge's attention. He ignored it; he permitted the entire testimony of Dell Ross before the grand jury to go in.

AFG: How did you hear about that decision?

Garry: I read all the "advance sheets."

AFG: Those are the weekly booklets of new court opinions, and they take hours of reading on a consistent basis. Do you have time?

Garry: Oh, I have to have time. As a matter of fact, I was the only person who was familiar with that case, and that point turned out to be one of the bases for the reversal of Huey's conviction by the court of appeal.

After the prosecution finished "refreshing" Dell Ross's memory by reading his whole grand-jury testimony, I started my cross-examination. I said, "Do you remember talking to me?"

"No."

"Did you ever see me before?"

"No."

So I carted out my tape of him. I had transcribed the entire tape and made twenty-five copies for the judge and jurors, and I played the tape in the courtroom so they could follow the written transcription and hear his voice at the same time. On the tape I had said, "Now, Mr. Ross, I want you to know I'm taping this, you understand that?"

"Yes, I do."

"You understand that you don't have to talk to me at all, unless you want to. All I'm trying to do is get to the truth, you understand that too, Mr. Ross?"

"Oh, yes."

"Now, you're not going to tell me anything that's not the truth, are you?" And I went on, "I want to call your attention to this portion of your testimony in the grand jury. Did you so testify?"

He said, "I don't remember what I said. I would say anything, because I was scared."

And he went right down the line, denying all of the things that he said to the grand jury, denying that Huey had said to him, "I've just shot two dudes," denying that he ever saw a gun.

AFG: Did the prosecution object to your playing a tape?

Garry: No. There's no way they could object to it; it would have been curtailing cross-examination.

AFG: What was Ross's reaction to your playing the tape?

Garry: None at all.

"Is that your voice?"

"I don't know nothing. I don't know nothing."

And at the conclusion of the tape, I moved that the entire testimony be stricken, and the judge told the jury to forget and discount that they had ever heard all this. The judge was really taken aback by what he heard on the tape, and the district attorney was just floored. The district attorney kept muttering how there should be an investigation of how this man came to my office, and all this kind of garbage.

AFG: Now, wait a minute—how *did* he come there?

Garry: I did not use a detective. I have found that white investigators are absolutely useless in cases of black men. The community will not talk to them. There were so many wild leads, I finally took over the investigation myself. I had the help of the Panthers and of several University of California Boalt Hall law students, who did invaluable work for me. A law student would have a Panther go with him—beautiful for investigation purposes.

AFG: How did you let the community know that you wanted their help and their information?

Garry: Well, this incident took place in the Skid Row part of Oakland—a kind of red-light district there—and at five o'clock in the morning. There were several whorehouses along the street there, hotels with prostitutes, and I made it a point to talk to many of these prostitutes and got all kinds of answers. One young lady told me that she saw the whole incident—that there was a third man who shot the police officer, and even went over and kicked him after he shot him, and then got away. But she also said some other things that didn't fit with the situation as we knew it factually. I weighed what she had to say and decided I couldn't use her.

It's important to remember that in a criminal case the district attorney has to prove what happened; the defense attorney only needs to show that there are questions the prosecution hasn't answered or to raise a doubt about the evidence against the defendant.

AFG: Would you have hesitated to call this woman because of her occupation?

Garry: No. As a matter of fact, during the time that the trial was going on her emotional involvement in the Huey Newton case was such that she gave up her profession. I understand she's gone back in business again. But she was very friendly to us.

You just have to evaluate whether you can receive more harm by certain testimony.

AFG: When do you go on these investigations?

Garry: You go whenever the people are available. If it meant carousing around at night and going to the whorehouses, we did it. To get cooperation, of course, we had to let the community know what the issues were. So when we made an attack on the grand jury—that the grand jury was hand-picked from the judges' cronies —we got a lot of publicity about the case and about the Panthers. This had a tremendous effect on the community, and we began to get friends from many many places. All I had to do was say that I was representing Huey Newton and the doors were wide open.

It got so that I could walk in any part of the ghetto by myself and get all kinds of help—the barrier broke down. I literally lived in the ghetto for months. I became a familiar sight there, and I interviewed hundreds of different people. Some of them would give me such wild yarns I'd think they must be smoking pot, but I had to listen to them and check the stories out.

Student: Did Ross's testimony from the tape stand up, or was the prosecution able to make him deny what was on the tape?

Garry: No, they didn't try. The judge ruled that there be a judgment of acquittal for the kidnapping. But, you see, the damage was already done; the jury had heard all this garbage, things that would connect Huey. The court of appeal ultimately used that as one of the grounds of reversal—that the judge permitted the jury's mind to be poisoned.

AFG: Did you make a motion for mistrial then?

Garry: I made motions for mistrial about fifteen times a day. Every day I would file a bunch of newspaper articles to show the inflammatory atmosphere of the court.

For instance, to give you a comical example, right in the middle of the trial a black doctor, Washington E. Garner, M.D., became a police commissioner in San Francisco. He's an old buddy of mine, socially, professionally, and in every other respect. And the first thing he did was to send me a badge making me an honorary San Francisco policeman—a nice little gold badge with a little blue card saying that's what I was. Well, the San Francisco Police Association heard about it, and they started raising hell. They called a press conference saying that here was the country's number-one cop hater receiving an honorary police badge. Then the Oakland Police Association came en masse to protest about this, and the mayor of Oakland started shooting off his mouth. Of course all of these things were on the radio and television. I would read these into the record, and attach the newspaper articles as court exhibits, and demand a mistrial because the atmosphere had been poisoned. This went on daily.

You've got to be prepared, you've got to know what's going on, because what you do in the courtroom becomes strategic. You won't be able to play on the facts if you don't know the facts.

Now, some of the facts in the Huey Newton case came right out of the books. The actual physical evidence was a very small thing.

Huey Newton testified for two days; of that time he spent only four minutes talking about the facts of what happened! The first question I asked was, "Did you kill Officer Frey?"

He said, "No, I didn't."

I said, "Cross-examine."

The judge said, "I think you'd better ask some more questions."

All a good lawyer can do in a courtroom, once he's well prepared, prepared to the nth degree, is use some showmanship and strategy and tactics, know when to cross-examine and when not to cross-examine, when to put on a witness and when not to put on a witness.

AFG: You talked about adverse publicity, but what effect do you think the whole "Free Huey" campaign had on the trial?

Garry: I think this all relates to what we call a public hearing, a public trial. The prosecution would have been very happy to try Huey in some star-chamber proceeding, where no one would hear anything about it; he would have been snuffed out in a day. The fact that we got a manslaughter conviction instead of first-degree murder was accomplished by the concern of the community. It's just as simple as that. So don't sell "Power to the people" short.

AFG: How did community interest help him, precisely?

Garry: Well, it was a positive public interest to offset the negative interest of Huey Newton's enemies. It created, for the first time, a balance—not a full, complete balance, but somewhat of a balance.

AFG: You mean the jury heard the community?

Garry: It heard the community. And those on the jury who had some feelings responded to what we were presenting.

AFG: You also represented some of the Oakland Seven antiwar protesters who were acquitted of conspiracy. Do you think the publicity affected the jury in that case?

Garry: Yes, it did. Sure. When we talk about publicity, we're talking about communication, about getting more people to understand the struggles of the day. Look, if it wasn't for the young people fighting against the war in Vietnam and Cambodia, God knows where our armed forces would be fighting today.

AFG: Are you saying you have some faith in the American people?

Garry: I have tremendous faith in the American people.

AFG: On juries?

Garry: No, I don't have any faith in juries. But I have more faith in juries than I have in the judge.

Sometimes you have to argue a controversial case in which the law is technically against you. Then you must rely on the jury to decide the case properly. In the case of Dr. Spock, the U.S. Court of Appeals for the First Circuit said that the jury was supposed to be "the conscience of the community" and was supposed to "look at more than logic," particularly in controversial areas, such as free-speech cases, where "a community standard or conscience was to be applied" by the jury.

That's not a new idea. When I first started practicing law, I relied on that all the time. I tried a lot of prostitution cases in those days, and I used to say, in closing argument, "Ladies and gentlemen of the jury, the judge will tell you that my client has violated the law by turning this trick. But I want you to forget about this judge. I want you to use your common sense. I know what the law is, but the law was made by men. My client had nothing to do with making the law; women have had no say in making this law. Now, ladies and gentlemen, there are twelve of you here, and no one has told you to leave your brains behind you when you walked into this courtroom. So I ask you: You know you can't turn a trick alone. Where is the man? This young lady is being prosecuted for trying to make a living, trying to give some sort of pleasure, and where is the man who hired her?"

I never lost a prostitution case.

AFG: But would you rather trust a judge instead of a jury in a complicated case in which you are developing legal points?

Garry: Well, let me give you two examples and you draw your own inferences.

In the 1950s I tried two murder cases in which I raised the issue of diminished responsibility. That's the area under the law between sanity, where you are fully responsible for the acts you commit and can be convicted and sentenced, and insanity, where you are not responsible for your acts and cannot be convicted or sent to prison but only to a mental hospital. If you have diminished responsibility for your acts because of your emotional state at the time, you can't be convicted of first-degree murder, because you didn't have the *intent* to commit murder that the law requires for this charge. To substantiate the diminished responsibility of my clients, I used an expert witness, Dr. Bernard Diamond. Dr. Diamond is a professor of law, a professor of criminology, and a psychiatrist.

In the first case my client had killed his wife and her alleged paramour, who was seventy-five years old! I tried that case with a jury. The evidence was clear that my client's wife had not had a sexual relationship with this old man. In fact, the old man's wife testified that he hadn't had an erection in almost twenty-five years. My client was charged with first-degree murder, and we were trying to get that reduced to manslaughter on the basis of his diminished responsibility. Well, the jury was out only two hours and brought in the verdict we wanted. And the reason they were out two hours was not that they were arguing over whether he was guilty of first-degree murder or just manslaughter, but that some of them wanted to acquit him, and the others argued, "If Garry wanted us to acquit him, he would have asked for an acquittal. All he asked for was a manslaughter verdict."

The other, similar, murder case in which I had to choose be-between judge and jury trial concerned a longshoreman charged with killing his gang boss. The case was assigned to a judge who seemed to me to be okay. I discussed it with several people, and we decided that it would be best to waive the jury in this case. There had been a fight going on in the longshoremen's union between two factions, and this gang boss was the leader of one, so a highly publicized jury trial for his murderer would just have made things worse.

The facts of the case were these: My client went to work at seven o'clock one night and he and his buddies were drinking. By ten o'clock he wasn't doing his work too well, and the gang boss cursed him out, in Russian, calling him a "no-good cocksucker." This terminology was a crucial factor in what happened. My client was Russian Orthodox, and at this insult he started telling the gang boss off. The gang boss, who was twenty years younger, then beat him up unmercifully and booted him. When my client got up again, he went home, got his gun (which he had never used before), fired it once to make sure it worked, came back, and shot the gang boss.

Now, I had Bernie Diamond testify in this case too. He spent many hours talking to my client in jail, recording their talks, and then studying the tapes. My client was known as Sleepy Nick, because he always drooped his eyelids. He would sit in meetings or other places with his eyes closed as if he were asleep. Nick told Diamond that when he closed his eyes like that he saw pictures on his eyelids—of angels having sexual intercourse! Every time he closed his eyes he saw a matinee! Diamond also learned that Nick's actual sexual relations with his wife had been on the side of impotence for a long time. So the gang boss's criticism of Nick's work, plus that particular Russian insult, plus the beating, triggered him off. Diamond testified that Nick lost all reason at that point and was brought back to reality only by killing his gang boss.

Now, at the conclusion of the case the judge said, "If I were to believe Dr. Diamond—and I do believe him—he has the only rational interpretation of what happened. But," he said, "the law does not permit me to believe him." So he found my client guilty of second-degree murder. Now, in that case, I believe a second-degree verdict was the *worst* I could have gotten from a jury, no matter how the judge had instructed them on the law.

So, do you take a jury or a judge? In this instance I made a mistake by accepting the judge.

The case was appealed, and although the higher courts didn't reverse the conviction, the California Supreme Court opinion clearly set forth diminished responsibility as the law in California.

So, from all this I hope you gather that I don't believe in trying cases with judges. I have no confidence in them, especially in political cases. Whenever the atmosphere is such that we have to resort to political tactics, then you must remember that the judge is the last person in the world you can rely upon.

AFG: Were these two cases political cases?

Garry: No.

AFG: Why did you take them?

Garry: Well, I was supposed to get paid for the first one, which was an optical illusion. The second one was related to our labor work.

AFG: Do you see any relationship between your early labor-union clients and your political clients today?

Garry: Sure I do. I remember when the labor movement was where the Black Panthers are today. I remember walking into a court to represent certain labor unions and being looked down upon with more vehemence than I am today walking in with a Panther.

The thing is that now labor unions have changed. They've forgotten that they're part of the class struggle, and they've started becoming part of the establishment. They've been bought off, bribed. Any time a union at the negotiating table worries about whether the boss is making money or not, it's no longer representing labor. In my day we used to say, "When the boss can't pay the wages, tell him to close up and join us, become a worker." But now they say, "Well, the boss has to make money, but we'd like a piece of that action."

AFG: Did you ever represent unions that committed acts of violence?

Garry: Sure. I've defended many a labor-union guy. Some of them were even *agents provocateurs,* actual agents of the company. By the time I found out, I was already committed to represent them. One guy I represented was involved in a five-and-ten-cent-store deal, and I found out he was an agent.

AFG: How?

Garry: He told me himself. He kept saying, "Don't worry about it, Garry. It's all greased." Well, the grease started slipping in the trial. Then he said to me, "Why, those son-of-a-bitch two-timing bastards! After paying me to do this, now they want me to go to prison!"

AFG: You talked about using Dr. Diamond as a witness in the murder cases. Did you use him or any other expert witnesses in the Newton trial?

Garry: Yes. We used Diamond to substantiate our voir-dire examination of prospective jurors to determine whether they had latent racism. I put Diamond on the witness stand and asked him, "Doctor, from your experience, do you think it is possible to pick an impartial jury that is free from racial prejudice and white racism?"
He said, "Absolutely not."
The judge leaned over and asked him, "Could you do it by studying them in your own clinic?"
"Perhaps, if I had forty-five or fifty hours with each person, and if they were willing to become patients and be honest in this regard."

The judge said, "That's ridiculous. We can't do that. You're lucky to get fifteen minutes with a prospective juror, much less forty-five or fifty hours in a psychiatric consultation room."

Then, on cross-examination, the district attorney asked, "Doctor, do you have any prejudices?"

"Indeed I do."

"What are some of your prejudices?"

"Well, I don't like lawyers, and because of this I make allowances when they become patients of mine, so that I will have an objective approach."

"What other prejudices do you have?"

"Well, being a Jew, I don't like Jews."

And the judge, it was Judge Friedman, said, "What's that again?"

The district attorney asked, "What other prejudices do you have, Doctor?"

"I don't like wealthy people." (The doctor himself is a very wealthy man.) "So I make allowances when they are patients of mine."

Diamond was very effective. We put on another expert, Professor Herman Blake, to testify about statements made by Huey that the prosecution had introduced to show that Huey was a cop killer. Blake was able to testify that when Huey Newton said so and so, what he meant was such and such, not what the white man understood it to mean. This is the rhetoric of the ghetto, the hyperbole of the ghetto; when you say X it means Y.

Herman Blake is a professor of sociology at the University of California at Santa Cruz, a very dynamic, outgoing person, very articulate. We had him on the stand, and he wrote the word "signify" on the blackboard.

I said, "Could you give us an example of what that means, Doctor?"

"Yes," he said. "On a beautiful Sunday afternoon, three of the brothers are sashaying down the street in their Sunday best, enjoying life. All at once they see on the porch a beautiful brown sister, extremely beautiful, sitting on a chair. The three brothers go up to where the sister is, and one says to the others, 'What beautiful legs that chair has.' This signifies something else—the beautiful legs of the chair, the beautiful legs of the girl."

This was a way of presenting an essential fact—that the language of the ghetto does not mean what a white prosecutor says it means.

AFG: Where did you get the idea that this needed to be brought out?

Garry: Newton said it to me, and I knew it to be true. I remembered the first Smith Act trial against the Communist Party leaders, the Dennis case. The prosecution had a stool-pigeon witness who testified that when the Communists used such and such a term, they were just trying to hoodwink the public with "Aesopian language" that really meant something else. So, I took a page out of that case, and I wanted the reverse. At first I didn't quite know what I wanted; it takes time to flounder around and figure out what things you want.

Student: I'm interested in relating the theory of diminished responsibility to property crimes. Are there any precedents for applying it to someone who is forced to steal in order not to starve?

Garry: You're confusing diminished responsibility with the constitutional right to eat. Don't confuse the two. Diminished responsibility applies only to crimes of passion, when a person does something because of his emotional condition at the time, without forming a specific intent with malice aforethought.

Now, what you're thinking about is the fact that certain things are constitutionally inalienable. You have the constitutional right to breathe, to walk the streets, to live. In order to live, you've got to be able to eat, and eat properly; you've got to have proper housing and atmosphere. These are part of the basic right to be a human being. No one can take the air away from you. And yet we have devised a system by which they can take the food away from you and say it's legal. And if you grab that food and eat it, you're guilty of a crime, although if you grab the air and breathe it you're not.

Student: But if diminished responsibility applies when there was no malice aforethought, can't it apply to a crime like stealing in which no malice is required? I'm sure hunger is just as strong a motivating force as intoxication.

Garry: What you're saying, without admitting it, is, How can we make a constitutional argument for socialism? I'm for it, if we can work it out. I've given this matter a lot of thought, but I haven't quite reached where you are yet. You may be on the right track.

Student: Mr. Garry, how do you think the establishment coordinates activities like the raids on Panther headquarters? There are a lot of people who seem to be part of a kind of racist conspiracy, and whenever I find anyone who might know anything about how it works I try to elicit this information. Would you like to make any comments on that?

Garry: Whatever comments I make are purely conjecture. I don't have any direct line on this, but it just seems that these activities are all coordinated. Basically it's because the policemen on the beat, whom my clients refer to as pigs, and the lawmakers, whom my clients refer to as pigs, and the judge and the prosecutor and some of the attorneys, whom they also refer to as pigs, are all working for the same employer. They all have the same mentality. That's why they're hired. And they all respond to anything that is a threat to their own security. Aren't the war in Vietnam, Korea, Laos, Cambodia, imperialism, and the war in the ghettos the same thing? They're all brought on by the fear of a people's movement to apportion the wealth democratically according to the needs of the people.

If you look at it that way, then you don't have to worry about whether there's a central system that gathers and coordinates everything, as the human nervous system does. These people all think alike. They look upon anything that deviates as a threat to their security, and they respond in a violent manner.

Student: But they don't have the same mentality. The families who are worth $7 million don't have the same mentality as the policemen on the beat. Yet somehow these distinct classes can work together on one main issue.

Garry: You're overlooking the fact that the policeman on the beat is hired to protect that property. He's hired to keep the so-called peace. And he thinks with that mentality or he wouldn't take that job.

They would never hire *me;* they would never make *me* a judge. Why not? I would never buy their method of doing business. Make me a judge and the district attorney would disqualify me in every case. In civil cases, where you have an individual pitted against an insurance company, basically, the insurance company lawyers would disqualify me. If they didn't, you know what I would do? I'd decide for the individual every time. I'd release every goddam guy who was jailed—on some writ of habeas corpus, some violation of his constitutional rights. Just present it to me and I'd release him.

They're careful about whom they pick. They pick the guys who will do their bidding. You've got to remember that. That's why I don't trust judges. If you became a judge tomorrow, under this system, I wouldn't trust you either; I'd watch you with a jaundiced eye. If I became a judge tomorrow, I wouldn't trust myself.

Student: Why did you go to law school?

Garry: Because I disliked capital punishment. As a kid I was an ardent reader, and every time I read about an execution it would make me shudder. I wanted to destroy capital punishment. I wasn't in law school but a year or two before I recognized that capital punishment was only one small part of our injustices. But that was what directed me to law school.

Student: Do you think being a lawyer is the best way to bring about social change?

Garry: I don't think it's the lawyer's role to make social change himself. I don't see how he can do it. The courts are the last place in the world to make social change.

You've got to understand the role of the courts and who the courts represent. Our judicial system represents the status quo, to keep big business where it can continue its exploitation. That being the case, all the lawyer can do is try to expose the court system: its chicanery, its inconsistency, its dishonesty, its degradation of human dignity, its function of trying to clean up the establishment's dirty linen by sending men and women to prison, rather than finding answers and making the democratic system work on an economic as well as a social basis.

I look upon the "movement" lawyer as a person who can keep

his client out of jail maybe one day, two days, three months, three years, so that the client can make the changes that are necessary on the street.

Now, that doesn't mean that the lawyer himself cannot participate in his individual capacity in making these social changes, but he doesn't do it as a lawyer, he doesn't do it because he is a lawyer; he does it because he's a citizen. But in that courtroom he has a special task to perform, and wherever he can he has to expose the system and tie it up. I don't have faith in the judicial system, but I do my work so that young people can change that system. All I can do is stall it, give them a temporary breathing spell.

You don't *win* anything. Carey McWilliams called me after Huey's case was reversed on appeal. You know, he was a California lawyer before he became the editor of *The Nation*. I knew him forty years ago when he was practicing law in Los Angeles.

"Charles," he said, "that was a tremendous victory. Do you think that the oppression is lessening?"

I said, "Carey, you can't be serious."

"Don't you think the Huey Newton case was a victory?"

"Carey, when a system requires an innocent man to spend two years in prison to have his case reversed, and then go back for another eight- or ten-week trial and have a million-dollar defense, that system's not working."

If the system requires a defense that would literally cost a quarter of a million dollars, as it did in the Oakland Seven, or the kind of a defense that Bobby Seale has to have, or Huey Newton, or Los Siete, or the Panther Twenty-one, or the Soledad Three—if it requires that kind of effort to get even a semblance of justice, then the system isn't working, and all of the platitudes that build up a lawyer's ego aren't going to hide what's going on in our judicial process.

All you have to do is go into our prisons, and you see nothing but black, brown, yellow, and red faces. In California, 17 percent of the prison population are brown people, 30 percent are black, and it's growing by leaps and bounds. Why? The system is not working.

I'm not saying for you not to become lawyers, I'm saying become lawyers who will change the system. You can't defend it, you've got to tear it down through political action and start over again. But in the meantime you've got to be in there plugging and doing your bit for your clients each day, as frustrating as it might be.

Student: Would you comment on the tactics used in the Chicago conspiracy trial, the use of contempt?

Garry: Yes, I'd be very happy to. As a matter of fact, I thought the conduct of Bill Kunstler and Leonard Weinglass was exemplary. They conducted that trial in one of the best and highest traditions of American law. As for disruption, you know, it wasn't until Bobby Seale was gagged, chained, and treated like an animal, that any kind of disruption took place in that court. And yet that judge had tried to disrupt that courtroom from the beginning. The day that I walked in there for pretrial proceedings, in April of 1969, that judge was goading and baiting everybody there.

I mentioned earlier that if a person is emotionally sick and has a psychiatric problem and is a little paranoid, it's pretty hard to deal or work with him. This judge is a classic example of that. This judge is a kook-box, he's paranoid, he's schizo, and he's mean, all combined. To have a man like that presiding over a courtroom is more than any lawyer can put up with. To give you an example, I appeared before him after the conspiracy trial was over, to set Bobby Seale's case for trial. I filed a motion to disqualify the judge for the trial.

AFG: Do you always do that?

Garry: With a judge like that, what else could I do? He had already held Bobby Seale in contempt of court and sentenced him to four years in prison! Well, he refused to disqualify himself, and he started baiting me. I said, "Your Honor, you might as well know this about me now, rather than later: I do not engage in repartee with judges."

"Fine. No repartee!"

So then he goes and starts baiting the United States attorney, Schultz. For the first time, Schultz didn't know what the hell to do. All during the conspiracy trial they had been buddies. Now he's berating Schultz. Schultz says, "I'm sorry."

"What are you sorry about?"

"Well, Your Honor, I'm sorry about . . ."

"What was that?"

He left me completely alone.

AFG: I understand you did get into some repartee in New Haven.

Garry: Well, the Connecticut grand jury almost floored me. Under the statute, the high sheriff picks the grand jury! In this particular case, the sheriff was a man about seventy-five years of age. The first question I asked him was, "What are your duties?"

The state's attorney objected, and the judge sustained it. Then the judge added, "You can have one of the local lawyers, Mr. Garry, read you the section that gives the duties."

I said, "I have read the duties, Your Honor. I wanted to know if the high sheriff knows his duties."

And the sheriff says, "Of course I do!"

The judge says to the high sheriff, "Mr. Sheriff, I would suggest you wait until there is a question."

Then I said, "Judge, I'm trying to find out whether, as out in the West, we have here a two-gun sheriff or what."

He said, "Mr. Garry, we're more civilized out here. We don't have our sheriffs running around with guns."

After all the kidding around was done, I said, "Mr. High Sheriff, would you tell us how you go about picking the grand jury? Do you pick them from your own cronies?"

"Cronies? I don't have any cronies!"

"How about your friends?"

"I don't have any friends!"

And the judge said, "I've always wondered how Mr. Slavin ever got elected without any cronies or friends over these thirty-five years. Now I know."

So I went down the list of the jurors who were called, and I asked, "Now, how did you get hold of this character?"

"He's an old friend of mine."

"Been on a grand jury before?"

"Oh, five or six times."

"Is he an elector?" (That's the only qualification for a grand juror—to be an elector.)

"Of course he is."

"How do you know he is?"

"Well, he wouldn't have been at the Democratic conclave if he wasn't."

"Did you check the voters' list to see if he was an elector?"

"Yes, I did."

"Did you do it on the day that this man became a grand juror, in August?"

"I don't know."

"Isn't it a fact that you didn't do it until February of this year? You thought that you were going to be questioned about this by some of the other lawyers, and you started checking that. Isn't it a fact that you were checking them this morning at eight o'clock?"

"No, I wasn't here at eight o'clock."

"How about eight-fifteen?"

This went on about each and every person. One guy, I asked, "How'd you get ahold of this one?"

And he said, "He's my barber."

"Is he a good barber?"

"Of course he is, or I wouldn't be going fifteen miles for a haircut."

And the judge and everybody were just rolling in the aisles.

The next one: "How'd you get ahold of this character?"

"Why, he owns the barbershop."

A third guy I remember asking him about, "Well, he was a lawyer. We needed one more grand juror, and this lawyer was going into the court. I said to him, 'Bill, how would you like to make a fast ten bucks?' "

And the judge said, "Why, that's below the minimum fee schedule here!"

At one point I said to the judge, "Can I get a responsive answer from this witness?"

The judge said, "Well, you can try!"

AFG: Do you enjoy what you're doing?"

Garry: Of course I do.

Student: Do you think there will be more repression against attorneys like yourself who represent political clients, to stifle what you do by using contempt citations?

Garry: Yes, they'll try to do that. But, you see, that's why it's important to have the lawyers also work with the guys on the street, a bilateral relationship, so that our forces will grow.

If they can isolate us and keep us small, of course they're going to stifle us. But I expect us to get stronger, not to be static or get defeated. We're growing; we're a lot stronger today than we were a year ago. We're certainly a lot stronger today than we were two years ago. You see, the struggle makes us strong, the struggle and the oppression teach people. The young people who went South in 1964 were committed to peaceful picketing and vocal dissent. They learned by practice and experience. Now some of them are criticizing the young people today who are not yet committed to anything beyond vocal dissent. As Huey said recently, "They better take a page from their own lessons and not be so critical of people who are just joining the struggle."

Student: Eldridge Cleaver said it, too—"They got to go through it."

Student: What do you think of Jerry Rubin's tactics of clowning around, wearing a crazy uniform and making jokes when he was called before the House Un-American Activities Committee?

Garry: I think Jerry Rubin's tactics or any other tactics that expose HUAC are excellent. Actually, it's not HUAC anymore, it's HISC—House Internal Security Committee—but it's still in the same dirty business. I'm in favor of anything that will expose this business of thought control, of trying to find out what a person is thinking, of harassing people for ideas in their minds. That's what the First Amendment was enacted to protect against. If they try to make it a crime to express what your views are on certain things, because they don't like those views, then you've got to use whatever you can to protect yourself.

There's no nice way of trying a First Amendment case. There's no nice way of trying a political case. The trial of political ideas belongs in the court of public opinion, not the criminal courts.

I think, since we're talking in this general philosophical area, I might as well tell you that I don't look upon any person's act against this so-called society as a crime. I don't believe in jails or prisons. I don't believe in punitive measures for acts committed by individuals—particularly black individuals.

We have had at least two commissions—the Kerner Commission and the Eisenhower Commission on Violence—say that America has two nations within itself, White America and Black America, with White America superimposing its own will and destiny and determination upon Black America without Black America having anything to say about its own future or its own conduct. If that's the case, and it is, then it substantiates the concept that the black community is like a colony being oppressed by its mother country. If the mother country has declared war on the colony, when does the colony stop just defending itself and start liberating itself?

These are questions that I'm not prepared to answer fully. My clients, black scholars, will have to find answers to them. I'm not steeped enough in black history to be able to give some of these answers, but I'm hopeful that others may do the research.

Student: Do you think there's any possibility of preventive law to keep political people out of jail? Can a lawyer advise people what to do or not to do? Like when David Hilliard was arrested because he used some rhetoric about killing the President—can you tell him what he shouldn't say in order not to get busted for a speech?

Garry: I see your point, but let me tell you what's wrong with it. What you're really saying is: Is there some way we can carry on this revolution in a safe manner? The answer is no, you can't do it. You've got to be able to say the things that you want to say. You've got to be able to say that the system is rotten, that there have to be sharp changes, that there has to be a revolution. Now, that doesn't mean a violent revolution or a physical revolution.

You can't set patterns for how much to say; there's no nice way of doing it. Be as careful and cautious as you can without limiting your activities. Use your head; don't take any unnecessary risks. But that doesn't mean you don't take any risks.

Student: Do you think there is any possibility that Huey will be acquitted?

Garry: I always thought the first trial would be reversed; I never had any doubt about it. No matter how rotten the system may be, and how punitive, they're not prepared to overthrow all the precedents. There are certain things they're not prepared to do. That's why you have to understand the role we lawyers are playing. I agree with many of the things that the young militants are doing. But I think that our work has to be done, too. You can't separate them.

Student: Let many flowers bloom.

TRIAL OF A CONSCIENTIOUS OBJECTOR
Allan Brotsky

AFG: Al Brotsky is a trial lawyer who worked first as an employee of other lawyers, then as a partner, a sole practitioner, and now as a partner again. He tangled with the California State Bar Association in his pioneering efforts to establish low-cost legal services for union members. I have asked him to give a trial lawyer's view of a draft case.

Brotsky: First I want to say that the mystique about the law now taught in law schools is anachronistic. I think that a year and a half or two years of academic work, leading into the kind of practical experience that a medical student gets commencing with his third year in medical school, would be a hell of a lot better legal education than what is now provided.

If you look at the law as a weapon, as a tool in the service of the movement for social change—which is today the counterpart of the labor movement when I was in law school—then clearly all you really must know to practice law is how to analyze a legal problem, how to decide what the legal issues are, how to find the law on these issues, and how to bring this law into the arena of the courtroom or the administrative agency. This means finding out how to get into court in the first place, what to do when you get there, and what kind of papers to prepare. These are the things a carpenter or an electrician does with his tools. These are the areas

98

that it seems to me law schools should be concentrating on; they should be revising their curriculums to teach these basic skills.

If you take this approach when you start practicing law, it will become apparent to you that, in the use of all of these tools and knowledge, you gradually acquire a capacity for making sound legal judgments. And this is why clients come to you, rather than relying on themselves or going to a nonlawyer or even going to some other lawyer—they want you to make sound legal judgments in their cases.

Every legal problem, like almost every problem in life, confronts people with alternatives. I consider the end product of a sound legal education and many years of legal practice to be the ability to make a decision on which alternative to adopt; to accept the fact that you have made the decision (whether it be right or wrong); and to act on it.

One of the best illustrations of what I'm talking about is the defense of draft resisters in criminal proceedings under the Selective Service Act. Let me give as an example the case of Austin Penney.

Penney was a conscientious objector who got to that point through the long and very serious process of examining the society in which he lived, the kind of values it had, and ultimately what war means. He concluded that war has no values, and that he could not kill under any circumstances. He became a CO at twenty-one, three years after he had registered for the draft and while the administrative process was going on. He filed his application for CO when the law still provided for a Justice Department investigation of each CO applicant. The report of the investigation on Penney was uniformly in favor of his being granted CO status. The people interviewed by the FBI said he was a man of the utmost sincerity, with deep convictions and ideals. All of his friends, his teachers, and his employer agreed that he had come to his view properly and sincerely, and recommended that he be granted CO status.

In those days, the notorious T. Oscar Smith of the Justice Department had the final say on all CO applications, based on the reports prepared by the FBI. T. Oscar Smith had his own standards. He concluded that Austin Penney did not qualify for CO for two reasons. First, the fact that he had not said on his initial questionnaire that he was a CO was clear proof that he was insincere when he did apply. The obvious question—how can you claim to be a CO when you register if you're not a CO when you register?—never bothered T. Oscar Smith. The second point he made was that Penney really was not a religiously based CO—he didn't believe in a Supreme Being in the traditional classical sense. This was before the Supreme Court decided the Seeger case, holding that a sincere person need not believe in a Supreme Being to qualify for CO.

Austin Penney, feeling as strongly as he did, believed that in declining to go into the service he had to do more than just go through the processing and then refuse to step forward. So, the day he was ordered to report for induction, he came down to the Oakland induction center with a batch of leaflets. He wanted to explain to other people why, as a conscientious objector, he could not allow himself to be inducted into the Army even though this meant possible imprisonment. He wrote a very clear and simple explanation of why he was a CO, and he called on the other people at the induction center to join him in declining to step forward if they felt the way he did. The Oakland Stop-the-Draft Week demonstrations had just taken place (leading to the Oakland Seven case), and, needless to say, the Army people were very uptight about this sort of activity. So when he entered the induction center, after having distributed leaflets outside to the busloads of draftees as they arrived, the authorities immediately grabbed him and said he couldn't distribute them.

He said, "Why not? I have a right to free speech and freedom of the press, and that's all I'm doing. I'm perfectly willing to be processed. I'm not going to interfere with it, but I'd like to distribute these leaflets stating my viewpoint and giving these other people the benefit of my ideas on this subject."

Well, they had a big conference and came back and said, "We're sorry, but you cannot distribute the leaflets. Now you have three alternatives: You can give us the leaflets, go ahead and be processed, and we'll give them back to you afterward. Or you can refuse, at this point, to be processed and go on home. Or you can throw the leaflets away, and just go on and be inducted, and that would be the best idea."

So he said, "I believe very deeply in what I'm doing. I refuse to do any of those things. I would be delighted to go ahead with the processing, but I will not give the leaflets up to you."

Whereupon they called the Oakland police, and after he had gone through a couple steps in the processing they arrested him for disturbing the peace. Ken Kawaichi, an Oakland lawyer who is active in the Lawyers Guild, defended him in the disturbing-the-peace case. The prosecution forced him to go to court two or three times, which they always do, to disrupt your life, and then the day it was supposed to go to trial the DA got up and said, "For various reasons we move for dismissal of this prosecution." So the judge dismissed the case.

When Penney was indicted for violation of the draft law, Ken asked me to work on the case with him, and I agreed to do so.

Even before we could consider what specific defenses we were going to rely on, we had to adopt an approach to our overall defense of this charge of refusing induction. For whatever it's worth, here was our approach: In the first place, the war in Southeast Asia is the most unpopular war this country has ever waged. It has caused more young people to leave the country to avoid service than ever before in history. It has caused thousands of young Americans to consider conscientious objection seriously for the first time, and probably under circumstances that would not be repeated were the war a popular one. In the second place, decisions on draft refusal handed down during more popular wars hold that the court and the jury cannot consider the real issue leading to draft refusal. This led us to conclude that it is the job of the lawyer to uncover and deal with the real issue, the nature of this war, in every Selective Service case.

AFG: Why should the lawyer and not the client uncover and deal with this issue?

Brotsky: Well, what I mean is that the lawyer has to make the decision on how to do it. Obviously the client is the one whose very activities have injected the nature of the war into the prosecution of the case. He would not be before the bar of justice were it not for his opposition to the war, whether it was a full-blown political opposition, a pacifist opposition, or some other form. The lawyer must take that opposition and translate it into legal terms, while utilizing the defenses available under the Selective Service Act and the decisions.

Student: Do you come to that conclusion after you investigate the file and find what technical defenses are available, or do you follow that approach regardless of whether you might win on a narrower attack?

Brotsky: You start out with that broad approach. However, you always utilize every defense, including the most technical, to show that your client is innocent. The technical defenses are not at all inconsistent with these broad underlying approaches; they are actually complementary.

AFG: What if a client has really changed his mind between the time he applied for CO or refused induction and the time he comes to you? What if he really just wants you to get him off and he doesn't want you to raise these broader questions? He's afraid, or his parents are afraid. Do you raise them anyway?

Brotsky: No. I think the lawyer has a duty to represent the client as the client wants to be represented, or to decline to represent him when there are so many basic differences between your approach and his that you cannot fairly and adequately do a job for him.

But, interestingly enough, as I talk to every draft defendant and learn just what motivated him, I have never yet found one that did not have, at the very nub of his feelings, his opposition to the war. And I have not found one yet who didn't agree that this approach was exactly what he wanted presented in court, even those who had never spelled it out until I presented it to them.

When a person is indicted in the San Francisco federal court, the judge issues a standard discovery order at the arraignment. In draft cases, this order entitles the defense to a full copy of the Selective Service file, a copy of any statement that the defendant has given to anybody connected with the government (including the FBI), and the names and counties of residence of the draft-board members.

So we got the file. Naturally the next problem, when you're defending someone charged with a felony that can carry a penalty of five years and $5,000 fine, is, what are his possible defenses? We found these by going very carefully through the file, and then talking to the client about what had happened at the induction center.

In Penney's case, we had the technical defenses that his draft board had failed to grant him a personal appearance after he was classified, and failed to reopen his classification when that was warranted. In addition, we had two basic points. First, he had been improperly denied CO classification. Second, he really had not refused to step forward; the Army had prevented him from being processed, because he was exercising his constitutional right of freedom of the press. This was beautiful from the point of view of blending constitutional issues with the issues in his draft case. Believe me, it's a rare case where you have such juicy issues to work on.

In every prosecution a decision has to be made whether to have trial by a jury or by a judge. Before I had tried my first draft case, I had concluded that, generally speaking, every case should have a jury.

Student: Why did you feel that way?

Brotsky: First of all, a judge is unlikely to give the draftee the benefit of the doubt the way twelve jurors will if they can. Secondly, I think the courtroom can be an educational forum. In trying a case to twelve jurors, you're educating them on matters that are vital to them, but on which they may never have been educated before—namely, the attitude of these young people toward the draft, the reasons for their opposition to the war, and their hatred of war. You have a captive audience that has to sit there and listen to you. And, believe me, after every draft case that I've tried, at least one or two jurors have come up and thanked me and said, "We really had no idea how deeply the young people felt about this until we sat through this case."

Now, you might ask, "Well, what the hell does that have to do with defending your client? After all, you don't have an independent duty to educate people."

Of course we don't. But we have learned that only if the jurors are educated during the case about the political issues in the war and the political opposition of the defendant to the war will they really be able to give him deliberation that is free of the narrow-mindedness, know-nothingism, and prejudice that is present when they haven't had this kind of education.

Another reason for a jury is that, to the extent that it represents a cross section of the community, it has on it people who are opposed to the war. They therefore have the understandable and proper tendency to hear the evidence and the judge's instructions in that frame of reference.

Draft cases are political cases. Where but in a situation such as we have in America today would you have the finest, most idealistic, most high-minded young men charged with serious crimes? Don't take my word for it. Most of the federal judges in San Francisco have said this when sentencing some of these young men.

I define a political case as one in which a person is being prosecuted primarily because of his political outlook, as narrowly or broadly as that may be defined. So a jury can take the community standards that they reflect and apply them to the political issue involved in a draft prosecution. We all recognize that feelings and divisions about this war do exist in this part of the country, and that makes it easier to decide to have a jury trial than in other cases. Clearly you do not want a jury in a draft case if there is no feeling in the community that the war is terrible or criminal.

Another advantage of having a jury is that many things are the subject of rulings of record by the judge in a jury case that he never has to rule on of record in a nonjury case. This means there is more chance of appealable error. For example, the voir-dire questions can be the subject of error. The judge's instructions to the jury are a matter of record in a jury case, and they often provide grounds for reversal on appeal. In a nonjury case, the judge makes no record of the instructions that he gives to himself. A ruling on evidence may be held to be prejudicial in a jury trial because the jury is composed of laymen not learned in the law, whereas the admission of that same evidence might be excused in a nonjury trial because the judge is presumed not to be affected by evidence that is prejudicial or that raises all kinds of emotional overtones. That's one of the many myths the law cultivates, which lawyers like us have to try to expose and break down.

Student: Are there any disadvantages in a jury trial?

Brotsky: Yes. The first disadvantage is that it takes much longer to try. A judge can try a case in one day; a jury trial usually takes three days. It's more work for the lawyer. He has to prepare the voir-dire questions to ask the prospective jurors to see whether they are biased or fair-minded. He also has to prepare the jury instructions and submit them to the court. He can skip both these steps if he tries the case to a judge.

There is always a possibility, although in San Francisco this is minimal, that because you have asked for a jury trial the judge will penalize your client by imposing a heavier sentence if he's found guilty. Many, many judges throughout the country improperly force the defendant to waive a jury by threatening that if he is convicted they will give him a heavier sentence because he asked for a jury. If ever there was a clearly unconstitutional, unlawful way of running a court, that's it.

Student: Can't something be done about it?

Brotsky: If a proper record has been made, the conviction gets reversed. But most of the time the judge will say this off the record and deny it later. A bar association can confront the judge with his unlawful procedure and get him to back down, which was done successfully in the Oakland municipal court.

Okay. We've been exercising legal judgments. We've made a decision about the approach we want to take, and a decision on whether we want a jury or a judge. Our next step in the Penney case was to prepare our voir-dire questions. They were keyed primarily to finding out if the prospective jurors had strong feelings about the war in Vietnam. If they did, by the use of one or two other judicious questions, and in the light of their background, occupation, and so forth, we could pretty well decide whether these feelings were for our client or against him. For example, if someone was a member of the Veterans of Foreign Wars, or had a relative in law-enforcement work, and also had strong feelings about the war in Vietnam, we didn't have to do much heavy guessing to realize that he or she was not the kind of person we wanted on the jury. Some of the jurors are always honest about it; they say, "Look, we simply couldn't be fair in a case like this. We think everybody should serve in the Army." So you get a fair number of jurors excused for cause.

Now we go into the trial. By the way, all the prosecution has to do is introduce the defendant's Selective Service file and prove he declined to be inducted.

Student: And nothing more?

Brotsky: Well, I should make this correction. If the file contains evidence that the man was at the induction center, went through the processing, then refused to step forward, and was taken aside, that the consequences of the refusal were explained to him, and that he nonetheless refused to step forward—if all this is in the draft file, that's all the government needs. If it isn't all in the file, then they'll put on the FBI agent who was at the induction center and witnessed his refusal. That completes their prima facie case according to the present state of the law.

Student: What about the presumption that the defendant in every criminal case is innocent? Does the file constitute proof by the government that he's guilty beyond a reasonable doubt?

Brotsky: All of the lawyers in the San Francisco Selective Service Panel would raise that question, because we feel that the presumption of innocence has been destroyed in these cases and also that the proper standard of proof is not met. To make that point, we move for judgment of acquittal in each case after the prosecution has rested. So far nobody has succeeded in getting a judgment of acquittal granted on the ground that the file itself is insufficient to overcome the presumption of innocence.

AFG: What you really have is a presumption that all Selective Service proceedings are conducted properly, a "presumption of regularity." Is that a proper presumption in a criminal case?

Brotsky: I don't think so. I think that it's a typical political decision cutting away at constitutional rights in an area where hysteria and national defense are involved. If property rights were involved in a prosecution for a violation, say, of a regulation of the Federal Trade Commission or the Interstate Commerce Commission, could you see the judges saying that the "presumption of regularity" would satisfy all the requirements necessary to prove that the regulation was properly arrived at?

Student: How do you overcome the argument that these are the limitations Congress has built into the act and that the courts should be reluctant to tamper with a congressional determination?

Brotsky: Well, the first answer is that "presumption of regularity" is a judge-made rule. There's no "presumption of regularity" written into the Selective Service Act. The second answer is that Congress cannot in this field, any more than it can in the free-speech field, take away constitutional liberties by passing legislation. Were the courts as jealous of constitutional liberties in this field as they are in others, they would strike down the whole present standard of proof in draft cases as an unconstitutional violation of the right to due process in a criminal case.

Student: Exactly what is due process?

AFG: Ah, my favorite question. Al, you won't mind if I answer it, will you?

I think due process is the issue that decides most political cases, even when the issue *seems* to be the right to freedom of expression under the First Amendment.

Due process of law in a criminal case requires that the defendant be acquitted (or retried) unless he was treated fairly at every stage in the proceedings—from the moment he was suspected of being involved right through arrest, bail, pretrial, trial, and verdict. Fairness is the test; that means following the procedures for investigation and proof at trial that our society has decided are fair.

Lawyers have found that many jurors do try to be fair, even when they can't accept the defendant's politics. They don't want to be part of a procedure to send him to prison in an unfair manner. Even in a repressive period when jurors are able to forget about the guarantee of freedom of expression, they are sometimes upset about informers, perjured testimony, denial of bail, wiretaps, unfair comments by the judge, and so forth.

Sometimes due-process defenses are looked down on as being

less revolutionary or principled than defenses based on freedom of expression. I think that's just falling for the line Joe McCarthy pushed during the 1950s—that a "Fifth Amendment Communist" was somehow worse than a "First Amendment Communist" who defended himself only on the ground that he had a right to do and say what he did. I think McCarthy just wanted to stop the victories on Fifth Amendment grounds.

Sir John Lilburn is really the model of the First Amendment man who uses Fifth Amendment defenses. He more or less invented the privilege against self-incrimination in seventeenth-century England when he tried to stay out of the Tower of London after receiving heretical tracts from Holland. He was quite a man. He wrote "Jonah's Cry Out of the Whale's Belly" while in prison and passed out copies as he was being whipped through the streets of London. (I found him in the *Dictionary of British Biography*.)

Now due process is guaranteed by the Fifth Amendment in criminal cases and also in cases before administrative agencies. So one of the major questions in draft cases is whether a registrant was treated fairly and according to the rules by the Selective Service System, which is an administrative agency. The rules for fairness in criminal trials are older and more strict than the rules for fairness in hearings before administrative agencies, but there *are* rules for such agencies, and radical lawyers have taken on a series of such agencies over the years—from the Immigration Service to juvenile courts—and tried to force them to provide due process.

Now our target is the Selective Service System, which has always thought that the people dealing with it—registrants eighteen to twenty-six—have no power and can be handled summarily, without regard to fair procedures.

Student: Mr. Brotsky, did you put in a defense in the Penney case?

Brotsky: Oh, yes. We had already gone into what happened at the induction center. The military witnesses first said Penney had disrupted the processing of other registrants, that he was causing an uproar all over the place. On cross-examination, that turned out to be untrue. The same number of men were processed during the period that he was there as were processed in similar periods before and after. They finally wound up with no factual basis for that contention.

Then we had the question of how to handle the CO issue. We had to make a legal judgment: should we subject our client to cross-examination by the U.S. attorney, who would try to show the jury that he was insincere, a draft dodger, and perhaps a coward? We made the judgment that it was critically important that the jury hear from our client's own lips why he was a CO. It was easy in our case to make that judgment, because our fellow was completely sincere and he was bright. In other cases, where your client is not so articulate and where he has to agonizingly tell the jury these things, it sometimes is a grueling and unpleasant ordeal for him. But the thing that is so ever present in these cases is that the men are absolutely honest and straightforward; this shines through in their testimony no matter how hard it is for them.

In these cases the judges absolutely refuse to allow the war to become an issue in the defendant's case. So in making my argument to the jury, I said, "Now, the judge has told you that the war in Vietnam is not an issue in this case, and of course we are bound by the law. My client doesn't really agree on this, but he is bound by the law. So whether you believe that the war in Vietnam is a criminal undertaking which is causing the destruction of an entire people," and I run on for five minutes on whether they believe that or the other (and I take only about thirty seconds for the other), "that has nothing to do with this case according to the court."

Obviously this refreshes the minds of the jurors on the basic issues that really are involved in this case.

There was one other point we had to fight on in this case that I think was critical in the decision of the jury. Assuming you get twelve men and women on a jury who are fair-minded, who are not out to hang the defendant, that group has a tremendous respect for and desire to follow the judge's instructions. You'd be amazed at how those jurors analyze those instructions, worry about them, and, in a close case, try to follow them.

In every criminal case the judge must give an instruction on the intent with which the defendant did the act that is allegedly illegal. A defendant is guilty only if he did an illegal act *and* he did it with intent. One instruction that is often given says that "intent" is the doing of an act with the specific intent to do something unlawful with knowledge that it is unlawful and out of a bad motive. If the judge will give that instruction in a draft case you can make a strong argument on it.

In Penney's case I said, "Now, the judge is going to instruct you that one of the essential ingredients of this offense is to have done this act with the following intent," and I read the instruction to them. I said, " 'Bad motive'—what does that mean? After all, this draft act was designed to punish men who wanted to evade the draft, men who were draft dodgers. Is that the kind of man my client is? Obviously when a draft dodger refuses to be inducted, he is doing it out of what is defined in the instruction as a 'bad motive.' Our man did it out of the highest principles, out of the deepest convictions, and from the most lofty motives. How could he then be guilty of the bad intent that is required?"

The jury went out, and they deliberated and deliberated.

In most jury cases at that time, the jury was coming in within thirty minutes; an hour was a long time. That jury had been out for five hours.

The judge called us in and asked, "What do you think we ought to do?"

I said, "Why don't we give them another hour, Judge, and see how they feel about it?"

He said, "Well, I'm going to lock them up for the night, anyway."

I thought, "It's unheard of to lock a jury up for the night after they've deliberated for five hours on issues as simple as those involved in this case. If they're deadlocked, they're deadlocked, and they ought to be discharged—it's just a hung jury." In the federal court, by the way, it's improper for the judge to inquire how the jury stands.

So they were called back in after the hour, and he asked the foreman if they thought they could arrive at a verdict.

The foreman hesitated, and finally he said, "I don't really think so, Judge."

We had to make a judgment, based on what this foreman said, whether there was a good chance of eventually getting an acquittal if we stuck it out with this jury or whether we should push for discharging the jury and hope that the U.S. attorney would decide not to retry the case. We made the decision on the basis of the foreman's background—he was a librarian—and because we no-

ticed that he had nodded his head when I was telling the jury that
the war in Vietnam was not an issue even though it was the worst
thing that ever happened to this country. We decided that he was
with us and that if he felt that this jury couldn't reach a verdict, we
wouldn't get an acquittal.

The judge said, "I'm going to lock you ladies and gentlemen up
for the night."

A couple of them groaned.

The judge asked, "What's the matter?"

One juror said, "We parked our cars, Judge, at a garage that
locks up for the night at eleven, and they'll be there overnight, and
no one will tell our families." And so forth.

At that point we had to make another judgment: Should we now
fight to get this jury discharged? If the foreman was with us and he
didn't feel they could reach a verdict, then we didn't want the hard-
bitten warmongers on the jury to wear some of the others down
and come out with nine to three for conviction, or ten to two, or
even eleven to one. Both sides are always told afterward how the
vote went, and the U.S. attorneys will rarely retry a case where it's
been a majority or better for acquittal. As a matter of policy, they
figure if they couldn't get a conviction the first time, there's no use
wasting more time.

So I said, "Judge, it seems to me that it would subject these
jurors to a great deal of hardship. The foreman has said he doesn't
think they're going to reach a verdict. I think the U.S. attorney
would agree with me that they ought to be discharged at this
point."

We knew he didn't give a damn on that. He had other things to
do in the morning, anyway.

The judge said to the jury, "Let's have a show of hands." And
they voted eleven to one to be discharged that night. Sure enough,
we found out that there was a hard core of people who wouldn't
have voted for acquittal under any circumstances. They were lying
under oath when they had said they had open minds. The other
seven were hanging tight up to that point, but they were beginning
to weaken. Several of them said to us later, "We told the people in
there that although we couldn't consider the war itself, we can't
ignore it. Obviously it had something to do with the case!"

So there you have the gamut of legal judgments in one case, all the way from how to approach the case, whether to have a jury, whether to put your client on the stand, and, finally, how to judge facial expressions of jurors as they're listening to you.

AFG: Turning to another problem, Al, will you tell us about the case of *Brotsky v. California State Bar?* How did it come about, and what was the outcome?

Brotsky: The firm I was with in 1961 had been retained by a trade-union local in San Francisco, the ship clerks' local of the International Longshoremen's and Warehousemen's Union. The arrangement with them was, in fact, being followed by many, many labor attorneys in town: their monthly retainer to us covered the right of any member to have one consultation in our office on any legal problem without charge. So far, no one had had the guts to reduce this arrangement to writing. We finally decided that we were going to take this issue on, because there was absolutely no reason why labor unions couldn't provide group legal services for their members like this at an extremely reasonable cost. So we signed an agreement with the local union to provide this service for a very small retainer, only about seventy-five dollars a month.

Well, the State Bar somehow got wind of this agreement and they brought charges against me for unlawful solicitation, practicing through an intermediary, and several other violations of the rules of professional conduct.

AFG: Did you get a hearing?

Brotsky: Yes. A disciplinary hearing is initiated in California by complaint from an individual or some other source. This was one of the questions we wanted answered—the source from which the complaint emanated. The State Bar refused to tell us, although we were told there was no individual complaint.

The lawyer is given an opportunity to reply to the complaint. If his reply is unsatisfactory to the State Bar, a local administrative committee informally hears the matter without a record being made. That local administrative committee itself has the authority to recommend that the matter be dropped. Of course, in this case, with these issues, no such recommendation ensued.

The next step was the issuance of a complaint and a formal

hearing before a formal administrative committee of the State Bar. We made motions for discovery and filed answers before that committee.

The law in this area was pretty much in its infancy when my case started, back in 1961. There were no good United States Supreme Court decisions. So, as always in the kind of cases we handle, the defense in my case was an offense. We denied that there had been a violation. We said that, to the extent that the rules made this conduct a violation, the rules were unconstitutional under the First Amendment right of association, because it includes the right of associations to provide legal services to their members. The Sixth Amendment right to counsel was involved secondarily.

We went on to say that what we had been doing was something that other groups and lodges, including the California State Automobile Association, had been doing for years, and that therefore the application of these rules to us was an unconstitutional discrimination in violation of the equal-protection clause of the Fourteenth Amendment to the Constitution.

In order to prove this, we had to use the discovery procedure, which had just been adopted about a year before in civil cases. It was modeled after the federal discovery procedure. So we served on the State Bar a complete sct of interrogatories—a list of questions—asking what their records showed about the number of organizations that had been doing the same thing that the ship clerks' local had been doing, what complaints had been received, and what had been done about them.

The State Bar had been the great champion of discovery, and had sponsored the state discovery legislation. But, astonishingly, the State Bar came to the administrative hearings and said, "This is unheard of. We don't have to give discovery. You don't have a right to it under the law. It's against public policy." It relied on all of the reactionary arguments that its opposition had used in fighting against discovery. The local administrative committee obediently accepted the position of the State Bar. At that juncture, we filed an extraordinary petition in the Supreme Court of California asking them to review the committee's decision then and there, without waiting until the administrative proceeding was over.

The court issued what is called an order to show cause, telling the State Bar to explain why it shouldn't have to answer our interrogatories. The State Bar filed an answer, and briefs were then filed, and the matter was argued before the California Supreme Court. There was no argument about the facts: they admitted that we had filed the papers showing we needed the questions answered and that they had refused. Their position was that we didn't have a legal right to the answers.

The California Supreme Court ruled that in State Bar matters, particularly where a lawyer's license is at stake, it was essential that the lawyer have the right to discovery, and they ordered that the State Bar answer the questions pursuant to such rules and regulations as the State Bar might make concerning discovery.

By then it was 1962. A year and three months later, the State Bar hadn't lifted a finger to issue any such regulations or to move my case ahead. It just lay there.

So I had a discussion with my lawyer and made a determination that the time had come to move to dismiss my case for lack of prosecution. That motion was made; the State Bar resisted it. We had a full hearing before the board of governors of the State Bar, and the State Bar staff looked just silly. Here fifteen months had gone by, and they hadn't even issued the regulations governing discovery, let alone answered the interrogatories the California Supreme Court had said we had a right to have answered. The board of governors listened to the argument, and two days later we got the order from the State Bar: proceeding dismissed. So that was the end of the entire substantive proceeding.

Now, the postscript is interesting.

By the time my case was decided, the United States Supreme Court had been faced with a similar problem. The Virginia chapter of the National Association for the Advancement of Colored People had been attacked for advising members to go to particular lawyers on civil-rights problems, and sometimes paying these lawyers out of organizational funds. In 1963 the Court held that, under the First Amendment, people had a right "to join together and assist one another in the assertion of their legal rights by collectively hiring an attorney to handle their claims." By the way, the Court also recognized in that case that litigation is sometimes a form of political action.

From there, the U.S. Supreme Court in 1964 decided that the Virginia Brotherhood of Railroad Trainmen could help its members by "channeling legal employment" to lawyers they considered competent in the very technical area of railroad personal-injury litigation.

For some reason, the Illinois State Bar Association chose that moment to go after the United Mineworkers for hiring a lawyer to handle its members' claims to workmen's compensation. The union had been doing this since 1913, and there had been no complaints by union members that they had been badly represented or that a union official had been paid off by the attorney for referring cases. But under the Illinois Canons of Legal Ethics it was deemed unethical for an organization to hire an attorney to handle cases involving individual members, rather than cases concerning the organization as such. In 1967, the case reached the United States Supreme Court, which rejected the Illinois State Bar position, apparently recognizing that all union members have a common interest in being adequately represented in damage suits for on-the-job injuries, even though their individual suits do not constitute general union business.

These cases showed the obvious need for some kind of group legal insurance or prepaid legal practice so that many lower-middle-class people and working people could get legal services they couldn't afford otherwise. Finally, the California State Bar itself proposed a group-legal-practice rule to the state Supreme Court, and as of January 1, 1970, the Supreme Court adopted a rule that legalized in its entirety the arrangement that I had had with this union ten years before.

BLOOD,
SWEAT,
AND
TEARS

LABOR RADICAL DEFENDANT
Archie Brown

AFG: Archie Brown is here as a client, not a lawyer—although he once represented himself in court. As a result of organizing on the waterfront, he's been in all the major struggles since the 1930s, and he's been a client several times: in the 1930s he was charged with disturbing the peace in San Pedro, and with murder in San Francisco; in the 1950s he was called before the House Committee on Un-American Activities; and in the 1960s he was arrested for being a Communist union official. He's learned quite a bit about prisoners' rights and the underground.

I know these legal cases weren't the most important fights in your life, Archie, but, can you give us some background on the charges, and then describe the trials?

Brown: Well, I'll telescope everything as much as I can.

Beginning in 1929, when the stock market crashed, there was a considerable amount of turmoil in the country. It was somewhat similar to the recent down turns in the stock market, only in 1929 it continued down and stayed down. Businessmen really did jump out of windows. But the real burden was on the people of the country, who were very much confused. Like now, the workers and farmers were pretty conservative. But soon they, and the young people, became radical and, maybe in a different way than now, revolutionary. There was a tremendous amount of unemployment and a tremendous growth of left-wing organizations and later on of unions, and the Communist Party probably had its greatest

119

influence in the thirties and on through World War II in the forties.

The problems of the young people and the older people were somewhat the same in those days, but not exactly like it is now. It was a question of poverty and hunger, unemployment. The generation gap took the form of kids leaving home, where there was no food and a lot of dissension. I know. I took off when I was quite young.

AFG: How young?

Brown: I was thirteen years old. I came from a working-class family. My parents were immigrants. They settled in Iowa and raised eight kids there. My father had problems just like any other worker. He was a teamster for small outfits—he drove a horse and wagon. In 1926 I took a freight train out here to California. On the way I met a lot of Wobblies and ex-Wobblies—Industrial Workers of the World. I learned a lot of things and became radical from that time on.

In the early 1930s the left evolved a program advocating the organization of unemployed councils to fight for the rights of the unemployed, for food, for unemployment insurance; it also advocated organizing unorganized workers. The labor movement at that time was pretty moribund, dominated by William Green, president of the AFL, who was something like George Meany, president of the AFL-CIO at the present time. Green wouldn't even permit a campaign in his unions on unemployment insurance; he said, "That's not only socialistic, it's un-American. Americans stand on their own feet; they are rugged individualists." He agreed with President Hoover on this. But most people turned out to be *ragged* individualists, and they didn't go for that anymore. So a huge campaign broke through in the unions and among the unemployed for unemployment insurance.

After the bottom of the depression had been reached and things began to pick up a little bit, the people were rehired into plants. These were the same people who had been in the unemployed movements and had learned organization, particularly from the Communists and the radicals. They went into the shops and began to organize. There was a tremendous organizing movement from 1933 right up to World War II and through the war. In the background there was terror on the part of the police, like you have now—killings, shooting of strikers, mass funerals, fighting back; the West Virginia miners, for example, fought the National Guard with guns in 1934. There were battles, rocks thrown, trucks over-turned, trains dynamited, and so on. That's nothing new for workers in the labor movement. Some people may try to picture it otherwise, but it's not new.

The upsurge in organizing led to the establishment of new unions and new kinds of unions, industrial instead of craft. For years the policy had been—and still is in the building trades—to organize electricians, plumbers, and others based on crafts, and each craft would worry only about its own workers. When there was a strike of one craft, the other crafts would scab on them. Well, in the mass industries like steel and auto and chemical there was so much overlapping with the new machinery that many crafts had been practically wiped out. These craft unions really stood in the way, and workers in the mass industries were not organized. These were the lowest-paid workers, and in those days a huge number of foreign-born were at the bottom of the scale—Italians, Poles, various other whites, but also, of course, the Mexican-American people, the Chicanos as they call themselves nowadays, and the blacks.

In 1929 William Foster and others helped set up the Trade Union Unity League, a left organization with Communists and other militants and radicals, because the regular unions wouldn't move. The League idea was to organize the unorganized into industrial unions for the most economic effect. Later on the unions formed by the TUUL merged with the AFL, and from this new base the TUUL militants played a vital role in the subsequent CIO upsurge. Then in the 1950s the AFL and the CIO got together.

Most of the craft unions were all white, but there was a fight for integration in the industrial unions from the beginning. Working people began to see that it wasn't a question of race at all; it was a question of the system. They didn't always understand it clearly and thoroughly, but they understood it instinctively. The rich were rich and the poor were poor, and the poor included white, black, brown, and everybody else. So they learned, just from those few years of experience, and were much more willing to get together into integrated unions. It didn't always work out 100 percent, don't you believe that, but great strides were made during those days.

AFG: It was really an uphill struggle to organize at that time. It wasn't until 1940 that the United States Supreme Court said that picketing, *peaceful* picketing, is a form of free speech. All of the things we assume now—that you can always picket peacefully, with no trouble, even in large numbers—weren't true when the unions were organized in the 1930s. You could be arrested for peaceful picketing.

Brown: And we were, and went to jail for it. Usually the company would go to court and ask for an injunction against all picketing, and when we violated the injunction we were thrown in the clink. Where we had the power, we would just establish ourselves on the picket line anyway.

After all, we were the voters, and we began to take political action against judges and city administrators who were antilabor. You see, whole sections of the cities were just destitute. Some of these judges became concerned and began to take the side of the people, at least to some extent. It wasn't that they were good people, but the situation and the power of the organized people *made* them good, in many respects. Like if you talk about good employers, I know that in 1934 we made a lot of good employers. They weren't before.

Now, getting on to the waterfront, organizing began in the early thirties in San Francisco with such people as Henry Schmidt, Harry Bridges, Germaine Bulcke, and Len Greer. Greer was a black leader who helped break up what we called the checkerboard system in the San Francisco waterfront. They would have two or three all-black gangs of longshoremen, and then they would have the white gangs—meaning work gangs, not gangs who fight each other. On the waterfront, you work by gangs at a pier.

Student: Did the employers want separate black and white gangs?

Brown: Oh, sure. The checkerboard system, man, they loved that, because they would say to a white gang, "Those dirty black so-and-so's, they're beating you. They've put out so many tons! You want to come back tomorrow? Let's see you hustle." And they just kept everybody killing himself trying to outdo the other gang.

Student: You mean the men worked just day by day?

Brown: Work on the waterfront even now is not steady. You work day by day, although now we've got some seniority, and they can't pull all the crap they used to. Each day the man told you if you could come back tomorrow or not. Before the strike, the long-shoremen would have to do favors for the boss—bring him a jug of wine, wash his car, clip his lawn, paint his house, and all that jazz, or give him a couple of dollars every time he put the man to work. That's why there was such a revolt.

I was a member of the Young Communist League at the time, and in 1933 we launched a campaign to build the YCL and help to organize the unorganized. We did what we called concentration work. We put all the force that we possibly could into the water-front unions.

Toward the end of 1933, I was delegated to organize at San Pedro, next to Los Angeles. We used to hold meetings and dances in San Pedro, charging fifteen cents, which was a lot of money in those days. But we would get several hundred to our affairs—mainly youngsters, but also seamen, longshoremen, cannery workers.

At that time Los Angeles had a red squad headed by a guy by the name of Red Hynes. It was vicious, like the Tactical Squad in the San Francisco police today, only they looked for political people. The red squad would come to San Pedro and tell our hall owners, "Cancel and don't give them the hall," and they would do it at the last minute. So one time in January 1934 we rented two halls. When people came to the first hall, we just handed them a leaflet that said to go to the other hall. Then, when we were all at the second hall, in walked the local post of the American Legion and the Los Angeles red squad to break up the dance. We told them, "If you want to wreck the place, you're going to have some-thing on your hands." Finally, though, because we wanted to organize these kids, we decided to make a deal: They would leave the dance alone and they would arrest two of us. We said, "If the American Legion stays, they have to pay fifteen cents apiece."

So, anyway, the dance went on and I went to the clink.

AFG: Was there a feeling that the movement of trade unionists should be nonviolent, a Martin Luther King–type period?

Brown: We *were* nonviolent then! We never looked for any trouble or any fights. The quieter we could keep things, the easier it was for us to organize. Our problem was that they would come and provoke us, like at that dance. What the hell for? Then they charged *us* with disturbing the peace.

We felt that we'd win the case, though in those days we didn't have too many illusions. But the International Labor Defense was just being organized in that area then, and they sent us some lawyers.

AFG: The ILD was a legal-defense organization that found lawyers for strikers and for unemployed people who got evicted and were arrested when they moved their furniture back into their apartments. It publicized cases of aliens arrested for deportation and blacks arrested on frame-up charges.

Brown: In San Pedro they sent us inexperienced lawyers, because the organization itself was new. Our trial lasted one day or so, and the jury found us guilty. The judge gave me the maximum, ninety days; he gave the other guy forty-five days. I was bailed out pending the appeal.

AFG: One of the main functions of the International Labor Defense was raising money for a bail fund. Workers and middle-class people loaned money to the fund, and it was put up as bail. The people could get their loans back when they needed the money. Hundreds of thousands of dollars were put up as bail in California alone.

Brown: In my case, I wasn't out on bail very long. There was a period of ten or fifteen days in which to file an appeal, but, to show you how new and inexperienced the lawyers were, they didn't get it filed in time. So the appeal was thrown out for being late, with no decision on the merits. And I served every bit of the ninety days.

Student: How was it in the jail?

Brown: Well, we had a bunch of belly robbers. They robbed the prisoners of even the little bit they were supposed to spend for the food, and pocketed it.

Student: To harass the men, or just because they wanted the money?

Brown: Just corruption. We protested the thing. We took the tin cups and the plates and raised hell in the jail for hours at a time. Then they took us ringleaders, myself particularly, and threw us in what they called the hole. I lost my good time and spent thirty days in the hole. They gave me a rough time for a while, but they didn't continue—there was too much exposure on the outside. I've seen them beat up other prisoners when there's no one to let anyone know about it, but in my case they didn't dare do it, because the news would be out the next day and our people would picket the houses of the judges and the cops. There was a lot of activity like that.

Student: When you're in solitary confinement, what do you actually do? How do you maintain your sanity?

Brown: First thing you do, you get yourself a routine. You get up in the morning and do exercises. Before you go to bed at night, do exercises. Keep yourself in shape. Usually you don't have anything to read—except that I did. Somebody over the course of years had knocked a hole in the wall to the next cell, and these clowns didn't know about it. I used to send notes to the guy in the next cell, and I'd share the food my friends sent in. So he'd send me a banana or an orange once in a while, and reading matter. Then I'd send it back to him, so when they came to search my cell there was nothing there. I was fortunate in that way.

But in many cases you don't get anything, so you count and do things by memory. And you figure, "Screw them." You try not to let yourself be broken or excited. And every time you can, you protest. For instance, the Salvation Army used to come and sing to us. So we had a little song that went:

> The Starvation Army comes around to save our souls,
> Why don't they come around to clean the toilet bowls?
> They say that Christ died for the likes of you and me.
> But we still need sugar in our tea.

We used to sing that back to them. You utilize all the situations you possibly can, which don't come very often.

The only person who could visit me was my attorney, Leo Gallagher. He was the chief attorney for the International Labor Defense in Los Angeles at that time, and he'd come and visit me as often as he could.

While I was in jail in San Pedro the big strike was starting on the waterfront. The waterfront workers had finally organized and presented demands to the shipowners. The demands were refused, particularly the demand to recognize the union. And the strike was on, May 10, 1934. The whole kit and caboodle was on strike, seamen, longshoremen, inland boatmen, all up and down the coast—Seattle, Portland, San Francisco, San Pedro, the upriver ports, including Vancouver, British Columbia. I was in jail during the entire strike, including the general strike. The strike was settled in August; I came out in September. The longshoremen won ninety-five cents an hour and recognition of their union, the International Longshoremen's Association (ILA), which in 1937 became the International Longshoremen's and Warehousemen's Union (ILWU). (This union is totally different from the ILA on the East Coast, by the way.)

Several crafts weren't able to settle, including the bargemen and the scalers. The scalers stayed out on strike for another whole year, 1934–1935, and that got me into my next trial.

The ship scalers and painters chipped and painted above the waterline and cleaned out the fire room and the boilers. Nowadays you don't have that so much; it's almost all automatic. But the oil burners used to leave a lot of soot, and these guys used to have to crawl into these holds when it was still hot in there and scrape the soot and put it in sacks and take them out. Just horrible conditions, for which they were paid the lowest type of starvation wages. The longshoremen had just won ninety-five cents an hour, and we were striking for $3.75 a day. In addition, these poor people were from Central and South America, many of them; they didn't know from anything about the United States. The contractors had them under their thumb, even to this extent: If a man wanted a job, and the contractor liked the man's wife or daughter, he had to permit the contractor to sleep with his wife or daughter. I'm not kidding you.

AFG: How did the contractors work?

Brown: The shipowners would hire a contractor to do a job, and he would hire men to work for him. There were kickbacks of all kinds. That's why the men were so angry.

The scalers had the support of the longshoremen, but the seamen sometimes would scab on us by chipping paint on their time in port, and we had to fight against that. The shipowners got the scaling done even cheaper in Hong Kong and Singapore, but all the ships couldn't go there, so sooner or later the strike had to be settled.

After we'd been on strike for a year longer than everybody else, divisions were created in the union. The contractors told some of the guys, "What do you want to listen to the union for? You can go to work for us any time you want. Don't let them keep you out. You're only starving your family." And, you know, after a year it gets pretty difficult. So some guys figured they should go back to work like everybody else, and they became stooges for the con- tractors. The scalers' union had a democratic procedure. It only took forty signatures to call a special meeting, so these guys called one to consider an agreement that had been offered by the con- tractors.

Everybody knew there was a lot of ill feeling and hatred. So the union searched everyone coming into the meeting as best they could and they took away any weapons, in order to have an orderly meeting. Most of the members did not want this particular agreement, but they figured they had a majority and all they had to do was vote it down. Still there was tension, particularly from the other side, and as the meeting progressed they began calling each other names, and one guy accused another of being a contractor's agent, and one thing led to another and some fights erupted. Sure enough, these guys pulled out knives and razors from wherever they had them hidden, and several of the guys got cut. The hall was being renovated and there was some lumber around, and every- body who could picked up some sticks and the battle was on.

The hall was quite large, but it was in an old, dilapidated build- ing with a very narrow stairway. Our meeting was on the second floor. One older man by the name of Torres worked his way through all this fighting out to where the stairs were, but they were pretty crowded and he didn't try to leave by the stairs. When you looked out of the windows from the hall down to the street you could see a marquee. We always thought the roof of this marquee was made of iron, because it was painted black. There was a drop of about four feet from the windowsill to the marquee, and another ten feet to the ground. So Torres jumped onto this marquee, but it didn't hold him. It actually was made of glass. He fell to the ground and was taken to the hospital.

The fighting went on and people were going in and out. The whole fight lasted maybe five or six minutes, and then it was over.

AFG: What happened to the rest of the meeting?

Brown: We reconvened the meeting, but our president went to the emergency hospital to see what had happened to the men, and they arrested him for fighting. Someone else was arrested for using a hammer on somebody, but subsequently he was found not guilty.

AFG: What happened to the proposed agreement to end the strike?

Brown: After we reconvened the meeting, we voted status quo— keep the strike going.

At that time I was chairman of the relief committee, Jiminez was chairman of the overall strike committee, Ville was chairman of the legal committee, and Canales was chairman of another committee. Eight or ten days after the meeting, we four were arrested and charged with attempted murder for throwing this man Torres out of the window. While we were in jail, he got pneumonia on top of his injuries from the fall, and died, so they changed it to murder.

We were in jail eighty days without bail. We were able to see people, and we had conferences with our attorneys, Leo Gallagher and George Andersen from the International Labor Defense.

AFG: Would it have helped you prepare the case if you had been out on bail?

Brown: Oh, sure, I could have gone to see people, witnesses, and followed my own leads. I told the attorneys some facts I had, and some of my leads were followed and some weren't.

AFG: What about your family? What happens to a family when there's a murder charge?

Brown: Well, in my case my brothers knew about it. But they just told my mother and father that I was away.

As a matter of fact, the public generally didn't know about the case. In this instance, instead of ballyhooing about murderers and strikers, there wasn't a word in the newspapers—not one stinking word, except the day we were arrested and the day we were arraigned, and then just a paragraph. Even when the trial was on, nothing was reported. They were going to kill it with silence.

Student: What about the families of the other three men?

Brown: The union saw to it that they were taken care of. Everybody was suffering because of the strike, but if there was anything to eat, those families got it also. We had a relief program based on collecting donations, and we tried to help people get on welfare or emergency relief, although it wasn't so easy if you were on strike. The longshoremen were working at the time, and we got donations through the union.

Jiminez had a big family. They used to come to see him en masse. They were splendid. They had revolutionary traditions from Mexico, so they weren't bluffed. They figured their old man was a hero. Canales was single, and he was a radical guy. I think Ville had a family, too; I didn't know too much about him. And then the community would rally around these people, the Latino community.

At that time I wasn't as aware of the importance of that kind of community support, because I was young. The trial didn't bother me, and I didn't know why the hell it should bother anybody else. That's how I saw it then. I figured the revolution was coming anyway, and their time was limited, so screw them.

AFG: How soon did you think it was coming, Archie?

Brown: Oh, I don't know. People all over the world were in revolt, and I didn't think it was very far off at the time. I guess I was a youngster, impatient like some young people are nowadays. We really had some evidence of the thing at the time, but later on we found out better.

Getting back to our trial—I suppose you are acquainted with the Mooney-Billings case? Two San Francisco labor leaders were charged with bombing a Preparedness Day parade before U.S. entry into World War I. It was a complete frame-up. They were in jail from 1916 on. It was a famous case, and there were protests every once in a while, particularly in San Francisco, and the district attorney in 1935 had run on a platform that there would be no more Mooney cases. We charged before and during our trial that this was another Mooney case, another frame-up. They were very touchy about that. "No, this is not another Mooney case," they kept saying. "We've really got the evidence."

The judge spoke to me three times about it. He said, "I have received letters and telegrams from all over the world demanding that this be a fair trial, demanding that the charges be dismissed, demanding this, demanding that. You're going to have a fair trial. What's the matter with you people?"

I'll tell you, this had a terrific effect. When anybody asks, "What's the use of sending a telegram or a letter?" you can tell them they have a terrific effect on the people in the establishment.

Student: An affirmative effect?

Brown: Oh, yes! It certainly did in this case.

Student: How did everyone know about your case?

Brown: The International Labor Defense was really international!

AFG: The ILD had connections with something known as International Red Aid, with headquarters in Moscow. Similar defense organizations existed in England, Japan, the Soviet Union, and even underground in Hitler Germany.

Brown: One of the facts we stressed very strongly in our case was that this was a battle—a war, if you want—going on between the bosses and the workers. The fact is that people get killed in racial and political struggles, and also in labor struggles. We said this was class warfare with casualties on both sides. And even if someone killed a man, that wasn't premeditated murder—it was done in the course of a struggle for his rights and for establishing the union. That's been the basis for the defense in a number of cases in the labor movement, like the Haywood case involving the murder of the ex-governor of Idaho in 1907. He didn't just plead that he wasn't there and he didn't do it and that kind of stuff.

Usually when people get killed or hurt in a class struggle there are attempts made not just to get the person who did it, but also to frame the leadership of the struggle, those whom the employers and the police and the courts consider to be most dangerous. If they can get the leadership out of the way, they'll have a better chance to quash the revolt, to keep the union from being organized, so they won't have to pay higher wages and give better conditions.

AFG: Don't you think it's elitist to say that?

Brown: That if you can get the leadership you can smash the group? Well, I don't think so. I think it works to a certain extent until new people come forward. You know, nobody is a born leader, and maybe some people have better qualities of leadership than others. I don't know. But it takes time, and I know in the 1934 strike if they had removed Harry Bridges it would have been a big blow. It wouldn't have stopped us, but it would have demoralized many people.

After all, how are strikes broken? By running in scabs, taking away people's jobs, discrediting the leadership one way or another. Those are some of the elements. One thing is to make people think the union leaders are out of their cotton pickin' minds. "What are they doing, going around killing people, blowing up trucks, and that kind of stuff? They shouldn't do it that way, even if there should be a union."

We made the opposite argument in defending our case. We said that if we were going to pick on anybody who was playing the contractors' game, we would pick on the leaders who had organized this back-to-work movement, we wouldn't pick on this old man, Torres. He wasn't a leader. There was no need to pick on him. He was just one of the forty-three signers of the petition to hold the special union meeting, and of course his group was getting the worst of it during the fight, because the majority of the men were against them.

Student: Did the two attorneys represent all four defendants?

Brown: Well, before the trial opened we discussed how to proceed, and the attorneys were of the opinion that if I represented myself I would be able to do a number of things in the trial which attorneys cannot do because they're supposed to be officers of the court. That was a subsidiary reason. The main reason was that at that time, just like now, we had thousands of cases going and in many instances just couldn't afford or didn't have attorneys. We thought this would be a good case to set an example of a person defending himself in court. And, of course, I couldn't make too many mistakes, because the other attorneys were there, so it was fairly safe.

Looking back on it, it made a difference in a couple of important things. First, we put people on the stand to testify as to what the issues were in the strike, what the conditions were that led up to the strike, and why the men fought like they did. The prosecuting attorney would try to prevent this from being revealed. But because I was acting as my own lawyer I was able to put a lot of that before the jury. Of course they would stop me too, but I would just keep going, and that was important, I thought.

On the other side of the coin, both Andersen and Gallagher had enough legal experience to know that when a man is injured and is taken to a hospital he is immediately questioned, "What happened to you? Who hit you? How come you're in this condition?" In our case, certain documents were presented by the prosecution, but this hospital-bed statement was missing. It just stuck out like a sore thumb.

Their evidence consisted mainly of two people who said they actually saw us pick this man up and throw him out the window; others who said they saw him near the window, saw us with our hands on him, and that kind of stuff; people who'd seen him on the sidewalk; and, of course, the police officers who found him in a certain position.

Then, on the eleventh day of the trial, we learned from one of our witnesses who knew one of their witnesses, that Torres had told his son that he had jumped out of the window. Torres' son had testified at our trial that his father had said we had thrown him out the window. But when we heard this other story, we figured Torres had probably told the truth when he was questioned at the hospital.

So we said, "Well, let's have that statement, whatever it is."

They refused to bring it in. So Gallagher and Andersen went to the next higher court with a subpoena. But before the appellate court had a chance to act, something else happened. The waterfront had a shutdown protest about us being arrested for murder, and demanded our release.

AFG: What kind of a strike would you call that?

Brown: Well, I'd say it was sort of a political strike. All it was was an extended lunch hour—a couple hours. But that got in the newspapers, because there was a lot of stuff in the papers in those days about wildcat strikes and violation of the contract, and what a bunch of bums these longshoremen and waterfront workers were. When they stopped work, that was news, and the reason they stopped work was our trial. That busted it wide open.

Then the prosecutor came in with the document. We thought that was very interesting, and a lesson that wasn't lost on the people later (particularly in connection with Harry Bridges' trial, when Hawaii was shut down during one of his four trials for deportation).

When that document was brought in we felt much better. By that time, man, we were pretty worried. My brothers and my friends and my wife-to-be—they were all anxious and concerned. Well, in the hospital records Torres stated that he had jumped. His statement was made in Spanish through an interpreter and was written down in English.

So that's another element in a frame-up—to find people who will say things that are not true or just half true and to withhold evidence that would help the defendants, and maybe even clear them.

Anyway, the trial finally ended, and the jury was charged. They took us back from the courtroom to the cells, which took about eight minutes. By the time we got to the cells the jury had come back to the courtroom. They had taken only one ballot. It was such an open-and-shut case, each of the twelve jurors found us not guilty, even the daughter of a shipper. They called us right back, and we were dismissed. Christmas Eve, 1935. And then, I don't know where they all came from, how they all knew it, but there was a big crowd to greet us after we came out!

Then I went to Spain—

AFG: Wait a minute! Let us ask a few questions. Would you say that in this case the big issue was the facts, not the law, and the facts went to the jury?

Brown: No, not exactly. The lawyers and I, whenever possible, kept making a big point about what kind of a fight it was. Suppose there hadn't been that document! We had to defend on other grounds.

AFG: Did the newspapers report that you won the case?

Brown: Oh, yeah. I'm sure the ILWU library has clippings.

Student: Isn't there some way to compel the prosecution to produce testimony?

AFG: Yes. You move to make them produce it, and that's what the defense attorneys did. But if they don't want to give it to you, they don't; they say it doesn't exist, it's lost, it never existed, and how are you going to prove differently?

Student: Okay, so in this case it was found that there was a document, after the DA denied it. Wasn't there any way to press charges against him, for prosecuting someone when his own evidence showed that the defendants were not guilty?

AFG: Prosecutors cannot be sued for malicious prosecution. You can make a complaint and try to bring criminal charges. But the very DA or U.S. attorney who did the criminal act is the guy who would have to bring charges against himself or his assistant, and it won't happen.

Student: Were there other murder trials in the period?

Brown: The *King-Ramsey-Connor* case came in '36, and then the dynamite case in Modesto.

All right, let me continue. The scalers' strike was ended. The better times started setting in. There was still continual turmoil. The CIO was being organized; there were many strikes, and I stayed down on the waterfront. I went into the longshoremen's union after that and helped with organizing, particularly the lettuce workers in Salinas in 1936 and 1937.

Then in '38 I went to Spain. When I came back from Spain, I went back to the longshoremen's union—

Student: What did you do in Spain?

Brown: I fought with the Abraham Lincoln Brigade against the fascists—the Spanish Civil War, you know?

Student: Did you find that an eventful experience?

Brown: It was eventful. People in this country were in support of the republic established in Spain by election; they were against Franco. We got tremendous support from the unions, and hundreds of recruits. I was in the machine-gun company made up mainly of seamen and longshoremen, East and West Coast. There were 3,000 people who went; 1,800 people stayed there, killed, in the Lincoln Brigade. Recently one of the vets, Arthur Landis, wrote a book about it, called *The Abraham Lincoln Brigade.*

AFG: I just want to put one legal footnote to this. Did you have trouble getting back into the United States after Spain?

Brown: Well, not exactly trouble, since I was born in the U.S., but this cat from the United States embassy wanted to know how I'd gotten there, because I had no passport. I had to stow away to get to France, and then the French organization took us into Spain.

AFG: Many people who went to fight in Spain were either naturalized citizens or aliens who had not been able to get American citizenship. When they tried to return to the United States, they had trouble, and there are still deportation cases pending today of people who went to fight fascism in Spain in 1936.

You know, any political upheaval like that has huge legal ramifications, not only in terms of criminal charges, contempt citations, injunctions, and attacks on the organization and its leaders, but also in the individual lives of the people who participate. There will be divorces, suits over child custody, problems with getting an estate settled, difficulty getting back into the country, and so forth. A broad movement, even a run-of-the-mill strike, means a lot of little lawsuits also, on seemingly unrelated issues.

Brown: After I returned from Spain, I went to Europe to fight in the U.S. Army against the German and Italian fascists. They were the ones who really defeated us in Spain.

After World War II there was another upsurge in the country and the world, with some countries, as you know, going socialist, and a large Communist Party being built in countries like France and Italy and Indonesia. And in the United States a similar upsurge took place, with a lot of militant strikes by veterans who had returned to the shops.

Then Winston Churchill came to the United States to make his Fulton speech constructing the Iron Curtain, and they started a counterattack—"they" meaning the reactionaries, the ruling class. They attacked the unions and the people's movements generally, and civil liberties and civil rights. So there was a double thing going on, a rising struggle for civil rights and an attack upon civil rights, both taking place at the same time, which is not unusual; that's the dialectics of the situation.

The Taft-Hartley Act was pushed through Congress in 1947 to regulate the labor unions, to make them report on their financial affairs, to restrict certain types of strikes and picketing, to require the unions to register and list their officers, and especially to kick out the left-wingers.

AFG: Under Section 9(h) of the Taft-Hartley Law, no one who was a member of or affiliated with the Communist Party in the past five years could hold a position in a union. So the people who were allegedly Communist Party members or considered "fellow travelers" either had to stop being leaders of their unions or they had to file a statement resigning from the Communist Party, or they had to in effect say, "I'm not a Communist," and be subject to a possible perjury charge. People tried each of those alternatives.

Brown: The next year, the left unions were kicked out of the CIO, including my union, the International Longshoremen's and Warehousemen's Union.

Then Joe McCarthy arose, along with Richard Nixon, and I want to say that McCarthyism was very effective. Also the left, including the Communist Party, made mistakes in judging what the situation was in 1951 when the Supreme Court upheld the Smith Act, in the Dennis case, which in effect seemed to outlaw the Communist Party for the first time. The Communist Party thought that this was the beginning of fascism or a form of fascism in the United States.

As a result, the reactionaries demoralized and disarmed and disoriented the radical revolutionary movement to a considerable extent. Part of the problem was that the government began to arrest the entire leadership of the party. This has to do with what Ann was talking about, this elitism. There had been a whole corps of experienced, knowledgeable, and dedicated people who were left-wingers—some of them members and leaders of the Communist Party and some not, some sympathizers of the socialist world and some not. The general campaign was conducted against all of them, and the labor and radical movement was beheaded. It was very effective. There was even a split within the Communist Party, and the whole ideological fervor and understanding went down. There was a battle to maintain oneself, to save as much as possible.

Some people have made a study of this period and written on it, but there has not been enough investigation, if you ask me. In any event, a lot of fear had been engendered, and that was the situation by the end of the fifties.

Some of us, myself included, took off so they couldn't arrest us, with the idea that some way or another we would be able to supply some leadership while these people were being thrown in jail. I just wasn't present. Actually I never left the country, if you want to know, never went outside the boundaries of the United States.

AFG: Archie, would you care to say anything about that period?

Brown: A couple of things. Hindsight shows us that making ourselves scarce should have been done on a much smaller scale, first of all. Secondly, our judgment about the oncoming of fascism was wrong. There was a threat, all right, but it wasn't to the extent we thought. It was not wrong that some people took off, because there was no need for them to be in jail when they could be outside doing certain things, helping with the movement.

AFG: How did your confinement in the underground differ from your earlier confinements in jail?

Brown: If you go away you just have to live like a refugee, like a fugitive. And stay here or there, wherever you can, under an assumed name maybe—all that kind of stuff. There was a problem of identification, a problem of work.

I was gone from right after the Dennis decision in July 1951 to September 1955, about four years.

AFG: What did it do to your family?

Brown: Well, I was just going to say I had a wife and four children at the time. The baby was a couple months old when I took off. I had a discussion with my wife about what to do.

Now, you talk about hounding! She was hounded! Three cars on her for twenty-four hours a day—you know, a car every eight hours, changed off.

Student: For how long?

Brown: Whole time, whole bloody time!

I saw my family about three times during those years, and it took quite a procedure to do it. You want to learn about the highways and byways of San Francisco and the Bay Area—I know them. You go over to Berkeley and there are all these little paths. You stop on one street, walk down some stairs and it's another street, and the cats don't know you're going to do it. Another car is waiting and off you go. You do that a couple of times, and you check, and the family had to do the same goddam thing. Finally I saw them on a couple of vacations. That was the way we helped keep our sanity.

Otherwise my wife was followed twenty-four hours a day. Then, of course, they knew when something was going on. They would try to trace it and see how she came back. Anyway there were strains and stresses in the family. She protested about it, "How long is this going to last?" And then, during that time, of all things, she had an operation on her back. She was in a harness for a long time before that, and we had to make a decision. I talked to her about it. We decided that I would not come in and that she was strong enough to take it. I know it was tough on her.

It was so impossible in San Francisco she moved from there to her folks' place in southern California, a small town. They put the cops on her down there, and they usually took pictures of everybody. One time, my brother-in-law got a camera and began taking pictures of them. So they cut it out for a while.

They never asked her directly, "Why don't you tell us where your husband is?" What they did try was to find out the process by which we met. They sent her a couple of telegrams signed "Archie," but they made a mistake. They sent them to "Mrs. Archie Brown." Now, there never was a Mrs. Archie Brown, as far as I was concerned. You know, I always objected to this whole goddam procedure of the woman takes the man's name—not only his last name, but his first name. It's out of this world. I would never go for that. So when the telegram came for Mrs. Archie Brown, she says, "What a phony!" The FBI never was wise to that.

Anyway, after that period came what they called the Silent Fifties. It wasn't really silent—we were making all the noise we could. But the students and the young people who had been quite active in the forties were silent in the fifties. The movement within the unions and among middle-class people had died down, for a number of reasons. The left unions were isolated, kicked out of the CIO, and unable to use the National Labor Relations Board; left-wingers in other unions were kicked out or silenced. This began to tell on the labor movement, because the yeast was missing. It debilitated the whole labor movement.

But in the sixties things began to perk up. A few of the obvious reasons were the realization of the meaning of the atom bomb and the development of the fight against it, and the reaction against the McCarthy period. Things opened up in the schools, where so many of the students and professors saw a threat to academic freedom. People began to tell them what to teach, and there was a revolt against that.

In 1961 I was arrested by two federal agents while I was coming off the job, taken to prison, and booked. When I asked, "What am I charged with?" they didn't know. The law they charged me under had never been used before. This was the Landrum-Griffin Act, which was a successor to the non-Communist oath in the Taft-Hartley Law.

AFG: Few union officials ever went to jail for signing Taft-Hartley oaths, because, after years of litigation, their lawyers often proved that the FBI or other government agents had violated the rights of the defendants. The Supreme Court reversed their convictions, although it held the loyalty oath constitutional.

Brown: So Congress passed Section 504 of the Landrum-Griffin Act to replace Section 9(h) of the Taft-Hartley Act. This Section 504 said in effect that if you had been a member of the Communist Party or imprisoned within the past five years, you could not hold office in a union.

AFG: It was made a crime. Before, it had been a loyalty oath, and the crime would arise only if you committed perjury. Now they made it a crime to be simultaneously a member of the Communist Party and an elected union official.

Brown: When that law was passed in 1959, I had been a member of my local longshoremen's union executive board for several years, along with another fellow who's now retired. Both of us were known Communists in the ILWU, both elected to the executive board every year by secret ballot. We had a conference with the attorneys and the international-union leadership, to discuss whether I should run, and decided I should. We were going to challenge the law. George Andersen, who had been in the murder trial, was one of the attorneys, with Norman Leonard and Richard Gladstein.

I ran and was elected. They let it pass for a while, but in 1961 I was arrested on this Section 504 and released on $5,000 bail, which the union furnished.

There are a few interesting things about that trial. First, our attorneys proceeded to show that I was a member of the Communist Party and showed the number of votes I got to win the union election. Present and past union officials testified as to my character, and that I was a good union member.

AFG: It got a little sticky for the government at one point. The defense was trying to put into evidence a letter from the NAACP to the executive board of the Longshoremen's Union asking for money for the NAACP. On the letterhead was the name of Cecil Poole as a member of the NAACP executive board. And Poole was the U.S. attorney prosecuting this case.

Brown: And I made the motion to give them the money. That's what killed them.

AFG: The argument behind passing the Taft-Hartley oath and the Landrum-Griffin Law was that Communists would disrupt the flow of industry by causing "political strikes," that is, strikes for non-economic reasons. So one of the issues in the case was whether the longshoremen's union ever conducted political strikes, and, if so, had Archie been involved in them? The trial got into union politics while testing the constitutionality of a statute.

Brown: But the government didn't want to talk about a couple of our political strikes! Like when the Nazi ship came into the port of San Francisco in 1938 and the longshoremen's union had a short strike in protest. And then, early in 1941, the Chinese people of San Francisco and many others, including the lieutenant governor, came down to the port and picketed against scrap iron going to Japan, which had invaded their country for a decade. The long-shoremen respected the picket line, and there was a big how-de-do about that. Well, they did not want these things in the case, or the fact that I participated in both of these political strikes.

Our union has always had a democratic constitution, and our lawyers brought out the fact that I was only one of thirty-five members on the local-union executive board. I couldn't call a political strike if I wanted to. Furthermore, any strike is a coast-wide issue. The question would have to go to the international executive board, and everybody else would have to look at it. It's impossible for one man to call a political strike.

The other important thing about this case is the instructions to the jury. The judge told the jury, "It is not within your realm to decide whether a law is right or wrong, constitutional or unconsti-tutional. All you have to decide is whether Archie Brown is a member of the Communist Party and is he at the same time a member of the union executive board?" Well, then they had no choice. They decided and found me guilty.

Next it went to the U.S. Court of Appeals for the Ninth Circuit, which ruled that the law was unconstitutional, based on the First and Fifth Amendments. It was a divided vote. What's interesting is that the government appealed that decision to the United States Supreme Court. The Supreme Court didn't even monkey with the First and Fifth Amendments. By a five to four vote, they said the law was a bill of attainder, and therefore Section 504 was out.

Student: What is a bill of attainder, exactly?

Brown: Well, as I gather, it's a special law convicting an individual, and it was forbidden when our Constitution was set up. England had passed special laws against individuals that the king or somebody didn't like, and this was made illegal in the U.S.—the law has to apply to everybody.

AFG: "Attainder" means to taint or attaint the blood of a person without trial. In feudal England, Parliament would proclaim a law saying that Sir John Lilburn, or whoever, was guilty of treason, and he was attainted, which made it legal to execute him, for the king to take all his land and money, and to prevent all his heirs from having titles or privileges.

In 1940, some Congressmen were so mad at the president of Archie's union, Harry Bridges, that the House of Representatives actually passed a bill that simply said, "Harry Bridges shall be deported." That was another bill of attainder. It never passed the Senate, but it shows that attainder is not a new weapon for reactionaries.

Brown: So those were my three trials.

AFG: I'll add a cultural note here. Most of the dramatic events Archie has described, the Mooney-Billings case, the shape-up on the waterfront, the '34 general strike, are all in the mural by Anton Refregier in the Rincon Annex Post Office. You may want to see it next time you go to San Francisco.

Student: Are there many differences between the radical movement today and in the 1930s?

Brown: Well, I think the 1970s are not the 1930s. The world situation is different; people have different experiences. And in the United States, maybe also in other countries, one big difference is in the labor movement. In the 1930s it played a leading role and had a lot of prestige. It doesn't have it nowadays, and deservedly not. As a result, all kinds of ideas arise based on having no faith in the labor movement and making the revolution without the labor movement, or with the labor movement playing only a small part in the change. We had all kinds of adventurist ideas in the 1930s, but not to the extent that they exist nowadays.

I believe that things are changing now, that the labor movement is coming back. Not to the same position that it had in the thirties, because that's impossible. But there are rank-and-file movements growing in many unions. And I see more of a joining together of the various movements and ideas nowadays, leading to a much more stable and more effective program and struggle.

I'm a Communist. I'm in the Communist Party. Never quit.

Student: How long do we have to wait for the revolution?

Brown: That's a question!

FIGHTING MURDER AND
RACISM IN UNIONS
Francis J. McTernan

AFG: Frank McTernan is probably a classic example of what is now called an old left lawyer. He started practicing labor law in the New Deal establishment, went into private practice representing established unions, and recently has represented dissident rank-and-file union movements, with some victories and some tragedies.

McTernan: When I was a student back in the thirties, labor law was the glamour field for the young committed law students. Those were the days of organizing the unorganized, the development of the CIO, the great strikes—the San Francisco waterfront strike, the Little Steel strike and the Chicago Massacre in 1937, the sit-down strikes in General Motors, and later the organization of Ford Motor Company. Very exciting days! I was a much envied person because I was able to walk out of law school and get a job with the National Labor Relations Board, the glamour agency of the New Deal to young radical-minded lawyers.

AFG: Did you think of yourself as a radical then?

McTernan: Not as much as I do today. I think I've learned over the years. Maybe I shouldn't have used the word "radical." Probably I wasn't even a radical. I was caught up in the New Deal and its promises.

144

AFG: Why did you quit the NLRB and go into private practice?

McTernan: I didn't quit; I was fired. The NLRB was under increasing attacks from employer groups and was subjected to an unfriendly congressional investigation by Southern reactionaries and anti-Administration Republicans. One result of the attacks was a sharply decreased appropriation for the NLRB, and a lot of the junior people were laid off.

In those days, making a living was a very difficult thing. Salaries were very low, and professional jobs were impossible to find. War prosperity hadn't started yet, and I was blacklisted in Washington because none of the other agencies wanted to have anything to do with anybody who'd been on the Labor Board. So I came West.

In the 1930s most of the fellows doing the really hard organizing were probably members of the Communist Party and other radical political organizations. But as the unions became organized they became an establishment, and we hadn't finished the decade of the forties before the establishment started to purge the unions of all radical elements and individuals. Nine international unions were thrown out of the CIO because of their alleged Communist leadership. Some of them are still out of the CIO. Interestingly enough, some of the guys who organized the cases against the left-wing unions because of their "Communist domination" are present-day radicals.

AFG: I think at least one of them now says he was wrong and shouldn't have done it.

McTernan: Maybe. I think that those who won the right to organize in the late 1930s, particularly in the automobile industry, by engaging in sit-down strikes and some illegalities, are among those who yell out loudest now about students who sit in. And today, as you know, the establishment of the labor movement, including the head of the AFL-CIO, supports the President on Southeast Asia. Organized labor, as it is now operating, is politically irrelevant to the problems of the day.

Except that unions are composed of people, and these people are not irrelevant. Lots of them are in good jobs and get good wages and conditions because of the unions, but lots of them don't get what they should be getting. Lots of them are dues-paying people who just contribute their dues to support a bunch of fat cats sitting around in their offices.

This situation exists in most of the big trade unions today, but there are always some people who don't like it and try to do something about it. They are the shit-stirrers.

Perhaps one of the most undemocratic of the established unions is the Brotherhood of Painters, Decorators and Paperhangers of America, an old-line craft union that was ruled for so many years with such dictatorial power by a man named Raftery that when he retired he was able to have his son "elected" his successor.

I became involved with this union in the early 1960s when I had the good fortune to meet Dow Wilson, a member of the painters' union in San Francisco. He had been at sea during World War II, was a radical, had been a Communist, but threw in his Communist Party membership in the early 1950s over an ideological struggle within the waterfront part of the party. Dow Wilson was extremely able, a real charismatic leader who understood the labor movement, understood political economy, and understood workers. He learned how to paint aboard ship and drifted out of the waterfront into house painting. Eventually he started to lead a rank-and-file movement within the painters' local in San Francisco.

At that point the union had a classic kind of organization: the constitution and the bylaws were designed to keep those in power entrenched. Elections were stolen; undemocratic representation in councils and conventions made it very difficult for the rank and file to get organized. Dow won his first election in the San Francisco local when his group prevailed upon the local to use the San Francisco County voting machines for their election. He probably had won several elections before that, but they were taken away from him when his ballots were thrown into the wastebasket.

One of the recurrent issues in the painting industry is what they call tool restrictions, and one of the principal restrictions in this area is against spray painting. There are two reasons for the restriction. One is that you can spray paint on much faster than you can brush it on, so it cuts employment. But another is that the fumes from epoxy and other paints generated by the spray gun constitute a serious health hazard. You can't use a spray gun without a mask, and even with a mask you get some of these fumes.

They get in the air you breathe, damage your lungs, and generally poison your system.

Painters are generally considered to be heavy drinkers, and there's always talk about all the alcoholics in the painters' union, but a good part of that is a myth. These guys are not alcoholics. They're dying of blood poisoning rather than of alcohol, and perhaps they drink a little more than they should to try to make life a little pleasant for a few hours a day.

Dow Wilson made a famous statement on tool restrictions. The employers always say, "The tool restrictions are killing us. They not only have a restriction on what you can spray; they have a list of things about the size of brush you can use and the size of roller you can use to roll the paint on." But the fact is that in nonunion areas they have rollers two to three feet wide and about thirty-six inches around, and one man has to handle the whole thing. That's terribly hard work, but you can paint a room awfully fast with it.

Wilson used to say, "Pay us decent wages, give us pensions and security for ourselves and our families, give us a proper share of the profits of this industry, and we'll put the paint on with a mop if you want us to."

Student: How many months a year does the average painter work?

McTernan: We had some statistics in one case I handled. They show that the average annual earnings in 1957 were $5,200 for 1,600 hours' work; in 1966, the average annual earnings were $7,200 for 1,290 hours' work. However, I think that if you compare that with the increase in the cost of living you'll find that the painter probably earned less in 1966 than he did in 1957.

Student: If you work fifty weeks a year at forty hours a week, you'd have an average of 2,000 hours; so these guys were working only 1,290 hours out of 2,000 possible.

McTernan: As with many other trades, the painters' trade is dying. That's one of the reasons for those decreased hours. Modern methods of decoration are replacing painting with plastics and other things that are manufactured in a plant and installed in the house or building. You look in any new public building and see how little paint there is. The employers say that's because the wages are so high that it's uneconomical to paint, but I don't think that's the real reason. It's part of the general automation of our society.

In any event, no sooner had Dow Wilson emerged into the leadership of his local than he gradually moved out into leadership in the San Francisco Bay Area. One of the methods of keeping the painters' union officials in power was to have several small local unions in the cities surrounding San Francisco, and even to have two separate locals in a single city. This made no sense organizationally, but it made it easier for the establishment to maintain control of these locals from on top and more difficult for anyone from below to challenge that power. Thus, as Dow started reaching out into these locals, the attack came on him.

Wilson had a good expression. He'd be in a union meeting and some guy would want to speak against him. Wilson would get up and say, "OK, buster, take your best shot." And when the guy got through complaining about something, Wilson would ask, "Is that the best shot you've got? Forget it!" And the union members would laugh.

Often someone would charge, "You're a Communist!"

"You're goddam right I'm a Communist. What's your next shot, buster?" That would break up the meeting. Everybody would laugh and think Wilson was the greatest guy that ever lived. He appealed to the average guy because he could end the debate with a crushing bon mot—a thing we all dream of doing, but seldom do.

One of the things Wilson was able to use as an organizing tool was a challenge to the international and local officialdom on the use of dues money—not in terms of theft or embezzlement but in terms of not using the money as laid out in the bylaws.

One of the first big fights was over a dues increase. Part of the Landrum-Griffin Act of 1959 is known as "labor's bill of rights." It requires notice of the meeting and its purpose when an increase in dues is to be voted, and a vote by secret ballot. The piecards adopted some gimmick—

Student: What's a piecard?

McTernan: Someone on the staff of the union who gets paid a salary. It's a derogatory term used for union officials who just sit around the office and get paid without doing any work. In other words, the guy's union job is a ticket (card) to live well (eat pie).

The painters' international requires these various locals to belong to district councils, with five delegates from each local union whether it has fifty members or two thousand. Under the bylaws of the council, dues are increased automatically every time the painters get a pay increase. But the automatic increase is so large as to be ridiculous, and the bylaws thus provide that the delegates to the council can decide how much of the automatic increase goes into effect. So the delegates to the council actually decide what dues the local members have to pay. In 1966, the delegates to one council raised dues by $1.75 per month for four thousand painters. The decision was made by thirty-four delegates voting eighteen to sixteen for the increase.

One of the big rallying cries was that the automatic dues increase was illegal. The union officers went to their lawyer, who depended on them for his livelihood, and said, "Wilson says this dues increase is no good. Write an opinion saying it's all right."

So the lawyer writes an opinion saying it's all right. Then Wilson's guys come to me and ask, "Is this right?"

I said, "No, I don't think under Landrum-Griffin they can do that."

"Well, what can we do? We won't pay it." And they didn't pay it, and we filed suit in 1966.

AFG: Did you have any qualms about going into a capitalist court to settle an intra-union beef?

McTernan: It was the only legal forum we had.

Of course, this brings up the question of what purpose does the lawyer serve? The argument I have with a lot of young radical lawyers is that I think the lawyer's job, until the revolution starts, is to be a lawyer, to keep the revolutionaries on the streets and out of jail. In the trade-union business the unions themselves are capitalist organizations. They're a part of capitalism just as much as the capitalists are. But within the trade unions there is an opportunity to restore control to the rank and file. This provides the best chance for the trade unions to really advance radical and progressive goals.

Certainly I had some hesitancy in going into a court that normally is thought of as leaning toward the employers. But that's not necessarily true today. We went into the federal district court in San Francisco because we were operating under a federal statute, and those judges are not necessarily all employer-oriented. They respond to the charges of union bossism and how the officers screw the rank and file out of what they're supposed to get and how they live fat and fancy off the dues of the working members of the unions.

AFG: But how could you use the Landrum-Griffin Act on your side when it's an antilabor law?

McTernan: I distinguished between two parts of the act. One part was antilabor. The other part spelled out rights of union members against undemocratic procedures, unfair disciplinary action by union officials, and undemocratic dues increases, and the rights of locals against unfair discipline by internationals. The unions opposed the whole act when it was before Congress, and at that time I went along with them, thinking it could be used to disrupt and break up unions. But my experience, particularly in the painters' union cases, has convinced me that the second part of it is not an antilabor act, that it can and should be used by dissident groups within unions, by rank-and-file movements, as a shield against being crushed by the union establishment.

For example, those who were in favor of this dues increase just crushed all the opposition talk within the established union, and it was only through our lawsuit that we were able to prevent this increase from becoming effective. It was only through the other provisions of Landrum-Griffin that we could protect the members who were taking on the establishment. Otherwise they would have been thrown out of office without legal cause and suspended from membership. Instead, we won the case in the federal district court and the court of appeals. The international union tried to get the United States Supreme Court to hear it, but they lost.

AFG: How long did their appeal take?

McTernan: Four years. Meanwhile, Dow Wilson continued the struggle and built strong local leadership on both sides of the bay.

The union in this period made some significant gains. Let me give you an example, to show what a union under good leadership can do.

The Golden Gate Bridge has to be painted constantly. I was told that it takes a crew of thirty painters nine years to paint it completely. The weather out there, with that driving fog and the salt in the air swept up from the bay by the wind, is very corrosive to the steel, so it's a continual battle to keep the bridge from rusting away. It's tough, hard work. The painters are hanging from scaffolds two hundred to three hundred feet over the water with that fog rolling in and blowing, and it's cold, half raining. All the work is outside, but it pays well. Under the California statute they have to be paid the journeyman's rate, which includes special premiums for the "high work." The painter who was getting about 1,300 hours of work a year in 1966 made $7,200, but the Golden Gate Bridge painter worked forty hours a week, fifty-two weeks a year, and with the high work premiums he made $12,000 to $13,000 a year in 1966. Despite the hard work and bad working conditions, it's a pretty good job.

There had never been a black man employed as a painter on the Golden Gate Bridge up until about 1966. There had been an arrangement with the bridge management that when they needed painters they would seek them out of the painters' hiring hall. Dow Wilson decided it was time to break the color bar on the bridge. He had previously brought a large number of black painters and apprentices into the union, and locally it's one of the best integrated of the old building-trades unions. He finally found a guy who had the records to prove his experience in painting on steel, which is necessary for bridge painting. When the bridge called in for two painters, one black guy and one white guy were sent down.

They were given the test they gave all painters, and they said the black guy failed the test. So he went back to the union and they sent him down to the state Fair Employment Practices Commission, to file a complaint.

Now I'm doing a little guessing, but I think the bridge management went to a member of the union establishment and said, "You've got to find a black guy to put to work on the bridge." Maybe this man went into one of these automatic car washes and said to one of the black guys working there, "Do you know anything about painting?" Anyway, we do know that the next day a black man was hired to paint on the Golden Gate Bridge, and he had never had a paintbrush in his hand in his life. His only work experience had been as a car washer.

Then the management got afraid again and let the first black man, the union man, go to work, and fired the second one. The second black man saw he was being used and came to us. We sent him down to the FEPC.

They let the first man work a few months and then they fired him. They had put a watch on him, and every time he'd turn around and spit they'd make a notation. You see, when you're working out there on the bridge and the call of nature comes, you just get in the right direction of the wind and let it go. They were complaining that he was not getting in the right direction of the wind.

In order to try to erase the claim of discrimination, when these two guys were both off during the FEPC hearing, management hired a third black painter.

We had a long hearing before FEPC. The union paid for my services to appear on behalf of the two black complainants, along with the FEPC attorney. And the union business agents were practically at my beck and call as investigators. This is what a good leadership can do.

We half won and half lost that one. The first black painter was an aggressive, no-shit guy. The second was kind of passive; he allowed himself to be used. By this time Reagan was governor and had put his men on the FEPC. The FEPC decided that the militant one had done unsatisfactory work, but the passive man, who had never had a paintbrush in his hand before this, had done satisfactory work: he was ordered reinstated. With the decision of the FEPC forcing the second man back, the color bar was broken. Now there are three or four black painters out of the thirty on the bridge.

This was a very important breakthrough in a small way. The union, with the proper leadership, used the tools of a lawyer to achieve an important social gain. The reason the state acted in this case was that there was a union banging on their door, not just an individual. That made a qualitative difference. And with the financial backing of the union a private lawyer was hired, putting an aggressive advocate on the case to buck up the bureaucratic lawyer for the FEPC. Moreover, the union's advocate did not hold his job at the pleasure of a governor or the chairman of an administrative body. I hold my job as long as I do effective work for my client.

Now, in the case of Dow Wilson, I suddenly lost my client in the most tragic way. He was attending endless meetings on both sides of the bay, to strengthen his movement. One night as he left a meeting, he was shot and killed. A month later, a reform leader in the East Bay was also murdered.

Student: Did they ever find out who did it?

McTernan: Yes—two small painting contractors from Sacramento who had been acting on behalf of Ben Rasnik, the top painters' union leader in Alameda County and an avowed enemy of Wilson. All three were convicted of murder and are now serving sentences. The two contractors did the killing, according to the testimony of one of them, after they were promised a reward by Rasnik. And it turned out that the contractors had also been looting the welfare fund in the Sacramento local, over $100,000 worth.

When Dow Wilson was murdered and the head of the district council was arrested for murder, the international president moved in. He put the district council under trusteeship, which meant that he would send his representative into the council, take over its books, records, and bank account, suspend all officers, and run the council dictatorially until it got back in line. This made some sense, because the head of it had just been arrested for murder.

But he also attempted to put under trusteeship the three local unions in the East Bay that supported Wilson. This led us to turn to the Landrum-Griffin Act once again. The act provides that you can't impose a trusteeship without having a reason. The reason the international president gave was that they weren't paying the dues they were supposed to be paying to the district council. We weren't paying the increased dues because we contended that the increase had been enacted illegally. But we also weren't paying the dues that were assessed before the increase. This was because we contended that some of the money that was going into the painters' district council from those assessments was being used for purposes that were not proper under the bylaws.

Now, under the law a union is an unincorporated association, and a member of an association has a contract with the other members and with the association as a whole. The constitution and bylaws constitute this contract. If you don't follow the rules set down in the constitution and bylaws, you've violated your contract. If you don't pay your dues you've violated your contract, and the association has the right to sue you for that breach of contract and collect the dues. Many trade unions have done that, and do it. They sue in small-claims court to collect their dues from guys who refuse to pay. There are guys like that who take all the benefits of the organization and won't pay the dues.

So the international president said that we had violated our contract and had to be put under trusteeship. Again, we used the law and wrote to the district council, saying, "You're violating your contract with us. You're using this money for general purposes when it's supposed to be used for a specific purpose, as set forth in the bylaws." They ignored us. Then we went on up to the international, and the international ruled that we were wrong. So we said, "Well, we're sorry, but we'll just have to stop paying you, because you violated your contract with us."

So here's the international president with all this power designating a trustee. What do we do?

I took the position (and the more I practice law the more I think it's a sound maxim) that possession is nine points of the law. We had possession of the union offices, the books, and the records —we had the muscle. We set up a twenty-four-hour guard on each of the three local offices. We took all the bank accounts out of the bank they had been in and put them in a new bank, and only a few trusted officers knew where they were. Then we said, "Come and get it." We used Dow Wilson's tactic. We in effect told the president, Raftery, "Take your best shot."

He responded with a series of lawsuits in the state court, seeking injunctions to require us to comply with his trusteeship order, and we responded with a complaint to the Department of Labor under the Landrum-Griffin Act that the attempt to impose this trusteeship was illegal. But the international union's officials in Washington had the ear of the Department of Labor, and our complaint was thrown out with no consideration at all.

Student: Why didn't you go into the courts instead of to the Department of Labor?

McTernan: We had nothing to go to court about. If we had turned the stuff over and then gone to the court, we'd have been dead, because by the time we got the final decision from the court it would have been all over.

Our position was, "We're going to make you go to court." We went to the Department of Labor because the law says you can; we didn't expect anything helpful.

Meanwhile, for some reason, the international stalled its own case in the state court. Then they suddenly dismissed it and sued in federal court.

Now, we had refused to pay both the basic dues and the increase. I wasn't worried about not paying the increased dues, but I got a little afraid about our financial responsibility for nonpayment of the basic assessment. The international was arguing that it couldn't run and this and that, because we refused to pay these dues.

So I brought into court checks totaling about $25,000, which is all the money we could have owed in basic dues, and I said, "Your Honor, if the international's lawyer is afraid they can't operate, we offer to pay the legal part of the assessment right here and now. Here are the checks." And I turned around to the counsel table. "Do you want them, Mr. Brundage?"

He said, "No."

He was on the spot. He had to refuse, I think, from a political point of view. But from a legal point of view he lost his case right there, because his answer wasn't lost on the judge. Brundage later accused me of grandstanding—and I was, in a way, but it worked.

Student: Why do you think he couldn't take the money?

McTernan: The international wanted to get rid of the local leadership and take over; they wanted those trusteeships. If he took the money he knew the basis for the trusteeship was gone. We had a good-faith lawsuit going about the legality of the dues increase, and the judge said, "As long as they're fighting that increase in good faith, and I find that they are, they have a right to withhold payment until its legality is determined."

But we had no lawsuit going as to the legality of not paying that assessment, and it was a weakness in our case, since the inter-

national had already ruled we were wrong on that. Later the
district council sued the locals involved to collect the basic assessment. The Superior Court in Alameda County ruled recently that
the locals were correct in their contention that it was the council
and not the locals that had violated the bylaws. Thus the locals
never did have to pay the basic assessment.

I should tell the rest of the story. We won the case, but the
revolt in the painters' union was crushed by the murder of the two
principal leaders. The reform or dissident movement still exists
around the Bay Area, but it's falling apart and bickering within
itself.

AFG: Do you feel that over the long haul the New Deal labor
legislation has helped the unions in this country? I'm referring
mainly to the Wagner Labor Relations Act, which guaranteed the
right to organize unions and set up the National Labor Relations
Board.

McTernan: I have many thoughts on that. I think they helped, but
it was a fatal error of labor to allow itself to be placed at the mercy
of Congress and the NLRB. The way labor law has developed
now, I think the burdens of the act far outweigh its advantages.

Some unions have already proved this. They refused to have
their officers file non-Communist oaths required under the Taft-
Hartley law, so they went on for several years without being able
to use any of the services of the NLRB. They had a rough time,
because the right-wing unions tried to raid them and take contracts
away from them. But the ones that were really strong unions, that
were run in a democratic manner and fought for the members'
demands, did survive. That includes a left-led union like the longshoremen's on the West Coast, and an old-line union like the
typographers'.

But some of the other unions came to place too much reliance
on the Labor Act. For example, about a year ago I attended a
meeting in Washington of attorneys for local unions from around
the country. They were fighting to preserve the doctrine of accretion, which applies particularly to retail stores. Under this doctrine, when an employer has a union-shop contract with a union
and he opens a new store, the new store automatically comes
within the old contract. Recently there's been an attack on the

accretion doctrine. The gist of the attack is that the workers in the new store should have the right to determine whether they want to be members of the union.

Well, this was the biggest problem bothering these lawyers and international officials: that they might lose this method of getting new workers under contract without convincing them to join. This means dues payments coming in to the union, but it's not organizing workers.

This is one way the law makes for lazy union leaders. It makes them the tools of antilabor employers, because they are more interested in holding their jobs than in serving their members. Thus they don't want to rock the boat. Even among some of the good labor leaders, there's a tendency to want to find some way of organizing without going out and convincing that worker that he's better off in the union. That's hard work. They'd much rather sit in their offices and attend conferences and meetings and be looked upon as labor statesmen and community leaders.

Situations like that lend support to the theory that many hold, and I tend to agree with, that President Roosevelt was the greatest capitalist of them all, that he saved the whole goddam system for them. This was one of the ways he did it—through stabilizing labor relations by convincing big industry that they should accept organization, that they are better off with it.

Roosevelt was aware of this. In one of his speeches he said, "The criticisms they make of me remind me of the story of a fellow who was standing on the dock, well dressed, with a fur coat, and wearing a beautiful high silk hat. Something happened to him and he fell in the water. A young man saw him and dove into the water and swam out to him. He dragged him in and saved him from drowning. No sooner was the fellow back on the dock than he noticed that his hat was floating down the stream, and he gave his rescuer hell for losing the hat."

AFG: Frank, do you think your political views have affected your practice, especially in terms of union clients? For example, would you be willing to discuss whether you have ever been before an un-American committee or anything like that?

McTernan: I have been before un-American committees as a witness and as an attorney for other witnesses; two of my partners have been called before the committee, and undoubtedly our firm does not have labor-law clients that it should have because of our reputation.

Take one local union for which we have been attorneys for over twenty years. The head of the local union first came to my partner, Benjamin Dreyfus, in the 1940s and asked us to take over representation of his local because he was dissatisfied with the services being rendered by what was then, and still is, a leading establishment labor lawyer. He thought he was getting advice that was colored by political considerations from the wrong side of the political spectrum, and that the lawyer's loyalties were more to the higher echelons of the labor movement than to his local.

But when Dreyfus got involved in defense of the Communist leaders indicted in Los Angeles under the Smith Act in the Yates case, the international president came to the local president and said, "You'd better get rid of those lawyers, or we're going to take over your local."

Student: The same business of trusteeship!

McTernan: Right. That was before the Landrum-Griffin Act. The local president temporized with the international president and put him off. Finally the thing slipped by.

Another partner represented a certain local union before he came into our firm about three years ago, and he brought the client with him. A most lucrative client. Because of the peculiar nature of their work, the members often suffer severe injuries under circumstances that give rise to well-paying personal-injury suits. The injured workman tends to retain his union attorney in these cases.

AFG: Listen to him! Frank, you sound as if you're gloating over somebody's injuries!

McTernan: Those are the less glamorous sides of the law, Ann. You've got to make a living, you know. And it's out of these cases that you make it. Besides, a union attorney can understand the workman's problems better and thus do a better job for him.

This was a particularly good client from a money-making point of view. But we lost all that business, because that union is one of the most racist in this area. As soon as we were publicly identified with the Black Panthers they backed away. We get no work from them anymore.

Many of the trade unions are still represented by the older breed of labor lawyers who don't use imagination, just give pedestrian advice, but demand and get big fees for it. So, I'm sure we'd be representing a lot more unions if it weren't for our reputation.

AFG: By the way, when workers are laid off, the number of personal-injury suits for job injuries goes down. So that hits the lawyer's pocketbook, too.

Student: How does your office operate at this point?

McTernan: In the course of developing the kind of practice we now have, we have put together an institution that takes money to hold it together and keep it going. But it's an institution that provides the personnel and office machinery to take on these big, difficult legal struggles that can't be handled successfully by one or two lawyers who are scurrying around trying to survive or by lawyers in a commune who are committed to typing and answering the phone part of the time.

Take the struggle our firm put on in the Huey Newton case, led by Charlie Garry. That took resources that you just can't put together from scratch. The position we took is that you've got to find a way to keep sufficient dough coming in to keep the institution going, so that it is available when the need comes along in these political cases. And as long as we're trying to do any work in court it seems to me that this is the preferable way of doing it, rather than having the commune lawyer spend half his time doing community organizing, and part of his time doing movement legal work, never building any kind of organization in the law office with depth enough to take on big difficult litigation. Maybe I'm wrong, but I don't think the time has yet come when we can give up the law practice as we know it.

Student: I think the life style of many people today is incompatible with learning the trade and becoming good lawyers.

McTernan: I think it is. That's what I criticize about their approach.

Student: Isn't life style sort of irrelevant, though? I mean, you can't be a revolutionary through being a lawyer, but you can be used by the revolution. You are the tool. If you're willing to accept that, fine. If you're not, then you've got a problem.

McTernan: Yes, you can have a problem trying to be a lawyer, a practicing lawyer, and a revolutionary, because the two are incompatible.

AFG: A lot of people say that the Huey Newton case was a $100,000 case, and that your firm is rolling in wealth.

McTernan: Well, that's a lot of baloney. We have had times when we had to scrape hard for money to meet payrolls in the last few months. Right at the moment we have some cases that have brought some money in, but that wasn't Panther money that staved off the crisis; it was money from other cases.

AFG: Why did the Panther case cause such problems?

McTernan: Because it wasn't just one case or one lawyer. We received money from the Panthers, and I frankly don't know how much it was, but we were not paid in full for the effort we put in. The money just wasn't there. And the demands on the time of the lawyers in our firm was so great in the Panther cases that our other cases weren't being processed. Clients were complaining, "I see you on TV all the time. You obviously don't have any time for my case; you seem to have much more important things to do than worry about my case." The client might have a little personal-injury case that might be settled for $4,500, with a $1,500 fee. That is important to us. And I'm sure we didn't get cases that would otherwise have come to us, because people felt we were too busy.

Garry isn't doing anything but the Panther work now, and three or four of us have to argue pretrial motions in Panther cases and handle what Charlie calls his "mistakes" on appeal.

AFG: What did Charles do before that?

McTernan: Well, he was the best money-maker in the firm, although he did a lot of political work as well. But he was the guy who used to turn over the P-I cases that kept us going. So I'm denying the charge that lawyers are rolling in dough; we aren't. We may face a crisis where we're going to have to make some very, very important decisions on our life style if there's no money left to keep it going. And you ought to watch us and see which way we jump—whether in a pinch the middle class in us is going to win out or the revolution.

AFG: Do you think your kids will affect the decision you make?

McTernan: My kids are grown up, so I don't have any financial responsibilities for them. But I think that perhaps my children would influence me to jump the right way—or the left way, to be more accurate.

UNIONS ARE NEVER
ESTABLISHMENT
Victor Van Bourg

AFG: Victor Van Bourg is a partner in a large labor-law firm with offices in several cities. Vic, will you talk about being an establishment labor lawyer rather than a lawyer for a dissident caucus, about the life style of a labor lawyer, and how you got into that field?

Van Bourg: I think you ought to know a little bit about me personally so that you can evaluate what I say.

I am the product of a working-class home. My father was a well-known activist in southern California; my mother was an activist, too. She was an educated woman in Russia, which they left in the 1920s.

They were political people. They organized people, in the troubled times, into study groups. She taught English to people who couldn't speak English; she taught Russian to their kids, to keep the culture going. She was an organizer and a leader. My dad was very active in the union, but not on the paid union staff. Connected with the union there was a cultural group, chorus, dramatic group, and a mandolin and string-instrument group he was in. There were meetings constantly at the union hall or at the cultural center. Every weekend there was a picnic for a cause. My parents took me with them, and I got a tremendous exposure to what they were doing. Sometimes I slept in a union cloakroom

162

while the women were having a meeting and the men were having a meeting, and then they would come together and argue!

And that was my life. It was a very close family, and the group, the Ukrainians and Russians and Jews, kept together. To be frank with you, it was a communal setting. I am not acquainted with modern communes; this was an old-country type of communal setting, where the language and the culture brought us together, with some communal functions and some separate functions. The impact of what those people stood for was important to me. When I left home for college, the community had begun to disperse. But that's why I am what I am and why I'm doing what I'm doing.

I always worked for a living. I started when I was twelve as a bookbinder's apprentice. Later I drove a truck; I worked for meat companies and bottling companies in the summer. My father was a painter by trade, and I also worked as a painter and had a working card in that union. I teach classes now in various places, and since I consider it a requisite that I be a union member, I am a member of the American Federation of Teachers, which I also represent as a lawyer.

I have very strong feelings about unions, and since I was given the very uncomplimentary topic of speaking as the establishment union lawyer rather than the dissident union lawyer, I will say a few words about that.

There is no such thing as an establishment union and there is no such thing as a dissident union. A union is established to work in a nonrevolutionary sense, within the framework and laws established by society. There are unions whose rank and file are oriented in a conservative way, which reflects very much the society in which we live. There are unions whose leadership and membership are very progressive. There are also unions with progressive leadership but with very conservative membership, and the reverse exists as well.

However, in my view, the unions are the only institution in the country, the only nongovernmental, private institution, that represents masses of people. There is no other private organization in the country that has within its framework masses of people from every section of life.

It is my personal opinion that the worst union, no matter how bad it is, is better than the best boss, no matter how wonderful he is. That is based on a very simple economic premise: we live in a capitalist society; there must be a chasm between what working people see as their goal and aspirations and what the boss sees. When they find themselves working and competing for a piece of the same dollar, no matter how wonderful a man the boss is he is going to have to put down his workers to one degree or another. The weakest union, the union with the worst leadership, has got to set a collective goal of getting people together in order to take more of a share of society.

It's this very simple economic premise that led me to become a labor lawyer. I'm an anticapitalist. I'm anti-establishment in that sense. But I think I would be as much in trouble in a socialist society as I am here, because I do not like the show of force to put down the collective efforts of people, regardless of the system.

The combination of my trade-union background and my political background left me no choice. It required that I become a lawyer and that I represent working people in masses, in collective effort, rather than in individual cases. It required that I represent people who cannot pay, because that is what working people are all about. They don't have any money, and they're afraid. They have basic motivations: fear of losing their jobs, fear of dying—all kinds of things. And they have to operate with institutions that have been raped ever since they were established in this country.

Unions were illegal for the most part until our recent history. A few laws were enacted during the New Deal days that made it possible to say that being a union member was a lawful activity. But, even so, the unions do not have an easy existence in large regions of the country, particularly the South and the Far West, except for the coastal region.

The basic premise from which I operate is that the enemy is not other working people—no matter how racist they are, or how reactionary, or how dense, or how ignorant of the value of life and labor. In essence the enemy is the employer, and working people can never beat the employer in a capitalist society unless they're together, and they cannot get together if they exercise the luxury of fighting amongst themselves.

That's why I decided, when I became a lawyer, not to be sectarian, not to attempt to represent a few unions that had strong memberships and militant leadership. They needed my help least of all. The unions that I thought it best to represent are the unions in the AFL-CIO, the railroad brotherhoods, the teamsters, and so on, because they represent large numbers of people who in the long run make very little money, who do not share in this life, and whose collective-bargaining patterns are not creative.

We are in a bind in our collective-bargaining system in America. We do not negotiate rent trust funds so that the employer pays the rent of all of the people. We do not negotiate the requirement that the employer build a beautiful housing park with green spaces. We do not negotiate with the employer that he employ us four days a week and pay for three days of leisure and send our children to college and do other things that make for a good life. We don't negotiate for those things with the employer because we're afraid to, because the laws bind us to what is a mandatory subject for collective bargaining and what is not. We have a lot of problems in making trade unions creative and in making working people, who are decent people, creative in terms of how they deal with the massive power of the employer and, in particular, how they deal with the machine.

The machine, automation, and the great technology of this country is a creative force, and at the same time it is the force that will destroy working people if they don't begin to bridle it and to deal with the fact that efficiency for efficiency's sake is antihuman. Maybe we should have some inefficient machines if it will make people happy! We might have to negotiate into our contracts the basic concept that we want machines that break down every so often because we need work for people, and it's not progress to increase unemployment.

The only goal for which a machine should be created is to make human beings happy rather than to make profit for one man or one corporation. That's the only way that we can deal with the ten or twelve corporations that control the system in this country.

AFG: What happens when workers want to deal with subjects that are not normally subject to collective bargaining, like the quality of education, which the American Federation of Teachers has been talking about?

Van Bourg: Some unions do deal with such questions. Many union members want to get the unions involved in what they call community issues. Getting involved in those issues is not inimical to the institution of the union. As a matter of fact, most unions, contrary to popular belief, do get involved in these things.

The NAACP recently filed a suit to require a breakdown in the segregated pattern of school assignments in San Francisco. At a membership meeting the AFT authorized me to file an amicus brief or a parallel suit supporting the NAACP. I represent the social workers' union; one of the things that they've authorized me to do is to file suits on behalf of welfare recipients to prevent the constriction of benefits.

Student: So why doesn't the machinists' union or the teamsters' union authorize you to file a suit to support the NAACP on the question of equality of education? After all, it's their kids who are going to those schools. And many of those unions are industrial unions with a high percentage of black members. Why don't they do it? It would seem that it would be an issue that would be politically close to them.

Van Bourg: The reason is very simple. It's that the unions are not political animals. And they're not political animals because of the law passed in 1947 which denuded the trade-union movement of its intellectual force and of its progressive forces. In 1947 the Taft-Hartley Law was passed, with two insidious provisions: a union could not contribute to a political campaign, even though a hundred percent of the members wanted the contribution to be sent, and Communists could not hold union office. Since there were very few Communists in union office at that time, most of the people who were swept out by that legislation were not even close to being Communists, just solid trade-union progressives. For twenty-three years the trade-union movement has been virtually a eunuch, politically.

Congress didn't want working people organizing in a political sense after World War II. The reason bosses fear unions is not because of their collective effect on wages, hours, and conditions of employment, but because of their collective effect on the politics of the nation, which can seriously affect wages, hours, and conditions of employment. Now the employers have the ability to shut us down. General Electric can close a plant when we get strong, and they can move it down to Georgia, where we're weak. The runaway shop is a pattern of American history. Workers could stop runaway shops through legislation if they had strong political organization.

AFG: How strong are the unions today?

Van Bourg: There are about five rich unions in the country, and the minute there are layoffs they start hurting too, because dues payments go down immediately. More than 80 percent of all local unions have no office, have no secretary, have no telephone, and have nobody on their payroll. The officers of the union work full time for their employers with whom they have to deal on grievances. These unions often need tremendous help from the lawyer.

For example, I represent a local union in a major industry, a local whose officers all work in production. I go down with them to their safety meetings with the bosses, just to give them beef. Not just because I'm beefy, but because they have to show management, "Look, we're not alone!" That's not a traditional role of the lawyer, but I sit there and I start yelling at management. The burden is lifted off these guys who have to work for the same people every day. Management gets mad at me and therefore is no longer quite as mad at these guys. That way we get something done, like getting a fan in to get rid of noxious fumes.

At the bargaining table my role is much more dominant, because these guys come right out of the plant to the bargaining table. They don't even get the time off with pay—they get docked, and the union doesn't have any money to pay them. So the workers come right out of the plant with the noise of the machines still ringing in their heads, and they're dirty and not quite sure how to proceed, because management is sitting there all in suits, white shirts, and ties. They sit down to start bargaining on the conditions of the contract. A lawyer is very important to them at that point. They don't want him to take over, they don't consider that he is their intellectual superior, but they say to him, "You've got a suit and tie on and we need you here because their side also has people like that." They are very proud.

Then it becomes a battle. By afternoon they've forgotten that they're tired and we have caucuses and we smash it out toward the end of the time when the contract has to be negotiated. I'm already sitting over on the sidelines, and they are leading the fight in the negotiations. Invariably that happens if the lawyer is sensitive, if he doesn't inject his own ego into the negotiations.

Student: Does it help the union to have a lawyer who is skilled in arbitration do the arbitration work for an individual client or a union, or does it make the client come to depend entirely on the lawyer? Does this keep them from developing their own leadership ability to handle things and to have more confidence in themselves?

Van Bourg: Well, I'll answer it this way: Present-day arbitration is a very formal procedure, rather than informal, and there's a body of arbitration law, both state and federal—statutory and case law. I would say that a union should never take on an arbitration, even on a simple discharge case or a discipline case, without a lawyer.

The reasons are simple. The arbitrators by and large are lawyers. And the companies by and large are represented by lawyers. The leadership of trade unions are working people who have come up through the ranks. There is no such thing as a guy being a trade-union leader who's a businessman; he's elected, he's a politician. And even the most intelligent, articulate, and trained guy cannot handle two lawyers speaking to each other. When the arbitrator speaks legally to the company attorney, and the company attorney answers him legally, or when the company attorney asks questions of an adverse witness or a friendly witness in legalese, our people are lost. And that's the procedure; it's an adversary procedure.

Student: Is there a difference between representing your clients in arbitration and in negotiation?

Van Bourg: A tremendous difference. Arbitration is usually a step that takes place in the administration of a contract once it's been negotiated—unless you have arbitration over an impasse at the bargaining table. But negotiation is when, either for a first contract or for a normal contract reopening, we sit across the table from management and bargain on the terms of the contract. I have various ways of handling negotiations. If the leadership of the union is capable of doing it on their own, I don't even come to the negotiations. About 80 percent of my clients are that way. But when the company gives them some language, it's our arrangement that they don't sign the contract until they submit it to me to see if there are any legal hookers in it. And I also prepare contract language for the union to submit, and then before the whole contract is wrapped up I review it from top to bottom.

Student: Do you mean there isn't a lawyer on the other side in negotiation, as there is in arbitration?

Van Bourg: Usually there's a lawyer on the other side, but I have confidence in my clients' ability to know their own policy, and they don't need me to speak their policy. They know a nickel. They know a dime. They know a concept. They're as bright and as sharp as anybody here. What they can't do is joust with a judge or a lawyer in the language of the courtroom, and arbitration is a court proceeding, in essence.

But at the bargaining table my people can screw up those company lawyers something terrible. The management makes a mistake; the only people who know management's problems are the personnel-relations people or foremen, and they sit mute at the bargaining table while some lawyer comes in from an Eastern office and starts negotiating with our people, and he just gets smashed. I don't have to be there; our guys know how to do that fine. But some unions don't have that kind of leadership. Sometimes I'm spokesman at the negotiating table and sometimes I'm simply there to participate in caucuses or to watch what happens.

There *are* some parts of the contract that only lawyers negotiate normally, such as grievance and arbitration procedures, although the economic aspects were negotiated by the parties without lawyers. Other things, like hiring procedures, might be negotiated by lawyers because, although most of our people understand how their hiring halls operate, they don't understand how to put it all down on paper, and we do have that ability.

And now the question comes up, no matter whether you're representing trade unions or other groups of people, such as tenants' unions: How do you not usurp the leadership position? It takes a great deal of thinking as to how you're going to relate. If you're good technically, and the union wins, it's probably the first time these people have ever won anything in a formal procedure. Their victories are usually in the street. They just absolutely don't believe that anything can be won at arbitration or in court. So when you win for them consistently, because you're good, if they trust you the people will try to get you to make the decisions. This is the thing that we spend the most time with in our firm: the whole question of patronizing attitudes and how not to usurp the union position. We have an absolute rule, a prohibition, against getting involved in the policy decisions of the union. We're very firm with the client.

We say, "When you're asking, 'Should we do this?' that's a policy decision and you make up your mind. When you tell me what you want to do, then I'll tell you what the legal consequences might be which flow from it, which might make you reconsider your decision. But I want you to make your decision on the policy question first before you tell me about it. I'll tell you another thing: If you think it's important for the union to do a certain thing, I couldn't care less that it's illegal. You do it, and we'll get you out of trouble if possible. If it means the survival of the union, and it means attacking the boss, all you've got to lose is your treasury, which you don't have anyhow, so go ahead and do it."

Now, that's not a position that most lawyers will take. Remember, you have to be an officer of the court if you're admitted to the bar, and you have an obligation, under our very interesting system of Anglo-American jurisprudence, to advise people that what they're doing is illegal, and in essence to be a fink on your client. Well, I don't adhere to that. I am an officer of the court, and I tell the courts exactly what I'm telling you, and that is that if I perceive the law to be immoral and unconscionable, even if it has been upheld on its constitutionality, I will advise my client that I think it's an immoral law. And if I can tell them that something is illegal but that nobody can go to jail for doing it, and the most that can happen is that they can be sued for damages, I'll tell them that. Nobody's going to put me in a position of advising, "Don't do it because it's illegal," because I do not own my clients, and I do not tell them what to do or not to do.

You can only play the role I have just described when you have established yourself in the legal community. And you can only establish yourself by being in a position where you can whip the best of them on any given day, even when they hate your guts because they disagree with your politics.

I'm not preaching now, but the one crucial political shortage that we have now is young people who are progressive and who are also willing to take the time to become good mechanics at the trade. When I put a man or woman in the courtroom as a lawyer for our office, to defend a case on an issue that might affect 50,000 people, and the judge is against us and the laws are against us and the whole system is against us, I expect that person to win, and the only way he or she can win is by dominating the proceeding and pushing everybody around. And you can only do that if you know how, and it takes a long time to learn.

Student: Do you have any suggestions about learning to dominate the courtroom?

Van Bourg: Spend two or three years of your life immediately after law school working for somebody who knows his way around pleadings and procedure, and who will give you tremendous exposure to trials. Let me tell you why:

To represent poor people you need to be very efficient, because you can't charge them very much money, if any. You can't learn efficiency in law school. If you spend a couple of years in the Peace Corps, or even clerking for a judge, which is always a very romantic idea, you won't get the work habits. Going to work for the government will just destroy you as a lawyer. You have to get where the action is, and that's not in the government.

You must become a mechanic, so you are sure of yourself. You need to have good work habits, like reading the latest court opinions regularly. When I have to research a question, I don't have the luxury of time. I have to know the answer already or know exactly where to find it fast.

And, although it's a terrible thing to say, you must cut your hair if the majority of the people you want to help are straight. They won't trust you if you don't. It took me a long time to be able to grow a moustache, and I still get comments, not from the leadership but from the rank and file, black and white, "Hanh hanh, hippie, huh?"

Of course, it goes deeper than how long your hair is. For example, I worked for eight years for the general counsel of the state AFL-CIO. I got the broadest orientation and training imaginable. I drafted legislation; I lobbied; I did all kinds of litigation and appellate work in administrative and court cases. I took workmen's compensation cases, unemployment insurance cases, attended meetings at night. When I felt that if I stayed in that job I would forget what I was, I made my move. I went on my own and established a broad union base.

Student: What about caucuses in unions based on race or nationality?

Van Bourg: My own philosophy is in a state of transition right now on that question. I believe in a mass organizational approach to all collective activity: that the organizations where people find themselves must be built, not torn down; and that the institution must not be destroyed, it must be turned to good purposes. I'm not sure that's correct, but that's the premise from which I have always operated.

If it is correct to have integration—and I'm saying it that way because I'm not sure—if it is correct to have integration rather than a partnership of races and nationalities, then it doesn't make sense to have divisions on a racial or national basis within the unions. The black caucuses in the United Auto Workers in Detroit are not unique. We have had many such organizations. Primarily they started on a religious basis, with a Jewish group or a Catholic group. That has always been true in America. I guess it's been true in all institutions where different human beings gather. But what happens is that all of the energy and creativity of the members of the caucus are focused against the union or the organization, and again the enemy slips by on his own.

It's like a jurisdictional dispute—two unions fight over one job. Who benefits? The boss. I don't know how unions are going to get truly unified, because union membership really reflects the country, the working people. White working people don't want their daughters to marry black guys, and vice versa, and Japanese-American working people don't want their kids to marry anybody but Japanese-Americans, and Jewish working people don't want their kids to marry gentiles. That's the way it is. How do we overcome centuries of cultural tradition?

You must understand the culture of the unions that you deal with. Some have their own national and ethnic cultures built in; some have a subculture—like one of the construction unions has a very bad record in keeping out members of one minority ethnic group, but it has the highest percentage of members of another minority ethnic group. There is a union in Hawaii with substantial numbers of Filipinos and Japanese, and perhaps there is discrimination against Chinese and Portuguese.

In general, our trade-union movement is beset with the central issue of society—namely, can we live together as human beings? We're thrown into competition for jobs, since there are more of us than there are jobs. I'm not sure what some of the solutions are.

Student: I've noticed that one of the major factors keeping blacks from becoming more radicalized is the racism practiced by unions. Whenever black workers look from the historical or philosophical reasons for organizing workers, or for socialism, to the reality, they find that management somehow seems to be more responsive to black needs than the unions. The racism in unions is of the most blatant kind.

Van Bourg: Well, that's a blunt assertion. Don't put me in the position of being an apologist for racism among my clients or any other institution. But I think you're dead wrong. Let me tell you why:

We have now approximately eighteen million union workers in America. We have much more than two and a half million black union members. So that's a higher proportion of blacks in unions than in the society as a whole. How does a union get members? If it has a contract in a place of employment, it usually has what we call a union shop. This means that everybody who goes to work for the boss must become a member of the union. In order for him to become a member of the union, he's got to get hired, right? Which means that the employer has the absolute right to hire whomever he pleases and the union has no control.

Less than 15 percent of American workers secure their jobs through union hiring halls. In all other companies, management advertises and hires as it pleases when people come to the door for a job. The biggest employers are the huge manufacturing plants. You have no doubt that the Auto Workers are an integrated union?

Student: No.

Van Bourg: They have 1.8 million members. You can take another seventy-five unions and put them all together and they'll have fewer than 50,000 people. Even if all of them discriminate, the effect of that discrimination versus the 1.8 million people in the Auto Workers must be compared. Not to say that discrimination is good, but to consider what the results of discrimination by unions are.

Student: In the Auto Workers case, management hired more blacks than were hired through the union.

Van Bourg: That's right. The management hired blacks and the union did not resist it.

Student: I want to talk about the union practices—

Van Bourg: I'm willing to talk about it.

Student: —the fact that they have training programs, apprentice programs.

Van Bourg: Unions don't have many programs. That's the whole point, and that's what we've got to talk about—where the bodies are. Almost no unions have apprenticeship programs. If you could make every apprentice in the state of California today black, there would still be a comparatively small number.

Student: Why does it always come up when blacks try to get in the union?

Van Bourg: I think there is no point in talking about it unless you have the statistics. Again, I'm not apologizing for unions that are led by reactionaries or racists. I've got my own problems with them.

Let's talk about the 15 percent of unions which have hiring halls. The two largest unions in the Bay Area with hiring halls are the ILWU and the laborers' union. Neither one has an apprenticeship program.

You and I are subject to the same stereotyped attitudes that everyone else puts on. I represent the laborers' union. The normal attitude is that the laborer is not a skilled worker, right? Just a pick-and-shovel man. That's just not accurate. Much more than half of the classifications covered by the laborers' union contract are skilled classifications—machine operators, hand-tool operators, tunnel workers. Some locals in the laborers' union in the Bay Area have as high as 80 percent black members, some as low as 40 percent, none lower. The lowest is in San Jose, which has about 40 percent black and 40 percent Chicano. The leadership reflects the majority of the members, so there are black business agents, black presidents, and so on. That's in the building trades, the skilled crafts. Incidentally, the wage for laborers in the lowest classification is in excess of five dollars an hour. That's just to do pick-and-shovel work or cleanup work.

One of the highest-skilled building-trades unions is the plaster and cement masons. It has about the same percentage of blacks in this area as the laborers' union, and it has a hiring hall. It also has an apprenticeship program, and about 80 percent of the apprentices are black. The carpenters' union has 18,000 members in the Bay Area; it has a hiring hall, and, strange as it may seem to you, it has 1,800 black members. I represent that union. I represent a local of skilled mechanics in San Francisco; it has an apprenticeship program, and no hiring hall. This is an integrated local with 8,000 members who work at one industrial location.

And I represent a black local of the Paper, Pulp and Sulphite Workers in Bogalusa, Louisiana, working at Zellerbach Paper Company. There is also a white local; the president of that local at one point was head of the Ku Klux Klan in Bogalusa.

AFG: So what you're saying is that you wear many hats simultaneously.

Van Bourg: What I'm saying is that I've kept my pants on and I've kept my dignity, and nobody has made me somebody else's man. I've been able to keep my ideals and my beliefs, and nobody's taken them away from me.

Now let's take the problem a step further. There are very few blacks in the pressmen's union here. Why? There has been a seniority clause in collective-bargaining agreements with management since 1898. There are members of that union still working at machines who went to work in the 1920s, when there were virtually no blacks in this area. The seniority clause is something that working people have always fought for. And it takes a fantastic amount of education before you can say to them, "Give it up."

Now let's talk about the molders' union, which is predominantly black. Molders work in foundries. Foundries are always closely associated with shipyards. The first place that blacks came when they came to the shipyards in the Bay Area was to the foundries. So there are guys in the molders' union, blacks, with thirty years' seniority. And I would ask them to give up the seniority clause? Of course not.

Seniority is an issue of job security for a worker, black or white. How are we going to educate the people to give it up? It's the same problem we have between young and old workers. Old workers want pension plans. When they go on strike, they want a portion of that raise to go to the pension plan. The young workers say, "I'll never get old. I want it all on my paycheck now."

Student: Would you represent a group in one of these white unions, a group of blacks, say, who wanted to break through on this? That's the issue.

Van Bourg: Sure, and I have. I don't call that a dissident group. But I would pick and choose whether I would represent such a group, because one of the rules I have is that I will never sue a union. I've represented groups of minority workers in various unions against the union. But not in litigation, because I've been able to accomplish what I wanted without litigation.

AFG: What if you couldn't?

Van Bourg: I would sue, but I would first advise my clients that the purpose of the suit would be self-defeating. I also will not represent a union, even when it pays me a retainer, in any action against it before the Fair Employment Practices Commission, unless it's a frivolous action.

AFG: Would you represent a complainant against a union before a Fair Employment Practices Commission?

Van Bourg: Against a union that I represent? No, that would be a conflict of interest.

I wouldn't mind losing the client. I have kicked union clients out of the office because they were resisting taking in a black guy. Just because a person is a lawyer doesn't mean that he cannot take sides on philosophical and social questions, and I do all the time. There are unions that I will not represent even though they ask me every day, because I feel that their self-interests as they see them are incompatible with my ideas.

But I also feel this way: I am truly a believer in a united front. And I believe the reason that human beings have not yet seized the reins of their own power is that they have never stopped fighting among each other. I don't know what the answers are. But I do believe that management continually creates situations that get us into this box.

AFG: Do you mean that you never represent a union in a jurisdictional dispute with another union? And you wouldn't go to court in a jurisdictional dispute?

Van Bourg: I will not.

AFG: That's quite an important statement, because unions are always getting into fights with each other.

Van Bourg: I've had only one jurisdictional dispute before the National Labor Relations Board, and that had a peculiar issue. The union I represented had people out of work, and the union that was contending for the job had members who were already employed during the daytime and they wanted to work at night. I'm opposed to moonlighting. I believe a man should have his full rest. I thought it was very important to resolve that issue of moonlighting, and I fought on that issue and not on the issue of who had the God-given right to the work.

Student: How would you handle a situation like the one in Chicago, where the bus drivers, who are about 75 percent black, have gone out on strike twice in the last two years, and whites, including the union management, keep the system going as much as possible?

Van Bourg: You mean they're scabs? I'd deal with those scabs just like I'd deal with any other scabs.

Student: But they control the union!

Van Bourg: A scab is a scab. It really doesn't matter if he's a black scab or a white scab; he's not really a human being. I really believe that. I mean, if a man makes a profit out of another man's suffering, he's as bad as or worse than the boss, because the boss—at least his interests are clear. This guy is not with the boss. He's been bought off. He's like a fink.

AFG: Can a labor lawyer play an educational role on the question of relations between men and women?

Van Bourg: Of course, Ann, and you do that by hiring women lawyers and showing the clients that you believe a woman lawyer can be as good as a man. Some of our toughest building-trades men become injured and a woman lawyer handles their cases. They say, "I never had a woman lawyer . . . ," but then they go down to the court and she whips the opposition, and they're convinced. That's probably the best thing we can do in a liberating way. Of the twenty-four lawyers in our various law offices around the state we have three women lawyers, one of whom is one of the top six partners.

Women lawyers have had a difficult time getting jobs, except in the domestic-relations field or in government. The only other place where there have been substantial numbers of women has been in labor firms. The women do hard-hitting, aggressive, cooperative work. My partner Arleigh Woods, a black woman, works out of the Los Angeles office. She has been considered one of the top workmen's-compensation lawyers in the state and is a good criminal lawyer.

In addition, we talk about these issues all the time. I inject my economic and political philosophy into every relationship I have.

Student: What about women in the unions?

Van Bourg: In some unions I represent, women predominate— waitresses, culinary workers of various types, and a lot of manu- facturing unions where there is sitting-down bench work on an assembly-line basis.

Student: Isn't that sometimes a problem in the same way that the conflict between old and young union members is? The conflict between men and women, like on maternity benefits?

Van Bourg: Yes, but where we have large numbers of women, such as in an office employees' union, maternity benefits are normally negotiated and the men kind of sheepishly say, "Yeah, yeah." The men usually have higher wage rates, so they concede on maternity benefits.

One of the big problems is that the foreman in a plant where there are a lot of women very often has liaisons with many women workers at one time. It's a real exploitation in the plant. And this comes up in collective bargaining. It is a very difficult situation to have women sitting on a negotiating committee at the collective-bargaining table across from the guys under whom they work and from whom favors are given on this very debased level.

Student: Do you think women are harder to organize into unions?

Van Bourg: No. The hardest people to organize are white-collar men and professional groups. Industrial women workers are some of the most militant people we have.

Student: I asked because I know a few people who work as stewardesses.

AFG: But that's another question—that's sexism too. They're hired because they're beautiful and a certain age. That's not the ordinary woman worker.

Van Bourg: Women aren't hard to organize. The groups that are most amenable to organization are all minority groups, if you think of that in the broad sense. The people who are not getting a fair shake in our society are easier to organize if they are aware of that. And most people who have a bond with other people on the basis of nationality or sex or something like that do a lot of talking among themselves; they have ties. And they are already organized when you get to them. You just have to convince them to join the union; you don't have to convince them to organize.

For example, take the farm workers. I went out into the delta in the San Joaquin area in the first organizational drive in the last fifteen years among the asparagus workers. The asparagus cutters are Filipinos, and they already had crews organized. They had a crew boss; they shared their earnings, and they all got exactly the same amount. You could always tell a Filipino camp because they all went out in one car or several cars which they shared; they were totally organized. The union sent a Filipino organizer to tell them what the union was about. They met, and they came into the union just like that. They still pay dues and they're still organized among themselves.

The same people who cut the asparagus also tie the grapevines and harvest the grapes. They used to drive up the prices even before they had a union. They'd simply cut the grapes and leave them on the ground, let them sit there, and wait for the boss to come out. You've got to cut the grapes early in the morning and get them boxed and into the cooling shed, because as the heat rises during the day the sugar content of the grapes changes. So they just sat there until the boss came out. It was no problem to sign these people up.

Student: Do you think union lawyers have a different approach to their clients than other lawyers?

Van Bourg: I can't speak for other labor lawyers. I'm a lawyer because of political conviction, and I'm not a religious zealot with a mission. But I do have some basic premises upon which I operate. I've told you about some of them.

I also think that man is basically good and not evil, no matter how terrible are all generalizations like that. But you have to have some general approach as a lawyer, because every guy that comes to you, you make a judgment about. If he's fired, and management says he was sleeping on the job and he says, "I wasn't sleeping on the job," you have to determine right then whether you're going to believe him, because if you take the case you will have to convince the judge later that he was awake.

Most lawyers are jaded and cynical from a very young age, and they don't believe people. And being able to believe somebody and at the same time be critical about his circumstances from a legal standpoint is not easy. You have to make a legal evaluation in rapid-fire order. Like after you've seen the guy for about five minutes, you're already making the decision on whether you are going to be able to convince the judge, or the arbitrator, or the trial examiner, about the facts of the case.

By the way, I think you're making a mistake, Ann. The guys that are coming to this Tom Paine School to talk are all cut out of the same tree. You ought to get a downtown lawyer here. I really think that radicals won't do anybody any good unless they know the face of the enemy, and I think you have to relate to them on a daily basis. When I'm representing a guy who's been fired who has worked for a company for eighteen years, and I know I'll lose the arbitration for some reason, I have to call up the management lawyer and say, "I want this guy put back. Please put him back." And if I can get him reinstated I'll spend some time talking to the company lawyer, take him to lunch and buy him a drink afterwards.

AFG: But what if McCarthyism really takes hold again? Could you settle cases that way with the company lawyers?

Van Bourg: Of course not. As a matter of fact, if I were attacked publicly because of my politics I'd lose my clients, about half of them.

Issues like that still come up. For example, I was the one who brought Walter Reuther to Delano and originally got the United Auto Workers and the farm workers' union together down there. There was a big rousing rally at the Filipino hall in Delano, and I sat on the same stage with Larry Itliong, who is a very good friend of mine. He's the Filipino guy in the United Farm Workers, the assistant director under Cesar Chavez. *American Opinion,* a John Birch Society magazine, wrote an article about him accusing him of being a Communist, and we filed libel suits.

A labor lawyer does all kinds of things. He has to be able to be a good trust lawyer, a good contracts lawyer. I get involved in libel actions all the time. Some of the biggest trials I've had have been on that.

But I missed the worst of McCarthyism, because I became a lawyer in 1956. And it's very clear that progressive lawyers of my generation are essentially alone in this world. You young guys have it over us—there are more like you. When I was in law school I was almost totally isolated. Now I think I'd be in the majority in some law schools; not many, but some.

I think this generation is tremendous. If I could get kids interested in unions, I would feel the battle was almost halfway won.

AFG: Interested in unions *affirmatively*. Some of them are interested in unions: they hate them!

Van Bourg: There is an anti-intellectual feeling on the part of working people. And an anti–working-people feeling on the part of intellectuals. You have to understand that in this area traditionally the strikebreakers were students.

AFG: Football players particularly.

Van Bourg: When the longshoremen struck the waterfront, students came in school buses and took their jobs. When the farm workers strike, high school students come down and scab. Don't be too hard on workers who remember who was scabbing on them a few years ago. And they don't understand you guys; they don't understand how come you're like you are. All this is new to them.

Student: How does your law firm operate? What's the structure?

Van Bourg: We have twenty-four lawyers, with offices in eight cities.

Student: Are the employees in your office in a union?

Van Bourg: Yes; they're paid union wages, and they sign a union contract with us.

And, while we don't make that much money individually, everyone in the firm makes a good living. There's a difference between making a living and becoming rich. In terms of the world's population, I earn something that puts me in the top 5 percent of the world. It's not hard to be there. You make more than twenty-five grand and you got it. And at the same time I don't have to screw people in order to get it.

Student: What's your perspective about law practice?

Van Bourg: After a couple of years of going through some real serious problems, I've decided to continue being a lawyer and to try to convince others to become lawyers. I would like to see 2,500 progressive lawyers in the state of California—250 could turn it upside down.

I'd like to hire every one of you. But by the time you graduate, we'll be in group legal practice. I think that as long as our legal institutions are about the same as they are now—that is, our statutory and common law, and our courts—we should move toward a prepaid legal system that operates on a very large basis, like a prepaid medical system.

WAR CRIMES AND COLD-WAR "CONSPIRACIES"
Mary Kaufman

AFG: Mary Kaufman is here on a trip from New York, and I asked her to come to tell about two unusual experiences she has had. One was representing the United States as a prosecuting attorney in the war crimes trials at Nuremberg after World War II. The other, on her return to New York, was participating as defense counsel in several of the important prosecutions of Communist Party leaders during the McCarthy period. And, of course, being a woman lawyer adds another dimension.

Kaufman: First, let me suggest that my involvements in the Nuremberg war crimes trials and in the Smith Act cases were not separate events. There has been a continuity about everything I've done in my legal career that I hope will come through to you. To put it another way, I think that time has a way of meshing history and biography. Of course, what is history to you is biography to me, because I lived through those events.

As I have been reflecting on what I would like to say to you, I recognized that the key to these events probably was the Cold War, which ran all through, and which has burst into a hot war within the period of your biography. What I will be talking about is my personal view of the Cold War, how I felt it and saw it. I haven't attempted to evaluate it from a historian's point of view, nor am I equipped to do that.

Let me start with Nuremberg. In 1965 I was preparing a conference to commemorate the twentieth anniversary of Nuremberg and to write about its significance in terms of present-day history—the Vietnam War. When I mentioned this to a very brilliant young woman attorney, she looked at me with a kind of annoyance and said, "God, why dig up all that old stuff about the killing of the Jews?" Then I recognized how important it was to discuss exactly what Nuremberg was. In my mind, and in your minds today, I'm sure, it means a great deal more than the slaughter of six million Jews.

First of all, it connotes the trial of the major German war criminals by the International Military Tribunal at Nuremberg. During the war, as early as 1943, when the barbarities being perpetrated by the Nazi war machine were brought to light, Churchill, Roosevelt, and Stalin got together and issued a proclamation saying, "We're going to punish the war criminals." That was the first time that idea was expressed.

Then, in 1945, the four major Allies, the United States, the Soviet Union, France, and England, set up a negotiating team that came up with the London Agreement and Charter. This document expressed the intent of prosecuting major war criminals, in a tribunal composed of representatives of the four Allies, and it defined the crimes with which they would be charged. In a sense it was the enabling act for the prosecutions.

It defined three categories of crimes: crimes against peace, crimes against humanity, and war crimes. The express definition of crimes against peace was new. Up until then, the making of aggressive war had not been specifically defined as a crime for which individuals could be punished. So the principle was now laid down that individuals could be punished for the making of aggressive war or war in violation of international treaties.

When the London Agreement and Charter was signed, Justice Jackson of the U.S. Supreme Court, who had been one of the participants in formulation of the treaty, said: "For the first time, four of the most powerful nations have agreed not only upon the principle of liability for war crimes of persecution, but also upon the principle of individual responsibility for the crime of attacking international peace. Repeatedly nations have united in declarations that the launching of aggressive war is illegal. They have condemned it by treaty, but now we have the concrete applications of these abstractions in a way which ought to make clear to the world that those who lead their nations into aggressive war face individual accountability for such acts."

The second innovation of the Nuremberg trials was most remarkable; that was to say that an individual had a responsibility under international law to refrain from committing crimes even though his government ordered him to commit them. The London Agreement and Charter expressly stated that it was no defense to say, "I was ordered to commit this act, and I had to obey those orders." In the words of the International Military Tribunal, "individuals have international duties which transcend the national obligations of obedience imposed by the individual state." So the principle of individual responsibility was formulated. The individual was given responsibility for making his own judgment on the fundamental question: "Is it a crime under international law for me to do what my government says for me to do?"

I think you will agree that the makers of the treaty had a very high purpose. Yet the prosecutions of war criminals were motivated, I think, by three forces. The world was horrified by the excesses of the war, particularly the barbarities of the German forces. In addition, our explosion of the atom bomb over Hiroshima and Nagasaki was so terrifying for many people all over the world that there was an enormous public clamor for some brake, some deterrent force to be exerted against potential future wars. The other force was the usual attempt of the victor to obtain control over the vanquished.

One of the things you'll find as I talk is that there is a kind of duality of things. On the one hand there is the force of what the people want and need in order to survive. On the other hand there is the force of people in power who have their own wants and interests. Now, I don't know where historians trace the beginning of the Cold War, but I know from personal experience that at the very moment when the principles of Nuremberg were being fashioned, the seeds of the Cold War were already sprouting: we had used that atom bomb on a civilian population for the purposes of intimidating the Soviet Union in the peace negotiations that followed.

AFG: When you talk about a duality, do you mean the same thing that Marxists talk about as "contradictions"?

Kaufman: Well, I said "duality" because people have a tendency to look at things as though they were monolithic. I see things as interrelating forces. It's a dialectical struggle—you're perfectly correct, Ann. After all, our government was a major force in setting up the principles of Nuremberg, while at the same time it was laying the groundwork for the Cold War, for a major struggle with the Soviet Union.

I want to get back to what Nuremberg really means. The concepts were first formulated in the London Agreement. Then there was the trial at Nuremberg of the top leadership of the Hitler government—those who were alive. It included Hermann Goering, Rudolf Hess, and others—the political leaders, the diplomats who had helped lay the groundwork for the war, the top echelons of the military, the organizations Hitler used to whip the country into a state where it could embark upon the war, the people who were in charge of the occupied areas where major atrocities occurred, and the organizations through which these atrocities were perpetrated.

Student: When you say the organizations, do you mean the leaders of the organizations?

Kaufman: No, the organizations themselves, the Reich Cabinet, the Gestapo, the SS, the SD (the intelligence agency), the SA, and the General Staff and High Command of the German Armed Forces. One provision in the London Agreement stated that certain organizations would be tried, that if these organizations as organizations were found to have committed the offenses, then individuals connected with them would be liable for the offenses.

The interesting thing is that the International Military Tribunal placed the same gloss upon that provision that the United States Supreme Court placed upon the language of the Smith Act many years later: an individual could not be held accountable for what the organization did unless he was a member with knowledge of the organization's illegal program.

AFG: Were there no industrialists in this first trial group?

Kaufman: Among the top leaders the one who came closest was Schacht, who was a financier and the treasurer for the Nazi war machine. There was one other industrialist named in that group, old man Krupp, but by that time he was sick or senile, so he was severed from the case.

But the London Agreement contemplated that there would be a series of trials of major war criminals. I have just described the first group. The second trials were to consist of a second major echelon: a designated group of industrialists, the Department of Justice, the ministers of justice, the medical corps, the doctors who had conducted some pretty hideous operations, the officers of the High Command, the *Einzatsgruppen,* which marched east as the German Army marched and did there what we have now learned was done at My Lai—they herded the population together and shot them indiscriminately (so that they wouldn't infect the purity of the Aryan race).

Well, the first echelon were tried, and the International Military Tribunal's decision is part of the meaning of Nuremberg. Later the United Nations, on U.S. sponsorship, unanimously affirmed and adopted the principles of Nuremberg as they had been defined in the London Agreement and Charter and the tribunal's opinion. And the U.N. then authorized its International Law Commission to define precisely what these principles were. They defined the nature of war crimes, the principle of individual responsibility, and the principle that one who aids and abets the venture knowing of its purpose is guilty as an accomplice.

The principles of Nuremberg are a complex of all these things.

Well, to go back, by the time the first trial ended, in 1946 I guess, the Cold War had begun to express itself so completely that the International Military Tribunal could not get together again in a joint body and make decisions. They did agree that each of the Allies was to try the major war criminals in its zone of occupation. And that's when I came into the picture.

AFG: How did you get involved?

Kaufman: I was working with the Wage Stabilization Board in Washington, D.C., in 1946, and that agency was closing down because the war was over. Somebody who was in Nuremberg and was scouting around for talent for the American prosecution team asked would I go. I said I would be delighted.

I went in February 1947, as a civilian employee of the United

States Army. I had to leave my five-year-old son behind until I found a house in Germany—Army rules. My parents brought him to Nuremberg in September, and they stayed and took care of him while I worked. I couldn't have done it without them.

I was to help prosecute one of the major industrial concerns— an international cartel, really: I. G. Farben. The people in the dock were its board of directors. This was the second echelon of war criminals, being prosecuted in separate trials in each of the occupied zones. The United States tried twelve such groups. And these should not be confused with the thousands upon thousands of war crimes trials that took place not only in Germany but in the countries of German occupation, prosecuting the foot soldiers and small men. In fact, they are still going on today, conducted by the Germans themselves in both East and West.

Well, I came to Germany to a very devastated, bombed-out area. The odor of death was in the air and in the rubble. The German people were living in holes, in beat-up old buildings. People were starving.

And I came there, a Jewish woman. Of course, the issue of racism was a dominant feature of the Nazi war. And being Jewish I couldn't help but respond to that fact, although before I got through I broadened my own vision as to its applications to many ethnic and political groups. But I had a sense of fear walking into this area where it was so bombed-out. Surely the Germans would just want to kill me. It was a very provincial response.

But I found something entirely different. They needed material things so much that there wasn't anything they wouldn't do to ingratiate themselves to get those things for survival and, at times, for profit.

AFG: Did you go there to be a trial lawyer or a brief writer or what?

Kaufman: It wasn't exactly clear what I was going to do when I went there.

AFG: In whose mind wasn't it clear?

Kaufman: Well, *I* was going there to be a trial lawyer, to be a prosecutor. The team for the I. G. Farben trial had already been more or less settled when I arrived. And I found myself waging a real battle, not with the head of the team, who was a rather nice guy, but with the subhead of the team.

Student: Why didn't he want you to be a trial lawyer?

Kaufman: I think it was because I was a woman. While it's true I came there with very limited trial experience, I had a background of considerable mature legal experience and skill. In any event, I simply didn't yield, and I was assigned as a trial lawyer.

I. G. Farben was charged with all the war crimes. We had a staff of six or seven prosecutors. There were twenty-four defendants in the dock, and they had about fifty German lawyers representing them, Nazi-oriented in the main. I witnessed quite an interesting development in these lawyers. In the beginning they would come walking into the courtroom very obsequiously, all fifty of them, bowing. But as time, and the Cold War, progressed, they stood more upright, became bolder, until they were arrogantly projecting the Nazi ideology and reaffirming the pretext for the whole Nazi invasion, namely the need to defeat the Communists.

The Cold War was having a profound effect on the prosecution side as well. We found ourselves in the peculiar position of working very hard to prosecute the industrialists and being impeded in every way by the failure of the State Department to support us. We didn't have adequate materials; our orders were countermanded; there were numerous incidents—I'll just give you two:

The documents that we dug out of the I. G. Farben files were the basic pieces of evidence against them. Farben was a major power in the world. In each country it operated either overtly or covertly to take control of the government and to dominate and exploit its economy. Millions of dollars' worth of books, pamphlets, newspaper clippings, and documents glorifying the master race and the Nazi state were sent abroad by Farben. It was all written down in those documents.

Now, the American consular official at Frankfurt had been there prior to the war and now was back. He had been a major force in uncovering the documents related to Farben's hidden assets. The United States had been eager to get its hands on those assets, to absorb them as enemy-alien property. If, for example, the U.S.

could show that an American company was really a hidden I. G. Farben asset, our government could freeze those assets and take charge of that property. In that context, this consular official had dug up many documents that I later needed for my prosecution. They showed that I. G. Farben's machinations all around the world were part of its espionage and sabotage activities in aid of the war effort. These documents included instructions from the specific defendants I was responsible for prosecuting—defendants in the economic department of I. G. Farben.

So I sent an investigator to Frankfurt to get this official to authenticate the documents, to say, "I found the document in this and this file." He refused.

My investigator asked, "But why?"

And he said, "Because I like these people. I know them very well; I've been to their homes. They're wonderful human beings. They're very cultured. I refuse to validate these papers. If you subpoena me, I am going to say what I think about the high moral character of these people."

These were the people whom even a Cold War tribunal found guilty of war crimes and crimes against humanity. These were the makers of the gas used for extermination; the procurers and users of slave labor from the infamous Auschwitz and elsewhere—used by Farben to the point of exhaustion and then sent to the extermination chambers. Even the two members of the tribunal who voted acquittal on some of these charges said, "With knowledge of the abuse and inhumane treatment meted out to the inmates by the SS, Farben aggravated the misery of these unfortunates in the way in which they used their labor." The not so respectful dissenter on the tribunal, who voted to convict, said that "it was no overstatement to conclude that Farben's working conditions resulted in the death of thousands of human beings."

These were the "wonderful human beings."

The investigator said to this consular official, "I don't understand you. You are the one who uncovered all these documents and prepared the basis for what I am now doing."

"Well," he said, "that was during wartime. But now we need these people." He really meant, "Before, we were trying to grab their assets, but now we need them in our Cold War against the Soviet Union."

This was our State Department, and it was as though we were dealing with another outfit.

Now the second incident. At one time during World War II a group of saboteurs were caught someplace in New Jersey. They had come here to commit sabotage in our factories. We tried them and sent them to jail. I had some information that these people had been trained by I. G. Farben. Now, in the midst of the Farben case, I suddenly learned that these saboteurs were being sent back to Germany before the termination of their sentences, to serve the rest of their time in the jail at Landsberg. I said, "My goodness, what a break," and I issued an order to have them brought to the jail at Nuremberg for interrogation. Then it was my intention to put them on the stand.

Shortly after they arrived, the chief of our trial team asked me, "What the hell did you do? Did you order those people from Landsberg to come down?"

I was amazed. "Sure," I said. "This is a hot piece of evidence." We needed it, too, because we knew then that we were fighting against odds.

He said, "You'd better send them right back. The State Department has been burning up the wires."

I didn't ask why. He didn't tell me why. I simply sent them back.

In speculation . . . well, let me just say one thing. Everything in Frankfurt was devastated by bombing, but there was one place that escaped totally intact: the I. G. Farben major office. Today it's functioning on a very high level.

AFG: You said that those saboteurs had been trained by Farben, not by the government?

Kaufman: Well, I. G. Farben was both an instrumentality *and* the government. It was a rather interesting structure, Hitler's whole war machine. It's really wrong to say that Hitler set it up, because what happened was that a group of industrialists got together and gave their support to him. Actually he was *their* instrumentality. It's similar to the way the military-industrial complex operates in this country with some dollar-a-year men and key government officials. I. G. Farben's members sat on the board .that did the economic planning. The industrialists constituted the important decision-making bodies running the country internally. They claimed that they were subject to its regulations, but they were making the regulations and were profiting by them.

Oh, what plans they had! They were going to move into this country and take over the economics of that country. I. G. Farben would get a piece of this, other companies would get a piece of that, and they'd distribute it. They called that the new order. And they were indeed found guilty of plundering the property of occupied countries.

So Farben was part of the government apparatus, in the same way that we can say the leaders of the military-industrial complex are part of our government.

AFG: It sounds to me like that famous quote—you know, when Charles Wilson, who was president of General Motors, was asked about possible conflicts if he became Secretary of Defense, and he said, "What's good for General Motors is good for the country." It's the same clear understanding of the relationship between government and industry.

Kaufman: Precisely. The Farben documents are a blueprint of how imperialism operates. They demonstrate the relationship between big business and government at home and in the exploited countries.

AFG: Who were the judges at Nuremberg?

Kaufman: For the International Military Tribunal, the judges represented each of the four Allied countries. In these later cases, they were judges from our U.S. courts. Three judges sat on a case and there was one alternate.

Student: What was the outcome of the I. G. Farben trial?

Kaufman: Well, by the time the verdict against I. G. Farben came out, the Cold War was in full blast. The Berlin airlift had already begun. So the Farben people first were acquitted of all charges of waging aggressive war, in spite of overwhelming evidence of their participation in it.

When it came to property rights, it is interesting to note that the tribunal was not so generous. It convicted all of the defendants for the war crime of plundering property in occupied Europe. Human beings did not figure so high in the scale of justice—at least for the two majority members. They found only some defendants guilty of the crime of the use of slave labor, although, as the dissenter pointed out, the evidence was abundant to convict all. The sentences ranged from one and a half years to a maximum of eight years. A range of four to eight years was given to those who participated in the crime of annihilating thousands of human beings.

When they read the judgment to us, we were in a state of utter shock.

Of course, the Allies had made agreements that never again would these industrial powers, I. G. Farben and Krupp, be allowed to emerge in that strong a form. And the Allied Control Commission had responsibility to see that the military forces were not rebuilt. But these agreements were not carried out. Today I. G. Farben and Krupp are as powerful as they ever were.

AFG: It's like the Tilden–Hayes compromise in this country after the Civil War. You know, the Thirteenth, Fourteenth, and Fifteenth Amendments to the U.S. Constitution were enacted to guarantee the rights of the former slaves in the South. And these blacks were beginning to vote and buy land during Reconstruction, while the federal troops occupied the South. But when the Tilden–Hayes election was thrown into the House of Representatives for decision, in 1876, one of the points worked out in the compromise was that the federal troops would leave the South. As a result, a wave of terror resumed in the Southern states, wiping out the gains in equality that the blacks had made, and restoring the white establishment to control.

In Germany, they didn't have to wait eleven years after the war for the losing powers to begin to regain control; it took only three or four years.

Student: You aren't saying that the judges at Nuremberg were coerced into deciding as they did?

Kaufman: Oh, no. It was simply that, as time went by, some of the judges in some of these cases began to socialize with the West Germans. And the Cold War affected some members of the tribunals.

AFG: You mean that economic or social class lines superseded national lines?

Kaufman: I would say that's true. Plus the factor of our involvement in the interlocking industrial complexes that had created the Nazi war machine.

AFG: Mary, if someone wanted to read the transcript of your trial in English, where would they find it?

Kaufman: In my home I have a complete transcript. But summaries of that case and the others were published in a series of volumes called *Trials of War Criminals before the Nuremberg Tribunals.* The I. G. Farben case, which is called *United States v. Krauch,* is Volume 8.

Student: What legal procedures were used in these trials? American?

Kaufman: No, the London Agreement set down the rules of evidence and the procedures to be followed, and they were a compromise between European and American procedures. So, for example, our opponents were given advance notice of everything we were going to use against them, as under some European systems. And to introduce documents we would simply make a brief oral summary of the document and offer it into evidence; its authentication was already noted. Our American principles of presumption of innocence, burden of proof, and other rules beneficial to the defendant were applied, including a very narrow interpretation of conspiracy.

Student: Was it an adversary proceeding?

Kaufman: Partially. Both sides had live witnesses and they were cross-examined by the oppposition. It was bilingual, through earphones: when we spoke in English, it was simultaneously translated into German, and vice versa.

AFG: Was there a personal relationship, across the languages?

Kaufman: Yes indeed. As a matter of fact, I believe they all understood English. These were the big industrialists—bigger than our Rockefellers, and much more trustified. They were very powerful, with companies throughout the world and substantial control in South America, China, various areas.

Student: Earlier you said that individuals were being held liable to international law, superseding the law of their country. But was there such a body of law during the war? It sort of bothers me that these people were being tried under a law that came into existence after the alleged crimes took place.

Kaufman: Well, there was a tremendous amount of controversy on that question: whether they were being tried under an ex post facto law, a law that came into existence after the acts had been done. That is forbidden in the United States Constitution and in other jurisdictions. The answer given was that the actual crimes charged were not newly formulated, nor was the principle of individual responsibility. What was newly formulated was the tribunal under which these people could be tried. In the past, you know, there were military courts that just disposed of people who were guilty of war crimes.

War crimes had existed for a long time. There was a large body of law on the customs of war, which said it just isn't right to do certain things. It was simply codified, put down in formal, orderly fashion, in the London Agreement and Charter. The crime against peace had never been codified, but it existed.

It's like our application of common-law principles. These were common-law crimes under international law, and some of them had already been codified. International law is defined pretty much the way our common law is defined—a growing body of principles that evolve out of the decisions in specific cases, and that "civilized" nations take into account. And the question of responsibility had also been established in the past. After World War I, for example, principles were formulated that the heads of the states were responsible for making the war. It's just that people were not interested in pursuing those principles against the individuals after World War I.

What was new here was that if you committed a crime it was no answer to say that your government told you to do it.

So the pros and cons were heavily debated. As a matter of fact, the defendants before the International Military Tribunal contended that the London Charter was ex post facto law. The tribunal rejected this argument and the challenge to its jurisdiction. It said it could ignore this contention and rely entirely upon the well-recognized power of countries to legislate for occupied territories. It could treat the London Charter as an exercise of that power by the countries to which Germany had unconditionally surrendered. But because of the importance of the ex post facto questions raised, it decided to deal with them.

It held that aggressive war had been a crime under international law since at least 1928, when the Kellogg-Briand Pact was signed in Paris. That pact "condemned recourse to war for the solution of international controversies and renounced it as an instrument of national policy in their relations to one another." Sixty-three nations, including Germany, signed the Kellogg-Briand Pact. The International Military Tribunal felt that this solemn renunciation of war necessarily included the proposition that war is illegal in international law and that those who plan and wage a war, with its inevitable and terrible consequences, are committing a crime.

The Hague Convention in 1907 had prohibited recourse to certain measures in waging war, and Germany was a participant in that convention. A whole series of other conventions and treaties were also referred to in the opinion. And the tribunal found that the provisions concerning individual responsibility had also been expressed in preexisting laws. So these were not new concepts.

AFG: Take this analogy: The concept in the Fifth Amendment is that you cannot be deprived of life or liberty or property "without due process of law." And the meaning of due process of law when that was enacted was the common-law meaning. Slowly we've written down what due process is. It wasn't until 1970 that the Supreme Court recorded (in the Winship case) that in a criminal case the standard of proof is "beyond a reasonable doubt," although the standard had been in existence for centuries.

And every nation has a stake in having rules of war, to cover prisoners of war, for example. So there had always been a recognition that you couldn't do just anything in a war, because the other side would do it to you, too.

Student: Precisely. War crimes have been perpetrated throughout history, and everybody recognized the fact that if you lost the war you could be held accountable, but only if you lost.

Kaufman: Now, the principle that you are enunciating is terribly important. Namely, up until that point or perhaps until this very day, when a body of laws defines war crimes, who gets punished? The loser gets punished, and the victor does the punishing.

In fact, it was very clear at that time. In my opinion, we committed war crimes when we dropped the atom bomb and when we fire-bombed Dresden. Actually, some of the charges against Nazi war criminals were simply thrown out because we had engaged in the identical conduct. So what you say is perfectly true. I am not trying to create the impression that we were the marvelous free country with clean hands, coming to the Nazis, saying, "Look, you barbarous people, at what you've done. We're going to punish you for it." Quite the contrary. We shared in some of the guilt.

So the question of guilt was a very serious one. You know, during the first trial of the major criminals, Justice Jackson said that "while this law is first applied against German aggressors, the law includes, and if it is to serve a useful purpose it must condemn, aggression by any other nations, including those which sit here now in judgment."

For example, we were very troubled by the fact that our U.S. industrialists had collaborated in many of the things that paved the way for World War II. This appears in the I. G. Farben indictment—only it is put in such a way as to indicate that Farben had "duped" our industrialists into collaborating. Farben had interrelations with some of our large corporations; there was a whole exchange of technical data about synthetic rubber and other stuff being used in the war machine. It was couched as though they were pulling the wool over the eyes of our corporations, and we were the innocent victims of deception. But I think if you read the evidence carefully you will extract a little better evaluation of the role these U.S. corporations played.

Now, what I have extracted from that for myself is this—and it's particularly relevant in this period with our escalation of the war in Vietnam: the principles of Nuremberg and the formation of the United Nations were designed to deter the making of aggressive war. But in practice they don't really act as a deterrent. Who is going to punish the United States for what it's doing in its adventures in Korea and in Indochina? How does one take a set of rules and transform it into an application to our own country, which appears on its surface to be impervious to the application of these principles? The United States is not a defeated nation that can be tried for its war crimes.

So, if the abstract law is not working, we must take up our individual responsibility. It then becomes our special obligation as people to see that the principles of Nuremberg are enforced insofar as our country is concerned.

And this proposition has already begun to be raised in a variety of fashions. I remember the early cases in which people refused to participate in the war in Vietnam, at first on the claim that the war was in violation of the principle against aggressive war and then later on the basis that we were engaged in war crimes, and if they got involved in Vietnam they would be required to commit war crimes. It was a question of how the individual resistance to these things could transform the principles of Nuremberg into a reality.

If we are concerned with the application of principles of law to everybody, not just to the losers, the basic and fundamental meaning of Nuremberg is that we must assume some personal responsibility for its enforcement. There are a variety of ways in which we can do it. The Fort Hood Three said, "You can't ship us to Vietnam, because you are committing war crimes there. We will not participate in war crimes. The principles of Nuremberg require us to say no. We have a right to refuse." Dr. Howard Levy refused to train medics for Vietnam under the principles of Nuremberg. Heroic actions on the part of many individuals were taking away from the government the power to say, "We can do anything we goddam please, in spite of the Nuremberg principles." There began to build up an insistence: "The Nuremberg principles are applicable to us." So that when the My Lai incident was exposed to the public there was a hue and a cry, "Let's examine responsibility." So let's look at what these principles were:

> Principle I. Any person who commits an act which constitutes a crime under international law is responsible therefor and liable for punishment.
> Principle II. The fact that internal law does not impose a penalty for the act which constitutes a crime under international law does not relieve the person who committed the act from responsibility under international law.
> Principle III. The fact that a person who committed an act which constitutes a crime under international law acted as Head of State or responsible government official does not relieve him from responsibility under international law.

(So you could prosecute Lyndon B. Johnson if you could show that he knew through the chain of command about the acts we were perpetrating in Indochina.)

> Principle IV. The fact that a person acted pursuant to order of his government or of a superior does not relieve him of responsibility under international law, provided a moral choice was in fact possible to him.
> Principle V. Any person charged with a crime under international law has a right to a fair trial on the facts and the law.

And then Principle VI defines the crimes, which are very interesting in terms of the My Lai incident:

> (a) Crimes against peace:
> (i) Planning, preparation, initiation or waging of a war of aggression or a war in violation of international treaties, agreements or assurances;
> (ii) Participation in a common plan or conspiracy for the accomplishment of any of the acts mentioned under (i).
> (b) War crimes:
> Violations of the laws or customs of war which include . . . murder, ill-treatment or deportation . . . of civilian population . . . , murder or ill-treatment of prisoners of war or persons on the seas, killing of hostages, plunder of public or private property, wanton destruction of cities, . . . or devastation not justified by military necessity.

(c) Crimes against humanity:

Murder, extermination, enslavement, deportation and other inhuman acts done against any civilian population, or persecutions on political, racial or religious grounds, when such acts are done or such persecutions are carried on in execution of or in connection with any crime against peace or any war crime.

And the final principle, which is very important to us, is Principle VII: "Complicity in the commission of a crime against peace, a war crime, or a crime against humanity as set forth in Principle VI, is a crime under international law."

AFG: I think one thing is clear. Even if you are uncertain whether the Nazis who were tried in Germany were tried under ex post facto laws, certainly everyone in the American military complex by 1965 was well aware of these provisions.

Kaufman: No doubt of it, because the Nuremberg principles are also incorporated into our military manual. Our Army Field Manual sets forth precisely all the things that constitute war crimes and crimes against peace as well as the Nuremberg principle of individual responsibility.

AFG: The one that strikes me most sharply at this moment is the question of deportation. We have caused the deportation in Korea and Vietnam of hundreds of thousands of people. Another thing worth mentioning is defoliation.

Kaufman: The analogies with Vietnam are remarkable—even the word "pacification" was used in Nazi Germany. And these principles, this body of law in our military manual, is the basis on which charges have been brought against some of our soldiers in the My Lai incident.

The massacre at My Lai took place some time in 1968 and was first brought to our attention in the latter part of 1969. We have all seen the photographs of the women and children lying in heaps on the ground. That gave rise to a whole lot of questioning by people about the meaning of these atrocities and their relationship to the Nuremberg principles.

At the end of World War II, when the pictures of the heaps of dead people were released, everybody went around saying to the

German people, "Where were *you* when all of this happened?" It was a cry of anguish. There was considerable discussion and confusion as to where guilt lay. Was the whole world responsible for the crimes charged at Nuremberg, because we fostered and permitted the building up of the war machinery? If the whole world was responsible, was nobody really guilty?

Now, in this My Lai incident, we are confronted with the same question. Where does the guilt start? I take the position that the participants, those who wielded the gun and followed the orders, are guilty. I do not find them innocent. I think that sadism is sadism no matter what circumstances breed it; I think that there were men who couldn't do the shooting and there were men who did it. As one mother said, "I sent them a good soldier and they made him into a murderer."

The next question is: How far up does that guilt go? I say it goes all the way up to the top. The very nature of the war we are engaged in compels the form of brutality that was shockingly shown in the My Lai incident.

We are trying to conquer a people who are trying to save their country from us. We have violated every one of the rules of war. We've defoliated wide areas beyond repair for years to come in the country we are supposed to be rehabilitating. We have napalmed human beings. We've adopted antipersonnel weapons that shoot out indiscriminately. We've adopted chemical warfare that forces the people out of their huts, and then we shoot them. We've moved whole populations out of their villages, destroyed their villages, and put them behind concentration-camp fences in other areas.

So, you see, the guilt is inherent within the whole chain of command. Some people say that the foot soldier is to be held innocent because he's just carrying out orders. I would not say that. It is he as well as our whole war machine.

There is one other thing: the question of knowledge. The Nuremberg decisions turned on that question. Many of the German people said they didn't know that all these crimes were being committed. We in the United States can't take that position. We see it every single day on television, in our newspapers. We know.

Therefore, I would say that our guilt is much wider, and we have got to stop this war. Our war crimes begin with the factory worker who is making the war machinery. That is complicity. I don't think he can be punished for it, but surely refusal to participate in a war that is in violation of the principles of Nuremberg is a justifiable position. I think eventually we are going to get around to that.

AFG: Tell us what happened after the Nuremberg trial.

Kaufman: I came back to the United States in September of 1948. While I was in Germany I had been immersed in the events there from 1933 until the end of the war. I had been living in the past, watching the whole rise of Hitlerism. The technique that was used was selection of a big enemy around which the Nazi Party consolidated all its efforts. The Communists were the first target. Then came the union members, then the Jews, then everyone else.

While I was away in Germany the Cold War was unleashed in the United States. There were the loyalty oaths and the witch hunts and people being tried for their political beliefs. I had been insulated from this until I came back in September 1948.

AFG: There's one point I should make about Mary. Unlike most lawyers in private practice, Mary does one thing at a time. She does not have more than one client at a time or work on one case after another each day. Her life is a history of doing one thing to the fullest, wherever it took her. This has created certain economic problems.

Kaufman: Let me just add that this one thing has always been the same thing. I went from one case to the next as a logical step in the struggles of the people of our country. So, when I came back, the first thing that popped up was the indictment of the national leaders of the Communist Party under the Smith Act.

Student: What is the Smith Act?

Kaufman: It was passed by Congress in 1940 and it made it a crime to teach and advocate the violent overthrow of the government of the United States or to organize or be a member of a group that did that.

When I saw that the Communist Party was under attack, and saw the pervasive propaganda about the "red menace," I was horrified. And I decided that the next logical step in my career was to go fight what I thought might be the rise of fascism in this country. The attack seemed so analogous to the attack in Germany, beginning with the Reichstag fire, which was used to attack Communist Party leaders and was the pretext for suspension of all constitutional guarantees.

A drastic change was taking place in this country. During the war, we had been such friends with the Soviet Union, such allies. Then, while I was away, we began an open struggle against the Soviet Union on many levels. It became necessary to indoctrinate the American people that the Soviet Union led a worldwide conspiracy and that the American Communist Party was a tool of this conspiracy to overthrow democracy in our country.

How do you do that to a people who have just experienced a feeling of great admiration for a country that had suffered so deeply from the war and that had turned the tide in the battle of Stalingrad? Why was it possible for the phenomenon of McCarthyism to settle in our country? I believe we had come through a war feeling highly moral. We were defenders of democracy. We had defeated fascism. We didn't even examine the atom bomb very closely. We didn't see what we had done very clearly. We felt very virtuous—unlike today.

Then material things became important to us. People had a stake in the rebuilding of our country. With jobs becoming terribly important, it was possible to use the tactic that Hitler used—divide and conquer. So they split the trade-union movement and kicked out the radicals.

People didn't have the conflicts that young people have today. They were satisfied with the morality of their country, and they began to believe the propaganda that was hurled at them that the Commies were just a bunch of saboteurs and agents.

Student: Who was hurling this propaganda?

Kaufman: First the House Un-American Activities Committee, by calling in the Hollywood writers who had done films during the war years emphasizing the evils of fascism. Suddenly they were called in and asked, "Are you a Communist?"

Then there was the Truman loyalty oath: in order to get a job with the government you had to swear you'd never been a member of the Communist Party. Then Nixon fathered a bill that said the

Communist Party was an agent of the Soviet Union and was full of spies and saboteurs; the bill was a forerunner of the 1950 McCarran Internal Security Act. The Democratic Party itself was being labeled a party of treason. Many people got scared and ran for cover.

Well, on my return I encountered the Smith Act prosecutions and I offered to work on the Dennis case. The trial lawyers decided I would be useful in the preparation rather than in the trial, and I agreed. You see, the techniques of the trial in Nuremberg were quite different from our court system. I hadn't had any American trial experience, having worked mainly for administrative agencies—I started from the top and worked my way down. In the Dennis case they had an outstanding team of trial lawyers, really magnificent people with extensive trial experience: Harry Sacher, Richard Gladstein, Louis McCabe, George Crockett, and Abraham Isserman.

The format of the Dennis case was the format that was followed in every Smith Act case.

AFG: It was like the national company and the rest were the road shows.

Kaufman: Right, with maybe a change of personality here and there. The evidence was always the books, the quotations from Marxist-Leninist classics. The prosecution's evidence went way back to 1919.

The prosecution would have a witness on the stand who would say, "I went to National Training School, where I was given this book" (no reference to what was done with the book), and then the prosecution would select sections to read—out of context, in context, in a variety of ways.

Then there were what we called the "blood and thunder" statements. Prosecution witnesses testified that they had attended a meeting where someone had said, "The streets will run red with blood." The statements were never related to the defendants, but they were related to the Communist Party, and the government's theory was that the defendants were responsible for anything said by anybody who had ever been a member of the Communist Party, because it claimed the party was the conspiracy.

AFG: Are you saying that the law of conspiracy wipes out the requirement of proof of individual guilt?

Kaufman: Yes, I think I would say so. For example, the defendants in *Dennis* were charged with conspiracy to teach and advocate the overthrow of the government by force and violence, and to organize an organization that advocated that prohibited doctrine.

AFG: An organization that *would* advocate it in the future.

Kaufman: Right. If anyone was a member of the Communist Party, his acts and declarations could be introduced into evidence. By that I mean Joe Blow could say, "I attended a meeting in Michigan. None of the defendants were present. And at that meeting John Doe said, 'The streets will run red with blood.' " Now, we couldn't cross-examine John Doe; he was not on the stand.

Ordinarily such statements are excluded as hearsay; they are statements made out of court. But the judge treated the Communist Party as the nub of the conspiracy and allowed into evidence anything any member of the party ever said anywhere.

"In the end," the judge said, "we will strike out any remarks that are not connected with the defendants."

The judge instructed the jury, "First you must find by the independent statements and acts of the defendants that they were parties to that conspiracy; then in determining their guilt or innocence you may consider all the acts and declarations made by other members of that conspiracy."

Today some judges think they've done away with that rule altogether. Almost anything goes in a conspiracy case now. Anything the judge allows in as evidence the jury is free to consider in determining the guilt of the defendant. They don't have to first find that he was a participant in the conspiracy by his own acts and declarations. Of course, no big political conspiracy case has gone to the Supreme Court to test this new rule so far.

But even with the rule in the Dennis case, it was not difficult for the jury to find the defendants guilty, because when the Communist Party was reorganized in 1945 these defendants, who were members of the party's national committee and executive board, had made speeches criticizing the positions of the party during the war. They claimed that the party had abandoned the principles of Marxism-Leninism, and they reconstituted the Communist Party based on those principles.

Now, these were abstract political discussions. Nothing in any of these documents went anywhere near saying "We've got to go out now and do this by force." It just was not there.

AFG: Was it in *any* of the evidence?

Kaufman: The prosecution put a person named Budenz on the stand. Louis Budenz had been a member of the Communist Party and an editor of its newspaper. Then he turned to a more lucrative career: he became a star witness against the party. He wrote books; he testified before congressional committees about the "red menace"; and he testified in the Smith Act cases. He said, "These speeches are double-talk." He called it "Aesopian language."

"When they say, 'We will revert back to the principles of Marxism-Leninism,'" Budenz explained, "they really mean, 'We will revert back to the position of advocating change by force and violence.'"

I'm simplifying a bit, but once the jury accepted Budenz's theory of Aesopian double-talk, it was very easy to convert innocuous statements into a theory that change had to be adopted through force and violence. "If the Communists said they wanted peace, it meant they wanted war." You can't lose with that kind of an approach. I'm not kidding. Many years later, when we were permitted to see his statements to the FBI, we were able to discredit much of his testimony as inconsistent with them.

AFG: How could a jury absorb a case as complicated as a Smith Act case, in which questions of ideology, history, and freedom of speech were all intertwined?

Kaufman: We argued consistently that they couldn't. No jury of twelve ordinary people can sit and listen to theoretical political quotations and come up with a conclusion about what their content is. Philosophers and political scientists and others disagree on the meaning of a body of political thought. So how can a jury come up with a conclusion after hearing one side read one quote and the other side another?

AFG: It was a period in which no juror in the country, in my opinion, would have dared acquit. The judge actually accepted the jury instructions proposed by the defense, but the jury knew perfectly well, by the judge's tone of voice and the way he treated the defendants and their counsel during this nine-month trial, that he wanted a conviction. He could have given them almost any instruction and they still would have convicted.

Student: What was the instruction he gave?

Kaufman: There was a rule that in order for teaching and advocacy to be criminal one had to show that it was not protected by the First Amendment. At that time, unless the language used created a clear and present danger of the imminent commission of violent action, it was protected by the First Amendment. So we asked for an instruction that the jury had to find that the defendants by their advocacy had incited to violent action.

We should have won on the basis that the evidence in the case did not show they had incited to violent action. But we come back to the fact that here were these lay jurors listening to quotations from Marx that you've got to "seize and smash state power." This was abstract teaching, not telling people to go out into the streets and overturn the government. But the jury, looking at these Marxist classics, did not have the intellectual training to distinguish one from the other.

We tried to explain exactly what the Communist Party's position and program were, how it conceived of the road to socialism. But the prosecution walked in every day with three loaded book carts and thrust quotations at the jurors. The only things that stuck in their heads were the words of violence and the worry about Aesopian language. Besides, the Cold War propaganda and the fear it generated were already effective. All you had to do was say "Communist" and the jury was ready to say "guilty."

AFG: Mary then was chief trial counsel defending two cases in New York, one in St. Louis, and one in Denver.

Kaufman: Only in those days we did not have the concept of chief trial counsel; we were a team of trial lawyers. Some emerged in a more leading role than others. But none of us claimed to be "chief."

The prosecutions in these trials all followed the same pattern, even using the same evidence from the same witnesses and informers. A whole stable of informers popped out at that time.

AFG: Tell us about your favorite informer.

Kaufman: Oh, yes, in St. Louis. He was unlike the regular informers, who were mostly a bunch of unsavory characters. Some had joined the Communist Party at the request of the FBI, because the FBI had things on them—we proved this many times. Some had joined at the request of the FBI for the money. Others for one reason or another left the party and were induced to testify against it. Many were liars, and some were later found to have perjured themselves.

Student: They were paid?

Kaufman: They were all paid for everything. They were paid for each report they sent the FBI. At that time we were not permitted to see those reports. They were free to embellish them. It was only after the Jencks decision that we were able to compare their testimony with their written reports; this exposed how they had manufactured many of these stories.

My favorite informer was a man who had joined the Communist Party at the request of the St. Louis police red squad. He remained in the party from the 1930s until the time of the St. Louis trial in the 1950s. So for twenty years of his life he had been a good member of the Communist Party. His whole life was the party. He had no friends outside it. He did send in weekly reports, but he didn't lie.

Lo and behold, one day there he is on the stand testifying against his friends! One of them, who was acting as his own counsel, cross-examined him. He asked him, "Didn't I teach you how it was possible to have a peaceful transition to socialism? Didn't I teach you this?" and he went down the line.

And the informer answered, "Yes, that's right."

This informer was really like a witness for us, except for the prosecution saying the defendant had been using Aesopian language, which proved the conspiracy.

That poor old guy. After he testified, he just simply up and died, because his whole life was destroyed. But he was not the typical informer.

AFG: What did you do about government efforts to force your witnesses to become informers?

Kaufman: That was one of the big problems we had to face in the Smith Act cases. Once we put a witness on the stand he would be asked on cross-examination who else had attended the meeting he described. Yet a statute said it was a crime to be a member of the Communist Party. So it became a very serious problem for us. In fact, our witnesses were held in contempt of court for refusing to name names.

AFG: What about Harvey Matusow?

Kaufman: Matusow was a young man who testified in the trial of Elizabeth Gurley Flynn. He was without any kind of roots. He did a lot of unpleasant things without any consistency. He joined the Communist Party—I am not quite sure whether he was asked to by the FBI or whether he just floated into it—and he became a paid informer.

I cross-examined him in the Flynn case, and as these facts of his life emerged, this total lack of principle in him, I finished my cross-examination by saying, "Gee, you'd do anything for a buck, wouldn't you?"

He looked at me in a very funny way and said, "Yes."

Later he testified in other cases. Then, somehow or other, he met somebody who had an impact on his life and began an intense and enlightening relationship with him. In the end, Matusow decided he had been totally lacking in principle and wanted to make up for it. So first he recanted his testimony in a Taft-Hartley loyalty oath case. When I heard that—I was on the Denver case at that time—I went back East to visit him, and he then told me that he had lied in the Flynn case. He also told me that one of the prosecuting attorneys had put him up to it.

Matusow said that this assistant U.S. attorney had helped him create the story that he had testified to. I warned Matusow that if he recanted his testimony and incriminated the assistant U.S. attorney, he could be held for perjury if the attorney came forward and said, "I did not say that." If he left this man out of it, he wouldn't be liable for perjury.

Nevertheless he said, "I don't care. That's the fact and I'm going to say it."

So I got the affidavit for the motion for a new trial. I had to go back to the Denver case, and Harry Sacher handled the motion. He subpoenaed the assistant U.S. attorney and his work materials. He had dated memoranda of each meeting with Matusow. On the first date no mention would be made of an incident. On the second, there would be mention of some of the people. And we could see the story growing, blooming, and flowering, until in the final memo there it was, the lie full blown.

Well, the judge found that Matusow was a man "without regard for the truth, with a passion for the limelight, and with the need for a few dollars." He held that Matusow had lied on the first occasion, and he ordered a new trial against two of the defendants Matusow had testified against originally. But the judge did not conclude that the assistant U.S. attorney had participated in the lie—it's not easy for a judge to say that. So the grand jury promptly indicted Matusow for lying about this, and Matusow was convicted.

AFG: He served a five-year sentence.

Kaufman: Yet he emerged out of it a principled person. He was not bitter. This was in the height of McCarthyism. Matusow describes all this in his book *False Witness*.

Eventually, the Cold War changed. If you remember, Eisenhower went to a summit conference, and there was a kind of a *rapprochement*.

AFG: McCarthy got put down because he attacked the Army.

Kaufman: That was a big thing. When McCarthy was put down, there was a relaxation of the tensions. By then, Warren was Chief Justice and a whole lot of favorable decisions began coming out of the Supreme Court.

The Dennis case had come before the Court earlier in the McCarthy period. The Court refused to review the evidence; it only reviewed the statute. It affirmed the convictions and affirmed the constitutionality of the Smith Act. Justices Douglas and Black wrote wonderful dissenting opinions, though, saying the Smith Act violated the First Amendment and due process. Then the Court refused to hear two Smith Act appeals. But after a while, when the Yates case came to the Supreme Court in 1957, there was a fortuitous combination of circumstances that turned the tide—the skill of the lawyers in using the law and the facts to the hilt, the relaxation of tensions, Warren on the Supreme Court, and the fact that the trial judge had refused to instruct the jury that the advocacy had to incite to action. He had been relying on a heightened Cold War and the perversion of the clear-and-present-danger doctrine by the court of appeals in the Dennis case. So he said, "I don't have to give that instruction. The advocacy is enough to show guilt."

AFG: He was arrogant, in other words.

Kaufman: He was arrogant, and the Supreme Court reversed him. The defendants were acquitted or sent back for new trials. The government did not pursue most of the new trials and eventually stopped prosecuting under the Smith Act.

In all, there had been seventeen groups of defendants. Only 28 people served sentences; 104 were eventually acquitted or not prosecuted.

AFG: Mary, what was the value of all those years you spent on the Smith Act trials? Would you do it again?

Kaufman: There were several gains made by anyone involved in those cases, and especially by a lawyer who continued to be involved. In the process of the fight in the courtroom you learned how to be a political lawyer, which meant that you were educating a lot of people: the jurors, your co-counsel, and people outside the courtroom.

When I went out to Denver I was the only lawyer there who had had experience with Smith Act cases. The others were court-appointed counsel, most of whom came from the leading law firms, the "Wall Street" firms, of Denver. The Denver headlines said, "Redheaded Lady Lawyer Comes to Take Over Million Dollars' Worth of Talent." I had to educate these lawyers as to the myths surrounding Smith Act cases. At first they viewed me with enormous suspicion. But the dialectics of the case, the relationship I and the clients developed with these lawyers, the transparent shabbiness of the stable of informers, taught them the phoniness of the charges.

One of them was a rugged individualist about eighty years old. He was dedicated to laissez-faire, both in business and in human affairs. At the end of the case he got up and made a long, passionate speech to the jury about the First Amendment. It was magnificent. He literally had to be carried back to sit down afterward. And when the jury came back with a verdict of guilty, these twelve establishment lawyers were heartsick.

That was the educational process that was being carried on. It was part of the process that defeated McCarthyism.

AFG: You feel that the technical skill of a political lawyer is of some significance, then.

Kaufman: Of course! The political lawyer must know what he is doing and must gain the respect of the judge and the jurors. Above all, he needs to know how to project the political character of the case.

AFG: I thought the judge was the pig?

Kaufman: Well, in those days clients didn't use that expression. But if they had, they would have said there were pigs and there were pigs. Medina, the judge in the Dennis case, was considered an absolute pig. Judge Dimock was not a pig. He acquitted a couple of party leaders—he had the courage, although he was pretty much related to the establishment. The judges we dealt with were part of the period.

Toward the end of that era one judge told me, "If I had my own way, I would reverse. But I can't." This was before the Supreme Court reversed in *Yates*.

Later, while we were working on the appeal in that case, he

called me up and said, "Mary, I hear you are submitting a type-written brief."

"We don't have any money to have it printed," I told him.

He said, "Why didn't you tell me? That won't do. Call me back in fifteen minutes."

When I did he said, "You just take your brief to this printer and don't worry about the bill." I don't know who paid for it.

AFG: Have you ever been cited for contempt?

Kaufman: No.

AFG: Have you ever bawled out a judge?

Kaufman: I have, of course. There are ways and times of being very forthright, and I was in all the cases I tried. Once in St. Louis, while I was out of the courtroom the judge criticized what he suggested was my lack of attachment to the Constitution. When I came into court I just got up and, as an equal, not as "Your Honor," I said to him, "You took advantage of my absence," and I was very sharp with him. He apologized to me.

That is not to say that the lawyer is always in command. When an experienced political lawyer is cited for contempt, look at the transcript—the provocation comes from the judge. In some cases the defense is under such restraint and there is such a terror in the courtroom, you sit and you sit and you sit and finally you explode. In that kind of atmosphere you have to be made of iron to maintain your sense of cool.

Student: There seems to be a big conflict today about whether a defense lawyer should be more concerned with the broader educational aspects of the case or with trying to get his client off.

Kaufman: No, there is no conflict, although there is a controversy. The truth of the matter is that there are two correct ways to handle political cases. One is to get your client in and out of the courtroom as fast as possible with the least cost to him. The other is an actual extensive political trial. The judgment as to which tactic to pursue when the option is available is a political one. Sometimes the option is not available. Generally speaking, it is not productive to use the courtroom as a political forum. You can be much more effective in organizing outside the courtroom.

When someone is arrested for a political action, the first important question is this: Since a long-drawn-out trial is a waste as a political organizing tactic, what's the best way of handling this case? Can I get my client in and out of the courtroom fast, so he can continue to carry on his political activism outside the courtroom? I have yet to find a political activist who wants to spend his time arguing his politics in court. What they really want is just to negotiate those damn cases out. In the legal-defense office of the National Lawyers Guild in New York City, the main weight of our political action in the past few years was to get our clients out fast—when we could. We did it mostly by negotiating for dismissal.

But there are cases, political trials, that you can't negotiate out of existence. There is only one way to win those cases, and that's by handling them in a political fashion. You focus attention on the political aspects. The government always says, "This is not a political case." But in fact it is.

The thing that makes you a political lawyer is how you focus attention on the political issues and bring them out. And since it is a political case, the accused must become the accuser. That is a sound legal position, which takes legal skill and political acumen.

BLACKS,
BROWNS,
PRISONERS,
AND
JUVENILES

BLACK PEOPLE DON'T HAVE
LEGAL PROBLEMS
Edward A. Dawley

AFG: Ed Dawley comes from Lincoln University, University of Michigan Law School, and the University of Hard Knocks in Norfolk, Virginia, where he practiced for several years before the establishment had more than it could take of him. About ten years ago he came out to California, where he is now the director of the Neighborhood Legal Services Office (funded by OEO), in Hunter's Point, which is San Francisco's lowest-income black ghetto.

I think it's only fair to warn you that Ed is a very complicated guy, with a wide variety of interests, from opera to playing devil's advocate, and I never know what he's going to say next.

Dawley: James Baldwin once said, when you're talking about something, anything, you may be saying something about the thing you're talking about, but you're always really talking about yourself.

For me to try to tell you what the law is like is also analogous to the blind men and the elephant. You remember, each man got hold of a certain part of the elephant, and the man holding the tail said, "An elephant is like a snake," and so forth. You may be gathering your particular impression, thinking it is the universal description of what the law is like; even if you try to be objective you're misled, because you are *not* really objective.

You must realize, then, that my point of view is largely condi-

219

tioned by the fact that I'm a black lawyer, and that makes a lot of difference. My initial experience was gained practicing in the South, which is a bad place to start off. When I entered practice, I had a conception of the law as a sort of slot machine: cite a certain code section, the lid automatically opens, and out comes the right verdict. Of course, I soon learned that that was not the case.

One of the things that most shocked me when I first visited the offices of black lawyers in Virginia was that they had no books. Oh, they might have a few books on display for the client, some old, out-of-print books—some were even book fronts. That shocked me. How could they practice law without books? After practicing a while I could see very well why.

There were two basic reasons. First, most of their clients were poor people, and to a large extent poor people do not have legal problems. A person has to have some minimum contact with the mainstream to have a legal problem. He has to be buying something or engaging in some kind of activity. So, in a community where most of the people are not in the mainstream, most of their problems are not legal problems (except, of course, for the criminal cases). The things the lawyer does for these clients—contacting someone, or giving certain general information—don't require lawbooks, don't even require a lawyer. They require an educated man, that's all.

The second reason these lawyers didn't use lawbooks, I think, was that most of them had lost faith in the law as a magic key to solving problems. You see, the law is a masculine and intellectual profession. A lawyer is supposed to know what's going on and go and change things. In the South, of course, the goal of the establishment was to destroy the manhood of the black people. So imagine a black lawyer telling a white judge what the law was or disagreeing with him. It just could not be done. A black lawyer who wanted to survive in his profession simply did not do that. As a result he ceased being a lawyer.

A favorite story among Southern black attorneys was of the black lawyer who was to argue a case before the Mississippi Supreme Court. He had prepared his briefs with great precision and scholarship, and was quite confident that the law was in favor of his client—that is, as confident as a black lawyer can be in a

Southern court. However, in his concentration on the law, he had neglected to look up the proper way to address the Supreme Court before beginning his argument. A stylized, formal address is always used in speaking to an appellate court, differing from court to court, but it's usually some variation of "May it please the distinguished Chief Justice and the distinguished Associate Justices of this Honorable Court." Being forced to call upon his instinct for an improvised form of address, he arose, looked up and down the bench, and said, "Good morning, white folks." His brief could not have stated the issue of the case more realistically and precisely than this spontaneous greeting.

In my experience, I found that I could not practice law in the South until the conditions were changed. I am from the South originally. I had always expected that I would come North sometime, but I would have felt guilty if I had not gone back South after law school and practiced there; it would have been hanging over me. So I went back there to get it out of my system, so that I could have a clear conscience.

I think subconsciously I was trying to get run out, so that I'd have an excuse to leave. You know how sometimes you don't like to resign from a job but you don't like the work, so you do something to make the boss mad enough to fire you, and you can come out feeling good. When I look back on some of the things I did, I think subconsciously I was really trying to do that, so that I could come up North and say, "I was run out. If I hadn't been run out, I'd be back down there."

So there I was. And in order for me to live up to my vision of what a lawyer should be—according to what law school, the TV, movies, and the radio had taught me—some conditions had to be changed. I began to look at the conditions that kept me from practicing law—the conditions that all the judges were white, that all the jurors were white, that all the court officials were white, that all the police officers were white. In the police court they would call out the docket; every time they called a case they would call out the race of the party, "John Jones, defendant, white man on bail," "Bill Smith, black man in custody"—all day long, at the same time claiming that justice was blind and race made no difference.

As a black lawyer I faced certain practical problems as well. If I wanted to interview a white witness, I could not go into the white section of town or into a white hotel to interview him.

The typical Southern courthouse had signs on the restrooms, "Black Men," "White Men," "White Women," "Black Women"— right in the courthouse. So that even when a black lawyer got in the courtroom and did his thing just like everybody else, when he took a recess and went out into the hall and saw those signs, they rebutted the whole image he was trying to project of himself.

One of the problems black lawyers have had, one of the things they talked about in the black bar association meetings—they had segregated bar associations in Virginia—was that black clients went to white lawyers. Why? I think it was because they did not believe a black lawyer could do as much for them as a white lawyer. Now, that was bad—because it was true. Or if it wasn't true it certainly looked like it. Those distinctions and disadvantages were obvious to everyone who might be a client. Certainly everyone knew that those signs wouldn't be in the courthouse unless the judge condoned it. So the judge was in effect saying, "There's a difference between a black lawyer and a white lawyer."

It created a vicious circle. Black people didn't go to black lawyers, because they didn't think black lawyers could do a good job. Because the lawyers lost clients they weren't getting any money or any practice in their profession. And because they stopped practicing law, they in fact became inferior.

All this, I think, has kept the number of blacks in the legal profession small. It's because the black lawyer has not set a model for youth to imitate. The guys who were prosperous were not the black lawyers. The guys who were militant were not the black lawyers. So black youth went into other professions rather than the law.

Well, I felt the need to change those conditions. I think it was fortunate that I wanted to leave, because I suspect that if I had planned to stay in the South I wouldn't have done certain things. For example, I decided to file suits against the judges, challenging various forms of discrimination and segregation in the judicial system. I brought my ideas to the black bar association, because these questions were often discussed there. I was hoping that the bar association would bring the suits. If all of us did it, they wouldn't zero in on any one of us. But unfortunately the rest of the guys planned to stay there, so I could not get them to participate in these suits. As it ended up, I was the plaintiff.

Student: What about the NAACP and the ACLU and the other big institutions?

Dawley: Well, the American Civil Liberties Union did not operate in the South very much. The NAACP was concerned mostly with suits on education. It was ironic that the NAACP lawyers were trying to correct segregation and discrimination in the school systems, and they would not participate in these suits to clean up the area in which they practiced.

So I had to file these suits myself, and you can imagine the repercussions from bringing that kind of action: an investigation by the state un-American activities committee, a series of contempt citations, and day-to-day harassment in my practice. I couldn't even get a continuance, holding a case over from one day to the next so that I wouldn't have cases going on in two places at the same time—that kind of thing. I had to give up any idea of making money out of law practice under those conditions. Word gets around—if you need a lawyer, don't get Dawley. Actually, what I was doing was not practicing law; I was crusading. I could see no alternative if I wanted eventually to practice law as a lawyer and do any good.

Well, these desegregation suits didn't change anything but my reputation. So I was known as a troublemaker, and that led me to get a case from the Southern Christian Leadership Conference, when it was first active.

The SCLC formed a chapter in Hopewell, Virginia, and when people there began to agitate, the local newspaper wrote an editorial accusing them of being Communists and that type of thing. The SCLC chapter distributed leaflets asking the citizens to boycott the newspaper. So the newspaper brought a libel and slander suit against the leadership of the SCLC. This had been suggested as a new technique for Southerners to use to bankrupt the civil-rights movement. Remember when Sheriff Bull Connor of Birmingham and a series of other Southern officials sued the New York *Times* and Martin Luther King for slander? They got million-dollar judgments from the trial courts. So the Southerners said, "Aha! We've got a new technique. Every time one of these civil-rights movements crops up, we'll sue it for damages, and of course the jury will give us any kind of judgment we want, because they want to stop the movement."

Well, the SCLC hired me to defend this suit, and I made up my mind that we were not going to lose it. But I could see that the law was not going to apply in this case. The question I had to ask myself was: Do I play the role of lawyer or do I go outside the usual rules of the court system to win the case?

The lawyer representing the newspaper was going to need the testimony of all the people he was suing, to prove that they had been involved with the leaflets, since he hadn't seen them writing them. He was going to put them on the stand and ask them if they wrote the leaflets. If they said "Yes," his case was set at that point; if they said "No," he was going to get them for perjury. Whether he could make it stick or not, they would have to appeal to get a reversal and would use all their money defending themselves against perjury. Naturally, he assumed that all these people would be in court, since they were being sued for a tremendous sum of money. But when the case came to trial, there was nobody in the courthouse except me—no defendants. And when it came time to prove the allegation that the defendants had written the leaflets, the lawyer for the newspaper had no way to prove it.

If the judge had been fair in carrying out the law, he would have dismissed the case, because it was up to the newspaper's lawyer to subpoena the defendants, ordering them to appear in court, if they were necessary to his case. Instead of doing that, the judge permitted the lawyer to get a series of continuances postponing the rest of the trial while the lawyer tried to find these people. And of course the radio was announcing it: "Wanted, So and So; anyone knowing his whereabouts . . ." The sheriff tried at that point to serve the defendants with subpoenas, but he couldn't find them.

After the judge had permitted several continuances of the case, and they still couldn't find the defendants, I suggested that the newspaper might want to settle the case for something like twenty-five dollars. You see, the lawyer and the newspaper were being made fools of in the community. Well, he said, "If they will submit an apology, I will settle the case for a small sum." I suggested mutual apologies; so we came out with statements from both sides apologizing, and I gave him something like twenty-five or fifty dollars. The New York *Times* eventually won the libel suits against it, too, but it took four years of legal hassling, all the way up to the United States Supreme Court. When they got there, however, the Court wrote a very important opinion protecting free press and expression.

Now, in my case in Hopewell, after the order was signed dismissing the case, the judge called me in and asked whether I had had anything to do with the fact that these defendants had been unavailable. I knew exactly what he was doing, so instead of answering his question I asked *him* certain questions: Why was he asking me that, and what were the consequences of saying "Yes" and of saying "No," and what were the consequences of not answering at all? He refused to answer any of those questions, so I refused to answer his question. Then he had the district attorney draw up an "order to show cause" why I should not be held in contempt of court, and he held a hearing on that order.

It was my position that once he had signed the order dismissing the libel suit he had no more right to make me answer a question than anybody else on the street had, right? The judge can only act when he has a case pending before him.

My case came up for a hearing, and my partner, Len Holt, defended me. Naturally, the first thing we did was move that the judge disqualify himself from hearing the case, since he was prejudiced against us. He denied that motion. Then we moved for a change of venue—to have the case heard somewhere else because we couldn't get a fair trial, even with a jury, in Hopewell. The judge at that point held both of us in contempt of court for filing the motion for change of venue. Then the judge abandoned the original contempt charge against me, and we appealed the new contempt charge against both of us.

Eventually we got up to the United States Supreme Court, where we won. By that time, of course, both Holt and I had left Virginia.

AFG: What Ed has left out, though, is the fact that his pleadings in the motion for change of venue were so carefully and skillfully done that the Supreme Court just couldn't rule against him. Despite the fact that his actions in Virginia had got him branded as a no-good, troublemaking, radical lawyer, he drew up this motion in the most conservative, old-fashioned, polite way, following all the rules, using all the proper language, as far as the legal technicalities went. In fact, the Supreme Court opinion does little more than quote Ed's motion verbatim, to show that the pleading was perfectly proper and that the lawyers shouldn't have been held in contempt for it.

Well, so you and Holt left the South. But you had a partner who stayed.

Dawley: Yes. We were a three-man firm, and our partner Jordan remained. He was a veteran who had been injured in World War II, and he was confined to a wheelchair, because he's a paraplegic. So he didn't have the mobility or desire to leave that we had, and we always felt that he was in a safer position than the rest of us because they wouldn't lynch a veteran in a wheelchair who was paralyzed.

Jordan spent his time registering black voters while Holt and I filed lawsuits. He stayed on and even ran for office, for city councilman of Norfolk. After running six or seven times, he finally was elected, and is still serving. Today in an election he is able to deliver 90 percent of the black vote. So I think that represents something. It represents the value of persistence.

But his role on the City Council, naturally, is that of the maverick, the gadfly. He's always in a minority, six to one. Sort of the Adam Clayton Powell of Norfolk. He is the only black holding either an elected or an appointed political office in the city of Norfolk.

Student: Do you know how many black lawyers there are now in the South?

Dawley: No, I don't. I see statistics now and then. For instance, there weren't ten black lawyers in the whole state of Mississippi in the early sixties. In Virginia, we had sixteen in the city of Norfolk when I left, which is more, I understand, than are practicing in San Francisco today. Are you going South?

Student: Yes, Arkansas.

Dawley: Why do you want to go to the South?

Student: I grew up in Arkansas; it's just my home, you know. I feel comfortable there. I only hope I can learn enough out here to have a little edge on some of those Southern lawyers who go to the University of Arkansas. And I think I could tone my ego down enough to try to build a base, try to be politically active.

There are people of my father's generation whom I've promised, more or less, that I'll come back. Every time I come through the state I stop and see them, and they say, "You come back when you get your education." It's that kind of a thing. I've had second thoughts, but I can't think of anything I'd like to do any better than that.

Dawley: It's exciting. I think it's good. Go back there and get run out and you'll make some changes.

Student: How would you compare the typical practice down South with practicing in St. Louis or Chicago or San Francisco?

Dawley: I've never been in private practice in the North, so I don't have full information. I do think that in the North the judge could stand to be told that he was wrong. I think that in Chicago or Detroit it's possible to get a lot of blacks on the jury. The people in the North are better educated, more sophisticated, more cosmopolitan. They could see that a black person might have feelings, might be entitled to some damages, you know. A $100,000 verdict for a black man in a personal-injury case wouldn't be inconceivable to them.

I think blacks have more money in the North, they have better jobs, so they might hire a lawyer more often than in the South. On the other hand, blacks are thinking of running for office in the South, and this has an effect.

Student: What's happening with legal-services organizations in the South?

Dawley: I was back in Virginia about three months ago, and they did not have any legal-service program in Norfolk. The community has to ask for it. If the community doesn't want it, it won't get it. There are a lot of communities even in the North that don't ask for it.

AFG: Even in San Francisco there was a fight about the legal-service program coming in. The bar association wanted a very minimal program, and some lawyers handling low-income plaintiffs were worried that OEO legal services would cut into their clientele and income.

The bar association drew up its proposal for a limited program, but another group representing many organizations got together a different proposal, for a broader program with branches all over town. There was a fight in Washington about which one to fund, and this broader approach won. So the San Francisco program is not under the aegis of the city bar association.

Dawley: Right. The San Francisco Neighborhood Legal Assistance Foundation is a private corporation funded by the OEO Legal Services Program. It has a main office plus offices in five neighborhoods: Chinatown, the Mission, the Central City, the Western Addition, and Hunter's Point. Most of the administration is done at the main office. The neighborhood offices are supposed to be autonomous to a great degree, and, of course, they have different kinds of programs for the different sociologies that they deal with. You can see that Chinatown would have a little different problem than Hunter's Point.

Student: Did the legal-service offices cut into the so-called black establishment lawyer's pocket very much?

Dawley: I don't think so. To some extent, but not much. Most of the people we get couldn't pay a lawyer a decent fee anyway. A person who is poor generally isn't going to have a problem that involves a whole lot of money. I don't care what kind of problem it is—unless he gets hit by an automobile, and we don't handle a case like that. Under the terms of our grant, we have to turn that over to a private lawyer. That's one of the conditions: that we not take money out of the pockets of lawyers in private practice. If the guy hits someone else and doesn't have insurance and is being sued for some money, we can represent him. But if there's any possibility of making a fee out of the case we're not supposed to handle it. In other words, we get all the losers.

Certainly nobody in private practice would litigate some of the questions that we do, because it's economically not feasible. It's the same situation as in the South. Our clients' problems generally are not actually legal problems. For instance, if a tenant can't pay rent and the landlord puts him out, that's an economic problem really, not a legal problem, isn't it? I doubt there will ever be a law saying a man doesn't have to pay rent—unless you all get the revolution going. But when I was in the South in private practice, it would have been economically impossible for me to represent a guy who wasn't able to pay his rent and was being brought into court for nonpayment; he wouldn't even have thought of coming to me. There are many other questions that are uneconomical to litigate. How can you litigate a fine for ten dollars, even though it was completely wrong and against the law? Now, the legal-services program gives you that opportunity. I think that is a great contribution. Many questions are litigated that would never be litigated otherwise.

But it seems to me the value of the program in the future must be something more than that. Because I don't think the problem of the poor is primarily law; it is primarily poverty, and I think you do a disservice when you try to pose it as something else. If a man doesn't have any money, he's in trouble. You can pass all the laws you want, but if he doesn't have any money he's in trouble.

The people who come to our office are in that bind. And, you know, when people are in desperate straits they don't separate their problems into a legal problem, a medical problem, or a financial problem. They're just catching hell, see, and I imagine if they went to a doctor they would say, "My leg hurts." When they come to a lawyer they try to formulate it into a legal problem, and the entanglements they have just get to be unbelievable. I have a theory that these people create a personal soap opera to make life worth living—they intentionally get into one problem after another to give their lives meaning. I had an idiosyncrasy at one time that when I left the house I would never check to see whether I had my key; all the time I was out I could enjoy this suspense over whether I would be able to get back in or not. This added a big drama to my life, you see? I could see that my clients were doing the same thing that I had done, only to an outlandish degree.

How do you help a person like that? You can solve the particular problem he's got, but with this kind of psychological thrust going you really do no good. It all comes back to the effects of poverty. I could see being there a hundred years, letting people stay in apartments fifteen more days without paying rent, or letting them keep the TV, and then what would I have accomplished?

So in the Hunter's Point office we've tried to project our work into changing the sociology of the community. What can we do in this community to get people out of poverty? I was asked on a TV program once, "What is your office trying to do?" I said I was trying to get some stock fraud, price-fixing, antitrust, and other big criminal suits in the office—that is, to change the character of the problems that come in.

When you try to change the sociology in which you practice, you might say you're getting into a sort of revolutionary approach. Yet it is amazing how much you can do *within* the law. I think that to a large extent the law has not been sufficiently used to bring about change, because people who know about the law have not had a revolutionary attitude. The law is a very conservative profession in terms of its practitioners.

One thing that impressed me about legal education was that it teaches the value of the dialectic. I think it is unique that way. In other disciplines nobody's trying to knock the shovel out of your hand. The history professor lectures to you about history, and everybody tries to dig it. In science the same thing. But the field of law is always like a prize fight: someone is trying to disprove whatever you say or to show that the opposite is true. When you're in practice, you've got to think that way. In drawing up a contract you ask yourself, "Suppose the other lawyer gets hold of this paragraph. What is he going to do to it?" You always have an opponent. And I think that has a tendency to make you not only very sharp but also aware of other points of view.

The greatest contribution of the new socially conscious lawyers may be their ability to analyze how to do things with and within the law. I think that's the primary thing you get from legal training: the ability to analyze social situations, to analyze power— who has the power and how it's exercised.

When we started examining the power situation in Hunter's Point, one of the things our office started advocating was community control of police. We may actually bring a suit to accomplish that. Whether the suit wins or not, it shows another function of litigation—as political education. When a lawyer takes an idea out of left field and makes it into a lawsuit, it begins to be considered as a real alternative. The suit has an effect on the people's ability to bring about the idea politically.

Another problem we face in the ghettos is that the conditions they produce make it difficult to change them. The violence among the blacks themselves makes it impossible to solve economic problems. There can be no economic development in Hunter's Point now, because no one is going to build a building there and have it burned down the next day. We need technicians, but no technician is going to come out there if he can't be sure of his safety. So the question of law and order is especially crucial in Hunter's Point in terms of economic improvement.

Our theory of the situation is that you can't build while destruction is going on. We do need law and order. Now, if there has to be some ass-kicking in Hunter's Point, a white policeman cannot do it, because if he does it's going to start a riot. But someone has to do it. Our proposal is that the people in the community should hire and fire the police officers and that they should be black police officers. Police authorities themselves point out that a police force cannot operate unless it has the support of the community. Well, the present police force does not have the support of that community. Even if I were in favor of the police force that is in Hunter's Point today, there's no way in the world I could openly support it. But with community control of the police force, I could support it. That is not to say that a community-controlled police force will solve all the problems. If you've got a black cop kicking a black resident, it might still create some problems; but it's not a race problem that might lead to a riot.

Once you get law and order through community-controlled police, then you can begin to talk about economic development, conditions in the schools, and all the other social problems in the area. You cannot even begin to solve them with the present police force.

Student: Do you get much political pressure on you at Hunter's Point?

Dawley: Some people have not been able to get over the contradiction of the government paying someone to fight the government. I suppose you have to be somewhat sophisticated to understand that. But in a sense it's not a contradiction, because the government is giving a man an illusion that he can get at it; it is still dangling that carrot. There is a debate over whether these legal-service programs are really revolutionary or whether they just try to mislead the people.

It's a little like the question of whether Roosevelt really saved the capitalist system by his measures, rather than attacking it. I do think that a lot of criticism of the system made by the legal-service programs keeps other people from going too far, sort of keeps them in line. The government still controls the funds, and that's bound to act as a check.

AFG: Do you think it's good, in terms of the clients, to divide up the cases so that OEO offices can take only civil cases, and people who can't afford to pay a private lawyer to handle a criminal case have to go to the public defender's office?

Dawley: No. In fact, this created some problems for us in Hunter's Point. We found that many of the men in the community were dissatisfied with the legal-service office because we couldn't handle criminal cases, which are the only kind of legal problems they have. We were representing mostly women in divorce actions, and we were chasing the men to make them pay child support and that kind of thing. We were always *on* them, but when they needed us to do something *for* them, we had to turn them down.

I'd like to see these functions united, because the civil and criminal cases are often closely related. This touches on what I see as the function of a neighborhood legal-service office. You see, the poor today are not like the poor of old. The old poor were outside and downtrodden, but the poor now are arrogant and to some extent sophisticated. You can't give them a speech and have them be satisfied. They want money, food, something they can use. Otherwise they don't hear a thing you're saying.

So, if your office can solve an immediate problem for a guy, then you can talk to him. If a man is going to get six months in jail and you save him, then you can talk to him. And I think that is probably one of the main functions of having a neighborhood office: to do something for the guy and then he'll listen to you. But you can't just give him some lecture.

So we started a criminal thing, in order to reach the men.

AFG: Ed started a program to have private volunteer lawyers come to Hunter's Point to handle criminal cases. Although the attorneys in the Hunter's Point office were prohibited from taking criminal cases, these volunteers could give this service to people in the community who wouldn't go to a public defender.

Dawley: I proposed this volunteer program, of course, as a temporary measure. We didn't want to call just for more money to be appropriated for the public defender's office, because the black people at Hunter's Point looked on the public defender's office as part of the establishment. Their office is right where the police are. The prosecution department is there, too, and they all talk to each other.

That's something a lawyer should think about when he's in practice—that during the trial he and his opponent get to talking and laughing, and his client thinks that he's pulling some trick. Generally, lawyers don't take their legal fights personally. But this is not always understood by laymen. On the other hand, I guess bribery does go on, to some extent. It is important for lawyers to pay attention when people make these criticisms. I think it has hurt the public defender's office to be physically located in the police station. That doesn't seem like a wise choice if they want the people to think the public defender's office is independent.

AFG: Didn't you receive an award from the mayor for this voluntary criminal-law program?

Dawley: The Board of Supervisors liked the idea so much they decided to present our office with a certificate of merit. For one thing, it saved the city some money. The public defender's office was understaffed, and the city would have had to appropriate more money for it. So, by having lawyers in private practice volunteer to take up the slack, it saved them money.

They decided to present us with a certificate. And what day should they choose for me to come down and receive it but the day the people were having a big demonstration before the supervisors, trying to get the Board to pass a resolution against the war in Vietnam. Everyone's scowling and shouting all these revolutionary slogans. They wouldn't even let people inside City Hall because of the big ruckus inside the supervisors' chambers. All the leaders of the antiwar movement from both the black and the white communities were there doing their thing. And in the middle of all this, they call me in to get this certificate of merit, right in front of all my radical friends!

Student: There are black lawyers who do go the route of the establishment. Like in Oakland there are several black lawyers who, as I understand it, make around $50,000 a year. They're into black capitalism. You know, as a black lawyer it's very difficult to decide what you are going to do with your legal training. It may turn out that all that training is relevant only in the capitalist context, that it doesn't help you become an aggressive revolutionary at all.

Dawley: Well, that old revolution may not come around for another fifty years, so you might pose the problem as what do you do in the meantime?

I don't think you should completely knock the guys who become black capitalists. Someday you may need one of those guys. You might even need an Uncle Tom to get you out of trouble, whereas I couldn't do a thing for you. Take this example: Suppose your client is charged with murder and he's going to get the electric chair, but you could get him off by shuffling and grinning and acting like an Uncle Tom. Should you do that? Remember, one of the basic principles in law practice is that the first interest of a lawyer is his client's welfare.

Student: I guess if I felt it was going to save his life, I'd put on an act. But if every time I went into court I had to do that, it would be a different situation.

Dawley: It's a problem that comes up in many contexts. Suppose you are representing a guy, and politically you are part of the movement, yet you know the judge doesn't dig the movement. Do you yield to the establishment ideas or do you talk that movement talk? Which is more important—the movement or your client? That question is posed in practically every political context. When you're defending a draft case, do you get in there and tell the judge that you think the war is illegal, or do you use some kind of tactical defense that you think the establishment would dig? Is that a copout? Or is it putting the client's welfare above your politics?

Sometimes you talk to the client and ask him how he wants you to present his case. Then he says, "Well, lawyer, what do you think? I'll do whatever you think is best." You have to advise him, he's depending on you. Then you have a hellish responsibility to separate your politics from his welfare.

How do I deal with that situation? I can't defend my solution. I think it's very individual, and I couldn't blame anybody for criticizing it. I believe I should be frank. If I felt that it would help the guy for me to Uncle Tom, and I could not do it, I think I should at least have the honesty to say, "What you need is a guy who can go in there and shuffle and grin. I can't do that. I'm going to give you your money back, and you should get this guy down the street here. He's good at that kind of thing."

Now, if my client is the kind of cat who says, "Go in there and do your thing, and I'll take my chances—it's worth it," that's fine. But I don't think that I should mislead the client or fail to tell him what the situation is. It's very easy sometimes to try to convince your client that the best approach is to get up there and say the war is wrong. You could probably convince him. I think you should be very careful. At the least, you've got to tell him that if you go in there and do your thing, it will make a hell of a fine headline but it might cause him to lose the case.

One of the satisfying things about civil-rights cases in the South was that you knew you were going to lose, so you could really do what you wanted to do. You had nothing more to lose. In most other cases there's always a chance of winning, so you're cautious. But a lawyer can get a lot of pleasure trying a case he knows he's going to lose and saying all the things he wanted to say.

Of course, that raises another point you should think about. Coming out of law school, you tend to think in terms of appellate courts. All the cases they have you read in school are appellate-court cases. But you have to stop and realize that for most people the first court they walk into is the highest court in the land, because they are never going to go any further than that. The decision will never be appealed. That's why a good lawyer, I mean a lawyer who can get results for people, is a guy who's got good relations with the local establishment. No question about that.

The radical lawyer is the kind of guy a client goes to when he's got nothing to lose. This lawyer already has a bad name, nobody likes him. He's got nothing to lose, either. So he gets the client who committed a murder with ten cops watching him do it and with no extenuating reason.

On the other hand, I think radical lawyers do tend to be great technicians, because they don't get any breaks. When they've won a case, goddammit, they've won it. They learn right away that they're not going to get any breaks, so they cross every i and dot every t.

That's true of any business. If you're running a restaurant and the establishment doesn't like you, the health inspector will be coming around, and the fire inspector. If you're a lawyer, they will be watching your clients. Someone may even set up one of your clients to frame you. Sometimes you get all wrapped up in trying to save a client and you might do a little something that isn't exactly what you're supposed to do. And you think you're pretty safe because you're doing it for the guy's benefit, to keep him from going to jail. But he might blow the whistle on you. For instance, he'll claim that you told him to tell a lie when he got on the witness stand, and that's ground for disbarment. He can say you did that even if you didn't. So that's something you should be careful about—someone planting a client on you.

When the establishment gets down on you, you can't operate like other lawyers do. The judge can decide against you even though he knows he's wrong and is going to get reversed on appeal. But he has forced you to file a brief in every case in order to get the right verdict. That means extra money and time. And in many situations the judge sets your fee—for instance, when you're representing a minor. If you're an establishment guy, he'll give you a great big fee, but if he doesn't like you, you'll get hardly enough to cover your expenses. That's the kind of thing that's hard to correct, because the statutes say it is a matter of discretion for the trial judge to set the fee, and the appellate court will uphold whatever the trial judge decides, unless it is clearly shown that he has abused his discretion.

So, in all these ways a lawyer is right up against the establishment. A doctor can do his thing and nobody will bother him. If he performed his operation, he'll get his money. But the lawyer has a peculiar situation: Everything he does has to be passed on by somebody in the establishment. Being an outsider to the establishment is especially hard, *especially* hard for a lawyer.

Let me point out something else too. I don't know how this got in my mind—I guess you can tell I've got a very ragged mind. I think in choosing your spouse it's important to know what she's after. If you want to be a revolutionary and she wants the best things in life, you'll have problems there. Of course, many times you can't find out until after you're married, because before then when she finds out what *you* like, she'll say, "Oh, I dig that, too," you know? But I think that's a factor to consider, not only from the standpoint of whether your marriage is going to work, but also in terms of how *you* are going to turn out. You can't assume, "If she ain't like I think she is, I'm going to get rid of her." It might end up that you'll bow down to her will, because you love her and she has a lot of influence. She might talk you out of being a revolutionary—or into being *more* revolutionary. I know it doesn't help for me to tell you all this now, because it doesn't mean a thing when you fall in love. But it's something you can think back on, you know? "Oh, yeah, he told me that."

I thought about it because I was once in a political situation, getting ready to do my thing, and I happened to think, "If I do this I'll lose my job." And I just pictured my wife and what it would do to her. Of course, I didn't have that much faith in what I was about to do, anyway. That's one thing in this business: You're never sure that you're doing the right thing, that your motivations are pure and all that. So you always have these self-doubts, and you're very vulnerable. The slightest criticism can send you off. So I was thinking, "If I do this and I lose my job, will she think I'm a bum?" Then I told her about it, and she said, "Go on ahead and do it. We'll live." So I felt really good about it. Now I can do that and come home easy, you see? And as strong as I thought I was, that little thing made a tremendous difference.

Student: Do you have any fears about being disbarred as an attorney for things you might do in your personal life style?

Dawley: I don't have any specific fears of getting disbarred. Most things I want to do I think I can do without running that risk. But it's very easy to get into trouble. You know, there are so many laws to cover things, if they really want to get you. That's why the question of enforcement is so important. Did you know that in California it's a crime to tell a lie over the telephone? Bobby Seale was convicted on a charge of coming within so many feet of a courthouse with a gun. Remember that one? In other words, when they want to get you, all they have to do is have the district attorney go down the index of the code.

Another way they do it is to use the Internal Revenue Code. Who can answer every question about their finances? They ask you about something that happened four years back. Practically every lawyer who has been involved in the civil-rights movement has had trouble with the Internal Revenue, both federal and state.

So, in certain things you know you run risks. Another example: when I was practicing in Virginia, a person could not get a divorce in New York except on the ground of adultery. People who wanted divorces were coming to Virginia to get them. In order to get a divorce in Virginia they had to allege that they were residents of Virginia, but a lot of people never really left New York State. If it was an uncontested divorce, the other party wouldn't show up, and the lawyer in Virginia would simply allege that this person was a resident of Virginia. A lot of lawyers made Virginia a divorce mill. Establishment lawyers could do that, because they knew the man wasn't going to come down on them. I couldn't avail myself of this lucrative hustle for fear of getting disbarred.

So it ties in with making money. If you're with the establishment, you can do a lot of things that are right on the periphery of the law; you can get those goodies. But if you're a revolutionary lawyer you can't do those things, and eventually it looks as though you're not a very good lawyer, because everybody else is making money and you're not, you see?

Now, sometimes the establishment will call you in to *give* you a goody. But once you take it, then they've got you. They can always hold that over your head, you see? I think there are some guys who by nature would have been more militant, but once the man got something on them they could no longer be militant.

AFG: Did they ever offer you one of those goodies?

Dawley: A guy came in one time to get me to draw up a will for a man who was already dead. The man had died without a will, and left quite a bit of an estate. This guy offered to divide part of the proceeds with me. And I was hungry as hell at the time. I could have done that, but then that would have been the end of it—I could never have done another radical thing.

Now, on the other side of the coin, sometimes a guy will use the technique of being "revolutionary" to point himself out as a person to be bought off. He'll do something that's calculated to make the establishment say, "We've got to take care of him." So getting involved in militant things may be a way of selling yourself to the capitalist system, putting yourself up for bidding.

I guess everybody knows that fixes and corruption and bribes do occur. The lawyer I first practiced with was about seventy-two when I started. He was telling me about the first paying case he won, about 1906. He'd never won a case and recovered money before, and he thought he just didn't have that kind of ability, so he assumed the reason he had won was that the judge had fixed it—given him the verdict. He wanted to do the right thing by the judge, but he didn't know how you were supposed to do it. So he went to see the judge in his chambers, took a suitcase full of money, and dumped it out on the judge's desk. He said, "I don't know how things are done around here—I just started practicing. But I want to do the right thing. You take your part of it, whatever you think you're supposed to have, and I'll take the rest. I really appreciate what you did for me." The judge just sat there stunned for fifteen minutes. Finally he said, "If I thought you knew any better, this would be your last case. I know you must not know any better, so you put that money back in that suitcase and get out of here."

Now, it wasn't all that inconceivable for this lawyer to think that the only way he would win the case would be by some bribe. If you think about the law, you can see there are a whole lot of legal principles sitting up on the shelf, and you pull different ones out to use on particular situations. It all looks reasonable and correct, because you are following a principle. But the real question is, which one does the judge pull out? He can pull out one that will give judgment to the plaintiff and another one that will give judgment to the defendant. And whichever one he finally pulls out looks good, looks pretty, just like it's supposed to be.

The trouble is, it's difficult for the law to do its job when people in the society in which it operates do not have equal power or anywhere near equal power. The law can deal with people who are more or less paired. But in this society, where things are not distributed fairly, I don't see how the judicial system can possibly operate to result in fairness. Who gets to be a judge? It's bound to be a guy acceptable to the ruling powers, right? How else can you get to be a judge?

AFG: Well, there's George W. Crockett, the black judge of the Recorder's Court in Detroit. Do you have any comments about the role of a black judge?

Dawley: I think he's beautiful and long may he wave, but I don't think he's going to wave too long. I would like to think that if I were in his position I'd be doing the same things, like ensuring that blacks get on juries.

AFG: Would you want to be in his position? As a lawyer he did some radical things—he represented the Communist Party leaders in 1949 in the Dennis case and was jailed for contempt for four months. But at a certain point in his life, I think, he deliberately decided to go step by step to get to be a judge. Would you want to do that?

Dawley: I guess when I got to be his age I might. But between now and then, I think I could be more effective doing other things than being a judge.

Student: Why did you become an attorney?

Dawley: Well, there are a whole lot of bits and pieces. One of them is the influence of my father. He wanted to be a lawyer, and I suppose he put the idea in my head before I was ever aware of it. I think my first choice would have been to be a philosopher, but it doesn't make any sense for a poor black guy to be a philosopher. So I sort of had to get something that's close to that that I could still make a little money out of. I don't think I really ever wanted to be a lawyer in a very positive sense, but it had a certain appeal to me. I think I had a certain talent for it.

AFG: Would you hire one of these young, very militant lawyers to work for you in Hunter's Point?

Dawley: I've made sort of a general observation that some of the youngsters who are extremely militant would do a good job as the prime minister of some developing country, President of the

United States, or something like that. But in terms of solving some immediate problems like at Hunter's Point, it's a lot different. They follow Che Guevara, Karl Marx, and all that. They would be great if the revolution was tomorrow, the day after tomorrow. But what about the next six months or three months or this week, you know? They're not men of today.

Student: Tell me this: How do you get a historical perspective so you don't look at the short term, so you don't look for Che Guevara to come in and change everything overnight, so you can see that if you do this today, sooner or later you will reach that end?

Dawley: I don't know, because my historical perspective changes every week. It is actually rather easy to figure out the weaknesses of those proposals that are presented to me. It is very difficult to construct a sound proposal of my own. For instance, I was interviewing candidates for a job opening, and I asked each one, "Suppose you were the black man in charge of all the blacks. What would you do to get deliverance for us?"

AFG: I think I'd get up and walk out.

Dawley: One guy was saying he didn't believe in black separation, he believed in integration, but "militant integration." He said, "I think we're going to have to kick the white man's ass until things get better."

I said to him, "Doesn't that remind you of beating a woman up and then going to sleep next to her? Aren't you afraid to do that?"

I understand that the world isn't run by logic. But to work a guy over and call him a lot of nasty names and say he isn't worth a damn and shoot him and burn his house down, and then to integrate with him—that doesn't make a lot of sense to me.

Of course, separation—I don't have to point out the weaknesses to that.

AFG: Why don't you?

Dawley: Because everybody else wants to do it for me.

I suppose my world view is to keep a more or less open mind, maybe trying a little of this and a little of that. You try a combination of various methods, which is really a copout for not having an answer, you know?

In the end, I've come to the conclusion that anything you think of is going to have flaws in it, because basically we're dealing with an impossible situation from the start. I mean, how is a weak minority going to overcome a strong majority? So, if the situation starts off being impossible, any program you come up with is going to have weaknesses.

I'm reminded of the myth of Sisyphus. A guy is in this place like hell.

Student: He pushes the rock up the hill and it keeps on going back down again.

Dawley: When it gets to the top it rolls back down. In other words, it is impossible to push this rock over the hill. But if you *can* push it over, you're in Paradise. What do you do? If you try to push the rock over, you're trying to do something impossible. On the other hand, if you do nothing, why don't you even try?

Student: If you can't ever push it over, you might as well stop pushing.

Dawley: Some people are just the kind who would still try. Other people, because of their personality, would say, "It's impossible. I'm not going to waste my energy trying." How can you say one makes more sense than the other? I don't know, I can't say.

In terms of a world view, the final question is: Which kind of cat are you—a stone-pushing cat or a non–stone-pushing cat?

Student: Which one is the lawyer?

Dawley: It might be a question of individual personality. Some cats might just enjoy the exercise, you know? It may be a question of how you entertain yourself until you die.

But we do know this: No one yet has come up with an answer as to what should be done and how it should be done that they *know* will really work. NAACP—is that the answer? CORE, the same story. Anarchism doesn't completely satisfy. All of them have got a point, but have you ever heard of a world view that made you think, "This is *it*"? Certain ideas do grab you in certain directions, give you certain means, approaches. But you never get that feeling that what you are doing is 100 percent right, that it's a 100 percent solution.

That's what I'm depending on the youngsters for—to get rid of certain misconceptions that we had to fight or were surprised by. We wasted our energy on these wrong doctrines, and maybe by the time we get close to the true doctrine, whatever it is, we'll be too worn out. Maybe if the younger generation starts off with some truths, they can spend more of their time finding out what the real answer is.

On the other hand, it may be misleading to think in terms of progress. Think of the Jews: They really had it going, were highly educated. I mean, you couldn't say they were downtrodden, in a class sense, like the blacks. Germany was one of the most advanced nations in the world, and it reverted back 3,000 years and tried to exterminate the Jews. So what does progress mean? A black guy was saying that maybe one of the things that enabled the black man to survive was his weakness and his ineffectiveness. If he had really been effective and had some power, he might have been done away with like the Jews with the Germans.

Student: You don't really believe that, though, do you? He's playing devil's advocate, isn't he?

AFG: Yes. He's such a pragmatist, he has said—I'm quoting you, Dawley—that it is not wrong to say something you do not believe, if at a particular moment you think it will have the right effect on a mass of people, and then some other day you can tell them what you really think. He and I have gone round and round on that, and we're still arguing.

Dawley: Well, I take that position because I'm so impassioned and so weak and so inadequate that I can't afford to be perfectly pure. I don't have enough talent to always tell the truth.

AFG: Come on, Dawley, now how am I supposed to answer one like that?

Dawley: Talking about weakness, there's another side to that, too. An older black man I was talking to pointed out that perhaps if the youngsters in Greensboro who did the first sit-in had known their black history, had read about the lynchings and tortures, they never would have done it. I'm sure that if the elderly black people had advised those kids, they would have told them not to do it. And the reason they did do it is precisely because they didn't know what had happened in the past. It's a funny illustration of the saying that "those who do not understand history are doomed to repeat it."

AFG: Yes, but it works the other way, too. If they had read about Sojourner Truth, the slave who became an abolitionist preacher, they would have sat in five years earlier. History's got two sides. I think history would say do it and don't do it.

Dawley: Well, I'm talking about the other side to it. I think sometimes when you read things it paralyzes you. Like burning these damn cities. I mean, I would probably have told them, "Don't do it, because bad things will happen and no good will come of it." The only reason I might have told them to do it is because I'd have been happy to see it, you know? I guess those who did it hadn't read those books, so they ran around burning the cities. And as a result all kinds of things are happening.

AFG: For instance?

Dawley: Well, law firms are hiring black lawyers. They got the OEO program. The schools are opening up. They've got black-studies programs. Niggers are learning the law. Look, you've got black lawyers talking about their duty to their people and the revolution and all that kind of thing.

AFG: They weren't doing that before?

Dawley: No. There wasn't anybody doing that, no. All because of some people who hadn't read any history. So I think there are two sides even to that. On the one hand, some people will change things because they don't know enough not to. And on the other hand I think some of the youngsters will spend less time under illusions because of the reading they do—they'll profit from our mistakes, and chances are they might come up with some answers.

CALIFORNIA RURAL LEGAL
ASSISTANCE PRACTICE
Don Kates

AFG: Don Kates works for one of the best-known OEO legal-service offices in the country—California Rural Legal Assistance. He has participated in, and believes in, test cases, and in suing the police when necessary.

Why don't you start by describing CRLA, Don?

Kates: Well, let me begin with OEO legal services. I assume you're familiar with the Office of Economic Opportunity. It's a federal agency, created in 1964, that gives money under the war on poverty, and for about two years it had nothing to do with legal services. Then Edgar and Jean Cahn, who were early OEO operatives, wrote a lengthy article concerning the possibilities of having an OEO legal-services program. Eventually they got one funded. It provides legal representation to persons who are otherwise unable to pay for it—in civil cases.

AFG: Was there ever a thought of providing representation in criminal cases?

Kates: There was, but the act now forbids it. The ostensible reason for forbidding it was the existence of public defenders; the actual reason was a concern that rioters and all kinds of "inappropriate" persons might receive defense.

245

AFG: I've heard that some OEO legal-services offices were glad of the prohibition because they had been swamped with some kinds of criminal cases, like drunk driving.

Kates: Maybe so. Now, the structure is this: A nonprofit corporation is set up under state law and applies for federal funds. If it is granted the funds, it sets up a program of lawyers to defend people.

From the beginning, there have been a number of controversies about OEO legal services. The major one had to do with the kinds of cases it should take. There were two archetypes for legal-services programs, having quite different approaches.

California Rural Legal Assistance, by which I am employed, is one type. North Mississippi Rural Legal Services is a somewhat similar program, and there are others. CRLA was started by a guy named Jim Lorenz, who was just out of Harvard Law School and working for a prestigious Los Angeles firm. He became familiar with the Emergency Committee to Aid Farm Workers and with Cesar Chavez's work on behalf of the grape strikers, and he began to see the desperate need for legal assistance for farm workers and rural populations.

CRLA was funded, but with certain specifications. One was that no union could be represented as such, although we have no right to discriminate against an individual because he's a union member. We have nine regional offices in places you've probably never heard of, even if you were born and raised in California as I was. We have about forty-five lawyers, approximately four lawyers per office, and one office in San Francisco with about eight lawyers.

That was the genesis of CRLA. Now let me compare the genesis of Alameda County Legal Aid. That was a well-established Legal Aid Society program, one of the traditional programs across the country, sponsored by local bar associations. The program handled nothing controversial; it handled very few court cases, and usually only gave people advice. It was sort of a mill operation: when a person came in the door, he got hit by a fan that pushed him all the way out the exit, and someone gave him some advice as he passed by.

Alameda County Legal Aid requested and was granted OEO legal-service funds. Many of the OEO offices across the country are nothing more than funded former Legal Aid programs. That doesn't mean they're necessarily bad programs. In Alameda County, for example, Legal Aid hired a bunch of attorneys who just revolted and brought in community people, and the program is now one of the better ones in the country.

But there are basically two kinds of programs: those that used to be Legal Aid Societies, and those that started out as brand-new ideas. The old Legal Aid types, I think, may be characterized most affirmatively as being of the opinion that people vote with their feet. What is important to the community will be brought into the office by the clients. Therefore, the lawyer should handle whatever is brought in by his clients.

Now, in effect that meant he should handle nothing but divorces, because every legal-services program in the country was immediately swamped by divorces.

AFG: Wait. These were mainly women clients, not men, right?

Kates: Yes.

AFG: Have you ever thought about why all of them would be coming in for divorces?

Kates: There were several reasons. One was that they wanted to marry somebody else. Another was that, until we knocked it over, there was a rule in California that a woman could get welfare if she was separated from her husband for more than three months, but if it was less than three months she couldn't get welfare unless divorce proceedings had been filed. So lots of people came in to file for divorce because otherwise they couldn't get welfare and they might be starving. Now, the reaction of some legal-services programs was to get them divorces. Our reaction in CRLA was to knock over the rule.

AFG: How long did it take you to knock it over? And how high in the courts did you have to go?

Kates: This was my first case, and we filed a complaint in a three-judge federal court, which is a procedure we can use to cut through delays. The court threw me out on my ass for failure to exhaust administrative remedies, which was just absurd, clearly wrong. So, we took it to the U.S. Supreme Court. About six months later the Supreme Court ruled in our favor, in *Damico v. California*.

AFG: So it took less than a year?

Kates: Oh, no; that reversal was only on the issue of exhaustion of remedies, not on the substantive issue of the suit. It took the three-judge court another year and eight months to decide that question, finally throwing out the three-month separation requirement. Of course, that decision solved that particular problem for all the women clients needing welfare in California, not just our clients.

But your natural question is, "What happened to all those people in the meantime?" Let's go back to the theory question. What would have happened to them under the vote-with-your-feet theory? The problem with that theory, as we saw it, was that there is approximately one lawyer for every 640 people in the United States. There are only 4,000 lawyers at most for about 22 percent of the population—the poor in the United States.

AFG: Whom are you including in the 4,000?

Kates: I'm including legal-services attorneys who handle civil cases and public defenders who handle criminal ones. Not every state provides public defenders.

These 4,000 lawyers are all there are for the poor, and I use that term to describe people who make under $3,000 a year for a family of four. Of course, that doesn't include a huge number of poor people who make over that sum but have many children to support.

The idea that indigents are receiving free legal services because they can't afford to pay is in large part a joke, because *nobody* can afford to pay for legal services in this country except the very rich. Therefore, the American Civil Liberties Union and most private lawyers who handle charity cases are handling cases for middle-class people who can't pay, who are indigent in terms of legal representation.

The fact is that there are literally millions of people needing representation, and OEO legal services cannot possibly represent them all. We can represent maybe 25 percent. And in every case that a poor person brings in, if the lawyer sits down and explores with him the things connected with that case, he finds innumerable other cases.

Poor people are not like middle-class people. They are more like rich people in that they have class problems—problems that affect the poor as a class—in addition to hundreds of little individual problems, many more than the middle-class person has. One economic problem leads to another. For instance, a person comes in asking for a divorce. It may be that the reason she is asking for a divorce is that the welfare department has said, "Get child support or a divorce, or you'll get no welfare." The reason the family needs welfare may be that the husband's wages were constantly being garnished by a credit company, so his employer fired him.

The legal-services offices that adopted the vote-with-your-feet view immediately became overcrowded with clients with individual problems and began to use a welfare-department system of handling them one by one: the client comes in, you ask him what his problem is, you talk to him for three or four minutes, and you do your best to solve the problem. The difficulty is that the client may not understand what his problem is, or may not be able to articulate the real problem, or may not understand that there are legal solutions for some of his other problems. So the legal-services programs that purport to handle all the client's problems don't do so. They adopt various mechanisms for getting the client through the office and out before he's ever able to tell about all or sometimes any of his problems.

Now, CRLA takes the opposing view. We say: We have a finite number of legal-service hours. We can't handle anywhere near all the problems. Therefore we are going to handle only problems that affect the poor as a class.

Let me talk about a few of these class problems, to illustrate what I've been saying about people not recognizing the need for legal services. On one day in March 1970, my single office of CRLA invalidated two whole sections of the California constitution. The first required all voters to be literate in English. We established in the Castro case that it was sufficient to be literate in Spanish.

AFG: It's only fair to say that other lawyers have been trying to establish this for years, both here and in the East.

Kates: Right. They succeeded first in *Katzenbach v. Morgan*.

The other constitutional provision required that before public housing was built in a particular area the populace in that area had to vote on whether they wanted it. Several areas voted against public housing projects.

Now, no client is going to come to a lawyer and say, "I want you to sue to knock that provision out of the California constitution, because it's stopping me from getting public housing." He doesn't know anything about provisions of the California constitution. What he knows is that he has to live in a car or a shack because there is such a severe housing problem. That is the most severe problem we have in our area. We won that case, *James v. Valtierra,* in San Jose.

AFG: The U.S. Supreme Court could overturn that decision, though.

Kates: That's right, because the state appealed from our victory. Anyway, there are those two approaches to legal services.

AFG: I agree with your characterization in general, Don, but, like some of the statutes you have attacked, I think you painted with a brush that was overbroad. I know CRLA handles many so-called service cases, and Alameda County Legal Aid handles some important test cases, so there aren't really two distinct models anymore. Maybe what distinguishes CRLA is the publicity it gets on its big cases!

Student: I'd like to ask Ann what *she* thinks is the reason more women than men were asking for divorces.

AFG: I think very few people understand that when a woman is no longer living with the man who was her husband, she has a very strong desire to have the situation regularized. The women want a legal status that is equivalent to the reality. It is a significant moral question, apart from money or child support or getting on welfare or anything.

Kates: Actually, I think their moral views are nonsense, but that's not the reason we don't handle divorces. It's not my business to pass judgment on their moral views. But when I have to choose between a client who is being hounded by creditors and who can't get a job because they attach his wages every time and some woman who wants a divorce to regularize her moral relationships—well, bullshit! If I can handle only one of the two cases, I'm not going to handle her case—I'm going to get that guy out of bankruptcy.

AFG: Well, now, wait just a minute. Quite often another reason a woman wants a divorce is so that no man can come to her door and say, "I'm coming in here, and I can do what I want to with you and the children, because legally I am still your husband."

Kates: That's a misconception of what happens to poor people. He doesn't care about his legal status. If a husband beats his wife— Or I've even had a man come in and say his wife beat him! I told him that if he couldn't handle his wife, there wasn't anything that anyone could do. And it is equally true of women. I can get her a divorce and an order so that every time her husband comes and beats her up, the police will toss him in jail. He'll get out two months later and he'll come and beat her up again and be tossed in jail again and so on. The only effectual solution to that kind of thing is to move somewhere else and maybe change your name.

But I have a moral objection which I regard as decisive. I was put there to give people legal services. Now, the legal system, which is something I believe in, runs only to the extent that both people are represented. The rich are represented; the creditors are represented; as a result, the people who would be my clients, who in the past weren't represented, got royally fucked all the time. They had innumerable defenses that never were raised. Now, if I take a suit for a poor person that's against another poor person, I've just increased the number of people who are unrepresented. If I sue somebody who doesn't have representation, I'll win. I am neither God nor a judge; I have no right to judge between one poor person who tells me his or her story and some other poor person whom I haven't talked to. I'm not willing to do that; as far as I'm concerned it's just not proper.

AFG: But you are playing judge by turning those women away.

Kates: Yes, but I don't have to play it more than that.

AFG: Actually, the advisory committees that decide what cases the offices should handle have come to the same conclusion as Don. The poor people ultimately found that they couldn't get help on political issues because of all the divorce cases. But I think that if we had some welfare-rights women here we'd get another side to this story.

Student: Could you say something about the future of legal services two years from now? That's when I get out of law school.

Kates: It's impossible to tell what's going to happen to legal services. It's only a very minor part of OEO, and there are constant complaints about it. Governor Reagan complains all the time.

In terms of a good job for a new lawyer, you'll find some legal-services programs with very good administrators and some with every variety of gutlessness. There are programs where lawyers are not allowed to do anything but file divorces, suing other poor people. These programs are controlled by the local bar. There's nothing worse for a program than to be controlled by the local bar, because the first thing that happens is that influential members complain to the bar association about suits being filed against their clients, and that's the end of those suits. The federal government may be going more and more to local bar control. That may put an end to the best legal-services programs and representation that has been given by offices like ours.

Student: Doesn't Governor Reagan have veto power over CRLA funds?

Kates: The governor has a discretionary veto. That is to say, he can veto, but OEO can override his veto. Reagan has threatened to veto us. But the growers are for him anyway, so why should he antagonize the minorities and a lot of middle-class people by vetoing us? That doesn't mean he won't ever do it.

Student: Do you have many suits going about farm workers?

Kates: Yes. Most of our offices are rural, and many of our clients are farm workers, but we don't always file suits to solve their problems. For instance, suppose a guy comes in with financial problems and we find out he's earning only ten dollars a day. The first thing we can do is file a complaint with the labor commissioner, to get him a minimum wage. We also ask for penalty wages. We go down to the fields and spend a day talking to the workers. We file a complaint with the Department of Industrial Safety about the fact that the employer doesn't provide proper sanitation, toilets, and so on. We can even file a lawsuit for damages for lack of sanitation. If we keep constant pressure on people, we get some action. That's the way you have to work it.

We do file some suits. When people are fired for union activities, we have a standard suit we file. It's under the California Labor Code section that says you have a right to collective bargaining and therefore you cannot be fired for being a union member. We sued one grower for $450,000 for firing nine people. We sued both him and the growers' association. The growers' association had told him, "Those people are going to organize your workers. Keeping them will be a mistake." So he fired them. When we sued, he settled, and as compensatory damages he gave these farm workers $4,500 apiece every year for the rest of their lives, whether they work or not.

We were still free to sue for punitive damages against the growers' association. We lost that in the trial court, but we appealed, and the growers' association was furious.

We have a standard suit we file about wetbacks being brought in and taking jobs from American resident workers. We have a green-carder suit. Green-carders are people who come across the Mexican border to work. They are given a green card, which is a daily work permit. Now, we have 500 unemployed farm workers in the Imperial Valley while 5,000 green-carders come across the border every day to work, plus wetbacks—and they are willing to work for far less money, so the growers love them. We do our best to get rid of them, because they are killing our farm workers. We won some cases but lost *Diaz v. Kay-Dix Ranch* and *Gooch v. Mitchell,* although, again, they may be reversed on appeal. Fascinatingly enough, we have produced on the other side at least one expert law firm. It handles the defense of all these cases and is just as diligent as we are.

One thing we have going for us is an incredible series of in-service publications and communications. When a case on a particular question is won in the District of Columbia or the Southern

District of New York, we hear about it right away. Imagine being a lawyer for some landlord trying to evict a tenant, like for instance a lawyer I've been opposing. He filed a complaint. I filed an answer and a trial brief. My brief is thirty-five pages long, and it raises such issues as retaliatory eviction, the tenant's defense that the landlord has "unclean hands," or that there are improper conditions, which permit waiver of rent. By improper conditions, I mean housing violations and conditions not up to the housing-board standards. This poor lawyer has never heard of these questions.

AFG: What about the judge?

Kates: Well, he hasn't, either. But, you see, we're ready to back the case up. If the judge decides against us, we'll take it up to the California Supreme Court.

AFG: Do you tell the judge that?

Kates: I don't have to tell him. He knows I can do it.

AFG: This is very important. You will find that if it gets to be known that when you lose you'll go right upstairs, it has a tremendous effect. It is a confrontation approach, and as a result you may lose at the lowest level, but you are treated with a certain respect, and ultimately you often win. But when you take that approach, you'd better tell your client it may hurt him in a way. It may mean that you can't get a favor on a small point, but you may win more in the end. By "a favor" I mean, for example, if your client's mother is about to have an operation, you will want to arrange for a hearing to be postponed.

Of course, your client wants you to be smooth enough to talk the DA or the justice department into granting a personal favor. At the same time he wants you to be entirely militant and never consort with the enemy. It takes a skillful lawyer to play that double role, especially in a political case. It's possible, sometimes, if the lawyer on the other side also wants a favor for one of his witnesses.

Kates: Once again we're going to disagree. Maybe in the back-country practice, where I am, things are a lot more informal, but I never have any problem getting deals, and God knows I'm not very smooth. When the opposing lawyer knows the case is going to the U.S. Supreme Court, he is much more likely to compromise in general. Furthermore, even as to small matters he'll be willing to compromise, because he knows he's going to want a lot of favors from us over the long course of appeals.

Student: I take it you think CRLA is doing a pretty good job.

Kates: I think CRLA is the best legal-services program in the country.

AFG: And I think people who don't work for CRLA would agree that it is one of the best. I think its record is objectively that.

Kates: Why do we say that? Because CRLA handles and wins the big cases: we have the most competent lawyers, and our policies are such that we do the best job for our clients. However, in my opinion, CRLA would still be only a C-plus or B-minus legal-services program. That is to say, there is no A-level legal-services program.

But CRLA does give a lawyer a chance to do a good piece of work. For instance, I handled a case raising the following issue: If policemen engage in attacks against minority-group persons and are not arrested and prosecuted, can the prosecutors and police officials be held liable in damages, as well as ordered to arrest and prosecute the officers? I took a solid month to write an appellate brief, researching the entire legislative history of the 1866 and 1871 Civil Rights Acts and the Fourteenth Amendment. There are many legal-services programs in the country where a lawyer doesn't devote more than an hour to any single client, no matter who the client is, no matter what the case is. If it takes more time than that, he tells the client, "I'm sorry, we can't handle your case." And, although my case was mooted on appeal, attorneys around the country have been using various aspects of that research in scores of cases.

AFG: By "mooted on appeal" Don means that the case was never decided, because of some other factor.

Student: Do many private lawyers handle police suits?

Kates: Not enough. Private practitioners for many years have been very hesitant to sue the police. They raise a number of standard objections: first, police officers don't have any money, so even if you win you can't collect the judgment; second, their employer is a municipality, which is not liable, so it is not going to pay the judgment; third, the jury will be all white, and if you've got a minority client you're not going to get a judgment; fourth, even if you can somehow win, the jury won't give you a big enough judgment against a police officer to cover your fees, court costs, discovery costs, and all that. So most lawyers will tell a guy who comes in wanting to sue the police, "Sure, I'll take the case. Give me a $1,000 retainer, and I'm going to want successive retainers."

There's an answer to each of these objections. First of all, most cops are insured by the Patrolmen's Benevolent Society or some cognate organization, so you can in fact collect a judgment against them. But let's assume it isn't paid; what I would do is assign that judgment to a credit bureau that would hound that cop for years, and garnish his wages if he ever did any moonlighting, and threaten to tell his boss, because moonlighting is illegal. Boy, I'd love to do to those guys what happens to my clients all the time.

AFG: But you must also keep in mind that the client who sues the police may be suffering harassment throughout the time the suit is pending. He may lose his job or be refused credit. There will be a lot of publicity, and it will affect his wife and children and his whole life.

Kates: That is certainly true, and that's something that you've got to tell your client. He may be subjected to physical harassment, police cars watching his house, retaliatory prosecution, all kinds of bullshit. But assuming the client really wants to sue the police knowing the consequences, the question for the lawyer is whether litigation against the police can be successful.

The first thing to ask is, "What do you mean by successful? What is your object?" There are two objects. One is to recompense the client; the other is to control police malpractice. The objections I listed before have to do with recompensing the client, and whether the lawyer can afford to take the case. Obviously that doesn't have any application to a legal-services lawyer, because he isn't employed to make money on the case.

AFG: In fact, some OEO legal-service offices will not take these cases because they *may* engender a fee. OEO offices are not supposed to take fee-paying cases. In that instance, of course, the OEO lawyer can do what he does in other possible-fee cases: he asks a lawyer in private practice to take it, and when two or three have said "No" he has fulfilled his obligations, and he can take it himself.

Kates: The ordinary lawyer thinks, "Here my client got the shit beat out of him. It cost him $2,000 medical expenses; he's got pain, suffering, and so on. If I don't get $2,000 plus my fee, the suit is a failure." Even if he is willing to do the case free, he's not willing to spend $3,000 of his money paying deposition costs— which is scarcely an unreasonable position—and the client doesn't have the money to pay for them. It's such a gamble that an ordinary lawyer is going to be very hesitant to do it.

But you've got to remember the dual objective. If you're concerned with controlling the police, the final question is not how much it cost the victim, but how much it cost the cop. He didn't get $2,000 (plus a lawyer's fee) worth of pleasure out of beating somebody up. Just a $250 judgment against him may be far and away enough to deter him—and lots of cops he knows—from ever beating anybody up again.

I took a deposition from a cop for six hours once, and at the end of that deposition that cop was sweating blood. I think he is never going to beat anybody up again, just on the basis of that deposition. Cops are scared shitless when they have a suit dropped on them. It really bugs them.

AFG: And that is also an answer to the client's fear that suing the police will hurt him in his job and everything. The opposite is very common, too: once a lawsuit like this is filed against a particular cop or a number of cops or deputy sheriffs, they tend to straighten up and fly right, because they have to pay a private lawyer to represent them. In the South, suits like this often proved to be a good way of controlling the police for as long as the suit was pending.

The famous case on suing the police came out of Chicago. It is *Monroe v. Pape,* and you all ought to read it. The lawyers who handled that case worked on it for years. One worked for the ACLU, others were in private practice. Today a few of them seem to want to forget the whole thing. That one case almost knocked them out, not only out of the police-suit field, but out of the civil-liberties field in general. It was too heavy a thing to carry for too many years, and they simply wore out. But others are still filing police suits, and because of the victory in that case a whole group of other cases were filed in Chicago, and occasionally now one of them is settled without trial, or is won by the plaintiff and not appealed.

Student: So you feel it's worthwhile to bring these suits?

AFG: Certainly, if you have the facts. I wrote an article on police-misconduct litigation, which was published in *Am Jur Trials,* volume 15, in 1968, and since then many lawyers have written to me about cases they have won against cops and sheriffs all over the country.

Kates: If you're beaten up in Berkeley and sue in municipal court, you know what kind of a jury you're going to get? You're going to get a jury where half of them look like you. I mean, Berkeley is the only place in the country where police are sued and *they* remove the case to federal court. That has happened!

AFG: I just want to make one point clear about juries. In a criminal case, all you need is one juror. He can hang the jury up, and they cannot convict you. You may not get acquitted, but at least they have to go through a new trial if they want to keep you in jail, and the DA may not want to do it. But a police suit is a civil case, and in a civil case when you are the plaintiff you need twelve jurors to win in most places. You have to convince them all to vote for you, and that is very, very difficult. It is your word as the plaintiff versus these policemen. Now, to most people, you are in the wrong, because a policeman did something to you. So you are starting from way behind.

My own view is that the best lawyer to try a police-misconduct suit by a member of a minority group is a lawyer of the same minority group. The jurors are then faced, for example, with a black plaintiff who was beaten up and a black lawyer. In other words, they see a middle-class, professional, black person, who is very polite, speaks well, and fits in with their idea of acceptable society, as well as a ne'er-do-well, militant Black Panther, indigent, or whatever, from a class of society they want to be removed from. The black lawyer forces them to think about racism in a different way. It heightens the image. A white lawyer with a beard representing a white client with a beard has a similar effect.

The jurors tend to identify with different people in the room. The one they identify with immediately is the judge. The judge is their father or their teacher, and they want to do what he tells them to do. Then they identify with the lawyers on one side or the other. The ones they tend to identify with least are the clients on both sides, because the clients are involved with some problem, and people like to stay away from a problem. But between a client who is a cop and a client who says he has been beaten up by a cop, most jurors are going to identify with the cop. So, within this framework, you somehow have to build some identification between the jurors and your side.

Jim Herndon is a black lawyer who recently had a case like this, and he handled it brilliantly. One thing he did was this: The attorney representing the cop said that the plaintiff had provoked the policeman. So Jim Herndon said to the jury, "The history of black people is full of overseers from the days of slavery. And now in the black community the cops act like overseers. So the myths about overseers and cops are deep in our culture, and they are typified in a song. You know, my client is from Houston," he said. And then he starts singing:

> If you ever go to Houston, man, you'd better walk right,
> And you'd better not stagger, and you better not fight.
> 'Cause the sheriff will arrest you; he's gonna take you down.
> You can bet your bottom dollar, you're penitentiary bound.

"So," Herndon said, "you can see that this is part of the Negro culture. This plaintiff would never pick a fight with a white cop. It would never occur to him." He convinced the jury.

Student: Does CRLA try many jury cases?

Kates: No. CRLA usually isn't involved in cases that need a jury to decide what the facts were. When you file a test case, you usually don't have a factual dispute; you are practicing lawyer's law. It's paperwork, not people work. It's far easier to handle a case with straight legal issues, where you are attacking the application of a statute or regulation or its constitutionality. The trial isn't as dramatic, but often the decision packs more clout.

WHAT HAPPENS IN JUVENILE COURT
Manuel Nestle

AFG: Manuel Nestle was the editor in chief of a handbook for lawyers, called *California Juvenile Court Practice,* and has become an expert in handling the cases of kids who are busted in demonstrations or for being out on the streets late at night or for possession of marijuana.

I thought you might tell us what juvenile court is like, and how it differs from regular trial courts, Manny.

Nestle: I'd like to start with the origin of the juvenile courts. It seems they were started to help kids out by keeping them out of the adult criminal court. However, the criminologist Anthony Platt, in his book *The Child Savers,* says that the juvenile court was instituted by do-gooders who were seeking to impose their white, middle-class standards on nonwhite and immigrant kids around the turn of the century. The court deals not only with criminal acts but also with behavior that simply upsets middle-class values—for example, truancy and "idleness." In other words, people are supposed to go to school, get an education, work hard, and make a lot of money. If a kid doesn't do that, something's wrong, and society has to do something about it.

AFG: I wouldn't put it quite that way. The motives of Jane Addams and the other Hull House women who helped initiate juvenile courts can't be categorized quite so neatly. But we can argue that later.

Student: Juvenile court has jurisdiction up to what age?

Nestle: I should start out by saying that juvenile courts are obviously state courts. The law on specific points is different in each state, although some procedures are quite common. So when I describe juvenile-court practice, I am primarily talking about California practice. On the other hand, the U.S. Supreme Court has started handing down decisions in this field, and they have changed juvenile-court procedures all over the country. The leading case, of course, is *In re Gault*.

Gault was a kid who was busted in Arizona for making obscene phone calls. At the hearing, there were no witnesses and no real evidence, but they threw the book at him. He was fifteen, and the judge sent him to Juvenile Hall until he became an adult—essentially six years for a violation that would have amounted to a five- to fifty-dollar fine or not more than two months if an adult had been charged. It was so outrageous it got up to the Supreme Court, which then established that a juvenile has a right to counsel, a right to notice of the charges against him, and a right to confront and cross-examine witnesses against him.

Now, to get back to your question. In California, the juvenile court has jurisdiction over anyone under twenty-one years of age, but people between eighteen and twenty-one can be taken before either the juvenile or the adult court, and almost all go to the adult court. If a kid is between sixteen and eighteen, the juvenile court can say, "Well, you committed a heinous offense, so you will go to the adult court." Kids under sixteen must be handled by the juvenile court.

Student: If the voting age is lowered to eighteen, would that have any effect?

Nestle: Not directly. But the legislature would undoubtedly amend the statutes so that those over eighteen would come only before the adult court, and those under eighteen would come only before the juvenile court. Kids between sixteen and eighteen would probably be treated the same as they are now.

Several kinds of conduct come under the jurisdiction of the juvenile court. In California there are three kinds. The first is committing what would be a criminal offense if done by an adult, or a violation of a court order. The second is incorrigibility, where the minor refuses to obey his parents or guardian or school authorities, or he is a habitual truant from school, or he is "in danger of leading an idle, dissolute, or immoral life"; this is a catch-all statute that allows the court to say, "Well, something is wrong with you, and we are going to straighten you out."

The third is a completely different thing: dependency. That's when a child is in need of parental care and there is no one willing and able to give it to him. It might be because he's being neglected or mistreated, or his parents are committing immoral acts, or the home is so destitute that he isn't being provided with adequate food, clothing, and shelter, or—this may be peculiar to California—he is dangerous because of mental or physical deficiency. Now, dependency should not come under the juvenile court, because dependent kids are usually put in the same facilities as delinquent kids, although the statute says not to do this. This really should be handled as a social problem by the welfare department.

The juvenile-court process is sort of parallel to that of the adult criminal court, only they give things different names, with the idea that they don't want to stigmatize the kid for the rest of his life. So the kid is not "arrested"; he is "taken into custody." The police may decide just to give him a warning or a citation to appear, and not keep him in custody. If they do keep him, they have to turn him over to the juvenile probation department.

The juvenile is not entitled to make any phone calls from the detention hall, as an adult can do. But the officer is required by statute in California to notify the parents immediately. Many officers seem to be rather slow in notifying parents. They always have some excuse. The problem in trying to get the statute enforced is, what sanction can you impose for failure to notify immediately? In the adult criminal court you may be able to get the defendant off because the police violated his basic due-process rights. That's a good sanction. I don't know of any test of this as far as juveniles are concerned, and I don't know how a test could be successful, because of the philosophy in the juvenile court, which is, "We're here to help the juvenile, so let's not let these technicalities get in the way."

Once the juvenile is turned over to the probation department, the probation officer has to release him unless detention is necessary to protect him or others. If he has been arrested for some violent behavior, they can keep him. If he is shooting heroin, they keep him on the ground that he will be a danger to himself. Those are clear cases.

In California, if the probation officer wants to hold the kid, he is required to file a "petition." That's the same as an indictment or information or complaint in criminal court. Here they call it a petition, because it's supposed to be "on behalf of" the juvenile. It has to be filed within forty-eight hours of the time the kid was picked up, but judicial holidays are not counted in the forty-eight hours, which is a bad scene because most kids are picked up on Friday night. So they can be held for about five days; a lawyer can't even try to get the kid released until Monday, unless it's a big probation department that has an officer on duty day and night.

If an attorney comes down with concerned parents, the probation officer may decide to release the kid. Otherwise there is a detention hearing. There is no bail in juvenile court. Some people argue for bail. I'm not sure whether it would be a good thing, because bail is discriminatory in favor of people with money. Until we work out that problem with the adults, I think it may be unwise to press for it for juveniles.

AFG: Don't you achieve the same results, though? When the kid's parents are wealthy, don't they get him out right away?

Nestle: No, they don't get him out because they are wealthy, but because they are white and middle-class and say, "We are concerned about our kid."

The parallel to a bail proceeding in criminal court is the detention hearing in juvenile court. It is to determine whether to keep the kid incarcerated or release him pending further proceedings. You present the same argument that you gave to the probation officer: the kid ought to be released because he is not a danger to himself or to others. I had a kid who was picked up with Seconal and grass and a hype kit on him, but when the referee learned he hadn't actually been shooting heroin, he let him out. Shooting heroin will keep a kid in.

AFG: What will they do about it in terms of medical treatment?

Nestle: They just keep him away from the source of supply. They say, "What else are we going to do? We are not set up to handle the situation." If the kid gets sick, then they might take him to a hospital.

The "trial" in juvenile court is called a "jurisdictional hearing" or "adjudicatory hearing." The court determines whether it has jurisdiction, which means, "Did the juvenile commit an offense or is he an incorrigible?" So it is really a trial.

Student: Who presents the case against him for the state?

Nestle: It used to be presented by the probation officer. Then, as more and more juveniles were represented by attorneys, the probation officers felt their disadvantage, and they got the district attorney to come in. Now it varies from county to county and offense to offense whether the DA or the probation officer will carry the case. I think the more serious cases are usually put on by the DA.

Student: And who is present at the hearing?

Nestle: You have a judge or a referee, the probation officer in any event (even if the DA is handling the case), a clerk, a reporter, a bailiff, the juvenile, his parents, and whatever witnesses are brought in. That's all. The hearing is supposed to be closed to the public, unless the defense waives the secrecy. Sometimes criminology or sociology students ask to be present. In an important case, the press may ask to be present.

Not many cases are contested. Of course, not many criminal cases are contested, either.

AFG: What might be a ground for contesting jurisdiction?

Nestle: That they can't prove the juvenile committed an offense or is incorrigible.

AFG: Who has the burden of proof?

Nestle: The "prosecution" has the burden of proof. In 1970, the U.S. Supreme Court, in the Winship case, required "proof beyond a reasonable doubt" when a juvenile is charged with a penal offense. Until that decision, California, and probably forty-nine other states, did not require that standard of proof in juvenile cases. California just required a "preponderance of evidence"— the same standard used in civil cases.

If you are contesting jurisdiction, you handle the hearing as you would handle any criminal case. You raise every constitutional safeguard. You get witnesses. You do everything you can to challenge the DA's evidence. To do that you've got to keep up to date on due process in the juvenile field. Since the Supreme Court decision in *Gault,* some lower courts have handed down decisions following the due-process approach stated there.

Student: Don't you find that in juvenile court the evidence is often all circumstantial?

Nestle: Almost every kid that I've represented did what he was charged with, and the prosecution had substantial evidence. So I haven't found this. It's more a question of whether he should be punished for doing it. You see, after the court finds that it has jurisdiction, meaning that he did do it, then we get to the dispositional hearing, meaning what should we do with him? This is similar to sentencing in criminal court. At this point the defense attorney usually can bring in affidavits of witnesses concerning the kid's potential for rehabilitation or whatever else may be helpful.

So you may not contest jurisdiction, but you try to argue on disposition. You talk to the judge in chambers beforehand, and often you can work the whole thing out before the hearing.

Community Worker: I'm from the valley, and a lot of the kids and parents who come to us are Chicanos. In our county, there's no chance of getting the judge to listen to our side. He's already against the kid.

Nestle: There are about three types of juvenile-court judges. The original judge who started juvenile courts in Denver, Ben Lindsey, was one conception—the guy who really wants to do something for kids, to keep them out of the criminal mill. I've met one like that. He's from the lower East Side in New York and essentially went through his period of juvenile delinquency. He understands the situations that come before him, and he's compassionate.

Then there's the kind of a guy who wants to be a juvenile-court judge because he wants to crack down on juvenile crime, get rid of the juvenile delinquents, and put them all in jail.

And then there's the judge who just doesn't care. In the California superior courts, if there's more than one judge in a county the judges get to pick what court they want, according to seniority. Juvenile court tends to be low on the totem pole, so the newest judge may get it. He usually just can't wait until another judge is appointed so he can get off it.

So you're lucky if you run up against a judge who *wants* to sit on the juvenile court because he wants to do something *for* the kids. Then you can work things out for the best interests of the juvenile.

Of course, the earlier you get into the case the better it is. There are decision-making points all along the line. Occasionally you get in before the kid has been transferred to the probation department; then you can talk to the police about letting him go with just a warning or a citation to appear before a juvenile probation officer. But you rarely get in that early.

Usually the first thing you do is get hold of the probation officer. He has a tremendous amount of power. He decides whether he's going to file a petition and what he's going to ask for in the way of disposition. He writes what he thinks of the kid in a report that the judge sees. So first you try to get him not to file a petition. What can he do instead? He can let the kid go—and chew him out if he wants to and if it makes him feel good. Or in some states he can put the kid on informal probation. This means that without making the kid go through all the court hearings, he can say, "I want you to sign an agreement that you will obey all laws and report to me once a month for the next six months for a talk," or whatever. This, of course, is desirable, if you can get the probation officer to agree to it. But usually they have fantastic caseloads and may honestly feel they can't handle anyone else on informal probation. Also, when you're dealing with new probation officers it's problematical to get it. If they're insecure, they're going to file a petition—and many of them are insecure.

Student: Is there a lot of variation among probation officers?

Nestle: That's an interesting thing. I've run into a lot of bright, creative, good probation officers on various committees and in other places, but I never ran into these guys when I was representing a juvenile. Finally I asked one of them about this, and he said, "Well, it's because the juvenile probation officers who know their stuff are handling casework. The ones you run into in court are the guys at intake, and they're often the newest people in the department." So they don't know much and may not be very perceptive. Essentially what you have to do is manipulate them.

I try to talk to the guy in a very easygoing way and respond to what he has to say. If you chew him out, he gets insecure. If you lord it over him because you're a lawyer and he's not, he gets defensive, and his only outlet is to do the kid in. My approach is to be patient and soft-spoken in trying to convince the probation officer to do what I want, and I've been fairly successful at it.

Now, before you try to talk to the probation officer, you've got to get the facts on the case. You talk to the parents and you talk to your client. It's been my experience that you get unbelievable stories from your client. If they're unbelievable to you, they're going to be unbelievable to the probation officer, the judge, and everybody else. It's a tough thing for a lawyer to get through to a kid—or to any client. To him you're just part of the whole process that's against him. So he's going to lie to you just as he lies to anyone else. You may get hold of the police report, either from the police department or at the juvenile probation department. In the police report you may find a signed confession by your client, admitting to all kinds of things besides the thing he's charged with.

At any rate, once you've got the facts, you talk to the probation officer. If you've got any basis to go on, you try to convince him that he shouldn't file a petition. If he decides to file one anyway, you try to convince him to let the kid out until the jurisdictional hearing. If he won't do it, then you've got to fight that out with the referee at the detention hearing.

One of the big questions is whether to let the juvenile talk to the probation officer. You have to decide that right at the outset, and it may make or break the whole case. If the kid doesn't talk, the probation officer is not going to write a good report on him. If the

kid talks and makes a bad impression, you blow the case. I can't
tell you what to do. It's a gut reaction. Generally, if I can't fight
jurisdiction (and as I said before, it's very rare that you can), I let
him talk.

The lawyer has a right to sit in on the discussion between the
probation officer and the juvenile. But you've got to talk to the kid
beforehand. You may have a probation officer who's not very
bright and a kid who will see that he's smarter than the probation
officer and will let him know it. I tell the kid he's not going to get
anywhere by doing that, and he should cool it. "Just answer the
questions," I tell him. "Don't volunteer any additional information, and don't show him how bright you are."

AFG: Are you *telling* the client what to do because you're some
kind of an expert? Are you trying to run the case?

Nestle: You tell your client the alternatives. You tell him what is
likely to happen if he says certain things. I don't know if that's
really running the case. I explain the situation and leave it up to
him.

AFG: Would you leave it up to an adult criminal to decide
whether he should talk to the police or not?

Nestle: Wait a minute. There's one basic difference between the
juvenile case and an adult criminal case. The adult does not go to
the probation department before trial. There is no probation report
on him until he is convicted and comes up for sentence. In a
criminal case you tell your client *not* to talk to the police; he has
nothing to gain and everything to lose by it. But in juvenile cases
the probation officers and the judges are extremely concerned
about "attitude." What's the kid like? Does he reject the system? If
he does, they say, "Well, he's all the more in need of treatment,"
and they keep him in custody.

AFG: In other words, it's almost exactly the reverse of a criminal
case.

Nestle: That's why, whenever there's a demonstration or a sit-in,
they always announce, "If there are any juveniles here, would you

please leave? We can't handle any juvenile arrests." Why? Because you can't really fight it out in juvenile court. It's too spongy. The right things don't happen.

For instance, the juveniles in the Free Speech Movement case in Berkeley in 1964 really fouled up the works. A few kids eighteen and under were tried in juvenile court long before the mass trial of the 750 others got underway. They tried to get the juvenile case put off until the adult trial took place, but they couldn't. So there was an adverse decision on the juvenile case, and the lawyers appealed it, but the court of appeal affirmed in one of the worst opinions I've ever seen—*In re Bacon.*

AFG: So there was a written opinion, based on a juvenile hearing, which was *not* a criminal trial with a jury and all the careful protections of rights.

Nestle: At that time the standard of proof in juvenile proceedings was not even "beyond a reasonable doubt," but just "a preponderance of the evidence."

AFG: And so the 750 adults lost in their trial, and they appealed. Guess what the appellate judges said? They wrote a one-paragraph opinion affirming the convictions, and cited, of course, the opinion in the juvenile-court appeal!

Nestle: The court of appeals used that juvenile case as a bootstrap in the adult cases. So this is one of the reasons it's a mess to have juveniles around in a political case.

Now, I should qualify that. I represented some kids who were busted at the Oakland induction center, and they were fine. They were very angry about certain things, of course, but rightly so. They wanted to tell the probation officer just how they felt about the war. I said, "Go ahead." No problem. We all knew what was going to happen to those cases. Nobody was going to get any more or less than anybody else. The DA and the police and the chief probation officer had apparently decided right at the outset exactly what they were going to ask for, and it was pretty clear that the judges would go along with it.

In a sense those kids didn't need a lawyer. I couldn't do anything for them as far as disposition was concerned. But in another sense they did need a lawyer, because kids with all their bragga-docio are still a little scared when they don't know what's happen-ing. Their parents are scared, too. So, if you can tell them exactly what's going on, so that they understand the process, it's a great relief to them. That's what a lawyer can do. But I have a hangup about charging a fee when I know there's nothing that I can do for the kid except relieve his mind.

The other major hangup that comes up is: whom do you repre-sent? You're called into the case by a parent, but in many, many cases you find that the parent and the juvenile are at odds. The parent is the one who's paying the fee, but you're representing the juvenile. No question about that in my mind. Sometimes you have to lay it clearly on the line to the parents that you're representing the kid, not them; you're going to do what he wants or what you think is best for him. If the parent doesn't like it, he can get a new lawyer.

Sometimes you can work a family thing out. If you find that the kid is acting out because he is fighting with his father, you may be able to convince him and the father or the whole family to go to one of the social-service agencies around and work it out together. I don't like to get too psychological about these cases, but some-times this is clearly called for. Then, when the court hearing comes up, you can tell the judge, "Look, we've got this kid and his father seeing these social workers about the problem."

Sometimes you might get the kid to see a psychiatrist. Or maybe getting the kid a job is what has to be done, to change the pattern of life that caused him to do the thing he did. Then you can argue with the judge, "Look, I got the kid this job. You don't want to put him in Juvenile Hall. You want to try to let him work it out. So give him straight probation." Nine times out of ten the judge will buy it, unless it's a really serious charge, like armed robbery or assault with a deadly weapon, where he would have been detained anyway.

Student: Suppose the kid threw a pop bottle at a cop during a riot. Can you take the approach, "Well, it's really the fault of his family"?

Nestle: No, I wouldn't do that in that case. I'd say, "Look, that was an exacerbating situation. This kid has no record. He did it under severe tension. The tension does not exist now. Why hold him? You are not going to be teaching him anything. The kid doesn't *need* to be straightened out. That incident was just an aberration."

I put it in terms of help, because that's what juvenile court is supposed to be all about. Other lawyers probably say something else.

AFG: Do you say all this in front of the kid?

Nestle: No. You see the judge in chambers. I've had no problem getting to see a judge in chambers, and I'm convinced it's worthwhile. You just try to present the judge with a case for better disposition in terms of what the minor's needs are and what would help him out. There are really no standards for disposition. The court can give the kid anything from straight probation to commitment to the Youth Authority.

Sometimes, depending on the situation, you can prepare alternative dispositions that will be acceptable to everybody. If it is clear that the kid's problems are related to his environment, I think the disposition should remove him from the environment. Maybe he has an uncle who owns a ranch in another state, or a sister living in another city who is willing to take him in. Your approach really has to be: what caused the situation and what is the reasonable way of avoiding it in the future, other than having this kid locked up for a year, which doesn't do anybody any good?

Student: Has there ever been a test case about a child being harmed emotionally or mentally by being warehoused at the juvenile authority?

Nestle: I don't know of any test case, but this is, of course, one of the arguments you make at the various stages of the procedure. The kid is taken away from his home environment, he's thrown into what amounts to solitary confinement with nothing to do, and it can be a terrifying experience. You want to get him out as soon as possible. But it's sort of hard to argue to county officials and probation officers that their facilities are doing this to the kid. The good ones realize this, but you're not talking to them very often.

If you're going to handle juvenile cases, you need to find out about all of the juvenile facilities in the county and what kinds of training each one offers. If the judge is going to send the kid to one of them, you can recommend the one with the best program for him.

Student: There's a lot of talk these days about the rising crime rate. Do you think juvenile crimes have gone up statistically?

Nestle: One thing: an increase in crimes may simply reflect better record-keeping. Also, narcotics, homosexuality, and some other sex offenses and consensual crimes are criminal simply because the state makes them criminal. Police like those crimes because they boost their statistics. For instance, when people report a burglary or a stolen car, police maybe make an arrest in 25 percent of those cases, so they have a 25 percent arrest–crime ratio. In narcotics cases, they have a 100 percent ratio, since no crime is reported until they make the arrest.

If you eliminate those kinds of crimes, I don't know what the general crime rate, or the juvenile crime rate, would look like. Before I would talk about the crime rate, I'd like to separate out the drug cases and those associated with drugs, like stealing to support habits. It has been asserted that if we dealt in a more positive way with the narcotics problem, non-narcotic offenses would go down drastically.

I want to be sure to mention the importance of juveniles getting their records expunged or wiped out when they successfully complete probation, if the laws of their state provide for expungement. This may make it possible to get a job or get into a job-training program that would be foreclosed if the person has to say he has a record.

AFG: Manny, why do you take these juvenile cases? Do you give more priority to helping a juvenile than, say, helping people already in prison?

Nestle: No. They all need help. I guess I do juvenile cases rather than regular trial work because I don't believe in the adversary system generally. I think people ought to be able to get together and work out a good solution, instead of being at each other's throats in a way that suppresses a lot of relevant matters. I find that I do a lot better with probation officers and referees and judges trying to work out something.

AFG: Well, do you think it will change the world?

Nestle: If somebody could draw me a nice little pattern of how whatever I do will change the world, I could pick and choose what will change it the fastest. But nobody can draw me that pattern. I think we each have to decide for ourselves what in society ought to be changed. If we all do our small things in different areas, to me that means changing the world.

AFG: Do you think that is a reformist's position?

Nestle: Depends on what your goal is.

AFG: What is your goal?

Nestle: I consider myself a radical, but my problem in the current situation is that I find it difficult to construct a model of the society that I want. I want to be sure that what I'm going to get by being a revolutionary is something positive. And if somebody says, "Come join the revolution," I ask him, "What are you going to create?" Not "What are you going to destroy?" I don't get any answers.

PRISONERS' RIGHTS AND
COMMUNITY CONCERN
Fay Stender

AFG: Fay Stender puts her whole self into the movement. In the summer of 1964 she went to Mississippi with the National Lawyers Guild Committee to Assist Southern Lawyers. She was part of the defense team for the first Huey Newton trial and wrote the brief that helped win that case. Now she is deep into prison cases, having started with pretrial work in defense of George Jackson, Fleeta Drumgo, and John Cluchette—three black inmates of Soledad Prison accused of killing a white guard.

Stender: I think everyone should find out about conditions in prisons, including Soledad. Every citizen in the country ought to do something about O Wing of Soledad and others like it. The only thing I can say is that it's the Dachau of America. (Sometimes I make the mistake of thinking that everybody still knows about Dachau. One of the hardest workers in our case, an eighteen-year-old girl who has been to Cuba to cut sugar cane, did not know about it. Dachau was one of the worst of the German concentration camps, where they found people who were essentially bones stacked up both alive and dead, waiting to be cremated.)

O Wing in Soledad is just a metal tier, with a continual din, night and day. It's the maximum-security row. There are people who have been locked up for years in the little cages there, with no exercise, no sun, no privileges, no nothing. They don't know how

275

long they'll be there; no one has ever heard of most of them, and probably no one ever will. There are people going crazy in there. They yell and scream all the time. That's O Wing at this prison.

Black inmates there have written a booklet about it that's devastating. They describe how the inmates' food is shoved through a slot in the door; how the guards let people bring food to people they hate, so that they put urine in the coffee. And so on. They describe two murders there besides the murder in the Soledad Brothers case. It's really a nightmare beyond description.

It's very hard to document the conditions. Twenty people tell you something, and the prison personnel say, "This just isn't true." And that's where it rests at the moment.

Because of these exacerbated conditions, there was tremendous racial conflict in O Wing.

Student: What evidence does the state have that the Soledad Three killed the guard?

Stender: On January 13, 1970, they let fifteen people, black and white, out together in the new exercise yard, and within a few minutes a scuffle developed. A lone guard in a tower fired four shots from a carbine rifle—no warning shots, no tear gas. With those four shots he killed three blacks and wounded a fourth inmate. The rumor was that they had set up two and that for the third they wanted the ranking Black Panther in the prison but by mistake they got a man who resembled him. One inmate died instantly; the guards wouldn't let the inmates carry the others to the hospital, so they died, too.

Within two days, that was declared justifiable homicide. A half hour after that decision came over the prison television in Y Wing, the non–maximum-security section, a guard was found killed in Y Wing. The Soledad Brothers are charged with killing him. At first the prison said that it was retaliation for the three blacks, but they don't say that anymore, because the court has held that the first killing is not an issue in the case—nothing is relevant except who killed the guard.

The three defendants were examined physically within hours after the incident, and there was no blood on them, no scars, nothing. The DA's witnesses are eight or nine inmates, all of whom will probably be flown out the moment they finish testifying. These witnesses are presumably going to say that the three men did it. It appears that that's all they have against them.

AFG: Why did the defense move for a change of venue?

Student: What's venue?

Stender: Venue determines the place where a case is to be tried. In criminal hearings, usually it is the county where the alleged crime occurred. When you move for a change of venue, you allege the defendant can't get a fair trial in that county.

Now, in the Huey Newton case we did *not* move for a change of venue. Although we didn't feel we could get a fair trial in the broad sense in Alameda County, we thought any other county would be even worse. So, we felt we should make our stand in the county where the Black Panther Party arose, in the west Oakland ghetto of which Newton was so much a part.

The Soledad case is very, very different in that respect. The three defendants are from Los Angeles. They are involuntarily in Soledad Prison. Soledad is in Monterey County, a valley with a rural, mostly unsophisticated population that has a great deal of hostility toward blacks, hippies, Communists, foreigners, urban people, and so on. Anything associated with the case, beginning with the defendants and ending with their lawyers, is generally hated. A large part of the county's Mexican-American population is not registered to vote, so almost everyone who would be even remotely a peer of a black ghetto defendant or prisoner isn't a potential juror. In addition, before the defense attorneys arrived on the scene the press printed all the information given out by the prison and the district attorney. So the populace of the county had already decided that the Soledad Three were guilty. There were extraordinarily good reasons for getting the case out of that county.

AFG: Are there any local lawyers in the case?

Stender: There is one lawyer from the county, Floyd Silliman. He's from a very well-known, wealthy, Republican Salinas family. He's under thirty, a liberal, an honest young man, and an extremely good lawyer. He is receiving an incredible amount of pressure from everyone. His family has constant phone calls. No one can understand what he is doing in this dreadful case.

AFG: But it is helpful to have him?

Stender: Oh, absolutely. Aside from the fact that he is a good lawyer, he knows the judges and he knows the people on the streets; he knows the local procedure, the county clerk, and the prison personnel. The other lawyers in the case at this point are Richard Silver of Carmel and John Thorne of San Jose.

AFG: How did the defense go about getting the change of venue?

Stender: Let's talk about the relation between the paperwork and what happened.

The lawyers prepared all the papers for the motion, written in the language of the statute, saying there was a reasonable probability that the defendants could not get a fair trial in Monterey County. We explained that both the victim and the defendants occupied special places in the community: the defendants are strangers, black, and prisoners, all categories that are not liked, and the victim was a guard who had a young wife and child; hundreds of people came to his funeral or gave to a community fund for his family. We collected newspaper articles saying that the defendants committed the murder, printing remarks by prison personnel that the defendants were karate experts and weight-lifters, stressing the "animality" of the crime. Then law students went around the county to beauty shops and shopping markets and so on, listening to comments and writing down what people said. One newspaper reporter also came forward and said he had heard a great many people say the defendants were guilty.

Then the defense enlisted the help of sociologists and survey research methodologists. They drew a sample that was accurate within 1.5 percent as a reflection of the total population of the county. They trained a staff of forty volunteers to conduct in-depth interviews and a telephone survey, and put it all together in a statistical analysis. The outcome was what we knew all along: an enormously high percentage of the population was prejudiced against the defendants, didn't believe that convicts would tell the truth, didn't like black people, and already believed that these people were guilty.

AFG: How did the defense find the people to do this study?

Stender: It was like the Newton case. People in all walks of life—psychologists, psychiatrists, sociologists, movie-makers, persons who do millions of different things—wanted to help.

If you work in the movement long enough you know everybody else in it. You meet people in one case that you can call on in another. I can call people in New York and say, "Would you please do such and such by tomorrow?" and they'll do it. That's just sort of the way it is.

AFG: You mean that if you run an "open" case, people will help you, right? I worked with a lawyer once who ran a really closed case.

Stender: Was it a movement case?

AFG: Yes.

Stender: I haven't had that experience. That seems to me to be absurd. I would say that's a movement case with a nonmovement lawyer.

AFG: He's just a loner who gives the impression he knows everything.

Stender: No lawyer knows how to take a valid statistical sample unless he's also a sociologist or a statistician. There are many things like that that a lawyer doesn't know.

Fortunately, the better—or more "radical"—sociologists of late really want to start doing things instead of studying things everybody knows the answers to anyway. In the Newton case the sociologists were enormously helpful: they did studies on racism, on how many blacks were registered to vote in the county, and on how many eligible blacks were not. This allowed us to show that blacks were underrepresented on the jury list. So we drew on these same sociologists and we also found others.

Once we decided to try to get the change, we poured a lot of resources into it, in order to win it on appeal, if not from the trial court. The first rule about appeals is that you win only when you have an overwhelming case. If you just have a 51 percent case, you won't win; the appellate court will simply say, "We might have decided it differently if we had heard it initially, but this was a matter for the trial judge to decide. Unless he really abused his discretion, we'll uphold him." So we had to make a spectacular case. But we didn't even know if the people being surveyed would be willing to give us affidavits. As it turned out, we got only one affidavit from a resident admitting prejudice. People were so prejudiced that they wouldn't give us affidavits saying they were prejudiced. We had to use the affidavit of the research worker who surveyed these people as to what they had said.

In addition, we assigned a law student to research the question of venue. He looked up every significant venue case in the state in the last year, went to the counties where they had arisen, and looked at the files and the decisions. They were mostly in small towns, because that's where people are often thinking about nothing but your case, and you usually can get a change of venue. In a large city it is harder to show that the whole population is aware of and biased about your case.

AFG: Did the other side put in anything in response?

Stender: They filed a three-page affidavit from one man who said that someone from the survey had phoned him and asked very ambiguous and silly questions; he said he felt that the survey was dishonest, that the answers were not valid, and that it didn't prove anything.

As it turned out, though, we didn't win it because of the hundred pages of documents. This is what happened: the first judge, in a very egotistical and neurotic way, was desperate to keep the case and put the defendants in the gas chamber. He overreached himself and lost his cool enough so that it was possible to get rid of him for cause—that is, we challenged him for actual bias. For instance, he said from the bench that he understood the dead guard was one of the most popular in the prison. Now, a judge is not supposed to collect evidence in a case; he's supposed to be impartial. Once he had said that, he himself realized that gave us grounds to win the case on appeal.

Then another judge was appointed who was older, very nine-teenth-century, very conservative, and racist without knowing it. He was one of those people who honestly think that the defense lawyers are crucifying the defendants, one of those people who feel, "Black, white, I don't mind, I'm not prejudiced, just give them a fair trial." You know? Very old-fashioned—he feels that Communists and hippies are ruining all the beautiful things this country contained.

This second judge was not sick like the first one; he didn't have a personal interest in keeping the case. Then he got a taste of what this trial was going to be like. The courtroom was packed—law students from Berkeley, people from Santa Cruz, a large number of county residents, both young and old, black and brown and white, hippie and straight, a very mixed group. And the four lawyers fought tenaciously over every point.

The county tried to figure out a way to control the defense. The atmosphere was very uptight. One young kid sold a Black Panther paper out in front of the courthouse, and the word spread that Black Panthers were there in force planning to burn down the town.

One thing the authorities did was to take moving pictures of every person entering the courtroom. It doesn't matter how radical you are, to have a bunch of deputy sheriffs taking a picture of you every day in court, following you around the parking lot and taking pictures, and taking down your license number, is an intimi-dating thing.

Then the authorities decided that one way of controlling the defense might be to limit the number of spectators. So they had a fire inspection of the court in March. They inspected all the rooms so as not to make it look like they were just doing ours, and they said that the courtroom we were in could hold ninety-two spec-tators, plus the court personnel, attorneys, defendants, jury, court clerk, court reporter, and so on.

Then this summer, on the day the judge was to rule on the motion for change of venue, two things happened. First, the defendants did not appear, and it transpired that the judge had told the prison not to bring them.

"I don't need them," he said. "I've read their affidavits, and I know what they're going to say."

This was really incredible! The idea that in a capital case you can have a proceeding and not have the defendants there is extraordinary! Just as the judge was beginning to realize that, the second thing happened.

After fifty people, including all the court personnel and people connected with the case, had entered the courtroom, they blocked off the door and said, "This room has been reinspected. It only holds fifty people." There were benches left open, but they refused to let people in. This judge really thought that by keeping the defendants in prison and by limiting the count to fifty people, he would be able to handle the hearing.

Well, you're not going to learn in law school what to do when they suddenly announce that only fifty people are allowed in a public courtroom; you just have to use your head. So the defense lawyers jumped up and demanded to know when the room had been reinspected, and what were the names of the people who had done the inspection, and wasn't it peculiar that it was just last week, and where was the ordinance, and where was the order, and had the judge signed it, and so on. We couldn't talk about venue at all; we just had to talk about the fire ordinance.

It seemed that the rationale for limiting the spectators was that all rooms with only one exit were to have only fifty people no matter how many seats there were. So we kept saying, as seemed visually quite obvious, "There are two exits to this room."

"No," the judge insisted, "there's only one exit." It was really Kafkaesque.

So finally I said, "Well, do you mind if I see?"

"Not at all," he said.

So I walked out an inner door into the judge's chambers, and around and about, and I came back in through the outer door. The courtroom burst into applause, and the judge was beside himself. He'd lost control.

He was able to see that controlling this case was going to be a major ordeal in his life, and he wasn't willing to do it. It just wasn't going to be worth it. So he granted the motion for change of venue. But why? Because there were in that courtroom fifty people who were acting as a single instrument. That judge knew perfectly well that they couldn't be intimidated. They had been to every hearing; they were going to be there all summer long; they were going to tell fifty newspapers everything that happened; they were willing to go to jail; they would check out that fire ordinance and everything else he did. In other words, he saw that it was going to be hopeless.

If somehow an angel had given the defendants' families $100,000 and they had gone to a straight establishment lawyer, who would have done an honest job of the case—but as a non-movement case—he would never in a million years have gotten the change of venue. It has to be absolutely understood not only that there is a role for everyone, but also that some things don't happen without the participation of many people, not just lawyers.

In the first place, it was this crowd of people who brought out the latent prejudice of the county, who conducted the survey, who lent their physical presence. They consistently got up at six in the morning to come to court. A lot of them cut their hair and wore ties so that the papers wouldn't call them hippies. They spent hours on the phone; they made sandwiches for rallies; they mimeographed pamphlets; they distributed literature up and down the highways from Salinas to San Jose. They knew the issues in the case; they knew the lawyers; they knew the defendants. They had a stake in the case.

Everyone was doing a lot of what we call shitwork, but no one more than another.

That gets into this issue of professionalism and the identity of lawyers and the identity of movement people. I notice when I look around at movement lawyers that I am in the middle age-range of the Lawyers Guild. The bulk of them either are over fifty, which means that they are of the old left and have been in it for years and years, or are under thirty-five and essentially of the new left. There are very, very few people of the middle range like me. This is partially because of the McCarthy period. I suppose there must be other explanations, too.

Anyway, I find that although I am personally not of the new cultural generation—I prefer books and classical music to rock and a lot of noise, I prefer liquor to dope—nevertheless I agree with most of the younger people's political ideas. I agree with their concepts of the law and of how to approach it. I think older people still think being a lawyer is a good thing in and of itself and they derive quite a sense of gratification and identity through being a lawyer.

That is tricky; a person's identity changes very slowly. The ideas of the younger lawyers and law students have changed my concept and my "self-identity." (I think that's a more important term than "life style," because life style is really a reflection of identity.) My identity is becoming almost antiprofessional and in some sort of way that of a political prisoner. In fact, I sometimes wonder whether my effectiveness will ultimately be enhanced or impaired.

I don't even enjoy cars and clothes anymore. I don't enjoy vacations. I don't live in that world anymore. I've got so schizy going back and forth that I really prefer to spend my working time in prison. In the most selfish way, I have a better time when I am talking to a prisoner. I enjoy myself more; I am more human; I feel more love than when I am in the Supreme Court being treated courteously and having the privileges of being a lawyer.

AFG: I don't think it's a question of age. There are many differences in each age group, as well as similarities. I'm in that middle group, too, but I never was interested in either cars or clothes, and I never learned to take vacations until the last few years. I happen to have been raised by radical parents, and this affected my life from the time I was born. Much of what you said I agree with, but I think it has to do with ideology. I was raised with the ideology that the present society has two major weaknesses, it causes wars and it causes depressions, and that these things cannot be solved until the system is changed, and that it is my responsibility, and my pleasure, to participate in the changing of the system. What I do is significant insofar as it helps this purpose. Within this I've lived my life. None of this has anything to do with age.

Stender: Well, in terms of age, though, it is one thing for an established lawyer to change his self-identity and then say, "Well, I'll still be a technician for the movement and use this skill that I have." It is another thing if you are in your twenties and in law school and ask yourself, "What is the best use of my talents?" I don't have any answer for that.

AFG: Do you really have to choose? I mean, Fay, when you've put down a really tight legal argument on paper, you must enjoy it; I don't think you could do it otherwise. I enjoy doing that. And I also enjoy listening and talking to every client and trying to be helpful. I enjoy wearing stockings and making an argument in court, and I enjoy wearing slacks and going on a walk. I enjoy many other things in life, like my kids and my husband, and so on.

I accept the notion that I must change my hat very frequently every day, and that each time I wear a different hat I must do it well. I know that I do not succeed. When I fail, I'm very sorry about it. But I'm willing to change my hat as well as I can as often as I must.

Stender: But while you're changing hats you have to have some basis. For example, I don't even use the expression "my clients" anymore. I don't think I could refer to Huey as my client. That expression is going out of my vocabulary and is certainly going out of my thinking. I feel that they are comrades.

Student: What is a political prisoner? Is that just a prisoner who is a member of an organized body engaged in political activity, like the Panthers? What about a guy who goes into a grocery store and accidentally shoots the owner in an attempt to rob him?

Stender: The term is used in different ways. We used to use it to mean people such as the Smith Act defendants, who hadn't committed "hard-core" crimes, who were in prison solely because of political beliefs. And then we broadened it to include people like Huey who were charged with hard-core criminal acts, such as murder, but under circumstances in which it was clear that the entire incident and charge grew out of political militancy. Then it was expanded to mean everybody in the movement. Then it included black people who were conscious of their oppression and reacted to it. Now some people use it to mean all minority people or even all prisoners.

One meaning is people who have a consciousness of it themselves. I think we are moving into a time when you could argue that everybody in prison is a political prisoner, but I don't know what meaning that would have. You certainly could argue that all blacks who have committed ghetto crimes or have records for being picked up in the ghetto are political prisoners, or all persons whose economic situation impelled or compelled the acts for which they are imprisoned. Everybody who has militant ideas and has been put in jail for them or kept in jail longer for them is certainly a political prisoner.

Student: What kind of guy is the prosecutor in the Soledad case?

Stender: The prosecutor is very courteous and decent, except that he permits terrible things to be done to the prisoners, without any investigation or apparent concern.

It's the prison people who are determined to get the defendants. They want to put down any kind of black identity or prideful inmate identity. What they're really afraid of is that the inmates will come to think of themselves as good people.

The prisons perpetuate a fear and shame complex. When the authorities see a real movement among the inmates for self-respect, when they see the people losing this slavish fear, it worries them, because that's how they run these institutions.

Student: I've done some work in a prison in the Middle West. What I'd like to see is more public awareness of what's happening day to day to the people there. Maybe law students or criminology students could maintain constant contact with different prisons, so we would have sort of a check and balance.

Stender: You're right, you can't do it as individuals; you've got to do it as a group. Right now, because I think O Wing is a little worse than some others, and because they want to put our three men in the gas chamber, and because you can't solve all the problems of the world at one time, I would like to see a real focal assault on O Wing to get some of those people fired or the guards changed. Then we can turn to the problem at large. If we win on O Wing, other groups will take up the rest of it. We have a real political problem there of the atrocities taking place, and we need a concerted political attack. I'm not talking just about seeking habeas corpus for individual people on O Wing—although I don't mean to put that down; we simply don't have the resources to do that. But possibly, by focusing all our resources on this one wing and this one prison for the moment, we can close down this Dachau. For example, I want to call every single inmate of O Wing and Y Wing into court to tell their stories and shine the light of day on that place.

One of the problems is that there aren't enough people to figure out how to use the resources that exist right now. There are more offers of help than can be used effectively.

What we really need is a coordinating group of some kind, to define goals and strategies so that the work can be done with maximum effectiveness. The group could combine a program of services to inmates with public education about what's going on. It could develop criteria for assessing which problems will yield to negotiation with prison staff, which will yield to lawsuits—individual or class actions—which to personal counseling, and which to public exposure.

Several lawsuits have already been filed. One very important case, *Cluchette v. Procunier,* seeks a variety of due-process rights for inmates before disciplinary disabilities are imposed. Another class action, *Hutchinson v. Procunier,* is on behalf of 265 inmates at San Quentin and 100 at San Luis Obispo and 200 at Soledad and some at Folsom, who want to give money to the Soledad Brothers Defense Fund. They won't let them, although they let inmates give funds to the guard's widow. Now, that should be a really interesting First Amendment case in the federal court.

One of the beautiful things that has happened is that I've been getting letters from prisoners. I got five letters from O Wing today. I'd like to just read you one, because it speaks for itself:

DEAR MRS. FAY STENDER,

I had a brief conversation with your client, George Jackson, at Soledad, and also I had the pleasure of meeting you personally on your short visit to Soledad's maximum row, which you might remember. Anyways I was pleased with your concern about us inmates of all races, and especially of those confined in Soledad's O Wing. Mrs. Stender, I've never lied in my life, maybe just twisted the truth a little for very concerned reasons, but not many times. You want information about Soledad prison, especially O Wing. First let me tell you a few things. On the crime I was taken to prison for I was told to sign my initials here, here, here, and here—a confession they called it, with their own handwriting—and they would drop another charge they had on me, the one I was originally locked up for. I said okay, but only because I wanted to be punished for beating up a man who I feared. I didn't know a thing about laws, courts, lawyers, prisons. . . .

Well, as time went by I became more paranoid at the lost life I was brought to. . . . I didn't want no part of being around guards that angered me on purpose just so I could get mad. But I didn't know that if you show a bad attitude you can't go home, so I land in the hole—O Wing, where guards beat on guys for almost nothing, where one doctor hack took convicts by force out of their cells and gave them shock treatments strapped on a common barbershop chair, where convicts were thrown gas bombs in their cells after being beaten, to subdue them they called it, where guards open convicts' cell doors on purpose when others knew they would fight or stab or kill each other, where guards would gas a convict just for refusing to come out of his cell.

I have been in Soledad five or six times, I know all the corruption it has among guard personnel. They create everything and lie. When one con hurts another, the guards cause it, and both pay— one by wounds or death, the other by the courts. And the guards lie. I know this for a fact and I can prove it. I myself have been set up to get killed or kill others or hurt or get hurt. I have been beaten, stomped, almost shot to death, shot at with gas, burned, clawed, dragged to cells called quiet cells and beaten, refused medical attention, sent to death row on a crime the guards purposely guided, attempted suicide three or four times to stop my own hell I was forced to live in. For five years I have not seen the sun—one in the hatch, one in death row, and the rest in the hole. I was found insane, and still I was forced to go right back to the hole, where I am now at. I've committed crimes but always was forced to plead guilty because I feared what waited if I didn't— a beating by guards. Who would like to live in this kind of life, in his right mind I mean? That's why I'm now going to court to get away from guards that are nuttier than I am. They don't put me in a hospital because they'd rather gas me at San Quentin. . . .

And he signs it, "A dead inmate that's gonna try to fight back or die again."

I also received a letter from a white inmate who wrote: "Listen, I'm supposed to be one of those so-called Nazis they talk about here, but that's another one of their tricks—to divide us all."

So people who were murdering each other are beginning to see that they've got to stop fighting each other and that it's the prison that's been setting this up all along. If a man can come to that while he's charged with a possible death-penalty offense and he's been locked up in a cage twenty-four hours a day for years, there may be some hope.

COMMUNITY-
ESTABLISHMENT
CONTRADICTIONS

AMBULANCE CHASING, OVERHEAD, AND POLITICAL DEFENSE
Marvin Stender

AFG: For many years Marvin Stender has represented seamen injured on vessels. He is one of the lawyers who represent plaintiffs in personal-injury cases and occasionally represent defendants in criminal cases, including some of the prominent political trials in this area. Will you tell us how you got into this business, how a personal-injury firm operates, and some of the contradictions in your present way of life?

Stender: When I got out of law school, I decided I didn't want to practice law. First I worked on a project to study the jury system, and then I came out to the University of California. I was going to integrate all the social sciences. But I didn't really like graduate school either. I taught for a while, but I didn't like teaching. So there was nothing left to do. I was sort of badly educated, and all I had was a law degree. So I had to practice law.

I worked with a labor and personal-injury lawyer and as a legal editor. Next I got a job with a general practitioner, and then went to work for a man doing almost exclusively personal-injury and admiralty law for injured seamen. After a few years, he and I and a third man formed the partnership we now have.

AFG: How did you get admiralty clients?

Stender: The office was in one of the seamen's union buildings. We represented the union in labor-law matters, and got a lot of personal-injury cases from members.

The whole question of getting clients in the personal-injury field is a difficult one and, to a lot of people, kind of upsetting. If you're going to specialize in personal-injury cases, you have only two main sources of clients. One is referral of cases from other lawyers who don't handle P-I work. They think of you as a specialist and will send you any chance personal-injury case that they get. But first you've got to make your name as a personal-injury lawyer. The other major way P-I work is funneled is through union officials.

The whole notion of ambulance chasing stems from this quest for clients. They don't just walk into your office. You have to seek them out. Until recently, under the canons of ethics approved by the American Bar Association and adopted as law in many states, the lawyer was supposed to sit there with his shingle hung out and wait for a client to come to his office. Of course, this was a myth; lawyers didn't do this in reality. They are forbidden to advertise openly in any way, so the ambulance-chasing notion was born.

P-I lawyers do chase ambulances, in a sense. They don't necessarily chase down the street after the ambulance, but they promote business in the same kind of aggressive way that business lawyers and insurance company lawyers promote business, by taking people to dinner, showing them what nice guys they are, and impressing them.

Some personal-injury lawyers are also labor lawyers. They represent local unions in contract negotiations, fighting injunctions, contempt citations, and so on. Very often the union members go to these lawyers with their private legal matters, including their personal-injury matters, just because they know them through the union. And union officials often send members with P-I cases to these lawyers, too.

Local unions usually have one key man who helps the members with their workmen's-compensation claims or state disability benefits. It may be the welfare officer or the secretary-treasurer. When an injured man comes in, this key person has it within his power to say, "Here's a good lawyer to go to." He may give the name of the union's lawyer or of a personal-injury lawyer the member has never heard of.

Usually there is no payoff in this situation. Of course, if the attorney does pay off the union official, there is no question that it is unethical. You are not supposed to either share fees with a nonattorney or compensate him for sending clients to you. But this is done all the time, although nobody will admit he does it.

People can be paid off directly in a fast commercial transaction: "You sent Joe Doakes in last week and that looks like a good case; here's some money." Or it can be done indirectly: a union official and his wife want to spend a few weeks in the Bahamas, and the lawyer may pay for the trip. Or a retired union official may do minimal consulting work in a law office at quite a high rate of pay.

A labor-union official *is* doing a service for union members by referring them to a competent personal-injury lawyer who will do a good job and will not cheat them. But if the union official is getting paid off by the lawyer for these cases, well, then his motivation to send these people to the best possible lawyer somehow isn't there anymore.

AFG: Do you think the personal-injury lawyers on the plaintiff's side are less ethical than the lawyers on the defense side?

Stender: From one point of view, yes; but from another point of view, no. By and large, the canons of ethics are fashioned so that they catch in their net these plaintiff's lawyers. You see, the defense lawyers are hired by insurance companies, not by the corporation that is being sued for damages by an injured person. So a corporation makes an arrangement to take out insurance with a particular insurance company, which is known to retain a particular law firm to defend damage actions. A lawyer from that firm may make that deal in the locker room of a golf club, with the understanding that the corporation executive who can swing the account to the particular insurance company will be taken care of in some way financially. I don't think that under any of the canons of ethics or court decisions this will be held to be unethical or illegal. But when the comparable thing is done on the plaintiff's side, it is specifically covered by the canons.

This is the complaint of personal-injury lawyers, that the canons are directed to what is traditionally called ambulance chasing, and not directed to genteel businessmen doing their thing in more polite surroundings.

AFG: There's a history of struggle about the ethics of getting clients. The anti–big-business lawyers, the labor and civil-rights lawyers, were often disciplined or disbarred for handling the personal legal problems of union members when they also represented the union on organizational matters. Al Brotsky discussed that, remember? The Supreme Court finally adopted a realistic approach and held that the right of association guaranteed in the First Amendment included the right to hire a lawyer to represent members of the organization.

Stender: The bar associations in several states are now discussing the whole question of prepaid legal insurance and group legal services provided by panels of attorneys similar to group medical clinics and hospitals. This is a complete turnabout from the law and ethics only twenty years ago.

Student: After you do get the client, what do you do next?

Stender: Other things being equal, you want to file a lawsuit in a personal-injury case as quickly as possible, because you make money by settling lawsuits, and you can't do that until the case gets close to trial.

Student: How long is it between filing suit and getting to trial?

Stender: Oh, in San Francisco Superior Court, if you push it hard, about two and a half years; in federal court, about a year and a half. If you're just a little bit lax, it takes longer. So if you sit around before you file the lawsuit, that's more "dead" time before the case cashes out.

Every time there is a mass bust, the civil actions pending in municipal court come almost to a standstill, because they transfer civil judges to the criminal calendar. This happened in 1964 on the mass picketing arrests at the Sheraton-Palace Hotel and Auto Row, when students were demanding more jobs for black people. And it has happened a few times since then. There is a comparable situation in federal court here. In the last two years the time for getting to trial has been extended by six or eight months, and there is no question in my mind that the increase is largely caused by draft cases.

Student: Are criminal cases tried before civil cases?

Stender: Yes, by statute, in almost all state and federal jurisdictions.

AFG: And under the 1967 draft law, draft-refusal cases come first in federal court.

Stender: Of course, there are many civil lawsuits going on in the courts other than personal-injury cases. Collection agencies are very unhappy when municipal courts get bogged down with criminal arrests. They are in court constantly, to get judgments against people who bought furniture and can't pay for it, that sort of thing. They are the biggest customers of the courts.

Let me talk now about the lawyer's relationship to the client.

There are two basic situations in which an injured person can get his medical bills paid, get compensation for time off work, and receive damages for injuries or illness. If he was injured on the job or was stricken by an occupational disease, he can file a claim for workmen's-compensation benefits with a state agency—it's often called the Industrial Accident Commission. Even if a fellow worker was careless or the injured worker was himself at fault, he can recover. Payments start almost immediately, and it is usually not necessary to go to court.

Student: Is that no-fault liability, like we've been reading about in the newspapers?

Stender: It's called workmen's compensation, but it's really no-fault liability in on-the-job cases, and it has existed since the 1910s. Now the papers are discussing the proposal for no-fault liability in the second situation in which you can recover for personal injuries—auto accidents. At present, in accidents not connected with work, the injured person says there *is* fault—another person caused the accident by his negligence. If that person's insurance company refuses to pay, the injured person sues the negligent person, and the company defends the action.

Now, the worker may not need a lawyer to file his workmen's-comp claim, although it is wise to get a lawyer in any complicated case or one where there is serious injury. Payment will be based on a fixed schedule—so much for an arm that is amputated, so much for a lost finger. For example, a person who is hurt on the job in California and is totally disabled, whose earnings have been up to a certain minimal level, now gets $87 a week in compensation for a certain number of weeks, depending on the extent of his disability. The lawyer's fees in comp cases are set by the commission and are kept low in all states. In California they are roughly 10 percent of what the lawyer gets for the client. Since payments are assured, so is the lawyer's fee.

In the personal-injury case against a negligent driver, on the other hand, the amount of recovery depends on the skill of the lawyer, and the lawyer's fee will be one third of the settlement or 40 percent of the recovery if the case is tried.

So the key to understanding the whole personal-injury business is an understanding of the contingent-fee contract. Almost without exception, personal-injury cases in this country are handled by the plaintiff's lawyer on a contingency basis: if no recovery is made, either by judgment or by settlement, the plaintiff's attorney does not get paid, and he doesn't get back the costs of the litigation, either. The defense attorney gets paid—he works for the insurance company on a per-diem or an hourly basis.

AFG: Does the attorney usually advance the costs of suing?

Stender: Yes. He pays filing fees, deposition costs, witness fees, costs for producing medical records. It doesn't take long, in even a small case, to run up $500 in costs. This is aside from general office overhead. The attorney is allowed to advance the costs of the litigation on his client's account. However, I don't think any attorney sues his client for the costs that have been paid on account of litigation if the case is lost. It would be very bad public relations. And then, not that many cases are lost.

The living expenses of the plaintiff are another cost. The plaintiff usually needs money to get along during the course of litigation. By definition he comes to you in a moment of crisis. He is hurt physically; he can't work, and he generally has little or no savings, but he has mortgage payments to make, a family to feed. Seamen typically come in broke, and say, "I'm catching another ship in two weeks, but I just can't pay my hotel rent." The lawyer gives the client some money and notes it down in the files, and then collects it when the case is settled or tried.

This goes against another ethical canon, but nobody gets terribly exercised about it, because virtually all lawyers who do a lot of plaintiffs' P-I work lend their clients money. It doesn't get out of hand, because there's a natural limit to it. In my office we have about 600 pending P-I files. If we started loaning a good percentage of those people living expenses, we would literally go broke. There are more of them than there are of us. So we treat them on a case-by-case basis, keeping two considerations in mind: the total amount of money we have to shell out and the possibility of loss.

One way to handle the problem is by an arrangement with a bank. Send the client to the bank, and telephone ahead to say, "Loan him x number of dollars; we will cosign the note." Then the bank will do it without making a credit investigation of the client. The advantage is that the lawyer doesn't have to shell out the money, unless the case hasn't been settled or tried when the time comes to pay the note and the bank won't renew the note.

AFG: What if you lose the case?

Stender: Then we try to get the plaintiff to pay the note. If he can't pay, then we have to pay. But if there is a very significant possibility of losing a client's case, I would think long and hard before I would cosign the note for him.

There are other considerations even if the case is a good one in terms of proving that the defendant is liable. For example, suppose my client comes in and tells me about his starving children, and I give him some money. At the end of two years he owes me around $1,000 and his case gets settled for about $1,500. After the costs and fees are paid, he gets about $1,000. So I hand him my accounting and say, "This shows all the money I advanced you in the course of the two years; now we're even. I've paid myself back." I give him no check and he goes away muttering. He can't really call me a liar, but he still feels done in, you know? He has been counting on this money, and the fact that he's gotten $1,000 from me in the course of these two years is not clearly in his head when we settle the case.

The relationship of the contingent-fee contract and the client's money problems requires a lot of tact and some watching of ethical requirements. However, these restrictions can also be a help. I often tell clients who want to borrow money from me that I can't lend it to them because lawyers are not allowed to do that. It's a way of saying no and softening it a little bit.

I'd like to say one other thing about contingent-fee contracts in product-liability cases. If a worker is injured on the job he can get workmen's-compensation benefits through his employer. But if he was injured while running a machine and the accident was caused by a defect in the machine, he can also sue the company that manufactured the machine for negligence in manufacture. That will be a court suit—a P-I case under a contingency contract. It's also one of those product-liability cases that Ralph Nader has made famous.

AFG: Barry Williams, a workmen's-comp lawyer in Oakland, explained how these came about. The payments in comp cases were so low that workers and their lawyers searched for some way to get payments that would really cover the income lost through accidents. They came up with these third-party suits.

Stender: The contingent-fee contract in such a case can become a built-in device to screw the client.

Take a typical situation: a truck driver is injured on the job. He gets a permanent partial disability, which means he is able to go back to work but he will have a permanent limp or pain as a result of this accident. Under the California workmen's-compensation laws, he is entitled to a permanent disability rating. His disability is rated on a scale from 1 percent to 100 percent, and for each 1 percent he gets about $250 in cash from the workmen's-compensation insurance company. That award is made regardless of fault or negligence.

Suppose the worker also has grounds for a lawsuit against a third party, not his employer, for negligence causing the accident. He asks his lawyer to represent him in both of these actions. He signs a contingent-fee contract in connection with the negligence action, but the fee in the workmen's-compensation matter will be set by the workmen's compensation board. His lawyer can either push the workmen's-comp claim and receive, say, 10 percent of a $10,000 award, that is, $1,000, or he can push the P-I case and receive $4,000 of the $10,000 voted by a jury. I know of nothing in the canons of ethics or statutes or decisions that says the lawyer can't do it the second way.

AFG: What if he loses in trial? Could he still get workmen's compensation?

Stender: Yes. He can then go back and get workmen's compensation.

Student: If there's only a fifty-fifty chance of winning the case, the lawyer might lose his whole fee.

Stender: Yes. But that bites both ways. It raises another problem that really has to do less with contingent-fee contracts and more with the whole strategy of negotiation. A situation often arises where the interests of the client might not exactly coincide with the interests of the attorney.

Let's say an attorney has a case that is getting close to trial. He thinks it will be a tough case to win, and he doesn't want to be out of the office ten days in trial. He has put in two years of time and $500 of his own money. His bank account is low, and it would be disastrous for him to risk two weeks in a trial and then to lose the case and get no money whatsoever. He may say, "I'd be much better off accepting this low settlement offer that the opposition has made and to get my $500 back and a modest fee."

I think even more commonly it works in just the opposite way. The attorney says to himself, "We have a tough case that we may either win or lose. But if we win, it has a really big potential. If we can convince the jury we are right, the award will probably go way up. The settlement offer is kind of low." He might very well decide that he can afford to take the risk of trying the case on the chance of making a name for himself as an attorney who gets big P-I awards. He has two hundred cases in his office, so if he loses this one it will average out in the course of the year. The client, of course, has only one case. It is disastrous for him to lose it.

There is no formula answer to that problem. There are three

separate factors you can analyze in deciding whether to accept a settlement offer or go to trial. First, what are the chances of winning? In other words, how clear is it that the other guy is liable for the injury? This is a matter of judgment. The second question is, assuming you go to trial and win, what is the expected range of recovery? What is the jury likely to give you? You can't say an exact amount, but, using your judgment and experience, you can arrive at a range. Then you can balance these two against the settlement offer. To put it crudely, in a case where you expect to get about $10,000 if you win, and you think you have a fifty-fifty chance of winning (if you tried the same case a thousand times, you would win it half the time), if the settlement offer is $5,000, rational calculus would tell you it's a fair offer.

That's a kind of mechanical approach, because it has neglected the third element that you have to consider: the client's specific interests and need. There are as many variables here as there are clients. Is it more important for the client to have a sure $5,000 or a 50 percent chance at $10,000? That's what you have to ask yourself and ask him—he is supposed to be involved in this dialogue.

AFG: Those are a few of the complexities and inequities of the present system. The insurance companies are always complaining about P-I lawyers and their exorbitant fees. But the people with serious injuries who lose their cases also complain. That's why there is a push now for no-fault liability in accident cases, to take the luck out of P-I verdicts, like workmen's comp for on-the-job injuries. The trouble with comp is that the legislatures set the benefits so low they don't truly compensate. If the same thing happened with a no-fault accident system, the injured person wouldn't be ahead very far. And, unless we're careful, the private insurance companies would have a bonanza.

Student: Wouldn't it be better if there were complete medical coverage for everyone in the country regardless of the cause of the injury or illness?

AFG: Yes, I think that would solve it. Plus guaranteed full employment, so that even if you are disabled you can get a job. That's one of the goals in the U.N. Universal Declaration of Human Rights.

Marvin, what about the client's psychological state in relation to collecting money for his injury? Is it ever psychologically bad for a client to have his case drag on and on?

Stender: I was going to come to that under the heading "litigation neurotic."

Insurance companies and their lawyers try to create the myth that the typical personal-injury client is out to get everything he can by hook or by crook in the course of bringing a suit. According to them he will needlessly prolong his medical treatment, because the higher the medical bills the greater the settlement value of the case; he will exaggerate his complaints to the doctors and over-emphasize his pains when he gets on the stand at the trial. Although this does happen, in my experience just the opposite happens even more often. That is, I have the greatest difficulty with the stoical client who won't complain.

To give a sort of absurd example, suppose a fellow loses his leg, and when he sees his doctor to get his prosthesis (you know, his false leg), the doctor says, "How are you getting along?"

He says, "I'm getting along just fine."

And the doctor will write that down on his report.

Then when you get to trial, the defense attorney reads to the jury, "Well, here, a month after the accident he told his own doctor he was getting along just fine."

What the client really means is, "Given the nature and the severity of my original injury and a month of efficacious treatment, I'm getting along reasonably well." He is certainly not saying, "I have no residual effects from this injury."

There is nothing about P-I litigation that makes most people dishonest. Some people are liars or cheats. More people in this situation tend to make it sound a little better than it is, not a little worse. By and large, most people react in a personal-injury context as they do in other aspects of their lives: they are reasonably honest in reporting their complaints, both to their doctors and at trial.

Having said all this, let me say I do also run into the person whose injury and lawsuit assume a very, very significant position in his psychic life. Almost by definition, these people are sort of neurotic to begin with, potentially ill in some way. And remember that a plaintiff's lawyer sees clients in moments of stress. They are hurt; they have financial problems; they are concerned about their well-being and about their families. This does not bring out the best in people.

At worst, you find clients who invest into their lawsuits their entire psyches and their entire lives. They feel something like "The world has been treating me wrong all my life, and the fact that this streetcar knocked me over is just the latest example." It can take various forms. Sometimes it's just "Goddammit, they're going to pay." But it can take a really sick manifestation such as "Well, I'm not going to get better. If I stay sick, then I can really screw that insurance company and get oodles of money for the rest of my life." That happens. But it is a very, very rare circumstance. And when it does happen, it really is easy to spot.

A more common occurrence is the one Ann implied, where you question whether to tell your client to stay off work after the accident. By definition, the longer he is off work, the more the case is worth. On the other hand, it may not be in the interests of his emotional well-being to remain off work longer than absolutely necessary from a medical standpoint.

The P-I lawyer who tries to milk every case to its maximum, getting the client to go to the doctor as often as possible and to get as many physiotherapy treatments as possible, when the client obviously doesn't need this from the medical point of view, is really doing his client a disservice. The medical bills and the wage loss, which are called the special damages, are proportional to the value of the case only in a $2,000 to $10,000 case. In a serious case, like when a man loses a leg, the value does not depend at all on the amount of the doctor bill—it is a small portion of the total damages. And clients themselves usually don't deliberately maximize their complaints, for a very practical reason: it's hard to maintain that you are very seriously injured once you are back at work, and very few people can afford to stay off work and make up aches and pains.

AFG: I would add that many people care about their jobs, crummy as they may be. They really worry about someone mess-ing up their work when they are away from the job. So lots of people go back to work because it is important to them.

Stender: The real problem in this connection is the way insurance companies use the two- and three-year calendar delays in the courts to pressure clients to settle. They keep people in economic bondage when the people really have a right to compensation for their injuries.

Student: How do you deal with what you call a litigation neurotic?

Stender: If it's a serious manifestation, you have to work very closely with the client's doctor. Take the doctor's word on the objective extent of the injury. If he thinks it is important for the man to terminate the litigation quickly, you try to settle the case. I have settled lawsuits for amounts less than I thought I could ultimately get, on the doctor's recommendation that it was bad for the client to let it drag on to the bitter end. But I do this only when I concur with the doctor's opinion, because you can't always trust doctors in this regard. They tend to be incredibly conservative about litigation.

You often run into situations where the client thinks you are not doing right by him and not getting him enough money. I have advised settlement to a client whom I considered a litigation neurotic, and had him absolutely refuse, saying, "I'm going to trial no matter what they offer. I don't care whether it's reasonable or not; I'm going to make them really pay." I tried to explain that P-I litigation has a single function, and that is to get money compensation for an injury. Any function beyond that—to get back at an insurance company—is both an illegitimate and a neurotic function. It doesn't do either of us any good in the long run.

AFG: I do think there is something to be said for seeking punitive damages in a product liability case, though, like the suits against automobile companies for producing cars that emit noxious fumes. Shouldn't they pay for conspiring to prevent the development of effective antipollution devices? I think we'll see a lot more product-liability cases in which a plaintiff who was injured by a defective product seeks money damages for himself, plus an injunction against further manufacture of the product until the defect has been corrected, and punitive damages to encourage better manufacture and testing of products before they are offered for sale.

Stender: That's a different matter entirely. But if a client in an ordinary P-I case insists on rejecting a reasonable offer, I tell him to go to another lawyer. And it happens. There are fallings out in the attorney–client relationship over whether a case should be settled or how a case should be handled or personality conflicts. An attorney shouldn't feel badly about them.

AFG: In your office, does one lawyer handle a case from beginning to end?

Stender: That's the ideal. When the case comes in, we decide which lawyer gets it, on the basis of how difficult a problem it is, how big a case it is, and any specific facts on which one lawyer may have particular expertise. In practice, though, there's a lot of reshuffling of cases. One lawyer gets too busy, so we take some cases from him and give them to another lawyer.

AFG: Is this ideal for preparing the case or for the client?

Stender: It's very important for the client, and lawyers who run personal-injury mills tend to forget this. If you have several lawyers in an office, when a client comes in to see his lawyer the lawyer may be handling another case, so the client will be told his case has changed hands. If every time the client comes in he sees a different person, he may get really upset, and he won't know whom to call when he has any problems.

The most economically feasible approach is to have an experienced lawyer and an inexperienced lawyer operating as a team handling a group of cases, with the experienced lawyer deciding the policy questions and the inexperienced lawyer doing the legwork. But you see really terrible examples of this in a lot of big P-I firms, where fellows have been there seven or eight years and are still just running errands and taking depositions for the boss. So we just don't do it in our office. When we hire a new lawyer, we do it for a while to give him a minimal amount of experience. But as soon as we think possible, usually within a year, the young lawyer is given his own case load. Invariably these are the smallest and simplest cases in the office, and he's encouraged to come to the other lawyers for help. If he doesn't, the other lawyers go to him to make sure that he's doing all right. But by and large he handles his own cases from the beginning until the time of trial.

AFG: What about a legal secretary who's been with the firm a long time? To what extent would she participate in decision-making about how the case should be handled? And if you think this question has overtones, you're right.

Stender: Those overtones are gushing over me.

AFG: I should have mentioned, in passing, that Marvin is president of the National Lawyers Guild chapter in San Francisco, where some discussion of this question has been going on, heatedly.

Stender: All right, let me try to deal with that. It's a very difficult problem. You see, I was elected president of the Guild chapter here not because I had any talent or expertise or anything else, but because I was born in a particular year, and I went to law school during a particular era, and I am supposed to bridge the generation gap. In fact, that is my total function.

AFG: I don't believe it.

Stender: And as you may know, a combination of things—the women's-liberation sentiments, the feeling on the part of legal movement people that the "star" system in legal defense is outmoded and has to change, the notion of integrating one's work and one's life—all of these things combined to raise the question of the position of legal secretaries and nonlawyers in law offices, in terms of both division of responsibility and salary.

For a traditional law office—not a commune or movement firm—to deal with those problems is really very difficult. Until people like Paul Harris and younger members of the Guild forced these questions on our attention, lawyers really didn't pay any attention to them. If they were nice to their secretaries, if they said, "Good morning" sweetly to them rather than barking, everything seemed to go fairly well. But policy questions are really being forced on us now. And to be quite frank, let me say not the least difficult of these problems is the legal secretaries themselves.

I know a secretary, for instance, who is young and very competent, but she is a right-winger. Now, I wouldn't want this woman participating in the decisions that I make, particularly on political cases, because her decision would be to throw all those black revolutionaries out.

Student: What reason would there be for her participating at all?

Stender: In terms of political cases, the notion is that although lawyers have training, expertise, and status, they don't necessarily have a higher level of political consciousness or better political judgment than nonlawyers.

Student: But most of the law isn't political trials. In a typical office, why should the secretary participate in any decisions? After all, what is a law firm there for? Who has a stake in the firm? Why should you talk to her about a legal question rather than some guy in the street?

Stender: The people pushing to involve nonlegal people in legal decision-making are those lawyers who don't want to practice "straight" law. They want to practice law that is by and large political law, oriented to social change. So they don't raise the issue in the context of my office as it is now. They are saying, in effect, "Change, Stender, because your ways of doing things are really outmoded." But that seems to me too facile a solution of the problem.

Even in a straight kind of commercial setting, when you're not talking about political legal work, you can make an argument against the rigid segregation of legal and nonlegal workers that exists now. I make a hell of a lot more money than the secretaries do. I make the important decisions; they do the shitwork. I bask in the glory of whatever success there is; they just have a job. From any viewpoint of how people should work together in a unit, the present system is not ideal. And there's no question about the fact that a law office is a unit—the lives of the people in that office are really connected and intertwined. We spend a lot of time together, we make decisions together, and we work with each other.

AFG: Socially are you a unit? Out of the office, too?

Stender: No. The lawyers to some extent are a social unit, and the secretaries among themselves are a social unit, but there is no crossing the dividing line. So, the question arises: Is that really the best way for people to live their lives or organize the little bit of society that they're involved in?

Student: You were talking about the lawyer and the secretary. What about the client, then? Whom does he want deciding and working with his case—the secretary or the lawyer?

Stender: I think you're putting the questions in such a way there's only one answer. It is not a matter of whether the lawyer or the secretary should try the case. In the context of purely commercial litigation such as personal injury, as distinct from political litigation, my secretary probably knows or, if I gave her a chance to, would probably know as much about the settlement value of a personal-injury case as I do. Her knowledge would come from the same place mine does—from experience.

AFG: Could she make as good a phone call to a lawyer to settle a case?

Stender: She could learn to, but she couldn't do it effectively; that is, the other lawyer wouldn't accept it.

AFG: Is one answer for legal secretaries to go to law school, and do they ever do it?

Stender: They do do it. I don't think that's an answer, though, to the people who say that law offices should break down the professional and economic distinctions.

AFG: I think you'll find that in offices that specialize in workmen's compensation, where the law is based strictly on statutes and regulations, there are many women who are called secretaries who really handle the cases almost exactly the way lawyers do, except they never take a case before the workmen's-compensation board. They prepare all the forms, contact the clients, obtain the necessary medical reports, and so forth. But they are paid as secretaries, not as lawyers.

Student: A lawyer friend of mine says that his daughter does all the probate work in his office.

AFG: This is very common in administrative law fields. Women prepare all the papers and no one is wiser.

On the general question, I think this argument will be taken seriously when women who consider themselves legal secretaries, who have done this work for a considerable period of time as a career and who are very competent—when *they* say they want a change in the office structure, then people will listen much more. Of course, I would encourage such women to go to law school if they want to stay in legal work.

On the other hand, I think there are periods in a woman's life when she has young kids or complicated family problems and she may want a job that pays well and takes her skill for eight hours a day and no more. She cannot afford to have a job that she takes home with her. For those years, some women may prefer the strain and responsibilities of being a legal secretary but not of sharing in all professional and legal decisions in the office.

I have a question on a somewhat related topic. Do you know any women or black lawyers who specialize in personal-injury cases?

Stender: I know one woman who is a very good maritime P-I lawyer. She represents longshoremen, gets great results, has a good reputation. But she is the only one I know or have ever heard of. I don't know of any black lawyers who do exclusively P-I work, and none of the big P-I mills here has any black P-I lawyers.

I'd like to talk a little about how a lawyer with a personal-injury practice can also do political legal work. The question is: Under what circumstances can an admiralty law firm like ours do political work when it depends for its clients on a certain sort of image, and depends for its results to some extent on the good will of federal

judges, since the majority of admiralty work is filed in federal
court and tried by judges, not juries?

The most obvious problem, which all personal-injury lawyers
face, is office overhead. A firm like ours has this problem acutely
since we have something like $25,000 a month overhead to pay
the salaried lawyers, the secretaries, the rent, the normal case
costs, the telephone bills, the loans to seamen. If we bring in only
$25,000, the three partners take home not one cent. You can get
along if you bring in less than that for a month or two, either by
not taking home anything or by borrowing money, or one way or
another. But that obviously can't go on for very long. This has all
sorts of implications as to how you structure your office. We could
cut down that $25,000 by having fewer salaried lawyers or fewer
secretaries. We have a secretary for every lawyer, and the secretaries are very good, so they're very well paid.

We structure the office in this way to run an efficient personal-
injury practice. But this has a political effect. Suppose somebody
says, "Stender, we want you to be the lawyer in a political case.
This trial will take four months, and it will take six months to
prepare for it, during which time you'll be able to do almost
nothing else." That means I can't bring in any money to meet this
$25,000 monthly overhead. My answer to them is obvious: "I
can't do it—not in the present structure of my law firm."

There is a more subtle problem: could we represent unpopular
clients and retain our personal-injury clients? Again, we kind of
muddle through. Several union officials on whom we rely to refer
clients have said to us, "I saw your name in the paper. You had a
rally on the steps of the courthouse in support of the Panthers," or
"You burned your State Bar certificate," or "You represented a
Panther in court. I don't understand how a guy like you could get
involved in that," or "You shouldn't do that." It comes out in
different ways.

AFG: Frequently personal-injury lawyers get cases referred to
them by the policeman who arrives at the scene right after the
accident. Some lawyers have said to me, "I get a lot of referrals of
money cases from policemen. I can't afford to take a hot political
criminal case in which I will have to cross-examine those same
policemen or their buddies."

Stender: One very specific thing happened to me. The calendar clerk in the federal court, until recently, was an absolutely key person to an attorney. Now the judges are assigned in turn when the case is filed, but she used to sign out the cases to individual judges just before trial. There are good "plaintiff" judges and bad "plaintiff" judges, and this woman used to have it within her absolute discretion to decide what judge we got for trial. So it was very important to keep her good will, which all attorneys did in a wide variety of ways.

Well, the Lawyers Selective Service Panel was formed in San Francisco to act as an arm of the federal criminal defenders' office, to represent the draft defendants who couldn't afford their own attorneys. I walked into court one day with a client I got from that panel, and the calendar clerk was there. She took one look, and she said, "Stender, are you representing that draft dodger?" or "that Commie," or something. I said, "Yes." She turned on her heel and walked out, and she has not said a word to me since. That was about two years ago.

However, I want to emphasize that it bites the other way, too. I really hate personal-injury lawyers who tell anecdotes, but I've got to tell this one as an example. You see, the latest thing in the Lawyers Guild is lawyers' demonstrations, and when the defendants and lawyers in the Chicago Eight conspiracy case got their contempt sentences, the Guild had a demonstration on the steps of the San Francisco federal courthouse. We burned our certificates of admission to the federal district court as a symbolic gesture, not giving up our right to practice in federal courts, but saying something about the federal courts. And, as the story goes, the judges had a meeting that afternoon to decide what to do about the fifteen or twenty lawyers who did this.

The initial response of even the liberal judges was to seriously consider disbarring us from practice in the federal district court. But when my name and the names of other older, more "respectable" lawyers were mentioned as among those who had burned their certificates, the judges began to reconsider. Instead of saying, "Well, that Stender must be a really radical rat Commie," they evidently felt, "Well, if that guy, who appears before us all the time in a suit and tie, and Your-Honors us and does all the right things, feels strongly enough about what happened in Chicago to do this absolutely outrageous and impossible act, we've got to rethink what this is about and who these other people are and what they are trying to say." As it turned out, the judges decided to do nothing.

The lawyers who spend most of their time just concerned with their own self-image and life style don't like this notion of the spy in the enemy camp, because there are aspects of it that are hypocritical and servile. It's easy for me to say that's the function I perform when I make a hell of a lot more money every year than the lawyer who goes to work in a community law office or confronts the judicial system in his courtroom style. So you have to question the motives of a lawyer who says, "Yeah, I'm really serving in the movement for radical change by being kind of square and straight and doing personal-injury work," because he's also serving his own interests when he does this.

AFG: Incidentally, has it affected your practice that your wife, Fay, is one of the lawyers for the Panthers and uses the same last name as you?

Stender: I don't think so.

AFG: That's good. In the McCarthy period I think it would have.

You talked earlier about secretaries doing shitwork. And you talked with such deep feeling about the $25,000 a month overhead.

Stender: Yes, I hate it. It's oppressive. I really feel personally weighted down by it.

AFG: Don't say any more. You gave just the answer I wanted. I think lots of lawyers feel the same. I suspect that anybody who thinks pounding a typewriter is worse shitwork than worrying about paying creditors has never had to raise money.

Stender: I think there is more to be said, though. There is a great change going on now. The best people coming out of law school appear not to have the same measures of success that lawyers have traditionally had. They are willing to live on what has been considered a sort of marginal subsistence income.

AFG: That's true. On the other hand, there are many more opportunities now to get a steady salary in an OEO legal-service office or to get a government fellowship at over $10,000 a year—and that's higher than subsistence.

Stender: But, you see, I don't think it's a matter of what you need to live on; it's almost that you live on whatever it is you make. And a law practice has a way of managing you; you don't manage it.

For various reasons the firm I'm in decided to specialize in personal-injury work, to do it very efficiently, using a big overhead, and therefore to create the need to bring in a lot of money all the time. Once you get yourself structured into that kind of situation, it seems inevitable. The overhead is there; you do your work well; and you make a lot of money.

I wouldn't know how to answer the question "What do you feel you need to live on right now?" The apparent answer is, I couldn't get along with a dime less than what I actually make. I have no money in the bank; I don't have a lot of expensive clothes; my one luxury is a sort of fancy car; I don't have stocks or bonds; I don't go on vacations abroad; and I have no money. Yet I make a lot of money.

But from another point of view, that's obviously ridiculous. For example, we eat out all the time. In part that's because my wife is very busy, and we live kind of a hectic family life. Since she has been involved in these big political cases—first the Newton case and then all the prisoner cases—her earnings have been kind of low, and now they're almost nonexistent. In addition, we spent a lot of money on the cases—I don't know how much.

I have two children, and my eleven-year-old son spent last year in Paris. We have some good friends living there who invited him to come, and he wanted to do that. Well, that costs a hell of a lot of money. If I were making half as much as I am now making, I couldn't have afforded to send him. And yet I don't continue working as I am in order to be able to do this, or at least I don't think I do.

Student: You were talking about whether it's effective to be a radical "spy in the enemy's camp." But do you think you can achieve radical change in the courts no matter what style you adopt? Do you think that even in mass-bust situations the courts can be a vehicle for achieving a political goal?

Stender: We like to think in San Francisco that we have learned a lot about mass-bust problems in the last six years. In the 1964 sit-in arrests on Auto Row and at the Sheraton-Palace Hotel, the legal strategy was to bring the judicial system to its knees. Like how in the hell were they going to give 500 people due process? This requires speedy trial, and providing lawyers and transcripts at public expense for indigent defendants, and lengthy questioning of prospective jurors in each case.

The defendants decided to put on a big push. Nobody was going to cop a plea (plead guilty); there was going to be a long trial for each defendant, bringing out all the political issues; they would not agree to one mass trial.

If we have learned anything, it is that the system brings the lawyers and defendants to their knees in these situations, and not the other way around. The court system is incredibly flexible. What happened was that over a period of a year and a half about two thirds of the judges who normally try civil cases were transferred to criminal cases, in addition to the regular criminal judges, and they just tried the sit-in cases in groups of eight to twelve defendants. When the defense lawyer took the time and effort to question the jurors for three weeks and then engage in a two-month trial, sometimes he won. What this meant was that an awful lot of lawyers literally went broke—lost their practices, lost their offices.

When it was all over, the calendar for civil cases was a little more crowded than it had been before, and there were a lot of unhappy people. Most of the defendants were convicted and became very alienated as a result of what they saw happening to them in the legal process. Lawyers became alienated because they felt that they had put on this incredible show, and for what? It didn't appear to advance the movement in any way. The system was not rusted and overgrown with weeds.

So it didn't work. And everybody was mad. The judges were mad; the DAs were mad; the court people were mad. But they were the ones who came out on top. They accommodated to the problem. It's my impression that now everybody agrees you can't bring the judicial system to its knees in a mass-bust situation by putting on that kind of show. They have more resources than we have.

When the Free Speech Movement arose at the University of California in Berkeley later in 1964, there were about 780 people arrested. This time the lawyers and defendants decided not to fall into the trap of endless small trials that would exhaust our resources. So we proposed a mass trial. The other side refused, and then a series of compromises was worked out. We ended up with a single "representative" trial of 155 defendants carefully selected to be representative of the 780, and the others agreed to accept the outcome of that one trial. But we had to give up a jury trial, and this, we learned, was a terrible mistake. The judge acquitted the defendants on one charge but found them guilty on two others, and imposed some very heavy sentences. So we learned that expediting the calendar may not be the answer, either, particularly if you have to give up a basic right. I don't think any of those lawyers would ever try a political bust without a jury again.

Now, on the general question of whether you can achieve changes in the law through the courts, I would say that it's very hard.

AFG: Norman Leonard makes an interesting point about that. He says that when you present a new legal idea in court, you really have two adversaries: the other lawyer, because the self-interest of his client requires that he oppose you, and the judge. He will also probably be an adversary, not necessarily because he's a bad guy, but because judges, even the best of them, tend to be conservative about the legal system. They've grown up in a legal establishment that has certain rules, which they know. If they are good judges, they know them well, because this has been their life's business. They are comfortable with those rules; they know how to operate within them and how to operate fairly with them.

So when something new is thrust at a judge who wants to be fair and conscientious about his job, it's almost inevitable that he's going to be suspicious, or at least uncomfortable, and to ask, "Where does this fit into the framework I'm familiar with?"

Norman concludes that the lawyer who comes up with a new idea won't succeed in having it adopted even by a fair judge unless he presents the kernel of the idea in a traditional manner and within the traditional forms. He says it's hard enough to get a judge to accept something new in content without at the same time kicking him in the teeth by the manner in which you present it.

Stender: We have a case now in our office in which I would like to get the courts to change the law. Precisely for the reason you mentioned, that probably means taking it all the way up to the California Supreme Court. It's kind of scary to go to trial, spend about a week's time and about $500 trying a case, pay expert witnesses to testify, and all for the sole purpose of appealing the case to the state Supreme Court to try to get them to change a rule with a hundred years of precedent. I'm not looking forward to it.

AFG: What if the other side offers an acceptable settlement— would you refuse, and stick to your guns to get the rule changed?

Stender: No, I'd advise my client to settle, and I'd wait for another case to change the rule.

AFG: This is why changing law by precedent is so terribly difficult. The courts are perhaps the slowest way to achieve changes.

Student: Maybe the laws shouldn't be changed through the courts, but through the legislatures. That's what they're there for.

AFG: Marvin, you answer that. Have you ever thought of going to the legislature on this issue?

Stender: No. Nobody would pay me, and if it took a lot of time and effort, it would cost me a great deal.

Student: What about going to your local representative?

Stender: Our office did that several years ago, in a matter that was very significant to our practice. The point I'm raising in the case I have now only comes up occasionally. But at that time we had a problem that involved our entire practice. It came up every time we had a seaman injured on a foreign-owned ship. We needed a little change in the law to make it much easier for us to sue in that situation. So my firm lobbied that thing through the legislature all by ourselves. We got all the San Francisco legislators to back it; we attended committee hearings, and we won.

The insurance companies opposed it, of course. They sent some very high-powered people to committee hearings, armed with arguments and statistics and dire predictions that foreign ships wouldn't come into this port anymore, but would go to Portland instead. That was the visible opposition. Whether anything went on behind the scenes or not, we don't know.

Student: Why do you think you won? It usually isn't easy, is it?

Stender: It depends on a lot of things. How public a controversy it is, for one. This wasn't public at all. Nobody was interested in it, except plaintiffs' lawyers and insurance companies. I was actually a little surprised that it passed, because we had absolutely no muscle other than the fact that we personally knew the San Francisco legislators. That helped. I think also that we sort of surprised the insurance industry. They didn't have time to mount the kind of campaign that they obviously could have mounted. I think it just happened too quickly.

AFG: Another thing is that it was a legal technicality, and most of the legislators are lawyers, so they could understand what you were talking about. If it had been a nonlawyer issue, you might have had a hell of a time.

Stender: That's right. And there already was a clearly analogous law covering automobile injuries, so there was really no reason not to have this kind of legislation to protect seamen. To make an appealing argument, we described it in terms of Aristotle Onassis versus the poor longshoreman.

AFG: I think that's great. You see, if they had done nothing, it never would have passed. I've always felt that if a radical lifts his pinky finger against the system it's amazing what he can do, because most of the time nobody does anything. If the issue had been more complex, more public, and less obvious, they might not have gotten it passed. But there are numerous small reforms that can be achieved exactly in this way.

Student: Are you involved in the case of the three Soledad Brothers?

Stender: Well, my wife is one of the pretrial lawyers in the case, and by virtue of that I've become sort of a pretrial, appellate, and federal court lawyer in the case. I challenged the constitutionality of certain orders the trial court issued, and went into federal court for an order to discover evidence that the DA had refused to divulge. I can work on this kind of thing because it doesn't take me out of the office for weeks or prevent my doing other things.

Student: Do you have any ideas about the direction the movement for prison reform should take?

Stender: One of the first things that has to be done is to cut down the massiveness of the problem by not sending so many people to prison. Don't send people to prison for dope violations. Don't revoke parole if a parolee just looks the wrong way at a cop. Make the so-called victimless crimes no longer crimes. Repeal the laws about homosexual activities. That will reduce the prison population to a more manageable level. At this time, almost half of California prisoners are black or brown. That says an awful lot about the reasons people are sent to prison. Now, community control of police may do something about that.

We need to increase communication with prisoners. I don't know why prisoners' mail should be censored, or why we should continue the rule that a prisoner can't get mail from more than ten people, who must be relatives, old friends, or a lawyer. None of these makes any sense.

But when you get involved in prison work, there is a great danger of falling into liberal solutions, because it's difficult to think beyond reform. For example, the big push now is to do something about the California indeterminate-sentence law, which puts absolute life-and-death power over prisoners into the hands of anonymous administrators with no standards for wielding this power. All right, let's say this effort wins, and the courts say there has to be due process in prisons. That means that before they can keep a guy in for thirty years instead of letting him out in a year, they have to manufacture reasons for doing this. Some people will benefit, but nobody can get terribly excited about that as a significant change.

The present theory behind the prison system seems to be to atomize people. Each inmate is locked in his own individual cell and considered dangerous. The image created is that, if given the chance, he would kill the guards, escape, loot, rob, and rape. People who manage to get into the prisons to talk to the men come away with an entirely different feeling about who the prisoners are and where they're at. There could be much more emphasis on useful work and less on punishment and oppression.

Student: Rehabilitation centers today are run more on that basis, with some cells but also with people working together.

Stender: But in California, and I think elsewhere, those centers don't really perform their function. Take San Luis Obispo. You can spend your time in San Luis strolling the pleasant gardens. But if you look at it realistically, that prison is a bribe for all the ass-lickers. You have to grovel and concede the legitimacy of your incarceration or you never get that reward. The people who end up there are not the kinds of characters who build a community movement; those guys end up in O Wing of Soledad.

Some people have speculated that the prisons of a society are an accurate mirror of the society outside. I suppose they are. But when you really get into it, better medical treatment or better food or better guards or more education for the administrators is not the solution. The inevitable conclusion is that you have to destroy the prisons. Conceptually that's a difficult problem. One approach is to look at revolutionary societies and see what they do about prisons. Cuba is a good example. Their prisons are not walled enclosures, but are sort of like rural communities. They are run more like consensual societies. People are put to work at jobs that they find satisfying. It's hard to visualize in twentieth-century American society. The United States obviously is not at that point now.

FROM JUDGE'S CLERK TO
COMMUNITY LAWYER
Paul Harris

AFG: Paul Harris graduated from law school in 1969, and for the past year has been law clerk to a federal district court judge. This gave him a glimpse from behind the bench of a lot of draft cases and how the judges view and decide the issues lawyers throw at them.

He is now starting a new law firm, on a communal basis, in the Mission District of San Francisco, an area largely populated by Chicanos and blue-collar workers. The firm intends to carry out many of the life-style ideas young lawyers have been discussing.

Paul, first would you comment on some significant trends in draft cases, and then describe how you hope your firm will function?

Harris: If I were going to teach a course in law school, I would choose draft law, because it shows in so many ways the influence of a lawyer, the factors outside the law that influence legal decisions, and the response of the courts and the law schools and the legal profession to legal arguments. Draft cases have come into prominence in the last four or five years, largely centered in New York and San Francisco, in terms of both numbers and the quality of the attacks on the draft law.

Ann has often brought up the point that from 1940 to 1960 draft law was done mainly by attorneys for Jehovah's Witnesses, and their efforts to keep their clients out of prison were framed

319

very narrowly within the language of the statute and regulations. Since then, radical and liberal attorneys have broadened the approach, attacking the system as they would attack any administrative agency, approaching draft trials as they would approach any criminal trial.

This has opened up a tremendous number of theories and methods for handling draft cases. For example, if you read all the innumerable draft regulations, you find that the agency doesn't follow them. No agency follows its regulations completely, and the draft board least of all. A number of cases have been won on the ground that the agency proceeded improperly under its own rules. I was talking to a U.S. attorney the other day and he said, "I remember when Ann Ginger and Norman Leonard first came in attacking the statute itself and the forms issued by Selective Service. At that time people always used the same old defense, and we just stomped all over them. Then those two started arguing their crazy theories. I had a good fight with them in that case. Of course, you know, Paul, many of those crazy theories are now law."

Let me give you an example of how "crazy theories" get turned into law. A major decision in the fall of 1969 dealt with the delinquency regulations. The Selective Service devised a series of regulations for classifying registrants as delinquent because they had turned in their draft cards, or burned them, or failed to send in new addresses. Having classified them as delinquent, the boards drafted them ahead of their turn and regardless of their deferments. The findings of delinquency were attacked over and over by attorneys, as a violation of the draft statute and the Constitution. Three circuit courts of appeals upheld the regulation in 1969. Then one district court judge decided in favor of a registrant, and as soon as he did a number of other district court judges here in San Francisco said, "Well, judicial precedent has been broken. Now we can do it." And in this district there had been a lot of delinquency inductions, because of all the draft-card burnings and turn-ins.

So six months before the United States Supreme Court decided this issue in favor of the registrants in the Breen case, half the judges in this district were already declaring delinquency inductions unconstitutional. And some of the other judges were persuaded to hold their cases in abeyance until the Supreme Court decided the point. Months before, in similar cases with exactly the same argument made, many of these judges had decided against the registrant.

AFG: Why do you think judges wait to follow the leader? Is it that they don't want to be reversed?

Harris: No. Judges are not afraid of being reversed. In fact, lots of them take refuge in the fact that they'll be reversed. When a judge's conscience bothers him about a decision he's made, he'll say, "Well, if I'm wrong, then the court above me will reverse me." The law clerk may say, "But the next higher court is more conservative than you are on this issue." And he'll say, "Well, then the Supreme Court will set it right." Very few of them really worry about getting reversed, and most of them don't get reversed that much. The ones who get reversed continually are the ones who don't give a damn anyway.

The reason they wait to follow the leader is that they just don't want to stick their necks out, in the eyes of their peers. All the judges eat lunch together, they're on judicial committees together. Just like any person relating to a peer group, no judge wants to be seen as an extremist.

In this district the peer group has a generally liberal, intellectual philosophy—they feel they should really think about and try to figure out legal theories. In some districts I'm sure it's the opposite. Whatever it is, no judge wants a national reputation of being a radical.

The peer group is a real political factor, too. The federal judges, who are appointed for life, don't get calls from the President or the mayor—at least not in this district. There's no real corruption, but there is an almost imperceptible direct political pressure that seems to come about because the system perpetuates itself by putting people into judgeships who have done well politically in that system. So the judges sit around and reminisce, "Remember how I wrote Earl Warren's speeches when he was still a California politician?"

And then the vast majority of these judges were prosecutors, many were U.S. attorneys. They may not have the kill instinct that the district attorneys today seem to have, but they do have a general feeling about who they think the good guys are. Time and again I've heard a judge say, "Well, there's a presumption of good faith on the part of the government," even though the file in the case and the proceedings in court have shown that there's no reason to give the government that presumption this time. Judges will hold cases over for ninety days, to give the government a chance to come up with a compromise plan, so that the judge won't have to order the government to do something.

Now, another factor that has influenced Selective Service cases has been the tremendous input of draft lawyers. Often a lawyer writes a really creative forty-page brief, and the judge will decide the case in his favor but on the most mundane point. The lawyer may get upset, but the reason the judge even bothered to look for some mundane point to decide on was because he was impressed and convinced by all the constitutional and innovative points.

AFG: Let me add, because Paul can't, that I believe the law clerks have done more to clean up draft law and make it honest than any other area of law. It's a shame that law clerks never worked that hard on other significant areas; it's because the others didn't touch their age group and didn't affect them personally. They could have done it in the civil-rights cases or deportation cases or labor law, and it would have been just as important to the world, I think.

On the other hand, it's magnificent that they've done this. It shows it can be done. When a group of intelligent, hard-working people straight out of law school concentrate on a subject, they can bring out all the dirty linen and insist that it be looked at.

Harris: Also the judges have really been affected by hearing the cases of all these young men, some with long hair, some looking pretty straight, who have refused induction. Some of the judges' children now have friends who have refused induction. One federal judge sentenced a tax evader to two years in jail and said, "Every day I'm sending young idealistic people to jail. Now here you come up, and why? Because you wouldn't pay your taxes! How can I give you anything less than I give them?"

Another big factor is that we're losing the war. There's no question that if we had won the war three years ago very little would have happened to change draft law. But it looks like the Viet Cong are winning. The people are getting more and more upset about the war as it drags on and on. This country is being torn apart, and the judges just aren't as ready to send people to jail about it. Very few people are going to jail in this district.

AFG: In *this* district—you have to emphasize that. Because in many places they're getting five years, the full sentence. One guy even got ten years, five and five, on two charges related to draft refusal.

Harris: Right. But in this district, if a person refused induction, the chances are 99 percent that he won't go to jail.

AFG: At this time.

Harris: At this time. Unless he's like David Harris, a militant pacifist, who calls a press conference so people will see his example. The judges think they've got to send those people to jail, for deterrent value. Draft refusers who applied for conscientious-objector status and didn't get it are usually given two to five years' probation, depending on the judge, and after two years they can ask for a modification. They're given probation to do two years' alternate service, work in the national interest, as determined by the probation office. So the guy who is denied CO status by his draft board gets CO status in effect from the court, but he gets a felony conviction on his record, too.

Student: I understand there's a panel of draft lawyers established in San Francisco to help expedite draft cases. Is there such a volume of these cases?

Harris: Oh, yes. The U.S. attorneys have 700 cases going now, and 3,000 Selective Service files that have to be handled. They simply can't do it; they're overwhelmed. They don't even argue the cases; they just insert the files into the record. So the judges have to rely on defense counsel to point up the issues in the cases.

Occupational and marital deferments have been just about abolished, but that leaves "extreme hardship." Now, that's an area I really want to get into. You see, draft law is made by lawyers. But poor people don't go to lawyers; the people with extreme hardship cases who are black, brown, American Indian, or poor white don't have lawyers. So the hardship area has never been developed in the law.

Aside from hardship, and of course physical disabilities, conscientious-objector status is really the only thing left. Except for procedural issues. The Supreme Court decision in *United States v. Mulloy* is very important on procedure.

AFG: Mulloy was an organizer for the Southern Conference Educational Fund. He organized the Kentucky coal miners' opposition to strip mining. He's a native Southerner who was raised as a Catholic, and he is a militant. His draft case was clearly a political case, but you'd never know it from reading the pure, clean procedural points the Supreme Court relied on to decide in Mulloy's favor. It's a perfect example of winning a political case on a due-process point rather than on a First Amendment point. The very judge, Stewart, who voted against broadening the definition of conscientious objector in another recent case wrote the opinion that allows reopening of CO claims on a procedural basis in *Mulloy*.

Harris: The Court ruled that the draft board must look at a person's case again, that is, reopen his case, if he states a claim that is valid on the face of it and adds new facts that the draft board has never considered. (That's called making a prima facie claim.) Then, once they reopen his case, if they deny the claim he has a right to appeal. Of course, in Kentucky his appeal goes to the Kentucky state appeal board; maybe he would be smart to get out of Kentucky.

AFG: No, he won't do that. These guys who believe in the South would no more come North or West than go to the moon. He would sooner go to jail.

Harris: Let me say one thing about draft counseling. There are some people I probably wouldn't counsel at all—people who aren't against the war but just don't want to lose their jobs or get shot. I would rather not spend my time; they can go somewhere else. But when you help a guy stay out of the Army, somebody goes in his place—mostly black, brown, or poor white people. Chicanos are 10 or 11 percent of the population of California; they are 22 or 23 percent of those killed in Vietnam. Blacks have comparable figures. Then there are Southern white kids, and working-class whites, who don't have draft counselors. I feel I can't counsel someone without putting that problem to him. And I won't counsel anyone anymore without a political discussion of some length, covering at least a few political ideas. It's taken me a long time to get to this point, because it's very hard to inject politics without being obnoxious or giving a lecture. But I feel I have to do that now.

Student: Do you think it makes any difference?

Harris: It makes me feel a lot better.

AFG: I think it does make a difference, but it isn't always apparent at the time. I have had men who sounded very sincere about their commitment who never did another thing on the draft after they got deferments, and others who were totally unconcerned about anything except their own lives, and years later I find out that they are doing draft counseling in the ghetto. So I don't think you can measure the input with the immediate outcome, and I think you're entitled to make the effort.

Now, what about life style?

Harris: I have seven or eight things to say about lawyers and life style. First, the lawyer's relationship with his client. I really believe that a lawyer plays the role that a priest does, to a large extent: he's put on a pedestal. Lawyers understand the mysteries of the law; they carry out the rituals; they understand its dogma, and they interpret it to the laymen, who find it very difficult to understand. It's not just lawyers; I think it's true to some degree of doctors and all professionals.

Not every lawyer plays this role with his clients, but it's typical of the legal profession, including the radical lawyers. We are taught in law school, and I have friends who tell me they were taught in medical school, that it's wrong somehow to let the client or the patient in on everything, for his own good and for efficiency's sake. My law school course in trial practice was taught by a practicing trial attorney, a younger guy, who should not be insensitive to these things. He said, "You do not tell your tactics to your client, because then he's going to have all these stupid theories that just mess things up. *You* have to run the case." I hear the same thing from radical lawyers. This is storeowner psychology: "I'm in business here, you come into my store; if you don't like my wares, you go next door. If you're a big enough buyer, then we'll talk longer."

One result is that the lawyer is treating people like shit. I was medically disabled and on welfare for a couple of years, and most of the doctors I had to deal with treated me the way most lawyers treat their clients. They would not explain things to me, they ran me through, did not take time to listen to what I said, and as a result several doctors did things that other doctors had tried and that hadn't worked. Some doctors in the same situation did spend time to talk and listen to me. Listening is very important. When you interview clients, a good percentage of what they say is irrelevant, but if you listen long enough you will find out things that do not come to light any other way.

I have a friend on welfare, a very intelligent girl. Her mother had some kind of court proceeding coming up and did not understand it. She was going to the OEO legal-service office. The daughter wanted to find out what procedure was going on, and I kept urging her to call the lawyer, but she didn't do it. Finally, she said, "If I call the lawyer it will be the same as when I call the welfare worker or any agency. Either the lawyer will tell me that he can't give out that information or he'll just rap on some things that I don't understand and then hang up." Many poor people have that feeling.

The second result of this behavior is political. When a person goes to a doctor or a lawyer usually he's in trouble; therefore he's dependent on them. Psychologically, when a person feels his own dependence, he either reacts with hostility or just sort of shrivels up, which is more common. When the lawyer rattles off the law and doesn't really explain things to the client and take time with his feelings, he's reinforcing the client's dependence on him. If the lawyer works in a poverty neighborhood, his clients are people who have been traditionally, historically dependent on other people. Their big problem is that they feel they have no power, they don't know how to use power, they are afraid, and they have no concept of their own resources. If, instead of developing his clients' political effectiveness, a lawyer reinforces their subservience and dependence, I think that is a really serious problem.

The lesson of the Student Nonviolent Coordinating Committee in the South was just that. White SNCC organizers would come down in the summer, they'd run the paper, they'd do all the activities themselves—because, of course, white college kids could do it better than poor black people—and at the end of the summer they'd leave, and the people didn't know what to do anymore because they hadn't done it themselves.

AFG: It would be foolish for me to argue that no radical lawyers treat their clients the way you have just described. But I must say that I have friends all over the country, lawyers my age and older, who have always been part of their communities and have always had respect for their clients, and therefore have treated them with respect—answered their questions fully, talked things over with them. I think they would tell you that they couldn't keep clients if they behaved any differently.

Harris: I'm not saying there are no such lawyers; we just disagree about how many of them there are.

AFG: Don Jelinek made an interesting point about the lawyer and the client in the courtroom. Don has represented the Alcatraz Indians since they took over the island, and he was in federal court with one of them. He noticed a lawyer sitting in a chair in the front of the courtroom in the area reserved for lawyers waiting for their cases to be called. When his turn came, he stood up and gestured to his client to come forward from the back where he was sitting alone on a bench. Don suddenly felt the status difference this indicated and decided in future always to sit with his client in the back till his case was called.

Harris: All right, let me give a third result of elitist behavior by the lawyer, a larger political effect: Test cases or court cases that you *win* can have bad effects.

For example, in 1963 the California legislature stopped the importation of braceros to serve as low-paid and easily exploitable farm laborers. However, the practice continued into 1967, at which time California Rural Legal Assistance got a temporary restraining order in federal court to force the Secretary of Labor to stop all importation of braceros. Then, what seemed like a great victory was avoided by the power of agri-business in California, which was able to misuse the provisions of the Immigration Act to allow Mexican laborers to come across the border as green-card commuters. CRLA attacked green-card commuters and lost in the Ninth Circuit Court and the case—the Gooch case—has to be appealed to the U.S. Supreme Court.

So the attorneys win a legal decision; the system is vindicated; people read about the decision; the liberal veneer continues; and nothing changes. In my view, the only way you can really change things is through organizations, in this case like the United Farm Workers Organizing Committee, instead of bringing test cases. Or, in the alternative, lawyers should work alongside organizations like the union, instead of bringing test cases without any organizational power.

A lot of young lawyers are really emotional about this; they don't like the law, and they say a big case just doesn't mean anything. I think big cases often do mean important things for people, but too often they mean very little.

One last example: There was a skillful union attorney working with a newly formed union. A new union invariably has some capable, creative people in it with leadership qualities and real potential for development, because they're the ones who created the union. In negotiations this lawyer did all the negotiating, as he often does—he's a good negotiator. The union leaders sat there in silence. The lawyer was emasculating that union leadership. I think that happens over and over again.

Okay. Second point: relations with staff—the secretary and the law students—and decision-making within the firm. Law students are exploited by lawyers to a large degree. They're not consciously exploited, but lawyers want them to do a lot of research. Now, it's always valuable—the more research you do, the more you learn. But it's not as good an experience as if the lawyer works through a case with the student—lets him sit in on the interviews and explains them afterwards, then takes him to court and discusses trial tactics with him.

I happened to work for a lawyer, C. B. King, in Georgia one summer. For years he has been the only black lawyer in southwest Georgia. Here is a man who has one of the heaviest case loads in the country, and yet he took the time to explain things to us. You see, when we're talking about life styles, we're talking about treating people as human beings. I'm starting a new firm now with another lawyer, Stan Zaks. We're going to have law students working for us, but we've made a commitment to them to do exactly this, even if it means less time for us to do other kinds of work, because that's how we feel we should deal with people.

Secretarial staff: You can't talk about secretaries without talking about the woman question, because the vast majority of secretaries are women. In some offices, apparently, the legal secretary actually does most of the legal work, and the lawyer brings in the clients. Even where the lawyer does most of the legal work, the legal secretary still does a lot of legal work, plus secretarial work. Our firm is going to have a policy that the legal secretary receives equal pay. I can see no reason whatsoever why I should get more money than a person doing a job that is equally essential and that I don't have the talent to do. I've done little bits of secretarial work and I'm not talented in that area.

Student: One thing strikes me there: If the lawyer has to pay back a big loan that he borrowed for his education, shouldn't he get more pay while he's paying off the loan, and after that the same pay as the others?

Harris: What you're talking about is paying people on the basis of their needs. Maybe the legal secretary has four children, in which case she has more needs than the lawyer who's trying to pay back the loan. So if you want to work on the communist principle of money according to one's needs, I think that's great. We're not ready to do it; we still have too many capitalist hangups. I don't want to worry about whether my partner needs more rent money than I do because he lives in a fancy place on Nob Hill and I live in the Mission District ghetto.

Equal decision-making power: We're talking about a political law firm that spends a lot of its time dealing with movement cases.

AFG: Does that include a divorce case for a client who is part of the movement?

Harris: If he needed a divorce so he could keep doing movement work, I guess you could say it was a movement-related case. I mean movement in the broadest sense possible: working with groups like Los Siete de la Raza, like the Panthers; a People's Park bust; military cases now are movement cases; class actions can be movement cases; and just dealing with people's problems.

AFG: Suppose a movement person likes and trusts you, and then he is injured in an auto accident. Should he come to you?

Harris: Just because we're a political law firm doesn't mean we won't take any other cases. You can't make a living doing only movement cases.

The reason I was making a distinction between movement and nonmovement is to explain what I meant by equal decision-making. When I go into the firm we're hoping to do free work 50 percent of the time, and decisions have to be made about that time—whose cases we will handle, whether we will bring a test case, whether we'll farm a case out to another lawyer. There's no reason why the other people in the office, the legal secretary, the community worker—if we can afford to have one—should not have an equal voice in those decisions. In fact, a person who has not gone through the brainwashing of law school may be a lot more insightful in deciding whether we should handle a certain case, and even whether we should handle it in a certain way. If the office people live in the community, they'll understand what kinds of cases are important to the community.

And I think that we have to formalize it. A lot of secretaries, even political secretaries, have been conditioned to feel they can't make those decisions, to the point where they don't want to make them. And for the lawyer to say, "Well, you're free now; you can make decisions," isn't going to do any good. So, in our firm—and other communal firms are also doing this—we close the office and spend two, three, four hours each week discussing the political objectives of the firm.

Next point: the kind of office you have. I think when a firm has a fancy office downtown in a big building on the fifteenth floor, where the people have to take an elevator up, that increases the alienation that the law creates.

Law and the courts have created a tremendous amount of alienation anyway. Bob Dylan talks about it, Kafka and Camus have written about it. A client comes into a fancy office and, especially if he's poor, he's intimidated. If he were making $30,000 and came into a fancy office, that would be great—that's his peer group, there's no alienation. But if he's poor, everywhere he goes, whether it's the welfare, administrators of this or that, they always have nice offices, and there's a certain aura that pervades these offices and affects people. Even Charles Garry's office creates alienation in a lot of people, but that firm has a lot of expertise that outweighs the alienation.

I'm not saying that all radical attorneys have to have a storefront office, but I do think the kind of office you have does have some effect.

Where you live: I think that's a critical question if you are going to have a "community law firm," relating primarily (but not exclusively) to a defined community. That's a life-style question, not just work style. If you live in a wealthy suburb and work in a poor community, that has a tendency to move you away from political cases. If you live in the neighborhood, you may realize that the PTA is important, because your kids go to the same schools in the community as everybody else's. You suffer the same kinds of problems, and I think that gives you a different kind of perception, and gives the people who come to you as a lawyer a different kind of perception of you. There's a lot of disrespect and hostility from the community for well-to-do lawyers who live in rich neighborhoods and come in to work.

AFG: There is also a lot of disrespect for lawyers who don't have fancy offices and who live in the neighborhood and are community workers.

Harris: That's right. Not only is there a lack of respect, a few people have walked out of our office because my partner wasn't wearing a tie, and it wasn't a fancy office. There are people, even poor people, who have been brought up with the capitalist notion that a tie and a fancy office mean a good lawyer.

AFG: They think you will be ineffective in court.

Harris: But just because that happens doesn't mean that you give up.

Working hours are another life-style problem. I think it's insane for me to work five days a week, eight hours a day, and see my child and my wife only when I'm tired. Consequently, we hope we can build into our firm, after a couple of years, a four-day work week, by keeping our income very low and just shutting down one day. And if that means fewer political cases, that's all right.

Student: What does "very low" mean?

Harris: For a family with one kid, $8,000; for a family with two kids, $10,000 or $12,000—that's a high figure.

AFG: Paul, what do you think a senior draftsman, fifty years old, earns today, in a major industrial concern?

Harris: I have no idea.

AFG: About $11,000 or $12,000. That's a skilled white-collar worker, fifty years old, and you're saying that what he earns after thirty years of work is what you call a low income.

Harris: But I'm talking in relation to what I could earn as a lawyer, as a radical lawyer, if I joined some of the firms around here. And it's obvious that in my first two years I'm not going to make $8,000. The firm wouldn't last six months if Stan's wife weren't working. I'm saying in relative terms—I mean relative to a farm worker I'm making a billion dollars. But I was talking with some lawyers in a radical firm in Los Angeles, and when I said, "You and your wife could live on $10,000 a year," they said, "That's impossible." That's what I'm relating to.

Maybe working only four days a week will never work out. But more important than that are the working hours. What I've seen happen in offices is that a person has to be there a certain number of hours, or other people don't think he's doing his work. Human beings are brought up in this society in such a way that we mistrust other people's dedication. In our firm, if I come in and work eight to twelve, I might get as much work done as I would by staying around all day. There's no reason to structure your life the way society has structured it for you.

AFG: As a young lawyer I had trouble learning the value in my being available by phone forty hours a week, even if I never got a phone call. I found the discipline of keeping in touch with my office very difficult. But what is your client to do in the four hours you're not available by phone?

Harris: That gets into personal life-style preferences, rather than political factors. We have an answering service, and my partner is willing to have his phone ring at all hours of the night and to go to a jail at midnight. I can't handle that. I come home and spend a lot of time with my child and my wife. I'm not willing to have somebody call at ten o'clock and say, "I'm in jail for something." I am willing to go to community meetings at night and to see clients on Saturday mornings, when most clients are free, especially working people. Why should I have to work Wednesday afternoons if I work Saturday mornings? If a client has a problem on Wednesday he can wait till Saturday, unless it's an emergency. The big firms often put clients off for weeks.

I have two more points. Clothes are one. I'm not going to sit around the office in a tie; I hate ties. An attorney I know was working with Chicano young people. He never wore his tie in the office, and he always made a big point of putting on his tie to go to court. Maybe in our firm we'll have a clothes rack for our ties and sportcoats, and it will be labeled "Courtroom Masquerade." One person walked out of our office because Stan was there in a dirty sweater on a day he didn't have to go to court. That's something we'll have to deal with.

Now the last thing about life style: I think it's significant that draft-counseling centers were not set up or run by lawyers. One of the more effective draft-counseling centers is the one across the street from the Oakland induction center. It was a brave thing to set one up there. Law students did that. Now, why didn't lawyers think of that? Or why, when it was done, didn't lawyers say, "I'll give you half a day a week"?

Student: Wouldn't the bar association have gone after them for soliciting clients? I mean, they were handing out leaflets in front of the center.

AFG: By the time that office was opened, most of the lawyers who knew anything about draft law were so inundated that they could not have offered to give a half a day. New lawyers might have.

Harris: Then why didn't the draft lawyers set it up two years before that?

AFG: Because at that time, most of those lawyers were trying to earn a living. Several firms were in deep economic trouble then, and they hadn't discovered that you can collect fees in many draft cases.

Harris: That may be true with regard to some, but there are lots of "radical" attorneys in this area who have been doing draft law for three years, and none of them thought of setting up that kind of thing.

Student: How come *you* aren't doing something more unusual than just starting another radical firm in the San Francisco Bay Area, where people say there are too many radical attorneys already?

Harris: I *was* going to go to Los Angeles. I thought there was a need there. But my wife and the two people with whom I was going to start the firm wouldn't go. Then some people persuaded me that there were communities here that needed a community law firm, that no one was servicing those communities the way we could. That was all the rationalization I needed.

Student: Why didn't you pick a place like Fremont or Richmond, instead of San Francisco?

Harris: We seriously considered Richmond. You know, there may be a lot of radical lawyers in a city, but they may service only certain communities, such as students or old-time union people. Around here it's the big political crises that keep left-wing lawyers busy all the time. Very little of their time goes into community work. And that's what our firm's purpose is: going into a community and servicing that community.

AFG: In 1937 and 1938, the National Lawyers Guild helped establish neighborhood law offices for precisely this reason. They flourished in Philadelphia and Brooklyn for several years, and at least one black Guild lawyer has stayed in such an office since he started in practice. Thirty years later this became the model for OEO legal-service offices.

Legal Secretary: I came tonight mainly because I'm interested in the draft. But I do have some comments on the life-style questions you've raised. I worked for a number of years as a legal secretary to a lawyer in Tucson named Ed Morgan, who does draft and criminal and constitutional cases, not only in Arizona but in Oklahoma and wherever they need a dedicated guy who is ready to stick his neck out for people and principles.

I want to immediately disenchant you of the idea, if you are really sincere about serving the people in the community, that you are going to be able to do it within certain prescribed hours. Ed's clients called at all hours of the day and night. As his secretary, it was not unusual for me to get phone calls from the answering service at one o'clock in the morning, and I made the decision whether to find him and send him down to get somebody out of jail right then. He worked sixty to seventy hours a week, and he didn't make any $11,000 or $15,000 or $20,000 a year.

I am very encouraged to hear you say that the lawyer and the community organizations are equally important, but somehow I have the feeling that you are underrating the lawyer's role. I agree that what happens in a community depends to a large extent on the quantity and quality of community organization. But the legal know-how of the community lawyer can add tremendously to the growth and maturity of the community organization; and a healthy relationship with the community organization can add tremendously to the growth and maturity of the community lawyer! Working together, they are an unbeatable combination. The big question is: How do you achieve this relationship of mutual confidence and respect?

Don't think that just sitting in a messy office in a dirty sweater is going to encourage the poor people in the community to come to you for the advice and very real help they need to handle problems they can't handle themselves. That's not going to do it. In fact, that sounds a little condescending, as if looking poor and sloppy makes you "one of the boys," and they shouldn't be scared of you because you are a lawyer. The fact is, you had to do a great deal of studying to know the law.

I am delighted to see law students coming out now who have

prepared themselves to really use the law as it is supposed to be used, for the benefit of the people. They want to solve some of the problems in the ghetto by using their skill and knowledge and training, which the people who live in the ghetto don't have, simply by virtue of living there. As lawyers they can do it. And I think their clients are going to appreciate that. What you do with your legal knowledge means more to these people than just rapping with them about all the things they want to do and about how to run the case. They are going to feel that you are a true friend and they will really have confidence in you, if you know what you are talking about, if you are really professional in your manner, and if you are a real lawyer.

Harris: I don't understand what you mean by "really professional in manner."

Legal Secretary: I mean this: It is fine to create an atmosphere where the client can come in and pour his heart out and be listened to seriously. By all means, get him to open up and talk to you, to the secretary. An awful lot of people come to lawyers because they need somebody who cares and who can do something about their problems. But if it's a matter of going into court with a case, *you* are the one who decides how the case is handled. It's a very dangerous thing to leave that to your client. He knows his problems, but you know the judges, you know how decisions are made, as you were describing to us earlier.

I agree that there shouldn't be alienation between lawyer and client. But I feel that the way to give your client confidence in you is not to toss the question into his lap and say, "Now, how do you think we should fight your case?" but rather, "Give me all the facts, and I'll use my training and my skill to win the case for you. You will do this, this, and this. This is the way you behave in court. This is what you do. You put on a tie, and I put on a tie."

Harris: Maybe I underplayed the role of the attorney, because so many attorneys overplay it.

Legal Secretary: Remember, you don't just have a relationship with your client. You also have a relationship with a whole milieu surrounding the court and the legal process. And there is no reason why you can't look just as respectable as some crooked corporation lawyer.

Harris: I don't think you would say that I have to shave my mustache in order to get into the milieu.

Legal Secretary: No, but I should think you also hope to influence other members of the bar. You are not just going to stay off in your community.

Harris: Why not?

Legal Secretary: Because that way you can't influence the legal community as a whole. You're not just interested in solving a few little problems for a few people in that area; you want to create some change in the whole system of law. It's even possible the American Bar Association may someday take a stand in the right direction.

Harris: I think that's true, and I'm glad that Guild attorneys in the state bar association go to the conferences and push for things. I'm not negating it. But there are other things that I'm going to put my energy into.

I'm going to explain very carefully to my client that we have to put on a tie and play a little game in court, that the judge is a real person who takes a nap every day, because his mind is not that clear without it, and that his secretary reminds him to put on his robe before he comes into court, because often he forgets. That's a political point I want to make to each of my clients—to do away with the mystique of the law and their fear of the law.

AFG: You really want a certain level of political maturity and emotional stability from your clients!

The thing I miss in your description is the concept that the lawyer is supposed to provide service to his client, whether it is an individual or a group. I know you believe in this, but it's not coming through to me in what you have said. For example, you said you could help a client better than many firms do even if you take off on Wednesday and he has to wait until Saturday to see you, "unless it is a real emergency." But what may be just another divorce case or even another political bust to you is extremely urgent to most clients.

And I have trouble with your criticisms of older radical lawyers for the way they deal with their clients and with law students who clerk for them. Most lawyers I know in small firms must constantly relate to so many people that they are harassed. They cut corners on all their relationships and come out looking like stinkers to their wives or husbands, their kids, their partners, their secretary, or their clients, let alone their law clerks or investigators.

Harris: What I don't like is the rationalization that this is the proper way of doing it or that there is no other way. They could at least say, "The way we treat clients or the way we run our office has bad political and human consequences, but there's no other way we've found of existing."

I wanted to ask, did you have an equal salary with the attorney you worked for?

Legal Secretary: I earned a *regular* salary, and it was probably more than my boss ended up with, because he was always spending thousands of dollars to run here and there defending capital cases and so forth.

I got well paid, and I earned every penny of it, because I was minding the store all the time. I was also doing an awful lot of legal work, but the clients never knew that. And I would always discuss it with the attorney. It would have been a mistake to do otherwise. When they come to a lawyer, they want the expertise and knowledge that somebody has gained over a period of years studying the law. Simply because a secretary can pound a typewriter doesn't make her knowledgeable in the subject she's typing.

I was fortunate in working with somebody who explained everything to me from the time I started. So I learned; I had a complete law course. I was more a legal assistant than a secretary. But I was still not the lawyer; there is a big difference. The nurse in the office is not the same as the doctor. They want the doctor.

Let me say one more thing. The reason I feel so strongly on this subject is because I'm so anxious for many of your ideas to succeed. This kind of thing is so needed by the people in the Mission, and I can see all the pitfalls I want you to avoid.

You mentioned how as a law student you appreciated working

for a lawyer who would take the time to help train you. I think that is probably the best thing that you can do for your law students and for your secretary. But don't expect or ask your secretary to start out on the basis that she gets equal pay and has equal say. She has certain talents; you have other talents. Pool them. If you help her understand why she's typing certain things and what they mean, she can help explain them to the client and relieve you of that, sometimes. From what I know of myself and other woman office workers, the thing we resent the most is being treated like an appendage to the typewriter and not as thinking people. If we understand what we're doing and if we're dedicated to what the lawyer is trying to do, we really enjoy the job and do it well. We're grateful to a tough boss who insists that everything be legally right and accurate, because then he's giving the best service to his clients and we're developing skills beyond just being stenographers.

I don't think it's a matter of equal pay, because the lawyer has had years of schooling—

Harris: The secretary should get paid more, if you want to use that argument. Why should a person deserve more money because he was lucky enough to go to college? It seems to me that if being a legal secretary is a much more onerous job, it should obviously be better paid. You sit there all day pounding a funky typewriter; I'd go out of my mind.

Legal Secretary: Well, I never had a dull moment in all those years.

Student: What educational requirements do you have for a legal secretary?

Harris: I think a legal secretary with no college education but four or five years' experience in a good office would fill the bill. But we decided it would be better for our office to have a Latino who spoke Spanish and who has relatively the same politics we do, even if she were less experienced. We are political people who are lawyers, and it's better for the movement if the office has a Latino person than if it has a white talented legal secretary.

Student: How much does a top-notch legal secretary make around here?

AFG: If she's a member of the union, it's over $4.50 an hour, $165 a week. That's a lot of money in overhead.

Student: You said that the secretary will help you in the decision-making, and yet you just said you didn't care whether she had four years of college. I don't quite understand that. If I were coming to you with a problem and I knew that the secretary was going to help make the decision, I would hope that— What kind of decisions are you talking about?

Harris: On the question of whether a suit has to be filed in San Francisco or in San Mateo County, I usually wouldn't discuss that with another lawyer and I'm not going to with the secretary either, if there are no political ramifications. But on the question of whether to try the Los Siete case in San Francisco or move for a change of venue because of prejudice, a legal secretary who is part of the community, even though she dropped out of high school, might have more insight than a lawyer.

The other kinds of decisions are moral decisions: Who pays when the lawyer is fined for contempt? Do we take draft cases of middle-class kids? Do we handle welfare mothers?

On the complicated legal problems, if she has a view on it, that's okay, but we're not going to sit down every week and discuss those. Whether we're going to have the office open on Saturday we *will* discuss, rather than having it open and asking the secretary to come in.

AFG: If she's in the union, the rules are clearly defined. The secretary does not work more than forty hours a week. If she does, she gets paid time and a half. She must have certain wages, hours, and treatment. She does not take the problems home with her at night.

Harris: It's obvious that those terms are a lot better for a lot of working people than what they could get otherswise. But it puts me in the position of a boss, and puts the secretary in the position of an employee with a strong union. With my political beliefs, that's putting capitalism into a socialist context. I'm not going to do that.

Student: I think you have kind of a VISTA or Peace Corps approach: "I'm going to live in the community and help these people. I'll lower my standard of living below what it could be if I were working in a capitalist firm. I'm going to make these sacrifices because I think it's good for myself and the community." Have you talked to the people in the community to find out how they feel about your living there? Some people really resent VISTA volunteers coming into the community as missionaries.

Harris: That's a valid point. One of the reasons we didn't go into a black community is that, whether you have a missionary complex or not, you're viewed that way.

For Stan and his wife, who is Chicana, the most logical place to be is the Mission community, because of her background and his interest. We don't have a VISTA approach. We don't live in the community because we want to help poor people. If I wanted to do that I would go into VISTA or the Peace Corps or Neighborhood Legal Services. To get really personal about it, I happen to like everyday people more than I like upper-middle-class.

Besides, when you live in the community, the people don't relate to you as a superhuman whose word has to be taken because you're a lawyer and you're white. When you work with black people you begin to realize that often they will listen to you because you're white. In a political framework it retards their own development and leads you to do all kinds of funny things sometimes.

We have discussed this over and over. When we set up the firm we didn't know for sure what the community's needs were. The general philosophy we came to was that no community is unified. There are people who want to be big capitalists, and there are people who are spending fourteen hours a day organizing community action. It was obvious we were going to relate to that second segment more than to the first.

Since we started, I've been amazed at the amount of trust and respect and the number of people who have come to the office. We're not viewed as missionaries. In three months there have been so many positive experiences that I don't think there will be a problem with that. When "brown power" gets as big as "black power," maybe there will be. Right now, people coming into the firm are working with us. The money's still a problem, but we're gaining the respect of the community. People see us around, in the park, shopping, living there. We are taking part in the community.

To some extent, we're suffering their problems. We exchange baby-sitters with our neighbors. When our kids grow up and we send them to the school in that area, not to a private school, the community's whole way of looking at us is affected.

AFG: I think that's critical. The kids democratize us all.

Legal Secretary: Also the fact that you don't move in there for two years and then move out.

Harris: Being part of the community is so important. A few of us who worked for C. B. King in Georgia were talking recently, and one guy who now works for OEO Legal Services said he hates it, he hates the shitwork he does for people who come in with their little problems. And he didn't understand why he should hate it, because when he was in Georgia he was doing the same kind of thing and really enjoyed looking up fifty years of who owned a piece of property for some guy. My partner put his finger on the difference: When we worked in Georgia we were part of the community; the people who came to us were real people to us. We didn't know everybody, but there was a community feeling, we were helping people with the same problems as the guy next door had. It's like when you're a law student—you do all kinds of work for your friends and you really enjoy looking up stupid little laws. A lot of the people who come to our office now are friends from the community or friends of friends. There is a community feeling. Consequently, Stan has found that he really enjoys doing the little bits of legal work and doing it well for people. Of course, as the case load gets bigger it's harder.

In Legal Aid or OEO Legal Services, people come in and are "processed" through an intake worker. He's dealing with only this much of their lives. He never sees them again. He doesn't know anything about them. Then they are turned over to an attorney, who considers them as files rather than as people because he has too many.

AFG: It doesn't have to be like that in Legal Aid. I think it depends on how capable a person is of building his own structure locally within the larger bureaucratic structure that he can't control. An "intake worker" can be a human being who is given time to show concern as he or she fills in a form. So can a lawyer. It isn't easy or automatic, but it can be done. Many private firms have as many clients coming in as an OEO office does.

Harris: We had a meeting of one of the Latino community groups, a defense organization, in our office. They saw the informality of the office, all our posters, and after a while people really began to take part in the discussion. In this general informal atmosphere you can bring people out, encourage their self-confidence.

At the same time, we don't pretend to be stupid. We come off as confident people, I think. Often we very specifically make a point that we have expertise in a particular area. And people feel confidence in us. We stand behind them with legal skills, to help build a movement of people struggling for change.

THE BREAD AND BUTTER OF PRACTICE
Henry Elson

AFG: Henry Elson is a lawyer, as opposed to a "rhetorician." He earns his living by the law—every day. The other day we had a role-playing session about an initial client interview, and none of these law students thought to ask the "client" about money or to mention fees. Finally one of the non–law students thought to bring that topic up. So I knew I was right to ask you to come talk about how a lawyer earns his living.

Elson: I really welcomed this opportunity, because it made me stop and think about what I'm doing professionally. But I also quickly got defensive, because I don't really like the idea of being the only person who will talk to you about money.

AFG: No, you aren't.

Elson: Good. Because I'm not really that good at making money, so it wouldn't be such a good education, and I'm not really that interested in it as a lawyer. I'm most interested in telling you what a general practitioner does.

Let me tell you a little bit about myself, so that you can get some idea of the context of my practice experience. I've been a lawyer for eighteen years, in Berkeley all the time. When I graduated I worked for one year for a black lawyer. At the end of that year,

1953, the House Un-American Activities Committee came to the San Francisco Bay Area. Some of my old friends were subpoenaed, and they asked me to represent them. I said of course I would. I checked with my employer, just to make sure it was okay with him. But it wasn't okay with him, because he felt that it would harm his practice. Those were the Joe McCarthy days, and everybody was nervous.

As a result I was fired, but that gave me the opportunity to open my own office, because I couldn't get a job. So for about five years I kind of hacked out a life on my own. It was an old-fashioned neighborhood practice in a neighborhood with a lot of working people and a lot of minority-group people. You had to walk up two flights of stairs to get there, and people would puff for the first few minutes of each interview.

After five years I formed a partnership with a friend of mine who was here in downtown Berkeley. It's a general practice. We handle personal injury, workmen's compensation, domestic relations (which includes divorce, annulment, and adoption), probate (which includes guardianships and estates), collection (where people are being hassled by collection agencies and where people are trying to hassle people who owe them money), wills and estate planning (and even trusts now, occasionally), income tax criminal cases, business cases (partnership agreements, buy and sell agreements), landlord–tenant law (which is big in Berkeley today), contracts (particularly construction contracts), administrative law (like permits for building houses, zoning, Public Utilities Commission problems), welfare-rights problems, real-estate transactions, and Selective Service matters.

Probably the major problem of being a general practitioner today is that you have to handle all those different areas, and it's too complicated to know everything. You don't want to turn down clients, because you'll chase them away, but sometimes if you handle them without a high degree of specialized knowledge you're afraid that you won't do a good job. The general practitioner has to make some very delicate judgments about when to handle a case himself and when to ask for assistance from someone who is more specialized. When you get a good personal-injury case, you hate like hell to have to call in a specialist and share the fee with him, especially since you can settle a lot of those cases very competently yourself without going to trial.

That area of judgment and discretion is something that lawyers, like all human beings who have responsibility, have to carefully develop. Wisdom is really what we're talking about. Common sense would be a less jazzy way of saying it. But that's where you really separate good lawyers from bad lawyers.

I wrote down a list of characteristics of a lawyer, good and bad. I really had some fun with this. I have on top of the "good" list: compassion. When a client comes to see a lawyer, there's usually something wrong. He doesn't usually go to see a lawyer because something good has happened. He's in trouble; he's scared that it's going to cost him a lot of money; he's not familiar with the law, and he's worried something bad is going to happen to him. A lot of lawyers forget about that entirely and proceed to treat the client as if he were coming in to buy two pounds of hamburger. I certainly hope that's something you think about as the years go by—that the client is not coming to you for a quantitative service. He's coming for something far more complicated and ephemeral. People see lawyers so seldom in their lives that it's a big event. If they're treated shabbily, or rudely, or superficially, not only does it give lawyers a lousy reputation, which is not so important, but it also damages both the client's and the lawyer's lives. That sounds a bit sentimental, but I think it's significant. It's easy to get angry at your client, to lose patience, not to believe him, to dismiss what he's saying as triviality or not worthy of consideration; but the person asking you for services has problems beyond the quantitative problems he presents to you.

Now, there is a point where compassion can be overdone and you can overidentify with a client. Then you cease to be useful, because if you quiver when he quivers, and quake when he quakes, he might as well stay home and do it himself.

In domestic relations, which I do more of than anything else, the human relationship is tremendously important. A person who comes to a lawyer wants more than just an accountant or an executioner—he really wants to be understood, to be loved, to be appreciated. It's very difficult to do that without interfering with the professional relationship. It takes some intuition and some restraint to get your own resources into operation.

Student: Is it necessary to have a lawyer in a divorce case?

Elson: It's not necessary to have a lawyer in any case; you can represent yourself *in propria persona.* But it's foolhardy not to have a lawyer these days, in my opinion. I have instructed people how to proceed without a lawyer, for economic reasons or in small-claims court. But when things get a little more complicated than that, when they will have long-range effects on a person or his children or his property or his rights, I would generally advise against it. Life is too complicated and lawyers are too skilled. Statistically I would say it would be overwhelmingly better to have a lawyer.

AFG: Essentially what happens in a divorce case is that human emotions are turned into money problems. You no longer ask your husband, "Do you love me?" because he's already left or you've kicked him out. Instead you're asking, "How much money is that bastard going to give me for the kids?" But what you're still fighting about is your feeling for him or his feeling for you.

Almost nobody is capable of looking at his own situation in any objective way at that time. Certainly no one's capable of projecting it objectively for the next eighteen years (if there are young children involved). You have to have an outside person. A priest or a minister or a social worker will worry about your psyche, but a lawyer should be able to think about both your psyche and the legal and financial relationships.

Elson: A lawyer's relationship with his client is a fiduciary rela-tionship—a confidential relationship with utmost trust, where he really has to carry a great burden. People take it for granted, and they forget how important it is.

Actually confidentiality doesn't work well, particularly in a town like Berkeley, where people have a lot of friends in common, belong to the same organizations, and go on the same peace marches. There's a tendency to start talking too freely under the influence of the third martini or the third joint.

That's a crucial problem, because when a guy walks into your office, he should have an absolute guarantee that what he tells you won't get out, even under torture. Well, when they offer you the lead enema, you may change your mind, but short of that a lawyer should be absolutely convinced of the importance of the confidential relationship. That means he doesn't tell his wife either. With my wife, I just simply laid down the rule that I would not talk about my cases at home. I told her, "For one thing, I'm not interested in talking about them anymore when I get home; for another, it's illegal and unethical to do that." She gets the gossip from her friends about who is getting divorced and who is shacking up with whom, or it comes out in court.

AFG: I asked to have Henry's wife come today, too, so that we could get her views. Why didn't she come, Henry?

Elson: Well, I thought it would be inappropriate, although she didn't think it would be a bad idea. If she were to describe herself, she would not call herself Mrs. Henry Elson. On the contrary, I could easily be called Mr. Evelyn Elson. She's a working mother; she has worked since we had children. She's brighter and more intelligent than I am, so I knew she'd end up monopolizing the whole conversation.

AFG: I think it's interesting that your wife is a teacher and so is Ed Dawley's, and Frank McTernan's, and Vic Van Bourg's, and several of the other lawyers' wives are also professional women.

Student: Getting back to the confidential relationship, do you tell your partners or your secretary what the client tells you?

Elson: You have to be able to talk to your partners about it. In fact, you have an obligation to. You might die, and your partner has to know what to do, what the subtleties of the case are. You don't write everything down in your files, for lots of reasons—because of laziness, or because the story is too interesting to write, or because people might get into your files illegally.

Your secretary is covered by your confidential relationship with the client, and you have to tell her that.

Student: You mean if your secretary is subpoenaed—

Elson: She has the same privilege of not having to disclose.

Student: How about a private detective?

Elson: I don't think that privilege extends to a detective. And that's a problem, because detectives know a lot of things about the client. Of course, they maintain that they'll never tell.

AFG: Social workers are not covered, either, which is a very serious matter.

Elson: That's right—particularly these days, when psychiatric social workers do the same thing as psychiatrists.

AFG: During the McCarthy period, some psychiatrists did tell about their patients in political cases.

Elson: Reliability is another thing on my list of good characteristics. You know the cliché about politicians: that if a politician says he's going to do something, he'll do it even though there's no written agreement, because if he doesn't follow through, nobody will ever believe him anymore.

Student: Maybe that's why nobody ever believes politicians.

Elson: Among themselves, though, they supposedly do honor those deals they make. And lawyers have to have the willingness to stick by their verbal promises. Without reliability in lawyers, it would be just a disaster. That's the oil that makes the wheels go. Honesty is always a good thing, but specifically it's very functional. With most lawyers, if they say, "That's a deal," it's a deal, and they'll fire a client if he backs out of his part. When the district attorney says, "Well, I won't bring this witness in if you don't bring that witness in," it's a deal. The punishment for violating that sort of thing is hard to calculate. It's your reputation, your future credibility, and the things you won't be able to get in the future.

I suppose that there might be times when a lawyer would have to forsake that for other values, but I haven't seen that time yet. It's your next client that you also have to think of. Suppose you represent to a judge, on a question of bail reduction, that your client has lived in the community for twenty years and is an upstanding member of the church. The judge reduces the bail, and then the guy jumps bail and it turns out that all the representations you made

weren't true. Next time you make a representation for bail reduction, the judge is not going to be very helpful.

I think you have to be honest with your clients too; that does
not mean you have to tell them everything, just as you don't tell
your kids everything, but you don't mislead them.

You should be honest with other lawyers and honest with your
creditors—that's important. Some lawyers never pay their bills. A
reporter will be hired to take down the transcript of a deposition,
and the lawyer won't pay him till the end of the case, months or
years later. When a lawyer just trades on other people's services
and pays at the last minute, he's really borrowing money without
paying interest to people who are also trying to make a living. You
can almost separate good and bad lawyers by the way they treat
the people to whom they owe money. One of our secretaries is very
meticulous. This woman pays the bills as they come in, you know,
and it's kind of terrifying. We say, "Why don't you wait till the first
of the month, in orderly fashion?" by which we really mean, "Just
give us another twenty days." It's kind of an office joke, but if I
really didn't like it I would tell her not to.

A crucial thing for a lawyer to be a good lawyer, to render good
service to his clients, is his ability and willingness to prepare his
case. That's the thing that I fondly wish I did better. You watch
some lawyers go into court, and when they call the case the guy's
so unprepared that the client has to nudge him, "That's us,
buddy."

You have to know the material. You have to know the facts, you
have to take detailed factual statements or get the client to do it
himself or herself. I've made it a practice recently to dictate memos
to myself. My files are full of memos recording what happened,
phone conversations, bringing things up to date. Because after a
while you get so busy you forget who your clients are. You see
them in the street, and they say hello and you think, "Who the hell
is that?" And then you realize that's the case that's coming up next
Wednesday! Well, that's an exaggeration, but it has some truth to it.

You have to know the law, and that's very difficult, because
there's so goddam much. But diligence and careful treatment of the
subject matter are essential. It's not easy. After a couple of years a
lawyer is wont to get sloppy. The pressure is so great, and you tend
to give your energy to the thing that's creating the most anxiety.
You tend to forget about or put off a lot.

That's probably the worst thing lawyers have to deal with: procrastination. Because when you're involved in a case it's your responsibility and you worry about it. And how do people treat the things they worry about? They tend to put them on the side, you know? They say, "I'll get to that a little bit later, when I have all my strength." Sometimes that will go on for weeks and months; if it weren't for the statute of limitations, it would go on forever. It's a problem you all face as students, I'm sure, about studying and doing papers. It is a crucial problem for lawyers.

AFG: On the other hand, a seasoned lawyer can help an inexperienced client by pointing out that every single bridge does not have to be crossed, because it may never be reached. I learned that with some difficulty from Victor Rabinowitz when I lived in New York. Some problems that might arise in litigation in fact never do. Of course, this can be carried to the extreme of never facing fundamental questions and always temporizing.

Elson: Right. A bad characteristic is litigiousness. That means an overdesire to go to court and fight. I think that usually it's bad for your client if you have to go to court, if you can't settle the case. Of course, some cases can't be settled.

AFG: They tried to settle the Oakland Seven antidraft conspiracy case. They came fairly close.

Student: How do you mean settle?

AFG: Agree to plead guilty if the charge were reduced to a misdemeanor.

Elson: We would have settled the Free Speech Movement case if the prosecutor had let us—no question about it. It is generally desirable to avoid litigation, as long as you don't give up any of your ammunition. In civil cases very often it's just a disaster to try cases. It's too expensive.

Some lawyers can't settle a case to save themselves. I mean, in a case that two little kids on the street could get together on, some lawyers are so proud or so dumb or so egocentric that they can't budge. Or they're so rushed they don't give any time to it. So they end up settling things at the courthouse steps, after going through depositions and raking everybody over the coals. The client is broke, he's completely pushed out of shape emotionally, and the case could have been settled at the beginning.

That's one thing I've done very well in; I'm an excellent case settler. In fact, I wonder whether I am doing something wrong to settle so many cases. But my associates and partners think I do very well. It's because I try to bring that spirit of understanding into a case. To a certain degree, it's personality, but you can learn it. Even with difficult people I've been able to reach agreements, just by perseverance, by reducing the hostility and not jumping so quickly when a lawyer says something I don't like—not getting into a combatant situation.

AFG: How much did you learn in law school about negotiating settlements?

Elson: I don't think it was ever mentioned. Law schools do not cover any of the things I've talked about so far. They are not oriented that way. They may be changing. Law students seem better than they used to be. They are certainly a better bunch than when I was there. God! I was the class radical. What a poverty-stricken bunch they were, ideologically.

Another bad characteristic is rudeness. That may seem like a minor thing, but it goes back to compassion. Just put yourself in the place of a client sitting in a lawyer's office, telling him about a situation in your life that is very painful for you to talk about, and very expensive to talk to him about. All of a sudden you hear a sharp buzz, and the lawyer turns around, picks up the phone, and proceeds to vanish out of your life for seventeen minutes while he's talking about somebody else's problem. This is inexcusable—unless it's an emergency or if you tell the client in advance, "I expect a phone call in about a half hour that I'm going to have to take."

AFG: So you have a rule that you won't take any calls during a conference?

Elson: That's right. Now, another characteristic goes along with that: failure to return telephone calls. Not answering letters is the same thing. That's part of procrastination, also.

There are a couple other little things. Tardiness is one—keeping a client waiting for twenty minutes or a half hour. Sometimes you can't help it; that's in the nature of things. But some lawyers are chronically late. And some clients, when they come to the lawyer's office, have to get baby-sitters or leave their business or miss school. It's a real inconvenience.

Nonattentiveness is another sin. You hear the same story over and over again, and, particularly at five o'clock in the afternoon when your blood-sugar level is low, your mind is elsewhere. Somebody is telling you the most important thing in his life and you're not paying attention to him. I find myself doing that more often as the years go by. I think young people may do it less, because they are not bored so easily; they haven't heard the stories so often. But it goes back to compassion again. If you understand that the person is there because he's in some sort of need, then it is disgraceful to ignore him.

There's a good characteristic here that I would assume you people all have. It's what I call courage. You know—to take unpopular cases. The opportunity will present itself, I assure you. These days even the big wealthy firms send a couple of lawyers out to do a little poverty stuff. It makes them feel better vicariously. Now the problem is reversing a little bit, and it takes some courage to represent people who are on the other side. In Berkeley, tenants' unions are a big thing, and it takes some guts to represent a landlord.

Student: How would you feel about representing some of the big-shot realtors?

AFG: Some people used to ask me when I was young, "You'll represent a Communist, but would you represent a fascist or a Nazi?" People think that lawyers are going to have these choices. Over the years you find out that the people on the other side don't come to you.

Elson: Some lawyers say they won't represent any landlords against tenants. There are all kinds of landlords and all kinds of tenants. One young lawyer told me that he just didn't like landlords. In his passion for justice, he forgot that there is another side. Landlords are people. There are even black landlords and poor landlords and Mexican-American landlords. The guy who fired me eighteen years ago just didn't like Communists. And there's the guy who just doesn't like blacks or doesn't like Jews or doesn't like some other bunch of people. The genius of the law in this country is that lawyers are to be available for people regardless of whether other people don't like them. You shouldn't draw any conclusions about the man who represents somebody.

It's true that when you represent somebody you don't like you may not do a good job for him. He should be made aware of that. But I think that we're getting to the stage now where young lawyers are so involved in social causes that they forget that the law has to have some integrity of its own as a professional service that is rendered.

The legal profession is a goddam good profession in many respects. In this country, I think, strangely enough, it's one of the best institutions that the system has developed. And I hope that if there is any great social change it's not discarded either by the people resisting the change or by the people making the change. It has worked out very well, I think. It has worked a hell of a lot better for well-to-do white people in this country, and it's terribly unfair to large numbers of people. It needs a tremendous amount of redoing. It needs a tremendous number of creative ideas to make it conform to the needs of the society today. But there's something about it that's good.

It works. I've represented a lot of unpopular people, in a very low-keyed way, without a lot of publicity, and it works. You go to court and present your case, and if you don't have a judge who's a complete son of a bitch you get places. By preparation, by sticking to your job and doing a good job, you can be successful. It's no substitute for the revolution. On the other hand, it doesn't have to be kicked out as an institution. Some people don't like it at all; I'm sorry about that.

"Lawyers' tools," I have written here—human and mechanical. I thought about using the word "tools." I thought I'd get some static about that. I wanted to use the word "armory," but I thought that these days it wasn't a good idea to use a military expression either. Let's leave the secretary and the human beings for a minute and get the easier ones out of the way first.

The telephone is a very interesting phenomenon, and, like all phenomena, it has its good points and bad. People still have a lot of old-fashioned ideas about long-distance calls. The telephone became part of my parents' lives as they were growing up, and it was a new, expensive thing to them. I'm used to the telephone, and long-distance calls are not an excessive expenditure to me. I've settled cases, cut through a lot of crap, by getting on the phone and talking to somebody in New York. It makes you realize that there's a person on the other end. It's not just a "Dear Mr. Smith, My client says that I'm going to have to destroy you and your entire office," you know? You get on the phone with some guy and find out he went to the same law school you did. So you get into a relationship, and you can get things done.

On the other hand, I know lawyers who use the telephone as an escape from responsibility. They get on the phone and they won't do anything else.

AFG: I've run into the opposite problem, and you people should watch out for this too if you are ever clients. Don't wait for your lawyer to call you; you call him, and keep calling till you finally get through to him. It's exasperating, but it has to be done.

Elson: There's another little problem about the phone, and that's the nosy secretary who insists on knowing a person's name, rank, and serial number, why he's calling, how much he has in the bank, and so on. The secretary may have good intentions, but it really can get a client very upset to have some stranger butt into his or her business.

Then there's that device on the telephone for conferences. It's all right when you have a number of people at one station who want to talk to somebody else. But some people use that all the time, and it sounds like you're talking to somebody in a tomb.

Recording devices, I think, are dangerous. Some people record telephone conversations. I think that's very bad, and it's illegal unless you tell people you're doing it. It also tends to discourage open discussions.

Other kinds of equipment: using dictating equipment rather than dictating to the secretary is really a time-saver. But I have mixed feelings about that. There's something about talking to a secretary personally that's helpful sometimes. When you're talking to somebody live you can work out your ideas better. And it's really great if you have the right person for that. The secretary is like a consultant. If you have an important problem, you ask what she thinks of it, what's her impression of the client. Of course, the responsibility is still basically yours. But when you're rushing around the office—and, you know, rushing and complications are the life that a lawyer leads—to have somebody who is quick and efficient and can take something down in shorthand is delightful.

I also wrote down "The lawyer as typist." The first year I was in practice, I was in that office with a few books and a desk and me and the telephone and very few clients, and I did all the typing. Funny, but I got a sense of satisfaction out of doing that typing. Every once in a while now I have to handle the probate of a will that I typed myself in those days. It's usually a pretty raunchy-looking document.

Copy machines: they are great. We have one that I think will fly if you push the right buttons. It really is helpful; it makes communication a lot better. It's expensive—but we do a lot of copy work, and we let friends and organizations and causes come in and use it.

Calendars: you've got to carry a calendar with you. I prefer the kind with a page for each month—where you can see a whole month of disaster at once, rather than just three or four days. You have to have a clear idea of where you are and where you have to be, or else they'll hold you in contempt of court.

There's a whole big thing about keeping track of your time. Some lawyers never write down what they did. I use a lawyer's diary, which has the day broken up into ten-minute periods, and I just write down everything I've done. We bill a lot of people on a time basis, and at the end of the month, if I want to bill somebody, it's awfully difficult to remember what I did eighteen days ago.

AFG: You don't charge flat fees?

Elson: Yes, I do for some things. But I keep track of that time so that when somebody says, "What do you mean, charging me that much money for that?" I can say, "Well, I did this amount of work." In other words, I have an account card for each case I take, and at the end of each month I transfer from my time book onto the account cards.

AFG: You do or your secretary does?

Elson: I do it. Because it is a very good check of my files. It means I go over each one of my cases each month. And I hate it. I hate it with a passion I can't describe. It's agony. I take it home and listen to the ball game while I'm doing it.

AFG: You hate keeping track of your time?

Elson: Yes. And fee-charging.

AFG: Do you earn all of your living by practicing law?

Elson: I don't do anything else, but my wife worked, and I have some investments.

AFG: But basically you earn your living by practicing law.

Elson: Oh, yeah, all my investments are losers.

AFG: So, obviously you live on the fees you collect. What is your broad approach? Do you establish what income you'd like to make every year and sort of work within that?

Elson: I see, you're asking more a philosophical question than a technical question.

AFG: Henry, if I knew how to charge fees, I would practice law.

Elson: Oh, well, there's not *that* much of a problem. Look, it's a relative thing, this business of income aspirations. I never really thought it through myself. I always knew I'd be a lawyer, and I always knew I'd make a good living. It just had to be, like it was written someplace. I knew I'd never make a lot of money, but I always knew I would be comfortable. No, actually I did have doubts about that, particularly when I got fired from that job in 1953. I had two children and no money at all. But I knew that my family could help me if I needed it, and fortunately I was able to recover quickly.

Money is a funny thing, though. I know—and it's some admission to make, especially with that bloody tape recorder going there—that sometimes when I'm feeling kind of good, there is a correlation with having some money in my bank account. Sometimes there's no change in my personal life, I haven't seen any good movies or any good ball games, I haven't had any political victories, and I feel good in spite of everything. That's because I feel comfortable economically, there's no doubt about it. If you're brought up in the system, as I was, money is an important thing, at least at certain stages of your life.

Some people are absolutely obsessed with money. Some get it from deprivation at childhood, and some get it from affluence at childhood. But you've got to figure out in your own life what you as a lawyer think about money.

AFG: Going back to the question of fee-charging, though, how do you find out if a guy has money?

Elson: That's no problem: I ask him.

AFG: And what if he says, "No"?

Elson: Then I decide whether I want to handle the case as a charity case.

AFG: But very often somebody who tells me he has no money will pay a fee to another lawyer. So there must be a difference in our understanding of the language.

Elson: You're probably a babe in the woods about fee-charging, Ann. I'll talk to you privately at my office, at my usual rates. We'll straighten you out.

A guy is sitting there opposite you; he wants something from you; he doesn't deserve it any more than anyone else does. You talk to him like it's a business transaction. You just say, "You want me, you pay for me."

Now, there are many ways of paying. I often make arrangements for people to pay me over a period of time. I've had people pay me ten dollars a month for five years—no interest, just what they can afford.

People should not come to a lawyer and expect a free ride, unless there's a good reason for it. A lot of clients have the same kind of financial problems that lawyers have, so that you have to watch them. There's a kind of intuitive thing that you develop about fee-charging.

I am not a good fee-charger, strangely enough. We have what looks like a good solid office, but we're not a rich office. We never have any luck on big cases, it seems to me. But we manage to do pretty well, because we're fair at it; C-plus I would give us for fee-charging. And often we screw the wrong people. The nice clients are the ones who pay, and the shrewd ones get away with it somehow.

Student: Is this what's called crying all the way to the bank? I mean I get the impression that lawyers think 20,000 bucks a year is pretty small change.

Elson: Well, I don't think that's small change. That's why I'm not a big-shot lawyer. A lot of my friends make $100,000 a year. And the day I discovered that, I was really appalled. I couldn't figure it out.

AFG: Well, I'm all for doing $100,000 worth of work.

Student: Nobody does $100,000 worth.

AFG: Listen, you can spend thousands of hours on a case over five or six years, if it goes to the Supreme Court.

Student: Oh, I'm not talking about the value of the effort you put in, but the good it does to the client.

AFG: No, that's no way to judge.

Student: I think that's the greatest lawyer's rationale for ripping people off that I've ever heard.

Elson: A lot of big money that lawyers make they make on contingent-fee cases, so they're not really ripping it off, they're pretty much sharing it with the client. That is, aside from guys who join the big firms and have the big clients—Standard Oil—and $150-an-hour billings. That's beyond me! But a lot of good honest lawyers make a lot of money in personal-injury work, and now in criminal work, particularly on narcotics charges.

AFG: Or, for instance, a lawyer will take one Mafia case a year for a high fee, and then the rest of the year he can do free or very low-paying work for political cases.

Elson: But part of the reason I resented the comment about laughing all our way to the bank is that we *earn* our money in our office. I get to the office at eight, eight-thirty every morning, leave five-thirty, six-thirty every night, and often work Saturdays and occasionally evenings. I'm comfortable. I have a nice home, and a home in the country, and a car, and a child in college. There's no complaint, but, on the other hand, no affluence, really.

I listed on my little sheet of paper various images of lawyers: the lawyer as legal adviser, technician, counselor, moral adviser, politician, fixer, political activist, and businessman. That's where a lot of them make their dough. They get in on the ground floor of a business through their clients, and they make a lot of money that way.

A lot of the *young* lawyers who are making it are criminal lawyers in the dope cases. There is a tremendous amount of cash money floating around this town in dope. These days a lawyer says, "I'll do what I can for you on this narcotics arrest, but it will cost $10,000 as a retainer," and people pay it! If somebody offered me $10,000 I would just pass out.

Student: What would a reasonable retainer be for possession—supposing it's a second offense, so it's a felony?

Elson: We don't do criminal work anymore. It got too specialized, and we decided we wouldn't handle it. But we would charge $250 to $1,000, depending on what the traffic will bear, to a certain degree—how aggravated the offense is, how nervous the client is, how much we need the money. Some lawyers will charge $5,000 for the same thing.

We charge forty dollars an hour. When I tell some twenty-one-year-old kid I charge forty dollars an hour, he really gets upset. But that's about what you need to make somewhere in the neighborhood of $30,000 a year. But you work for it. It's hard work.

AFG: I wasn't satisfied with your explanation of why your office got out of criminal law.

Elson: When I first had my own office, I did criminal cases. I had very few, because I didn't hustle them. Only a handful of lawyers do criminal cases constantly. It's a difficult field, and I didn't like the idea of doing it just on occasion, because I wouldn't be involved in the scene enough to do a good job and to bargain. So I stayed away from criminal cases except on rare occasions. Then when we formed the partnership I'm now in we had a much more business-oriented office. We just didn't have the time to do criminal work properly. At one point we hired a young lawyer out of the public defender's office, and we did some criminal practice then. After he left, I did criminal work only occasionally and on a very low-pitched level—shoplifting, drunk driving, that sort of stuff.

In criminal work, it's very, very important to have skilled people, and unless you do it regularly you're not skilled. Felony charges, jury trials—you can't possibly do that stuff unless you really know how to handle it.

The easiest way to become a criminal lawyer today is to work for a public defender for a couple of years. You try a million cases, and you screw up the first fifteen of them, but at least you're doing it for a big institution.

Student: So you aren't really screwing people?

AFG: Sure you are. They're going to jail. But there's no way out.

Elson: But I don't think that's being quite fair to the public defender's office. You do have supervision, at least theoretically, and they start you out with misdemeanors. But criminal cases are very difficult.

AFG: I agree. When a client of mine goes to jail, a piece of me is in that jail, too.

By the way, did you have "the lawyer as mouthpiece" in your list?

Elson: Well, that was the "fixer."

AFG: No, I meant in the way that Garry might consider himself a mouthpiece. The lawyer can put the client's ideas in language that the mass media and the judge and the jury can understand better and can accept.

Elson: I guess that's what I would call the technician. To call Garry a mouthpiece is kind of funny. He is a great folk hero now. Charlie is an excellent lawyer and deserves everything good that has been said about him. But today he is really operating as a political activist, in my estimation. He has filled the hiatus between the client and the lawyer, which is often a valuable hiatus—it allows the lawyer to be separate from the client. Garry identifies with the client because he loves the Panthers with a kind of emotional attachment. I don't know if that can be done or if that is desirable, unless you're a guy like Garry, who's an excellent lawyer as well as devoted. A guy who's not so able, and who gets that closely identified with a political client, often either gets charged with contempt or screws up the case. I don't think Charlie has ever had a client held in contempt, and he himself has never been held in contempt. I doubt if he ever will be.

Garry basically is, in my opinion, a sound lawyer in the old tradition: compassionate, understanding, a decent guy who's not trying to push everybody around but who gets tough where it's necessary to be tough. I think he's the ideal lawyer in a lot of respects. It does trouble me a little to see him talk in that street rhetoric like the Panthers do, because he's not a street person, although Garry is more of a street person than most lawyers we know. He's not a Harvard-graduate type by any means.

AFG: I think Garry's doing pretty much what he always did, but now that he's famous he gets more respect for it. Other lawyers used to pooh-pooh Garry because he wasn't an intellectual; he wasn't an appellate lawyer. It's a snobbery among lawyers, you know, that if you're an appellate lawyer that makes you nine times better than a trial lawyer. It's only recently that trial lawyers have been considered pretty good stuff.

You represented some Panthers, didn't you, Henry?

Elson: Yes, I did handle a few small matters for them in Richmond.

It makes sort of an interesting comparison. There were some street fights in Richmond, and the Panther group was being subjected to constant petty harassment by the police. Somehow my firm ended up doing some of the legal work. It was on a very different level, a pre–Huey Newton level—not chronologically but in terms of intensity. The police were still at the level of charging them with misdemeanors, for traffic violations and using obscene language.

We had a couple of successful jury trials. We handled them on a very low key. The Panthers asked if I wanted to have a crowd show up in the courtroom, and I said I didn't. I don't like to do things that way. I don't know why; my psychiatrist will tell you the reason.

So we had these two jury trials in the Richmond municipal court, raising the same issues that are being discussed in other trials on a much broader, more violent, more intense level. There was no heat; there were no large crowds outside; it was just the district attorney—some young guy who got stuck with the case—and me trying to reason with a very unimpressed jury. And it worked, it worked very successfully. The harassment pretty much stopped for a long period of time. The Panthers in Richmond cracked up for internal reasons, however, I'm told.

But it's that kind of experience that leads me to at least have mixed feelings about the viability of the system, to feel that under certain circumstances the system can work. It's helpful to have a good lawyer; but, with a certain juxtaposition of circumstances, with certain individuals who are willing to do things, the thing can work.

AFG: Your use of the phrase "the thing" reminds me of something an old radical lawyer used to say in describing judicial administration in the United States. The late Irvin Goodman of Portland said the courts are actually the sewer system of capitalism through which the unpleasant parts of the system are disposed of. So that turns lawyers into plumbers!

Elson: I'm not going to comment on that!

But the whole business of how you represent clients in political cases is a very interesting question. I think that most lawyers are not like Charlie Garry or the other people who are so committed to cause-type clients. They're more like I am—committed to a regular general practice, to making a living and living in the community. I'm not inactive politically in the community, but I'm not in the vanguard of political change.

AFG: But, Henry, I don't think you're being quite fair to yourself. When there are political problems in Berkeley, somehow people get to your office almost every time. They come for some reason.

Elson: I don't deny it. But there's a difference between the way I function and the way Charlie functions. Even in the Free Speech Movement case, which was a big, flamboyant type of case, we handled it on as low-keyed a level as we could. I mean the idea of having 800 clients is, in itself, overwhelming. And these were not very gentle people. If you said something they didn't like, they would blow up. They often did. They had a lot of criticisms. We had about sixty lawyers at the beginning, but it filtered down to about seven or eight of us.

Student: What were some of the criticisms?

Elson: The major charge from the more radical people was that we sold out by not insisting on having 700 separate jury trials. My God, we'd still be trying them! I think you'd probably find that the majority of the people think that was a mistake. I don't think so.

What we tried to do was find out what the clients wanted. That's always the first thing a lawyer should do, in my humble opinion. We had a tremendous logistics problem. Lawyers met with groups of clients, for months, and we took polls. The general idea that filtered down was that the vast majority of the defendants did not want to get involved in protracted legal proceedings. They wanted to go about their business, finish school, graduate. They thought they had made their point, and they didn't want to screw around in a long court fight. Once we determined that that was the majority feeling, we operated on that, and anybody who wanted to could easily have broken away and represented himself, as a few did. But later a lot of people felt that the lawyers had talked people into this. I certainly will never know the truth of that.

Student: How did it work out?

Elson: Well, we agreed on waiving a jury trial and had one trial for a group of about 150. Everybody had to waive the jury trial; it was really painful. I mean, each person had to be formally asked, and almost every person had something to say. It was just very unpleasant. Then we had a trial for six weeks, and they were all convicted, and we never got anyplace on appeal. The sentences were relatively low for the vast majority and high for the leaders.

Student: What did Mario Savio get?

Elson: He got 120 days. But the vast majority of people I assume went back to school and finished, or did whatever they were doing. A lot of them are still politically active, and I still see a lot of them.

The problems that were generated by that case could be very instructive to young lawyers: you have the problem of satisfying clients who are really obsessed with an idea; you have a legal system that you have to respect to a certain degree; and you have this vast number of people calling on you, for different things. You can't satisfy all of them. It's almost impossible to have a good situation with that many clients, just by definition.

Student: What do you think would have happened if you had refused to waive the right to speedy trial and held out for jury trial?

Elson: They would have brought judges in from the outside and had a series of jury trials. By the third or fourth month of them, somebody would have gotten tired, and there would have been some deals made. But our idea was to do what the defendants wanted. Of course, a number of the more radical leaders did not want to expedite things. They wanted chaos in the courtroom, and they tried to create that, as a matter of fact, on several occasions.

I'm very dubious about future trials if that approach wins out. If the Chicago conspiracy trial is the prototype of the future, the system will not survive.

Student: The legal system?

Elson: Yeah. It just won't work unless you have defendants who are willing to sit through a trial or not be pushed into courtroom activity.

Student: What do you suppose would have happened in Chicago if they had just played it straight?

Elson: I don't know. I read parts of the transcript and I'm confused about a lot of it. I'll tell you: my judgments about a lot of things, you can rely on. But my judgments about the left, the movement, politics—pay no attention to them at all. I've been wrong for so many years that I can't tell you how depressed I am about it. I'm a very conservative person in all my impulses, it seems, and I just don't know how to predict the future politically.

There's a lot of dissatisfaction in the world, though, and a lot of lawyers feel it. I think that's why so many lawyers are considering dropping out or changing. That's not a reflection of the legal system, but a reflection of the stirred-up nature of the world.

Lawyers are right on the edge; they get the first blows very often. They feel a lot more, and they see a lot more of the contradictions of the world. Lawyers like me, who are basically general practitioners but politically hip at the same time, find it very frustrating. A lot of the work we do somehow lacks significance in the face of people being shot down. We have doubts about the validity of what we're doing if we're not on the firing line all the time.

Plus the fact that we're living in a dying society, and lawyers have to act as if it's not dying, because our clients want to live and prosper, and we're supposed to run interference for them. There's something strange, almost bizarre, about doing that, if you have some of the political feelings that I personally have, so that the contradictions are very apparent to me. That would account for some of the disillusionment that I do feel personally. So I've decided to take a year off next year. I want to go abroad, get out of the scene here, and think about where I'm going and where I want to go—try to get some perspective about the future.

SOLO IN SOUL COUNTRY
John George

AFG: John George is in private practice in Oakland's black community, where he handles both civil and criminal cases—a general practice. I met him years ago when he was working on school integration in Oakland through the NAACP. Then he ran for Congress in 1968 in the Democratic primary. John is known for his subtle sense of humor; his friends listen for it, but acquaintances often miss it under the weight of his rhetoric!

After that introduction, John, tell us how you happened to go to law school.

George: I drifted through college in the Quiet Fifties, not knowing what I wanted to do. I was taking political science and economics, to learn what makes this country tick, why we are where we are. That was the eternal question being asked even during those Eisenhower years. But we didn't do anything about it. We would just sit around the coffee shops and talk.

Somebody came to me after 1954 and said, "The future of the black man is going to be decided in the courts of this country." That was because of the Supreme Court's opinion in *Brown v. Board of Education,* desegregating the schools and saying that separate is inherently unequal. That decision foreshadowed a generation of litigation. So I said, "Well, I guess I'll go to law school." Like if they had said the future of the black man was going to be decided in the schools of architecture, I would have gone to architecture school.

367

Legal education, even when I was coming through, answered all the questions that nobody was asking.

Student: That's a good line.

George: I came out of law school, and my first two years I worked for a lawyer who was also an inheritance-tax appraiser. But my motivation was to do something in civil rights, so I gravitated toward those kinds of cases, which in the West were demonstrations—like the Sheraton-Palace sit-ins.

What I want to tell you about those cases is not my experience in conducting the trials, but what those cases do to the legal system and how the court personnel react when you get involved in them.

You are walking around as a lawyer and you've had the routine case—that is, four counts of murder, two counts of robbery. The DA is your colleague and friend. You go down and discuss equitable disposition, maybe negotiate a plea.

The judge says, "Come on back in chambers," and "Well, what have we got here?"

"Well, Judge, my man has got this going for him," and you name some factors about his life, "and here's what we're trying to accomplish . . ." The judge is your colleague and friend in a certain sense, too.

Then the sit-in cases hit San Francisco. These were political cases. Well, the judges, the DAs, the court personnel just changed almost overnight in dealing with the lawyers on those cases. They treated those sit-ins as if they were hitting at the whole system and they were going to use everything they had to protect it.

Maybe they were perceptive.

See, a guy who goes and murders somebody or robs a store is not threatening the system as a whole; he's just a criminal to be given a jail sentence or probation. But those guys demonstrating were hitting at the very foundations. So all our dealings with the judges became different. And in the sentencing there was almost no talk about straight probation. Those guys were made to serve some time in jail.

I went from those cases to some in Oakland for a guy named Mark Comfort, who was a revolutionary in the early sixties, which was still a quiet time. I couldn't put on an elaborate political defense, because these were just misdemeanors, and we lost them.

Student: What kinds of charges were they?

George: One was a charge of tending to contribute to the delinquency of a minor. Mark was in a group of speakers that asked high school students to come down to a park to protest police brutality. Now, if a student is absent from school three times without excuse, he becomes a delinquent. So Mark was charged with tending toward contributing to delinquency, because the students were out of school that day without permission. He was found guilty.

Going by the rules, he would have been found guilty no matter what the skill of the lawyer had been. Remember, there is a tendency for radicals to say, "You cannot get justice out of the courts." Yet they want to go to court all the time as a method of focusing attention on the struggle. Then, as the trial comes on, I detect a lingering hope in them that they *are* going to receive justice—that they can beat the rap. They forget that the premise on which the arrest was made indicated that they would never win the case.

I also met Huey Newton at that time. He was going to college then, and we had a few misdemeanor cases. I think we won one and lost two or three. Then they formed the Panthers, and in May 1967 they went to Sacramento to demonstrate. They got arrested for carrying guns, and there was a hard struggle to raise bail money.

There was some talk about why they didn't choose a black lawyer to handle Newton's murder case. My view is that if there had been a skillful black lawyer around who could have handled a case of that magnitude, he would have been chosen. But no black lawyer had ever put himself out for Newton before that, and now that his life was at stake, this was no time for pussyfooting around.

Student: Does a lawyer have to be in a big firm to take a case like that?

George: Well, a top-notch criminal lawyer, even if he practices alone, would have access to investigators and other lawyers, to do research and legwork for him in a big political case. But the average lawyer would need a pool of resources to handle those cases or he would be wiped out economically.

There's another thing to consider, too. When you get known for doing public-service work, many, many cases come unto you. These clients don't think about your office expenses and bills; they think you are a great public servant, a lawyer, and you can afford it. Other lawyers can establish the image of saying, "You don't have money for me? I'm not going to give you a thing." But he who puts himself out as trying to do something for the community— much is expected of him, and he will receive the rap from people if he doesn't perform. He is like the auspicious intermeddler they tell about in law school: you are under no duty to save a person from drowning, but if you do go out to save him don't do it negligently or you will be sued, and it is no defense to say, "My intentions were good. I tried to do my best."

Student: How many black lawyers are there practicing in the black community here?

George: In the Bay Area there are about fifty-five admitted to practice.

AFG: Are all of them practicing?

George: Those are lawyers and judges practicing in government or whatever, but not those doing just real estate or some other business. In private practice there are about thirty or thirty-five. Then there are some with the public defender's office and with Neighborhood Legal Services.

The tragic thing is that there are only about two Mexican-American lawyers in Alameda County.

AFG: Do you know any black women lawyers? What problems of practice do they face?

George: There are a few in private practice in the Bay Area. One does mostly domestic relations and personal injury, not much criminal law. Another practices in the public defender's office, and one is with Legal Aid in San Francisco. Then there is Cherie Gaines, a brilliant lady lawyer who is now teaching law.

Not being a woman, I don't know the difficulties of women lawyers. I just think a woman lawyer may be handicapped in criminal law. You have to go into some nitty-gritty places. Even a middle-class man has problems walking into the criminal world. That's why not many middle-class lawyers, black or white, engage in criminal law—you're dealing in many instances with a bad element.

Student: Are white firms opening up to black lawyers today? Are there good opportunities there?

George: In my opinion, it's not prevalent. And it really depends on what the black lawyer wants to get out of a firm. If he goes into a firm that represents insurance companies, that's the experience he'll get, and if that kind of firm selects him it would probably be because his background indicates that he would fit in with that situation.

Jim Herndon is a black lawyer in a white firm, but it's a firm with "a social conscience," which means he can develop and pursue civil-liberties and other controversial cases. Now, if you go down to one of those big establishment firms in downtown San Francisco . . .

Student: One of the black activists at Boalt Law School took a job with a firm like that. That's why I asked.

George: I think he probably would have to either sell out or leave that kind of firm.

In the future, I think there is going to be more of a movement of black lawyers creating black firms. Of course, if your practice is based almost exclusively on the black community, that dictates how much you can do. It limits the financial resources you have for handling suits against insurance companies or the district attorney's office. Your clients cannot pay for "fringe benefits" like discovery and investigation costs. That's why these public defenders and Legal Aid offices are popping up, trying to fill the gap.

Money buys a lot of things in this country: housing, education, medicine, law. If you don't have enough money, you may not send for a witness down in Los Angeles; you might not even put an investigator on the case to look for a witness here. If the lawyer is not paid enough, he will not be as diligent in looking for the things that can help his client, even within the present court system. So, the times we could get better treatment within the present system, we miss out for lack of money.

When you are practicing law from a black perspective, you've

372 SOLO IN SOUL COUNTRY

got to know the community you come from. Otherwise you won't know what rules to apply in that community or how to conduct yourself. Black people are engaged in economic crimes, mostly: burglary, robbery, these type things. That's because the system has created a situation where they have to engage in that sort of conduct. I don't mean to say, "Just excuse that type conduct"; I'm not excusing it, I'm explaining it. The poor are not the cause of poverty; the system is the cause of poverty, and poverty is the cause of these crimes. Then when poor people are thrown in jail, they aren't fined and given probation the way other people would be, and a lot of talent is wasted. I see guys in county jail who might be some of the best material we have—just wasted.

One of the things we are up against is this: people create institutions and devices to make things more livable and convenient. The creation of these legal systems is a public political act. But the laws are drawn up in many instances to exclude, not to include.

It has been said that politics is the art of making some things impossible for outsiders. They make it impossible for you by putting you on the outside, and then they make rules against outsiders. They dare the outsider to break the rules, and when, on occasion, you break a rule for your survival, the people who judge you—the jury, the prosecutor, the judges—are more in tune with the people who made the rules to exclude you in the first place. You are judged by the rulemakers and you had no say in drawing up those rules. That's what makes it doubly difficult for black people. And if you're poor this falls on you, too.

AFG: For example?

George: You know how judges are appointed—they are lawyers who worked in a political party. In some instances they may pick a legal scholar, but usually the day before he was appointed the judge was a highly partisan political figure—a county chairman or an assemblyman, maybe. The next day he's the judge, and the lawyer who comes before him is looking for the even hand of justice.

There's also the social atmosphere that judges and lawyers engage in. When you pick up the phone and say to opposing counsel, "Hey, Jim, can we work this out?" and you've just seen him at a luncheon or some other social affair, it helps in your negotiations.

The organization that draws up the rules for the legal profession is the bar association. Now, the people who can be active in the association and can go to the bar conventions are usually the lawyers who are well off, who can take off a few weeks. So somehow it happens that they draw up the minimum-fee schedules based on the practice of most white lawyers. They say the minimum fee for a divorce is $300. Then black lawyers have to take that fee to the black community and try to make it work. Many black people can't afford $300.

Or take another example: a mother doesn't know her son is going to get arrested. She didn't schedule this in her budget. Suddenly one night she has to come up with $150, $200, or her son won't have legal representation. How can she find that money right like that? This is what gets me out there sometimes. Most lawyers won't take the case on credit, because once you become the attorney of record the court is looking to you to carry through on the case.

There is also what I call selective enforcement of the law. The district attorney has great power to select whom to prosecute. For example, in Oakland they've got a statute prohibiting gambling. It's all right to play cards, but not for money. Now, I've never seen any white gamblers being prosecuted. See, if you've got a private club where you go and gamble, then the police don't reach you. But they prosecute black gamblers. They've got experts in the language of gambling, and if you're down in someone's house they've got some informer there playing, too, or listening at the door, and later he comes in and testifies, "Yes, they were talking about money."

I've never seen white prostitutes being prosecuted in Oakland. The rare one who is may be working in black neighborhoods.

Student: Black people get discrimination instead of justice.

George: But remember: in the practice of criminal law, people are looking for you to get them off, not for justice. If the first words you say to a client are "I can save you from jail, man," then you can be as impatient and insensitive as you want. You can demand the attention and respect of your client. You have what they call great client control.

So, when you practice criminal law in a traditional manner, you strike up a relationship with the district attorney—you discuss matters with him. On a class basis, the black lawyer may be able to communicate better with the DA than he can with his own client who is from a different class. A lawyer has to be very skillful in human psychology to know how to communicate and be understood by his clients. You have to explain difficult things in simple terms. The client is usually in trouble, facing jail, and he does not want to engage in intellectual dialogue or abstract discussion. Even when you try to give him a hypothetical example to show how his case stacks up against others, he'll often say, "But that's not my case. Let's get back to what I did."

You've got 500 cases in your head. His case is the only case in the world to him.

AFG: Do you encourage your client to participate in making decisions about his case?

George: At a time like this, the routine client is not looking for participatory democracy.

You say to him, "What are we going to do with this case?"

He says, "Well, I came to *you* for that."

He wants you to make an arbitrary decision that you can save him, not to explore the doubts of his case.

He says, "I know I got a weak case; that's why I came to you."

Student: It sounds like you don't have many illusions about your clients.

George: Many of these guys are hustlers. Some of them are even hustling the lawyer. I had a guy come in, and I asked, "What have they got you charged with?"

"Burglary and receiving stolen property," he says. Then he sits down and says, "That's a nice dictating machine you got there. I like your typewriter." And I start getting leery of my own client.

"Do you know you are only *presumed* to be innocent, and presumptions are easily overcome?"

He says, "What's the retainer fee?"

"It's $200."

"I thought you were one of the brothers who was trying to help out," he says.

Then I look up and say, "You're guilty. The presumption is over."

Student: Do you get offered TV sets?

George: No, I don't get offered stuff from thieves. They've got other lawyers with a fast-buck reputation. Criminals will gravitate to those who engage in that kind of stuff. There are some lawyers who will take a second deed of trust on the client's house as security for their fee, and then when the client is off in prison they foreclose on that deed. Bail bondsmen do that, too.

Student: Do you think the bail system works? Is it economically feasible for the people engaged in it?

George: If you mean the bail bondsman, he makes more money than the lawyer. When a client is in custody he wants to get out. The person who can get him out is the bail bondsman, usually for 10 percent of the bail. So if bail is $2,000 and the client has $200, the bail bondsman will get it. If the lawyer can get the bail reduced to $1,000 or $500, he may get a chance at a fee out of part of that $200.

I don't think the bail system is absolutely necessary. It puts a financial criterion on whether justice will be done. Most people will show up for trial. You can determine whether a person has ties to the community and the nature of the crime he allegedly committed. Just make the penalty for not appearing in court stiffer than the bail and they'll appear. People don't run away. Or, if they do, the police can catch up with them—like they do with guys who don't pay traffic tickets.

When a person cannot raise bail he is denied his constitutional right to a lawyer of his own choosing. In a felony case, he'll be in custody at least ninety days. That means if his lawyer takes every step as quickly as he can, the procedures will carry over for at least that long.

Aside from the problem of bail, this system can crush a person to the extent that he gets fantastic notions. A guy will come to you and say, "Murder? I didn't do anything but pull the trigger and this fellow was standing in the way. I don't see why they have to charge me with this. Bunch of Gestapo pig cops!"

Some clients are realistic. A father will say, "I know I have to pay some child support. I just don't want to pay $200 a month when I'm only making $350." But some fathers say, "I'm not going to pay that woman nothing."

The lawyer says, "You're not paying the woman; you're paying the children."

"Well, I'm still not going to pay anything." He's unrealistic.

You know, a guy will let his traffic tickets mount up to $500. He gets ten warrants, and he doesn't know what to do, so he lets it go up to fifteen, then twenty. Then he comes to the lawyer and says, "Extricate me from this mess, you magician."

Or a guy comes in with fifteen witnesses against him, fingerprints against him, photographs against him, and says, "I don't want to go to jail."

You tell him you can't keep him out of jail, but you may be able to keep him out of state prison.

And he tells you, "You're selling me out." He thinks you ought to go down and pull some bamboozle over them. "Just tell them I wasn't in the area. It's my word against theirs, isn't it?"

No, it isn't. And he doesn't understand the service that you can perform for him. For example, in California if you are sent to prison on armed robbery, you are not even eligible for parole until seven years later. If the lawyer can get the arming clause dismissed, the guy will be eligible for parole within two or three years. The lawyer who does that has performed a great service within that context.

In criminal law, you just can't walk everybody out. All cases can't triumph. There's a little slogan going around these days: "You win some and you lose some and some are rained out."

Some crimes by their very nature are so ghastly that the accused cannot get what you would call a fair trial. The only thing the lawyer can do is try to get him the fairest trial possible under the circumstances, with all the supposed safeguards: challenges, motions, stuff like that. That means you've got to acquire the skills of a lawyer if you want to serve the cause. Otherwise, the cases may come to you but you won't be able to deliver.

A good place to get that skill, if you are sympathetic with the poor and the struggling, is in the public defender's office. Even in the district attorney's office you can learn some of the ropes of practicing law—it wouldn't be what you would call a waste of time, if you've got your perspective down right. In different counties the DAs are different, too. Some counties are not what you would call harsh.

Your study habits are very important, too. If you are sloppy in law school, you are going to be sloppy in practice. Don't think, "All I have to do is make it through school and the bar exam, and then I'll shape up and do things right." Your work habits from school will carry over into your practice.

You acquire a reputation for yourself. If you do personal-injury work and you are not well prepared, the insurance adjusters will treat you accordingly. If you are demanding $5,000 and they know you're not ready to go to trial, they are not going to respond too favorably to that demand; they figure they can drive you to the wall. You can acquire a good reputation in various ways: participating in community affairs; following through when you are given a task to perform; paying attention to detail in even the little misdemeanor cases.

Some students come out of law school and want to engage in dramatic cases as soon as they hit the streets. You are not going to do that. You sit in your office waiting for the big case to turn up. It never will unless you acquire the reputation of taking care of business.

When you prove yourself, then you can accomplish things. A black lawyer in Oakland, say, with a firm reputation will have a colleagial relationship with the judges. He will have a better entrée with them than a young white lawyer would have.

AFG: Getting back to political cases, we were talking the other day about a client who is arrested or beaten up and then the charges are dropped or he is acquitted. Do you think it's wise at that point to sue the police for misconduct in such a case?

Student: This fellow was arrested for selling the Panther paper on a busy intersection. They charged him with obstructing traffic, but he said he had been busted a number of times before for disorderly conduct, resisting arrest, that kind of thing—in other words, the police knew him as an activist in the community.

I was asking him, "What would you like to see happen in your case?"

He said, "If I have to do time, that won't please me. If I cop a plea, that won't please me. If I get an acquittal, even that won't please me." So we were trying to figure out some means of effecting change in the forces that are trying to suppress his freedom of expression.

George: I think that case ought to be fought to the end—especially if you can give it the treatment and attention it deserves. A move like that, against a guy for selling Panther papers, is political.

We had a similar situation of a girl putting Peace and Freedom Party posters on the telephone poles. They have a rule against posting on telephone poles, and they enforced it against her. But if someone goes around tacking up George Wallace's stuff, the police just don't see him.

Student: And the police are supposed to be working for the society at large, not the interests of any particular segment.

George: They don't do that.

Student: Of course not. But how can we force them to do it? Everybody pays taxes, after all, even the poor. And for them it's taxation without representation. I went to law school to find out how to work things out in ways other than using unreasonable force or having a revolution. Can it be done?

Student: The way I see it, there are limitations to what you can do in government.

George: Well, there are limitations to what you can do in the courtroom.

I think one of the most highly cherished values of white European culture is the right to take up arms when you feel all reasonable means of litigation have been exhausted.

Certain cases can be brought to court to extract certain benefits at the particular time, I think. But you cannot expect a legal case to bring about the fundamental changes that have to be brought about in this country.

Any system will pay the highest price to protect itself. So political cases are treated more harshly than ordinary criminal cases in many instances, because they are attacking the system. No system that can defend itself is going to lie down and keel over when it is threatened.

But practicing law is still a way of engaging in some service to the community, I think, although in the 1970s the salvation of black people may not necessarily rest with the lawyers. There are many more things opening up for blacks.

AFG: You ran for Congress in 1968. Why did you do it?

George: I did it because you can accomplish certain things for a community if you get into a position of some influence and relative power. This congressional district is in one of the largest counties in California, and that means that the statewide and even the national politicians cannot ignore it.

Bob Scheer ran for that seat in 1966, mainly on an antiwar platform, and did well. But we in the ghetto like to come at that question a little differently. We talk about community problems and then say how the war puts a limit on what can be done about them. We don't talk just about the moral outrage of this war. Scheer got 46 percent of the vote, and I thought that if I could tie the black community into what his campaign had put together, we could win.

But by 1968 things had changed. In January the Peace and Freedom Party was created, taking about 10,000 votes out of the Democratic primary, and then they ran Huey Newton for the seat on that ticket. I stayed in the primary to provide some opposition to the Democratic incumbent, but my political strategy and my motivation had been made somewhat obsolete by these two developments.

AFG: How did you do?

George: I got 40 percent of the vote. I don't consider that bad.

AFG: Not at all. Would you do it again?

George: Under the right circumstances. For Congress, now, that's no longer necessary, because we elected Dellums, who will be there for the next twenty-five years, if he is not elected President before then.

AFG: Quite a few progressives are running for Congress this year along with Dellums—Bella Abzug of New York, Father Drinan of Boston, and John Conyers of Detroit, who is up for reelection. They are all members of the Lawyers Guild, by the way. And there are other liberals trying to get Congress to actually do something about the people's needs.

Would you mind telling us whether you spent your own money in the campaign?

George: Not a lot. I spent around $18,000. Scheer had spent around $60,000 and I think he ended up with a deficit. By 1968 the district was 20,000 voters larger. Dellums spent $60,000 or $65,000. Both Scheer and Dellums ran in off years, though, not Presidential years. There's more concentration on the congressional seats in off years.

AFG: Are you in practice by yourself now?

George: Yes, but I share an office with two other lawyers, so we talk things over and we split the office expenses.

AFG: Would you like to have a bigger firm or a more specialized practice?

George: Yes, both. It's hard keeping up with just search-and-seizure law, much less all the rest of criminal law, domestic relations, patent law, corporations. Most black lawyers are general practitioners. We are corner grocery stores in the supermarket age.

I live from month to month. I don't know where the beans are going to come from in August or the rest of July. I'm hoping it will be like last July or last month, but right now I do not have the money to pay my bills, unless it comes in this week or next. And the office expenses have to be paid almost before the home expenses, because if you don't take care of the office, you may not have your home.

I've been practicing about five years now, and I can make it with a lot of scuffling and volume. But when the clientele you're practicing among is predominantly poor, to make $30,000 gross you've got to handle 500 cases. Compared to the guy who makes

$30,000 handling 10 or 100 cases, the service you are giving is another question.

AFG: One of the students was asking how a lawyer can be a decent human being if he has to spend so much of his time working at his profession. Can you ever get away from it, John? Can you relax with your family? Does your wife work? How do you manage?

George: My wife is a former science teacher. She doesn't work outside the home now. My three children are nine and seven years old and eighteen months.
   I'm involved in some political things that do keep me away from home sometimes. I think it's the quality of your relationship with your family that counts, not the quantity. That's my rationalization. I think your children have to be brought up so that they don't constantly have to have their parent around.
   You can't schedule robberies. A guy doesn't come to you and say, "I'm going to commit this crime on July eighth. Would you get ready?" You get phone calls at night, on weekends, and you have to go down to the jail. There's no point getting morally outraged when the guy calls you. It would be like a doctor getting mad at a patient for getting sick.
   Anyway, by the time your kids get to be fifteen or twenty years old they'll be gone.

AFG: But wait five years, until your nine-year-old is fourteen.

George: What happens then?

AFG: I found that a parent of teenagers in this time and place has to be in touch with his kid every day. I'm for self-reliance, and my kids do a lot of things on their own; but at a certain age, if you don't give them a chance to talk to you every day, they can get into the damnedest things you would ever dream of. And if a week goes by before you hear about it, it may be more serious by then.

George: Well, that's a problem, because a lawyer listens to troubles all day and is supposed to deal with them and resolve them as calmly as possible. So then he goes home and he has to listen to more troubles? Home is the place to relax and lounge.

You don't have to smile anymore. Your wife is the one person in the world of whom you can say, "She understands. We know each other's feelings and ways so well that I don't have to explain everything." I can come home and sit down and smoke and kind of shut out. That's true for everybody—teacher, lawyer, physician, bail bondsman, real-estate broker, operating engineer. Home has got to be that sanctuary.

DEATH
AND
TAXES

THE WONDERLAND OF TAX LAW

Harry Margolis

AFG: Some of you may think Harry Margolis is not a radical lawyer. He doesn't do political trial work, he does taxes, mainly for rich people. But after you listen to what he has to say about tax law, maybe you'll come to the conclusion I did—that Harry Margolis is one of the most radical lawyers I know.

Margolis: The field of taxation itself is a very young field. No course in taxation was taught at my law school until after I had graduated in 1943. The year I took the California bar exam there was an optional question on taxation for the first time, and of course I didn't dare try it.

The subject is one that I think is very badly misunderstood. As far as I'm concerned, the outstanding people in tax (with, perhaps, a few very strange exceptions) are those who are most broad. The more training they've had in various other areas of life, the more they are able to do in the field of taxation. Everything in life has some tax aspect. You can pick any subject, describe any goal, and I can translate it into a tax problem and a tax solution.

AFG: How did you become a tax specialist, Harry?

Margolis: It was entirely accidental. I went to work for a firm (the two partners are both judges now), and within the first thirty days a client walked in with an excise-tax problem. I knew nothing about it. I looked in the book and solved the problem. What I didn't realize was that I had solved a problem that involved 250,000 barrels of whiskey, of which my client had about 4, and before I knew it I was very popular with the people who had the remainder of the 250,000 barrels.

After that I found myself representing beer distributors, and I just learned as I went along by reading the statute books and the cases. In 1951 I became ill and gave up that work and started to do tax work for professionals—lawyers, accountants, doctors. It was mostly very small estates—small incomes, relatively speaking, but I could make a living out of that. For a person making $25,000, I could save about $3,000 a year and I could charge about $1,000 a year. So if I had twelve or fifteen clients, I could make a living for myself and my family.

I think that of all the fields of law, tax is the one in which the practitioner generally makes the most money. If you want to make as much money as possible practicing law, there are few choices. Of course, if you're related to wealthy people, it doesn't matter which field of the law you pick; you can do well. But if you're unrelated to wealth, then the probability of doing well on your own gets cut down very quickly.

If you're in the personal-injury field, it's how fast you can chase the case, and the race is indeed to the swift. But in the tax field, it's been possible up to this time for anyone who has the stuff to do well. You don't have to have millionaire clients. I've had only one client in my entire career who made a million dollars in one year; there are, believe it or not, a large number of people who at one point or another do. I've never had a corporation that made more than $500,000 in a year, and there are a lot of businesses that do. The nice thing, in the field of tax, is that if you have one major client or corporation that makes a million dollars a year, you can do enough for that client to make yourself a living. That type of outfit or individual nowadays will normally have a full-time person or a number of them working in the field of tax, as their general counsel or on the payroll.

I've had clients in the entertainment industry from time to time. I've represented a number who made $200,000 a year. They did the hard work and I did the tax planning, and at the end of the year we added up the money. It turns out that about 60 percent of what money they had left was a result of the tax planning and 40 percent was a result of their work.

It's always interesting. For example, I can take any taxpayer in any bracket and totally eliminate his tax, legally. This shows you the game theory of the subject. The tragedy is that elimination of tax for the lower-bracket taxpayer, if it's properly and legitimately done, costs him more for the services performed and the accounting work that has to be done and the books and records and the audit headaches, than it would to simply pay the tax.

So for the vast majority of our poorer people there is no oppression greater than the tax that they pay, because there is no relief from it. It's taken from them before they get their income, and they have no place to go to get it back. There's no one who can help them.

Then there is the $10,000 to $15,000 class. These people by poverty standards are well off; they are the great wonderful middle class of today. But insofar as taxation is concerned, they also have almost no place to turn. I would speculate that a person has to make somewhere around $35,000 a year before you can give him a break in the tax field.

I've often thought it would be a wonderful thing if OEO legal services or one of the new law communes would have someone really seriously spend some time on how to save tax for people making less than $35,000 a year. There is some money to be saved, although the standards are different than in tax work for the higher brackets.

Tax planning is pervasive. It almost has reached the point where it dominates every other consideration of life. And there is nothing more corrupting to our society than the system of taxation. I have no words strong enough to condemn the society in which we live in terms of taxation. We're constantly playing with a totally unreal world. In fact, to do very well in taxation you ought to be like Alice; you should be able to change your size. You should be able to get in under the transom. You should be able to jump over the fence. And you should be like the queen, ready to do the execution first and try the matter afterwards.

That's the wonderful thing about taxation, if you like fantasy and can overcome your feelings about what it does to society. What you do in taxation is to write your own scenario and then go live it, particularly if you do a good job. When I talk to lawyers who do a lot of personal-injury work, I point out to them that taxation is very much as if they got up in the morning and decided what accident they were going to plan for that day. They could plan an accident to take place at two o'clock, decide what street it would be on, who would be involved, what kind of vehicle, how fast it would go, what the weather conditions would be, who would be the witnesses, and arrange for their photography in advance. You could get some wonderful personal-injury cases if you could do that.

Literally what you do in taxation is plan future events within the rules of the game as Congress has given them to you at that moment. Now, there's nothing rational about those rules; they're totally irrational. In fact, if you want to destroy the corruption in taxation, what you have to do is make it a completely rational system. It's the interaction of absurd laws that makes the whole field of taxation possible.

It is very tough to go into taxation without getting corrupted. The real world is hard enough to face on a daily basis; if you get into an artificial world, which taxation is, it's almost impossible to keep your sense of social responsibility. I would hope you young people are going to law school with a very deeply felt intent to make a contribution to society. That was very rarely true in my generation. But it's wonderful to meet the recent graduates from law schools all over the country who don't care so much about degrees and material aspects but are resolved to do something about the social order.

I'm afraid I should say that taxation isn't the field for you, that it's a trap. For myself, I've had to recognize that I'm incompetent to do anything worthwhile, and therefore the only answer is to do as much work as possible and take the money and give it to causes that represent the things in which I believe but to which I can make no contribution.

AFG: Let me just say that in the course of years everybody learns that there's a Margolis Foundation. It isn't a very big foundation, but if you have a socially progressive cause that needs a certain amount of money, sometimes you can find just that amount right there. So I want you to understand how corrupt Harry is.

Margolis: The same is true of my clients, most of them. Believe it or not, of approximately 150 clients for whom I do consulting work, over 100 are people you would like. There *are* people who make a lot of money and who do care about social matters, thank heaven. But they never have enough for all the causes.

I would like to give you an illustration of a practical thing I did about fifteen years ago. I was giving a class for lawyers on taxation, and I wanted to show that I could take a relatively poor family and eliminate tax for them. We selected a Japanese-American family in Cupertino, where I lived. There were two brothers running a fruit stand. Between them they had eight children, and there was a grandmother, now gone, a wonderful woman. So, with Grandma, sons, wives, and children, there were thirteen people, and the family made something less than $12,000 a year.

If you've had your first course in taxation you can figure quite easily what I would do with such a group. I had a built-in advantage, of course, because of the children. The wonderful thing about children is that they give you deductions. Not only that, but a child is just as good a taxpayer as a person of any age, and one of the great tricks in a tax system that has a sliding scale is to divide the income among a number of people, to bring it down below the minimum income that is taxable. At that time, I think, it was $900 or $1,000, with exemptions and standard deductions. So a person with around $1,000 paid about ten dollars tax. And the state exemption was way above $1,000, so there would be no state tax.

Now, when I came to this family, only the two brothers were reporting their services for tax purposes, which meant $6,000 income in each family. Grandma wasn't reporting any income or tax, though she worked—as you can imagine if you know the Japanese-American family situation—as hard or harder than any other member of the family. So the first trick was very simple— how to make these people into thirteen taxpayers.

The way you make each child a taxpayer is to set up a trust for him. They don't have to be permanent trusts, just short-term trusts. If you do it legitimately you must in fact give the trust income to the children. The Japanese-American families are quite closely knit, so this arrangement will work without difficulty. You don't have to worry about whether they are going to stay to-gether—the probability of divorce is not great. You don't have to worry that if the trust income is used for family purposes the child is later going to holler, "Hey, policeman, Mama took my money." That does happen occasionally in trust situations. But all of those things were unlikely here.

So I had thirteen taxpayers dividing up $12,000, and you can see very quickly that I wouldn't pay any tax for anybody. That would have been the simple solution in this case. But we did things slightly different for other reasons. We set up eight children's trusts and put Grandma on the payroll. We did nothing about the wives, because filing joint returns already gave them as much tax benefit as possible. Now, the children can get some income in trusts, but if they don't spend it for their support they go right on being deduct-ible for Papa and Mama. So we can put about $800 into each trust without having to pay tax on that. And then each family can still take six exemptions, which meant that they could have an income of about $4,500 apiece and pay no tax. It wasn't a very difficult problem.

We did something special for Grandma. She had worked all these years and had never drawn any money as income. She was then in her early sixties. One of the first things we did, and it has always given me great satisfaction, was to qualify her for Social Security. We paid her a maximum salary, even though it meant she had to pay tax on it. As I recall, she had to pay $500 or $600 a year in taxes, but in three years or so (I've forgotten how long the requirement was then) we had qualified her to receive the maxi-mum Social Security benefits. So when she became sixty-five she could retire and receive an income of $80 or $100 a month. I've always been very pleased with that. She saved that money and finally made a trip to Japan that she had wanted to make all her life. That would never have been possible for her otherwise. (I've often been asked to qualify a wife for Social Security whose husband is already making $50,000 a year. You know how badly they need it.)

There was one problem: we had given the money to the chil-dren, but the family needed it to live on. This is a more difficult problem when the children are very young. Obviously, a youngster two or four or even six years old can hardly acquiesce in buying things for the family with his trust income. But by the time they

HARRY MARGOLIS 391

are twelve, thirteen, fourteen, they might decide that they want to buy the sofa for the house or the car or something else. Such choices can be legitimate and are not likely to be attacked on audit anywhere along the line.

We were audited in this particular case ultimately. The family had been paying about $1,500 a year in taxes, and all of a sudden they stopped paying taxes. So the government came out to take a look. But the money had been used with skill within the family. They had to be fairly carefully directed for the first four or five years in how they should distribute it. But after things got going, one of the husbands, quite an able guy, learned the technique, and I haven't paid any attention to it, other than to say hello, in the last ten years.

That's an illustration of what can be done with a poor family. The accountant and I did it for nothing, but it would have cost approximately $5,000 in fees to have that work done. We saved them something in the neighborhood of $3,000 in a little over two years, and they went on making savings. It's been worth a great deal to that family. Several of the children have gone to college. That's why I've suggested that there is some potential even in the lower-income office.

The short-term trust should be an automatic thing. When and if you have a child, conception of the child and conception of the trust should go together. It automatically makes your deduction double, and the earlier you start it the better. If it's legitimate, of course, that money belongs to the kid, which is sometimes difficult. One way to handle that is to get yourself a big whip and make awfully certain that the youngster grows up in fear of you. Another way, obviously, is to have a relationship with your child in which love and affection prevail.

Neither one is reliable, the whip or the love and affection. But there's a third way, the way that a planner uses, to take care of youngsters. You set up your trust to run up to the ideal age for children—normally, giving them enough time to get through college. Meanwhile, you start giving them small amounts of money at age thirteen or fourteen, and see what they do with it. If they behave, fine—you give them a little bit larger amounts. If they give you a bad time, if the youngster at eighteen makes a comment, "When I'm twenty-one, I'm going to get this $42,000 and I'm going to have a ball," the poor child will discover that six months before he reached twenty-one, the trustees decided to make a long-term investment under which the trust proceeds will be tied up for the next ninety-two years.

This is a planning device that can be used where you have to. In the vast majority of cases in which I've been involved, I'm pleased to say it hasn't been necessary. It is a step that you hope you'll never have to take, but as a planner you have to tell the parties, "These are the risks."

There was one other tool we had with the Japanese-American family—namely, property, which isn't always available with poor families. It's a natural for tax arrangements. It happened that they had about five acres of land that had been acquired when they came back from detention camp after World War II. They had paid $10,000 for it, but it was on the main highway and had gone up greatly in value, so it was now worth about $80,000. The rent paid to the family was about $6,500, and we wanted to divide that among the children, give each one about $800 a year, on which they wouldn't have to pay income tax.

Now, in the field of taxation, if you want to give away the fruit you must also give away the tree. You can't keep the bond and let someone else clip the coupon—you've got to give him the bond too, even if only for a short period. So we divided the land into $10,000 parcels and made short-term gifts of it to the children. You can give up to $30,000 in a child's lifetime without having to pay gift tax on it. With eight beneficiaries we had no problem staying under that limit.

One other advantage took place when pieces of the property were sold. The children could take the capital gain, and it too was divided into smaller amounts that were taxed at minimal rates. In the middle-class family today there's always some kind of property interest. They are always borrowing or buying something. The most common tax-saving techniques that are available in these situations are (1) depreciation, which is as ridiculous a concept as is imaginable, but nevertheless offsets your income, dollar for dollar, and (2) deduction of any interest you are paying. Putting these two together, one of the techniques is to take whatever assets you have, give them the largest possible value for depreciation, get the largest possible loan from within the family unit, and delay payment on the loan.

This may be a little bit complex. Let me explain the theory behind it. We used to say, "If you will give me the use of a dollar, at the end of eleven years I'll give you back your dollar and I'll have a dollar of my own," because a dollar invested at 6 percent interest will produce two dollars in eleven years and eight months. At 10 percent interest rates, a dollar doubles in about seven years. In the same way, if I can delay taxation for a number of years, so that I'm using the government's tax dollar during the interim, maybe something delightful will happen. If you carry this to the ultimate in tax planning you would arrange to die at just the right moment, when you've spent every nickel you've got, including the government's tax dollars. Then the tax collector has one impossible job. If I had terminal cancer, I think I would try to arrange it that way. That's a fairly cold-blooded way of looking at the world, but taxation is a fairly cold-blooded field.

Let's come back to our idea. How can I delay the payment of a tax dollar? The law gives me a lot of outs. One of them is to just not be able to pay it, to be broke at the right time. That's a little dangerous; it's hard to put together and always involves an element of fraud, which isn't a good idea. I don't like that one. But within a family group it's entirely possible to arrange it legitimately.

Lawyers in every field learn very early the advantages of being able to make their clients judgment-proof. If a lawyer is representing a defendant in a personal-injury case, and the client has $10,000 and nothing else, and he's likely to lose the case, if that lawyer doesn't see to it that that $10,000 comes within areas that are exempt from judgment he's not being a good lawyer.

Another way to delay payment, providing you are careful about relationships within the family, is to take an asset, sell it to someone who's close enough to you so you don't really lose the asset, and arrange to take payment for it over a period of years. Your tax on the payment is delayed over that period of years, and the person who takes the asset may also be getting several advantages.

Let's assume each of us has his own home. We can deduct taxes, interest, and so on for that home, but that's all. Now, if you move the houses around just once, so that I have your house and you have my house and we rent them back, then they are income property, which qualifies for depreciation; we can start playing around with interest deductions; we can create new values; we can delay payments. These arrangements are so extremely difficult for the person in the low-income bracket that it just isn't done.

One other opportunity for delaying tax suggests itself. It may be difficult to follow. There are two types of accounting: cash accounting and accrual accounting. The majority of taxpayers are cash-basis taxpayers who report income for the year in which they receive it and report deductions in the year in which payment is made. The accrual-basis taxpayer reports income and deductions without regard to when he gets or pays them. In accrual accounting, income and deductions are treated as such for all tax purposes as soon as their legal character as income or expense is fixed, without regard to receipt or payment. It is simply a form of accounting.

So if the buyer of a piece of property incorporates it, small as it is, and goes on accrual basis, he can end up with a situation in which he has a deduction of interest due on the property payments, even though he may not actually pay that interest to a cash-basis seller, who also wants to delay tax on his income. Now, this is a game for experts only. If you're going to cook up a transaction like this, it had better be cooked awfully carefully. The documents have to be done properly and you have to watch the relationships of your parties.

By combining these techniques, a family can easily get a few thousand dollars' worth of interest to deduct, plus a few thousand dollars in depreciation each year for eight or ten years, and delay those tax payments.

Actually, with people in the price class that I represent, with a man who makes $100,000 a year it is very easy for me to eliminate all tax. I deliberately do not do so. I don't want to rub it in too much. I prefer to have him pay tax on about $20,000 or $25,000 or whatever it costs him to live.

The problem for rich people is not so much income tax, but gift and estate tax—how to pass it on to their children without giving the government such a big chunk. For example, not too long ago in Texas a father who had an enormous amount of money wanted to do something for his children, but he had already given them as much as he could in tax-free gifts. (You know, the government allows you to give $3,000 a year plus $30,000 over a lifetime in tax-free gifts.) This father talked to his lawyers, who obviously were very bright, and they said, "For heaven's sake, lend your children your money, interest free." And so he did. The Du Ponts have been doing this for many years. It's one of their key techniques for moving money to their youngsters, and they've gotten away with it for a long, long time. You see, by loaning the children the money, the father gives them the value to be gotten from the use of that money. This particular father loaned his son and daughter enough so that they each picked up about $500,000 on the use of the money. Of course, since it was a loan, an essential feature was that it had to be returned.

The Internal Revenue Service contested this arrangement and said, "It's true that the kids did give back the money at the end of three or four years, but you've given them the use of the money without requiring them to pay interest." To make a long story short, the government lost the case. And under our law that's completely correct. Think of it in terms of ten dollars: If I borrowed ten dollars from you, I don't think that at the end of a couple of weeks you'd ask me to give you back $10.07 or something. You'd probably chase me and be very glad just to get your ten bucks back. But, as you can quickly see, in the case of the very rich, this becomes an interesting technique.

The problem with most rich people is that they would like to give the money and then forget about it. Then, of course, the IRS is going to win, because the whole thing is phony. But this man in Texas didn't do it halfway. He complied with the law and made the law work for him. And the courts upheld the point that you can give someone the use of money without paying tax as a gift.

Attorney's fees have all kinds of tax ramifications. Let me give you a typical illustration, a very simple one in the field of domestic relations. In a divorce, if the attorney's fee is paid by the wife it's deductible. If it's paid by the husband, it's not deductible. I don't think any of you have to go to law school to figure that one out: you make sure that the wife pays the lawyer and the husband gives the money back to the wife as alimony. Yet, in eight out of ten cases today or seven out of ten (they've learned something in the last few years—it used to be ten out of ten, even in the big firms), the husband is paying the attorney's fee. It's just absolute nonsense. I don't care how much they're at each other's throats, let the attorney's fee be paid by the wife and have it deductible.

Time after time, calling a thing by a different name, like this, can save you tax dollars. Let's take child support and deduction of the child as a dependent. Normally speaking, now, the divorce settlement specifies who gets the deduction, but why not specify both in such a way that you beat the IRS? Give the child deduction to the higher-bracket taxpayer, where it's most useful, and put the support in terms of alimony. Support isn't deductible, but alimony is. Or suppose, instead of support, we give the children some income through trusts. All of a sudden the support is deductible. You can structure your agreement to call it whatever you darn please.

From my position, it's strictly a matter of mathematics. How does tax apply to each side of the settlement? No matter what, there's a way of structuring that settlement better and dividing the savings.

Another example comes up in workmen's-compensation and personal-injury cases. The lawyers who try these cases have finally learned something about tax consequences. If a client recovers something for physical injury, no tax. If he recovers it for loss of earning power, watch out—it may be taxable as ordinary income. I've had situations where the parties were quite far apart and where I could settle the case because the tax consequences flowing from the name given to a certain payment made up the difference between them. This doesn't happen very often. But every personal-injury case that is filed does have some claim for loss of wages or earning power, and many a death case is calculated almost exclusively on that basis. The lawyer had better be sure that when that judgment or settlement is translated into specifics, payment is arranged in such a way that the tax collector gets as little as possible, and this depends largely on what you call it.

Let's take another example: a real-estate broker. His fees are generally ordinary income. If the deal is small and conventional, that 5 or 10 percent is not worth doing much about. But suppose he's getting a $50,000 fee for a large transaction; then it might pay to translate that ordinary income into capital gain, which is only 50 percent taxable—he'd pay tax on only half as much. It's not terribly difficult to do. To get a capital gain he has to own the asset. So the party who wants to sell the property sells it to the broker at the price he wants to get, minus the $50,000 that he would have paid the broker as a fee; he's satisfied. Now the broker can turn around, after fulfilling certain regulations on holding periods and other matters, and sell the property to the man who wanted to buy it, adding $50,000 to the price the broker paid the seller. Ordinary income is turned into a capital gain. It's done constantly. Normally, it's done not directly through the real-estate broker but indirectly through a separate corporation established for that purpose. Every large real-estate firm in the United States has some alter-ego entity that it uses for those purposes in very large transactions.

Sometimes you have opposite factors at work. The buyer may want to call it one thing so that it's immediately deductible, while the seller wants it to be called something else, so that he can take it as a capital gain. What you do is simply sit down with both parties and say, "Give me your tax returns and I'll tell you what it will be. Whatever comes out mathematically best for the two of you is what we'll call it. That's all." And in a sufficient number of cases the difference is large enough so that in twenty minutes or an hour or two, if the parties will cooperate, you can give them a choice that will involve tax savings.

Planning is what makes the difference. Here's another example —I always tell this because it's such a vivid one: you may or may not remember the Remington case several years ago involving an $8 million estate, on which they paid estate tax of $5 million! Just no tax-planning work had been done. A few years later, when John D. Rockefeller, Jr., died, he left a $150 million estate and paid no tax. The Rockefellers have always been very careful in the field of taxation. In his case it was absurdly simple. They did two things. They had him marry his nurse, which gave rise to the marital deduction, meaning that half—$75 million—was exempt from tax, and they gave the rest to charity. Eliminated the tax.

If they hadn't done this they'd have had infinitely less money. When the Ford family created the Ford Foundation they were not being generous at all. If they had failed to do so they might have lost the company. Instead, by giving rise to the foundation, they had enormous charitable deductions available to balance against their income. They eliminated the extra-high estate tax, and they kept control of the company. Before then, they influenced only the automobile market; after they formed the foundation, they influenced world politics. They really got value out of this money.

AFG: Does the personal quotient get mixed in with the tax? Or do people look at money as if it's just money and has nothing to do with human relationships?

Margolis: Let me give you an illustration concerning the differ- ences between men and women. In twenty-five years I have never yet had a case in which a man has said to me that he worried about his wife remarrying after he dies. I have had a large number in which the wife was concerned about the husband remarrying. The first time I ran into this the couple had just celebrated their fiftieth anniversary. We were discussing their wills. I knew them quite well, and I was blithely describing a fairly simple trust setup under which if one of them died the estate would go to the other with the power of appointment, and the woman said, "No, no, no. I'm not having that with this husband of mine. The minute I'm buried he'll hook up with some young chick and my children will be deprived of the property." It struck me very vividly because I had never experienced it before.

The woman is concerned about the children; she's still con- cerned that her husband will remarry and give away what belongs to the children. I've never had a husband who thought in those terms; I don't myself. But my wife does. She's thinking now of the grandchildren.

The human values are there, and as a tax practitioner you have to keep saying, "Taxes do not come first." How many academic solutions I've made during the years that fit the specific situation but were wrong from the human point of view! Very often in taxation there's a moral problem in that your client is so com- pletely at your mercy. The opportunity to cheat him is almost unlimited, and some lawyers do on occasion succumb. This is true in all fields of the law, but perhaps more in taxation because so much of what you do nobody really understands, and all you have to do is change a word here or there to get totally different results.

This creates another great temptation, particularly for young lawyers. It's so easy to give a superficial appearance of doing your job. There are so many fraudulent wills—I mean fraudulent in that the practitioner has just pulled something out of a book because he doesn't want to admit he doesn't know how to draw a will. But the client usually dies before the evidence comes to light. Regrettably, of the 30,000-odd members of the California bar, I don't think there are 1,000 who are competent to draw a will. They don't give enough thought to the client's problem, but the client does not know that. He sees a document an inch thick, lots of pages; he can't understand it anyway, and he just says, "Where do I sign?"

AFG: Do you tell your clients what to do or do you ask them what they want done?

Margolis: I'm not a good illustration, because in recent years I have been largely acting as a consultant to other attorneys and very seldom see the client. But the client will very rapidly build a relationship with you. You become his friend. Most people are looking for something to hold on to, and the lawyer assumes that position very quickly.

Student: Do you practice before the tax court?

Margolis: Yes, although I used to consider that when I got to tax court I had failed. In other words, since my job is to tell you today what's going to take place next November and to plan it, to control the facts, and to know the law, if I can't beat it—if I reach the tax court—then I'm not doing my job well enough. In the last few years, I've done consulting in half a dozen cases where the mistake was already made, and I'm doing the best I can with it. But in cases that I plan from the beginning, there is no excuse for violating the law; I don't have to.

Don't misunderstand me in the slightest—I would have no hesitation to violate every criminal statute in the field of taxation if I thought I could get away with it and do some good with it. I just can't. There's no morality to the field of taxation. (I've been criticized for expressing this point of view. I was a member of a nationwide committee concerned with taxation, and when, about the third meeting, I said that, I was politely dropped from the committee.) There's morality to dealing with people or dealing with issues, but there's no morality to our system of taxation. There is nothing more corrupt than the fact that the man who runs an oil well can get a tax break for doing it but a guy who works on the dock handling freight can't. Illustrations of the corrupt nature of our law are almost endless. So the only reason I don't violate the law is because I can sleep better at night and I can do a better job for the client by staying within the law. That's important, too, because after all the client ultimately will pay the most.

There's no excuse for sticking your neck out. You don't have to. The revolution is a different story; but if you're in the field of taxation, comply with the law. You can beat the taxation laws and do it honestly. I'm fairly cold-blooded about it, and I always keep my fingers crossed. I've never ultimately lost a major tax case in twenty-five years.

Recently I've been doing a great deal of tax-court work, primarily because I'm heavily in the foreign field and the government is after the foreign field now. We've reached the position where the lower-level Internal Revenue agents can no longer settle the disputes. In other words, we've harassed them badly enough so the only way they can harass us in return is to force us to court. We're going to beat them in court, because we've done our work right, but they're making it cost us more money and take more of our time.

Also, it's one of the techniques the government uses to get a change in the law out of Congress. First they go to Congress and ask for the change. Congress turns them down, because there are a half-dozen very rich people out in the boondocks someplace who tell Congress, "Don't you give it to them." Then the government goes out and loses a case. After they've lost three or four, they get up before a committee and say, "Well, this one cost us this much money and this one cost us that much money. We were here four years ago asking for this change, which would have avoided this, and you wouldn't give it to us." Along about then they get a law.

The political situation in this country is such that actually billions are controlled by relatively small amounts of money. Our whole political campaign structure can be run on about $200 million. That $200 million then controls everything else. Around $170 million of that comes from people who have interests in taxes. An Agnew who can raise $10 million will determine how $400 billion are spent. That's how little it takes. The key to that $400 billion is that $10 million, which comes from people who save it in taxes. They control where those destroyers are going to be built, what's going to happen to Israel, where the Arab planes are going to come from. Give them a fair tax system and Agnew wouldn't be able to raise money the same way. If it were even a little bit more proportional, it would cost these rich people half of what they get. But as it stands now, never has so much been bought so cheaply. It's being bought every day that cheaply. Nothing will happen without a basic change in the whole society. When you dig into this question, the society you uncover is a pretty sorry society.

I'll give you an interesting illustration: one of our richest men died with $100 million in trust in the Bahamas. Rumor goes, and I would not be surprised, that he paid no estate tax in the United States and that the operation had always been substantially free from tax in the U.S. How was it done? Remarkably simple device. And you know who paid for it? You and I.

This man set up a company in the Netherlands Antilles that bought products at a fair price from his company in the United States. This Antilles company then was the distributor for South America. South America has currency problems, as you probably know, and most of its governments have their currencies backed up on an annual basis by U.S. currency. In Brazil, where the biggest killing was made, the cruzeiro, the Brazilian currency, has constantly gone downhill in violent fluctuations.

What he did was, each December or January he entered into an agreement for the delivery of products to Brazil at the then value of the cruzeiro, which value was guaranteed by the U.S. government for the ensuing twelve months. Every time the cruzeiro went down in value, the man got more cruzeiros, but he could trade them in for dollars at the January cruzeiro value, which meant he got more dollars than on the market exchange rate. He had to pay 30 percent tax on this to the Netherlands Antilles, which he was perfectly willing to do.

Then he put the money in the Bahama central trust. Why in the Bahamas? There is no income tax or estate tax in the Bahamas. Why in a trust? A trust is like a corporation, a separate legal entity. This separate entity is a nonresident alien, and a nonresident alien can sell an asset in the United States with no tax. How delightful. Now, if that nonresident alien ties in with the distributing company in the Netherlands Antilles, which can earn interest in the U.S. without tax under certain circumstances, he has put together a perfect setup. He takes losses and deductions in the

U.S., and he takes gains and profits abroad, under a tax treaty. If it is done very carefully and set up right, the governments of the two countries actually compel him to take advantage of the law.

You think that any Congress we have is going to change the laws that allow that? Let's not kid ourselves. With those savings, the rich of this country can afford to buy the entire Senate if necessary.

Overseas trusts and investments are a large part of my work. By the way, I don't have to lead the parade in using the Bahamas for my clients. Sullivan and Cromwell, all the big corporate firms in the country, are doing it for me.

Even supposing Congress does take away a gimmick, as fast as Congress changes the law we find another gimmick. That's what's delightful about this game. (There is only one way to stop the game and that is to throw out the whole thing and start over again.) For example, a very common thing we used to do was to "capitalize" interest. Interest is ordinary income, taxed at 100 percent. A capital gain is taxed essentially at 50 percent. If I buy a house that costs $12,000, by the time I get through paying for it I will pay around $28,000, because of the interest. We used to talk to the buyer and the seller and say, "Why not pay $22,000 and no interest?" This was magnificent for the buyer, who would save $6,000. It was also magnificent for the seller, who had capital gain for the whole thing here and now. The only one it was bad for was the tax collector.

By 1963, the government had had enough of this. It was losing too much money, so it passed an "imputed interest" rule. Then you couldn't do this anymore. If you didn't have an interest factor in a transaction, they interpreted an interest factor for you. You could use a 4 percent factor if you wished; if you didn't, they'd interpret a 5 percent factor. You know what happened? The law hasn't been changed, but the interest rates have changed. So today, with 10 percent interest we put in a 4 percent factor and capitalize the other 6 percent.

Student: Suppose you have a client who's making money illegally—for instance, by making book or selling dope. He wants to put his money someplace so that he doesn't have it under his mattress and so that it's not reported income that he has to pay tax on. How do you go about setting up a Swiss bank account, and how does he get money out of that account when he wants to, so he can bring it back over here?

Margolis: I have fairly strong views on that subject. If it's holding up the Bank of America, maybe I would handle that case. Most other criminal matters that come across my desk I reject. I simply can't do work for the man who pushes the dope. I told you I'd violate any law, do anything else, throw the bomb in the revolution, but I won't support the man who pushes dope. This is where I happen to draw the line for myself.

But to answer your question on how to plan for these people. There are two basic ways that it's done: one by the Mafia, which is highly sophisticated, and another by the petty criminal. The man who steals from the cash register, as I like to describe him, has got it in cash. Once he gets it out of the United States, there's no trick to opening a Swiss bank account. You or I can walk into any bank in Switzerland and as long as we hand them the cash there are no questions asked.

Student: Is there any limit on how much?

Margolis: No limit, no nothing. The Swiss banks have no hesitation taking Franco's money or Himmler's money or anybody else's. Swiss bankers have a very simple rule: They'll take any money that's negotiable; they will respect the party's confidence, and they will act "honorably" in returning the money to that party. They set up techniques for the movement of money.

How do you move it? There's no legitimate way to move it, obviously. You can never take money that was corrupt, that was infected, and cure it simply by getting it out of the country in cash, putting it in a Swiss bank account, and then taking it out to spend it.

Student: What do you mean, the money can't be cured?

Margolis: Don't misunderstand me. It's very easy to spend, if you're willing to get out of the country and spend it. It's impossible to bring it back to the place where you got it in the first instance in any way that's safe. I would suggest spending it somewhere else. In other words, I don't think it would be a good idea to run guns in a country and go back there with the money you got from it.

If you bring it back here and you're living it up, with fourteen girl friends in various places, a number of fast automobiles, and some horses, and you're reporting $8,200 a year for taxes, the government will step in and say, "Explain yourself." Or they simply assess as your taxable income everything they think you're spending anyplace. Then the burden is on you to prove otherwise.

If you're talking about a man who's got an illegal $1,000, who cares? Although, forgive me: the man who's got $1,000 is the one who'll end up going to jail! The man who's got $1,000,000 will probably have a gimmick.

Let me tell you how the really sophisticated criminals work. They pay tax and they pay tax lawyers. They remember that Al Capone was picked up for tax evasion, not for any other criminal activity. They don't dirty their hands when they take the money from the dope pusher. They're running a legitimate business—a hotel, a laundry chain, a trucking firm, a housing development. They see to it that the illegal money comes through channels into this business, and then they go ahead and do exactly the same kind of tax planning I do. And they do pay tax on it, believe it or not. Once they've moved it from the criminal to the legitimate, they are the most honest taxpayers there are. They've gotten theirs. They're not going to chisel any more. They're taking no chances.

Student: How do they move it into legitimate businesses?

Margolis: There are many, many techniques. Actually you can't solve the first step, but you may bury it well enough so that it gets lost. That's the real technique. One of the oldest tricks in the world is to trade dollars. You get the cash to a particular area and then bring it back as a loan to a legitimate business or a capital investment. That's the way the big gamblers in Las Vegas do it primarily. All their skin money ends up as equity in something. The money is gotten out, very often to Hong Kong, and is used to set up a corporation there. Then it's loaned to some guy to build an apartment house in San Francisco for $5 million. That's obviously legitimate. He took the $5 million, he's got it, he owes it, his books are clear, and the company in Hong Kong has got an investment. From then on that money can be handled pretty freely.

It's a fascinating area, but I cannot emphasize too strongly that it's an extremely dangerous area. Number one, people who handle that kind of money at the lower levels occasionally end up in an alley dead. And, number two, the government does a better job on these guys than it is given credit for. Almost all of the small people are caught sooner or later. The "legitimate robbers," the big businessmen with Bahamas trusts, get away with it, and quite successfully, because they comply with the law, although what they do could not be more dishonest.

I like to think that I push hard on this subject of integrity to the client. If I find him stealing when I come into the picture, I stop him. He doesn't have to steal. By careful tax planning we can create deductions so that he can save honestly.

This means we have to do our homework. We must know everything there is to know about the client. We have to get the facts. Every case is different. That's another reason why the lower-income client is too hard to work for, because you can't afford to spend the time doing that kind of job. You get the tax returns, you examine the family relationships, you see the business, you look at the statements. You have to be supplemented by an accountant, and you yourself also have to have a keen eye for the statement. You should know intuitively how things look to the auditor. You should understand relationships of numbers. All of these things are essential. Every good lawyer—I've never known an exception—does his homework.

I have always given to the client a concern and attention that I do not give to myself. Therefore I've earned the client's trust. I can write a check on almost any of my clients' accounts in any amount at any time. I don't do it, of course. If there is anything that gives me pride in my work, it's the fact that the clients trust me and have cause to do so.

That has nothing to do with taxation. That ought to be true whether it's workmen's compensation, community work, architecture, or whatever, and it's awfully hard to do, whatever you are in. There is no way to do it except by delivering the goods. You've got to care.

AFG: How many hours a week do you work?

Margolis: I'm a very bad example. I work too many hours, because I don't have the sense to come in out of the rain, and because I don't know a darn thing about administration, and because I'm always fascinated by the problem. Name anything and I'll give you a tax plan around it. I don't care what it is—a piece of cheese, I'll have a whole factory going.

You actually can represent only about one client a month— twelve a year. That's probably too many for the first several years. You can ultimately do, with satisfactory service, about twenty-five or thirty and that's it. I'm thinking in terms of a client who is a $50,000-a-year physician. You cannot do more than thirty and do them conscientiously, no matter how you organize the work.

But the nice thing about taxation, you see, as opposed to the personal-injury field, is that you only have to chase the ambulance once. When you've caught him, you've got him. And when he dies you've got his family and when they die you've got someone else and when you die someone can inherit the case. It's much easier to build your portfolio.

Student: How do you handle 150 clients, then?

Margolis: I do largely consulting work, not direct handling of clients. I was no good at arguing cases and I'm very bad at hand-holding, because I always tell the client the truth and then the client hates me, so what happened to me was that I became a specialist in the field in which I was almost alone. Other lawyers with whom I have worked at one time or another, when they get a problem in my field, call on me. I don't work well with the client; I work well with ideas, and therefore I limit myself largely to consulting. It's a highly specialized role that is fairly unusual.

Tax planning is a wide-open field, simply because it is not being well done today. You could go into the biggest law-office building in any city and before you got up to the fifth floor you'd have enough clients to take care of you forever.

Student: You were talking about how the rich keep hold of their money and how the Ford family turned their money into power. I'm interested in finding out similar things about the trustees of my university. I'd like to know about the deals they make and what they're involved in. Do you know any ways I can find out these things?

Margolis: I know what you mean. Very tough question. The office that does the tax-planning work for any of the major interests in your community would probably know these things, but that information is protected by the confidential relationship. That is enormously important. There are occasions when I've respected a confidential relationship when I would very much have preferred not to do so.

Student: Yes, but in a tax case aren't there some things that have to remain public records?

AFG: One of the reasons many lawsuits are filed is for discovery. You file a lawsuit for some purpose, and the minute the suit is filed you have a right to see and ask questions about and get copies of a lot of things that the opposition would never reveal otherwise. The suit may never come to trial.

Margolis: One of the toughest areas of all to get into is a man's tax returns. A representative of the President can get anything he damn pleases, for obvious reasons. But out in the courts I think you would find that a trustee's tax return was a very difficult thing to get, and even if you got it I would be very surprised if you could understand it.

One of the things we do for major clients is design tax returns for them. Most of our clients are in the category of the physician who's reporting his taxes, so his return requires very little design. But, for example, it used to be that if there was something we didn't want the auditor to pick up we formed a partnership and put that item into the partnership return, because traditionally they never looked as carefully at the partnership returns. Any sense to it? None at all. If I were working for the government, the first thing I'd look at would be partnership returns.

This doesn't work as well anymore. Now we hide it in corporations. Actually we're not hiding. I've often said to a client, "I don't care if the IRS man is sitting here while I'm telling you what I'm going to do, but I prefer that he not be here simply because I'm not looking for the trouble." If it came to a court case I would win, because I stick within the law. But I don't want to have to win. It costs time. It costs money. It costs energy. If he's going to hit me on a small item, on the dinner that I paid for, and say it was nondeductible, what do I do? I can't afford to fight; I want to settle. This business of fighting on principles if one dollar is involved—don't go into taxation if you have that kind of attitude. Your attitude has to be that the auditor is entitled to something and you're entitled to something. My rule is roughly that he's entitled to 15 percent of what he ought to get. If he takes 20 percent I don't get mad. Anything over 20 percent I'll fight.

AFG: Are you advising these students to become tax lawyers, Harry?

Margolis: My advice to the law student is: If you want to make money, enjoy that course in taxation, take all you can, choose it as your field. You'll be able to live pretty much where you want to. You can really be quite independent. It's the easiest kind of work to chase.

Judging from the young lawyers I've known through the years, I would say that a lawyer fresh out of school in 1965 will have gone from $10,000 to $18,000 to $28,000 to $40,000 a year by 1970. There is no other field of law in which that can be done. It's corrupt, it's immoral, and it's fattening. That's the nature of taxation.

Now, you have to work; you have to have some judgment. But most of you, I'm sure, have that quality. I might point out, for those of you who are black, that the taxation field for the black lawyer is absolutely unlimited, if you want to make money.

You can make money in it, but I know of no way in which you can make a contribution to changing society by handling tax clients. The constructive work in taxation will be done in the political area, not in the client area. Not just tax reform—the war in Vietnam is tax-based. You could stop the war in Vietnam a darn sight quicker by doing something about the tax system in this country than by anything else you do. The real power of Congress to remake our system rests strongly in the field of taxation, in my opinion.

Taxation determines where businesses are located, how pollution is handled, where a roadway goes, where a subdivision goes, how a trade union operates. In every one of these things tax is more important than any other economic factor. So if you go into politics and you know a great deal about taxation and are willing to use it the right way, the contributions you could make to a better society are virtually unlimited.

Student: It seems to me that tax lawyers just serve politicians who create a tax structure that is beneficial to them for their purposes. So how can the tax structure be used to benefit poverty groups or poor people, who aren't getting that money to begin with or keeping it or paying it out in taxes?

Margolis: I hate that question, because normally it gets me off on a two-hour economic argument that nobody of any conventional political persuasion accepts. But let me try to be brief.

The ideal society will have no tax system as we know it. In this sense, the germ of the ideal society is being formed in the socialist states. At the present moment China comes closest, but it's rapidly losing it. The whole story of where we're at, where we're going, and what our values are, rests in a statement of the quality of life that we want. For me it's having enough to eat, a place to sleep, some education, a little freedom, and an opportunity to run away once in a while. But there's one obligation, and it's one that I find is extraordinarily difficult for young people: the obligation to work. I don't care if a person is a paraplegic or blind or has an IQ of seventy, he can work within his limits. In fact, to deny him the opportunity to make his own way within the limits of his competence is the worst insult you can give to any man. That's the ultimate of human corruption.

Once you've established that social system, taxation is abolished. Your work is the tax you pay to that society. There is no other tax on anything because there is no need for taxes. That society will produce as much as it possibly can within the limits of the quality of the life it wants. In the United States, there is plenty of capacity, if we would eat only a little less richly, if we would give kids a little more education, a little more help, if we wouldn't use people like Harry Margolis, who have talent, to do things that are absurd. Let me teach third-graders how to read; that's useful. And no lawyers and no law schools as we know them. Then indeed do we have a chance at a society in which the whole problem is one of production and distribution, and I don't care whether it's pot or alcohol or sex, providing it's not exploitative.

I know of no way of achieving that in my lifetime, or even in your lifetime. I wish I did. Therefore, what are the alternatives? How do we take politics and the field of taxation and do something worthwhile with them?

There are things that can be done within our society politically in the field of taxation. Ralph Nader is an example of how I think it has to come. I don't think it will come from any single one of us putting out a shingle. I would say very cynically that you've got to appeal to the worst elements of man's nature and just make it too damn expensive to do the wrong things. The great Greek play *Lysistrata,* where the women refuse to sleep with the men until they end the war, was written with acute knowledge of people, let me tell you.

Take the war in Vietnam. There is a genuine chance of making that war expensive. If the young people will take their position in society politically (whether they will or not I don't know), they could make war too goddam expensive from the point of view of taxation. If I have to work eighteen hours a day to support the war, I'm going to find a way to fight against that war, not for any moral reasons, but because I love myself!

We've never had a war as unpopular as this. We've never had this number of people refusing to fight. It is unheard of in this country. I think that, given the present climate, you could for the first time get through the Congress of the United States, if it were well handled, a law that would eliminate all profit on war. Oh, brother, then would you see a battle in this country!

AFG: He calls himself a cynic, and he believes this!

Margolis: You have to make it hurt. You have to make it cost. If it cost me ten dollars every time I went by a black man and didn't say hello, oh, brother, would I be running down the street to say hello to black men! I think you could design a tax system to accomplish almost anything, from rape of every woman to respect for every woman, from increasing homosexuality to abolishing it. If it cost Dow Chemical money to make napalm, they wouldn't make napalm. If it cost the universities money to have ROTC, there'd be no ROTC. That fight has got to be made, and the young people can do it.

A single tax, whatever its form, is a step in the right direction, simply because you can't foul up a single tax as badly as you can a bunch of them.

I have no optimism; I'm essentially cynical, but I think we ought to work toward a situation in which taxation is no longer taught in law school, in which there is no such animal anymore. I know of nothing politically more important.

There have been periods in our history when political parties have changed. Young people have an opportunity today, which I'm afraid they are not going to take—there is no evidence they are going to take it—of forming a life-style political party. Certainly you young people are smarter today, you are better informed, you live in a world that is moving much faster; the challenges are much greater.

I think it's a difference in our two ages. I'm pessimistic and discouraged. When my father was forty-five, I told him off quite comfortably, gave him my full views about what he stood for. He made one very quiet comment: "Harry, I ask you only one thing. When you're forty-five, will you say the same thing?" And if he had been alive when I was forty-five I would have had to apologize. (Incidentally, you'll do this, too, when you get older—you'll quote your own father. All our fathers get wonderful after they're gone.)

But I happen to be cynical. I think man is bent to destroy himself, despite all the affection I have for your generation.

Student: I'm cynical and pessimistic, too, and I think that is more prevalent in the younger generation today than it was in your time.

Margolis: It pays to go into the suburban areas and see what is happening there. The people are all real; they all have their eyes open; they are all drinking and functioning, worried about the things that are going on; and yet they are all dead. This is exactly Orwell's world, of course.

Life exists, in my observation, only in the ghetto (and not always there because of the struggle), and at the very highest levels, believe it or not, where there are people who are comfortable and nevertheless intellectually interested.

In my experience, it takes extreme circumstances to bring out the best in people. I wish it weren't true, but I think that if you keep the screws on tight, the amount of quality that comes through is unbelievable. I love very much to sit in the sun, I have to confess it. But a man fighting for his survival manages to put out just a little bit more than you ever thought he had. If you add a little bit of culture, of poetics, of sentimentality, of romanticism, then all of a sudden you find completely illiterate people who are more articulate than you are. You discover that a George Jackson in Soledad Prison with ten years of jail can write as Byron wrote. This is impossible. This man could not have written these letters. But he did. And if he had been free, he never would have written them.

Student: It can bring out the worst in people, too.

Margolis: Oh, yes, but the worst and the best are very much the same thing.

There is an awful lot to know about the human animal. We may discover that even in an ideal world there are certain types of pressures we have to keep on him to make him produce at his best.

When I was a kid, I always wanted to hang from a bar by my toes. Have you ever tried that? I would hang by my toes, fall on my head, and go home with a bloody mouth. My mother would give me hell. I don't know why I kept trying; but I wasn't satisfied until I could hang by my toes from anything, even from a six-story building where, if I fell, that was the end. Any sense? Not at all.

Who was it who said, "A man's reach should exceed his grasp, or what's a heaven for"? There ain't no heaven as far as I'm concerned, except that reach. There's no beauty except in that reach. There's nothing except in that reach. So reach!

Don't stop fighting, that's all I can say. I'll help every way I can. The best thing that could happen to me would be to have my usefulness destroyed, to have everything my practice stands for destroyed, and to have every single benefit my clients get outlawed.

DEATH ROW AND
SMALL-TOWN PRACTICE
Carl Shapiro

Shapiro: I'm Carl Shapiro of Marin County, a small-town lawyer.

AFG: Carl is a lot more than that. He does both trial and appellate work and he's always there when you need him. He takes cases for people on death row, and he knows a lot about habeas corpus. He opened his office in Marin County, and pretty soon there was a draft-information committee there.

Carl, first let's talk about death row. Some people don't seem to be as concerned about the death penalty these days, because there have been few executions recently, but there are something like ninety men on death row in California alone. And of course the basic issue in a death-row case is whether the defendant can do anything about some unfairness in his case, and that same problem arises in other criminal cases.

So, suppose you are asked to handle the case of a client who is set to be executed in twelve hours. Let us say it's in a place where you've never practiced before; and the defendant is a Black Panther. What would you do?

Shapiro: The main thing you've got to learn is how to ask for help. If you know how to ask for help, then you can get things done. The mechanics of finding out where to go may take somebody an hour, and if you have to do that yourself you've lost one twelfth of your time. You can't afford that. If there are two people working

413

414 DEATH ROW AND SMALL-TOWN PRACTICE

on it, one person can be finding the judge and the other can be preparing the next set of papers or seeing what to do with it.

One thing you must understand in this situation: Be prepared to work on this and only this right up to the last moment. You can't say, "Well, gee, I've got a case in the morning." This is a full-time and sole job. There is no time for anything else.

Another reason to have two lawyers is this: I'm a small-town lawyer, and although I have all the legal skills, I don't have all the influence with some of these federal judges that a prominent, well-established big-city lawyer will have. So I've brought in Charlie Garry and George Davis and other prestigious lawyers. They are often willing to help in these cases. And I've been brought in a couple of times. Mechanically, one person can't do it alone.

If somebody comes to you about handling the case of a prisoner in another area, you've got to find somebody in the district where the prisoner is located to handle the case with you.

AFG: There are always two problems in a lawsuit, and if you're in a hurry you've got to be very clear about both of them. One is where you go, and the other is what you say when you get there. It does you absolutely no good to find the law and prepare a good pleading if you don't know where to file it or what to do if it's turned down. So you can really divide the case into the procedural and the substantive aspects and, if you have two people, work out who's going to concentrate on each one. Since you have an absolute deadline, you'd better make a calendar. "My deadline is tomorrow at twelve o'clock, therefore by eleven o'clock I have to have accomplished thus and so, therefore by ten o'clock I've got to be at such and such place, and so on," all working back from the deadline.

Student: Isn't the common procedure in death-row cases an automatic appeal to the state supreme court?

Shapiro: Yes. Almost every place that I have read about has that automatic appeal without going to an intermediate appellate court. This is a right the state can't take away. Even when the defendant pleaded guilty, his appeal goes to the highest state court, and as a rule they have jurisdiction for all subsequent phases of that case.

Any single justice on the court would have the right to grant a stay of execution, and this can be done without any papers being filed. So that would be the first remedy you would try for if you had only twelve hours. Chances are you'd be coming into the case after working hours, so you have the problem of finding a justice. But you can find them. Now, I'll warn you that in California the supreme-court justices have decided among themselves not to do this individually. They convene the full court specially to consider a stay of execution.

Assuming you can't get a stay from a state supreme-court justice, the second place you would go is to the governor of the state. You try there next because you can always reach him, and there's a California statute saying that the governor can postpone an execution. That statute came about because of a case Charles Garry and I worked on that resulted in a hopeless mess because this was not available. The supreme-court justices' control of executions is part of their appellate jurisdiction and power of enforcement of judgment, but the governor's power comes directly from his pardoning power and can't be taken away by the legislature. So you call the State Capitol and try to get through to the governor's secretary, and you'll find somebody who can get you to the governor.

The third place you go is to the United States district court. This is generally done by filing for a writ of habeas corpus.

Student: Exactly what is habeas corpus?

Shapiro: Habeas corpus is a very old remedy dating from the struggle for the Magna Carta in 1215 in England. The United States Supreme Court described it in 1963 in a very important case, *Fay v. Noia:* "Its root principle is that in a civilized society, government must always be accountable to the judiciary for a man's imprisonment; if the imprisonment cannot be shown to conform with the fundamental requirements of law, the individual is entitled to his immediate release." So when you file a petition for a writ of habeas corpus, you are asking the judge to release the prisoner because something about his trial or conviction was unfair.

Obviously, a judge is not likely to issue such a writ lightly, because, by the time the case gets to him, several courts have already said that the trial and the conviction were fair. The most the judge is likely to do when he gets your petition is hold a hearing on whether he should issue the writ releasing the prisoner. Many judges will not want to go even that far. They will, instead, only want to hold a hearing at which the government should show cause why the habeas writ should not be granted. At such a hearing the prisoner need not be present, only the lawyers and the judge. At a habeas corpus hearing, the prisoner must be present as well. This may seem like a small distinction, but you can see that the presence of the prisoner would affect the mood of the hearing, particularly in a death-row case.

To file for habeas corpus does require the filing of papers, unlike the two techniques I just talked about. Basically you must file a petition for writ of habeas corpus and a brief or memorandum stating the facts in the case and the reasons for issuing the writ and describing similar cases in which other courts have issued writs. In many federal district courts, and in several state courts, blank petition forms are available from the court clerks. If you have a copy handy in an emergency, fine. If not, write your own and it will be accepted.

AFG: These forms were prepared so that prisoners could prepare their own petitions for habeas corpus writs. The 1963 decision Carl mentioned made it easier for a prisoner convicted by a state court to file such a petition in a federal court to review the fairness of the procedures in his case.

Shapiro: In addition to the petition for the writ, the lawyer actually prepares an order for the judge to sign if he agrees with it. This saves the time it would take the judge to dictate an order himself. Since a judge may be willing only to require the government to show cause why he should not issue the writ, the defense lawyer must prepare a proposed order saying that, too, and have both orders ready so that the judge can sign whichever he prefers.

Of course, in a death-row case, it is essential to get some judge to sign a temporary restraining order staying the execution until further order of the court.

Federal courts have the right to intervene in an execution if a federal question is involved, and, of course, federal questions are involved if any constitutional claim was made in any stage in the proceedings. The Constitution gives the federal courts the power to grant writs of habeas corpus.

My practical experience has been that it's exceedingly difficult to get habeas corpus except during working hours. You can find the governor or even a state supreme-court justice at night, but it's pretty hard to find a federal judge at night. What that means is that you have to stay up until you have prepared every paper you will need to take the case right up to the United States Supreme Court, assuming you get a denial each time. Then you'll be ready to go in the morning. You'll find that the federal courts are not reluctant to grant a stay of execution so that you can argue the legal questions raised in a petition for habeas corpus. You just have to convince the judge that you have a substantial legal question. He may not agree that the question justifies a reversal, but if he sees that it's a serious legal question he will sign what is called a certificate of probable cause. Then you're allowed to take the petition to the next higher court.

AFG: How would a new lawyer find out that he has to have that certificate?

Shapiro: If he's familiar with the Lawyers Guild, he can call one of the Guild lawyers. They would know the answer or how to get it.

The other major source of this kind of information is the clerks of the courts. They are generally most helpful, decent people.

AFG: They deserve a good deal of respect from lawyers. They will tell you truthfully everything they know. They will not tell you anything that is questionable. If you ask them, "Should I do this or that?" they won't tell you the answer, but they will give you enough information so that you can figure it out for yourself.

Shapiro: If you've never prepared a certificate of probable cause, for instance, you go down to the clerk's office and tell him what you need. He won't tell you how to fill it out, but he'll show you the file in a case that contains one.

Another way to find out how to draw up papers is from a form book. There are some excellent federal-practice form books. They are useful to tell you what you must put into pleadings, but they're written by unimaginative people and may even have bad grammar and bad writing. So just use them as an outline to get the idea.

You've got to persuade a judge that something wrong happened, that some deprivation of due process of law occurred during the course of the proceedings. Now, it's easy to put these things together and have a speech for a judge, but many judges are not going to accept your word for it. So you must have a transcript of the trial, marked.

AFG: In a habeas case you often have to show there was unfairness that the defendant's trial lawyer should have mentioned in the trial or the appeal. So you really have to show that the trial lawyer made a mistake that resulted in denial of the defendant's right to *effective* assistance of counsel, a constitutional right.

Shapiro: Lawyers face this problem all the time. As a trial lawyer you have to be willing to sacrifice your own personal pride. You have to turn the case over to somebody who either is more capable or has a fresher view, or will attack you in order to win. I've had this happen to me, and I've attacked other lawyers. The last death-row case I got was like that. The lawyer was one of the best trial lawyers in California, but he did an incompetent job. I wrote and told him that I was doing this and apologized, but there was no question in my mind that I had a duty to do it. If I did a poor job I would have no hesitancy about saying to another lawyer, "Look, attack me as incompetent for what I did." But it takes a different lawyer; I couldn't attack myself.

Okay. Let's assume that the federal district judge denies your petition for habeas or will not sign the order to show cause, or will sign the order but not the stay of execution. That's no help; an order to show cause after your client has been executed doesn't do very much good as far as he's concerned, although it may establish a very interesting legal point in the next case.

AFG: What if the judge says, "I have to think about this"? He won't grant it, and he won't deny it in writing.

Shapiro: You have to file a notice of appeal to the next higher court anyway.

There are district-court judges, particularly in the South, who do not want to go on record as executing somebody, but who are not willing to grant a writ either. When that happens, I would suggest that you just take your habeas papers and trot up to a circuit judge of the United States Court of Appeals.

AFG: How about going to another district-court judge, if there were several in the town?

Shapiro: If the second judge didn't know that the first judge had turned you down I suppose you could get away with it. But don't get caught at it, because judge-shopping is one of the sins judges hate the most. In most California districts, there's also a practical problem that makes judge-shopping very difficult. The judges rotate at sitting in the law and motion department, and these petitions come before that department. Whichever judge is having his turn there at the time your case comes up is the judge you'll get.

Student: Suppose you can't get in to see the judge—he's in court in the middle of another case.

Shapiro: Under those circumstances you go to the clerk. You tell him, "I've got three hours, and I have to see a judge." If it's crucial, the clerk will contact the courtroom clerk, who will pass the message up to the judge, who will call a recess.

AFG: I really want to emphasize that. Habeas corpus is called "the Great Writ." It's part of the Constitution—not the Bill of Rights, but the *body* of the Constitution. And everything Carl has said assumes that everyone in the legal system understands that. When you walk in with a petition for a writ of habeas corpus, you get treatment right now. Everybody does understand it, too. Even a very bad judge, if he does not take care of you immediately, knows perfectly well he is violating the basic constitutional law of this country. So you walk in with absolute self-confidence that they've got to stop what they are doing and pay attention to your case. If they don't, they are on the defensive and they know it.

Shapiro: Absolutely. Especially in a situation with a death penalty, where somebody is going to have on his shoulders the responsibility for executing a man if he doesn't act in time.

Student: Is it sometimes better to wait till the last minute so that the judges will feel more pressure?

Shapiro: But remember the price that you pay if it doesn't work. And you must realize that you don't have just one chance. You might have fifty chances.

AFG: Do you know how many times you can file a petition for habeas corpus? There is no limit.

Shapiro: Now, I'll tell you one of the things that does put pressure on a judge: the newspapers. One time George Davis and I were doing one of these last-minute death-row cases, and we were sweating out a judge of the U.S. Court of Appeals. George knew where the pressroom in that building was, and I knew where the library was, and I don't know which was more important. If you have newspaper reporters interested in your case, and they're sitting outside in the judge's waiting room while you're talking to the judge, you have somebody who's keeping that judge honest. He knows that what he does is promptly going to be put in the papers. This is a very important part of all political cases, especially these desperate last-minute things.

Student: How do you make sure the judge knows the reporters are out there?

Shapiro: Generally these things are done in the judge's chambers, not in the courtroom. So you mention to the judge that the reporters find this case awfully interesting, and would he mind if they wait out in the anteroom?

Remember the importance of the press. Have good contacts with the reporters in the courthouse, and give them good cases, tell them interesting things that are happening. I would never think of filing an interesting case without talking to the reporters about it, showing them the pleadings and so forth. If you can, you should have extra copies of your papers for the newspapers, so that they can get the names and details right. This is a practical asset you'll never find in the books.

So, now your time is really short, you're really under the gun, and you have to use one of your last resorts: a justice of the U.S.

Supreme Court. Each Supreme Court justice is assigned to a circuit, which usually includes several states. California's circuit
judge is Justice Douglas.

To reach Justice Douglas and get a stay of execution, there are
two ways of proceeding. One is to call a lawyer in Washington,
D.C., who will go see him. If you have time, of course, you would
go back yourself. But if you can't, you get a Washington colleague
to do it. He needs only the outline of the case and the points you
are making, which you can give him by phone. He doesn't have to
have the actual papers at this point. In fact, often in a capital case
a petition for a writ of certiorari or an earlier habeas-corpus
proceeding has already been brought before the Supreme Court, so
papers describing the case and previous appeals are already on file
in the clerk's office.

If you have a Washington connection who has enough status
and self-assurance to go see Justice Douglas over at the Court,
then that's the best approach, because a face-to-face confrontation
is very persuasive. This is when a political figure, especially if he's
a lawyer, can be a big help. Some prominent politician or legislator
has a far better chance of seeing a justice quickly and getting the
relief than somebody he has never heard of. And the lawyer will
probably also get more cooperation from the clerk and the court
personnel. That kind of a contact is a valuable asset.

Now, the other way to proceed is to reach Justice Douglas
yourself from here. One way is by phone. You call the Supreme
Court clerk and you explain the urgency and seriousness of your
case. That clerk has more respect for the importance of habeas
corpus than anyone else in the United States, and he will put you
right through to the proper justice. If Justice Douglas is off in Iran
in the wilderness (which happens not infrequently), another justice is assigned to this circuit. And it's amazing, you can reach a
justice of the U.S. Supreme Court by phone easier than you can
reach a municipal-court judge.

The other thing you can do is send a telegram, if there's time.
The advantages of a telegram are that it's in writing, it identifies
you and the case, and it's a permanent record. Again, you don't
have to file the habeas corpus papers or anything. A Supreme
Court justice can grant a stay of execution just on the basis of the
telegram or phone call.

Now, suppose Justice Douglas says, "This case has come before us three times, and you've got nothing new. I'm not going to interfere."

You've got nothing left except the governor of the state. You go back to him again and ask for a commutation or some other relief. You know, the governor of California, and I suspect it's true of every state, keeps a line open to the warden of the prison for an hour or two before any execution. And the warden is at his desk waiting for the governor to call.

You may have talked to the governor only eight hours ago, but now you have something new. You say, "Look, we can't get any relief in the courts, and we think we have a substantial question. If you don't give us some help, we'll never be able to raise it, and you're going to have the blood of this man on your shoulders."

So this is the last possible thing. While they're putting the man in the chair, you're calling the governor's office asking for a stay of execution. I've been through three governors, and I'll tell you the differences. When Pat Brown was governor it was possible to reach him personally and talk to him. With Reagan, you can talk only to his clemency secretary. When Knight was governor, all you could reach was the clemency secretary's secretary.

Even when it wasn't a last-minute plea there were differences between these governors. Under Knight, when you wanted to ask for clemency he said, "Write me a letter." So you wrote a letter. Then, generally speaking, his clemency secretary would call you up and say, "The governor has decided not to grant clemency." You never saw the governor or the secretary.

Pat Brown was opposed to the death penalty. His clemency secretary for a good period of time was Cecil Poole, who was not opposed to the death penalty, but who did a fabulous job. They held clemency hearings. I went to several of them, and I would bring witnesses and exhibits and put a regular case on. The governor had a summary of the case, and Cecil Poole knew more about the case than I did. He had read the transcripts carefully, had extracted from them the relevant things concerning clemency, had talked to witnesses, and often had talked to the defendant. He presented a report to the governor in the form of a book, which the governor read before the hearing. As a result, a large number of clemency petitions were granted.

Since Reagan has been governor, there has been only one execution and there have been two clemency hearings, one of which I handled. I got clemency from Reagan, but the hearing was an entirely different thing. In the first place, we all knew ahead of time that clemency was going to be granted.

Student: How did you know that?

Shapiro: Well, because Justice Douglas had already granted a stay of execution, and the governor's office called me and said, "We're going to have a clemency hearing regardless." So I knew they wouldn't have the hearing and *deny* clemency. The governor's secretary conducted the hearing, and it was purely pro forma.

AFG: Carl, tell us, why do you take these cases?

Shapiro: Well, I guess this is my way of fighting capital punishment.

AFG: And why does capital punishment matter?

Shapiro: It's the height of immorality for us to feel that we can officially, legally, and righteously take away somebody's life. There are so many things that you have to fight if you're going to be a lawyer. You have to be selective; you can't do everything. I was in Marin County, where San Quentin is, and that's where the executions take place. I got involved in death-row cases because there weren't very many people in the area who could do appellate work and were interested in this kind of case. I had some ability, some luck, or something, and I just kept doing it.

I agree that it's curing symptoms, not illnesses. The death penalty is only a symptom of a sick society. I'm not curing any of the ills by getting due process of law for people charged with murder, or getting cases reversed so they can be retried, or setting up better standards. I may be wasting my time, and I may not; I don't know.

But I do it and I enjoy it. Death cases have one big advantage: you can make better law in a death case, because there's more at stake. The same kind of substantive or procedural error might not be accepted by the court in a burglary case as a justification for making a new rule of law, but in a death case, where there is so much at stake, they might accept a smaller point.

I can take very few cases, because I have such limited facilities, practicing alone. I take one at a time now, and I've been doing a lot of draft work.

AFG: Tell about your draft-counseling service.

Shapiro: Well, we have a fascinating draft-counseling service that runs out of my office. We have regular draft counselors who come in two nights a week and see young men, and then we have a free legal clinic every Saturday morning. Any kid with a Selective Service problem can come in and talk to a lawyer about it. Until recently there were six of us, two lawyers and four counselors, and we were seeing around 150 kids a month. We don't do any publicity, and we don't have any committee backing us. Just a group of us did it. Of course, we're able to reach only some of the draft kids; we don't really reach very many. With more lawyers we'd be able to reach more.

Student: Many people I know have said that the Bay Area is tremendously overloaded with lawyers. You seem to be saying there's room for more.

Shapiro: Well, I don't think *any* area is overloaded with lawyers. It's the same old thing—there's underconsumption of lawyers. I do think it's easier for a person who wants his own practice to start out in a small town than in a city. For one thing, when there are only two or three other lawyers in town you're bound to get some of their clients who don't like them. Or they may not do trial work or criminal work, so you get those cases. In the city, there are so many other firms to turn to, you can't expect clients to come wandering in.

I was in a firm in the city at one time where the whole practice came from the publicity we got in the newspapers. Clients would line up, because my partner was one of the most flamboyant and best lawyers in San Francisco, and still is. However, that's a very unusual situation; it applies to only a few firms. Studies have shown that 75 or 80 percent of the people select their lawyers by going to a friend or being referred to one. If you go into private practice, you learn that whether you like it or not you'd better do a good job for your client, because you depend on him not only for a fee but also for referrals.

They don't teach you these things in law school, of course. It's the most ridiculous thing. You go through three years of law school, and when you come out and a client walks in your door, you have no idea what to do. It really gets me angry. What kind of a school is it that doesn't teach you what you have to know?

The worst thing that ever happened to law school in this country was the philosophy of a guy named Langdell, who was the dean of Harvard Law School. He developed the case system. That's the most inefficient way of teaching law in the world. They make you read thirty pages of gibberish in order to get one sentence of legal principle out of it. What other field of endeavor would make you do that?

Student: Yeah, why do they do that? About 85 percent of the stuff I read the first year seemed irrelevant.

Shapiro: Of course it is. The theory was that if you read cases you would learn how to analyze cases, so that you could then analyze your own case when you were up on appeal.

Student: I don't think that's true at all, though.

Shapiro: It isn't, but this was the theory. Did you ever go to the library in Harvard Law School? It's unbelievable. I was going to go to Harvard Law School, I had been admitted and made arrangements to go, and then I went up there one day and looked at that library. There were all these kids with eyeshades on sitting there, and nobody looked up—ever. I think they must be there still.

Student: You go to the library in Boalt Hall these days, and nobody's there.

Shapiro: I went to law school at Boalt Hall for one year. I hated it. When I was there, at the tail end of the thirties, it was a little tiny building. There were about 250 students in the whole school. And I hated it with such a passion that for the last month or so I never went to class. I couldn't stand the fact that law school was so encompassing; these kids I was going to school with ate, drank, slept, and smoked law. They couldn't break away from it. To me it wasn't that important or meaningful at that time. So I took the final exams and just quit. Ten years later I went back to law school.

AFG: I sometimes think the main reason I stayed in law school was that I thought the University of Michigan wouldn't want to have me as a graduate, and I was determined to get the best of them.

Where did you finish up, Carl?

Shapiro: University of San Francisco night school. I worked all day as a carpenter and drove over to the city at night to finish law school.

Night school is just a device to get permission to take the bar. Then you start to learn the law. Abe Lincoln learned how to be a lawyer by working in a law office, and that's the way it should be. Sure, it's important to know legal reasoning, but you don't teach it; a guy develops it if he has good attitudes and is bright enough to practice law. Not only that, if you teach legal reasoning you are teaching the preservation of things instead of change. So I'm all for the apprentice system.

Law school is changing now; the attitudes are changing. The modern generation is challenging these old ideas like the case system and the fact that you don't learn how to be a lawyer in law school. I had that experience myself. I figured you were supposed to be able to practice law after you graduated and passed the bar. So I opened an office, and a week later a guy came in who was being sued, and I didn't have any idea what to do. I was lucky I had some friends to help me.

AFG: You practice alone now, right?

Shapiro: Yes. But my wife and daughter work in my office. For a while my wife was the only secretary I had. Now she works in the office part of the time and goes to law school part time. My daughter works in the office three days a week, and she is going to law school, too.

I've been doing it for twenty years, and fourteen have been in small-town practice. I make a living, always have and always will, but I'll never get rich at it. Small-town practice is to me a very satisfying thing, but it's hopelessly outdated. It's the most unbelievably inefficient way to practice. My library costs me $200 a month for the rest of my life, but I have to have it to practice law. If I had five partners we'd each be paying $35 a month instead of $200. If I were in the city I'd probably be able to use the public law library.

The second thing about small-town practice is that you have to do cases that an expert could do better. You have to be able to handle everything that comes in. It's a very difficult way to practice, but a very satisfying way. In a small town, everybody knows all about you—how much you charge, what kind of a person you are, what kind of a lawyer you are, how easy you are to see, and so forth.

Now, when I was in San Francisco, we never saw a client a second time. They came in because they had a case, and they wanted our firm because we were well known; we did the one case, and that was all. In Marin I see clients I've had for twenty years. I see their children.

There aren't very many small-town practices left. The small-town lawyer fills a funny role in the community: he and the local priest do the things that the small-town doctor and policeman used to do. In other words, they are the town counselors. The policemen in these towns now are professional policemen; they are no longer part of the community, they're against the community. The small-town doctor, the general practitioner, is gone. So the people have only two places to turn—to their minister and the local attorney.

Student: Do you feel that the role of an attorney is expanding generally, not just in small towns?

Shapiro: Oh, yes. Law has changed significantly in the last five or seven years. The OEO programs have made a tremendous difference in the practice of law. They've made it possible for people to have lawyers without paying fees. But they also made for a different kind of law practice, in which the lawyers are part of the community rather than just limiting themselves to court matters.

Before the OEO started, a person coming out of law school, passing the bar, had a choice of opening an office, in which case he was a slave of the system, or working for one of the big firms, in which case he couldn't do anything meaningful, or working for the district attorney's office or the public defender's office, in which case he was a wage slave with so much to do and so many hours to do it in. Law was just like driving a taxi—it was just a job to bring in an income. Now it's very possible to do a meaningful thing. You're out in the neighborhood, doing things that are challenging, working with people, and you don't have the problem of extracting money from them for your services. The doctor under socialized medicine is a lot more free to do interesting things medically and personally than the doctor under our system who has to worry about whether his patient has insurance, is going to pay the bill, or is going to come back.

And the second big difference in law today is that a lot of these young people have brought imagination to law. There are new ideas in the law, new concepts about kinds of cases, and a lot of the rigidities are gone. It has pushed us older practitioners along, too. We have to do things better.

The level of practice today in San Francisco is probably higher than anyplace in the country except maybe New York and Miami.

Student: Why Miami?

Shapiro: Oh, a lot of bright lawyers have gone down there, and they have just raised the level of practice. They probably do better personal-injury work down in Miami than anyplace in the country. When I talk about new ideas, I don't mean just political ideas, but techniques for all kinds of cases. For instance, a Miami firm developed a technique for wrongful death actions. An action for the death of a housewife as a result of a wrongful injury used to get maybe a $12,000, $15,000 recovery. These lawyers came along and listed what a woman does that's useful around the house. And then they figured it out: To hire a woman to do the cooking would cost this much, to hire a nursemaid would cost this much, and they analyzed all the jobs and what it cost to do these things with paid employees. They were able to raise the level of recovery to about $120,000.

AFG: Remember that, the next time someone says housework is valueless work.

Shapiro: In San Francisco I see young fellows like Mike Kennedy and Dennis Roberts who have been involved in political work and community practice going into private practice now and bringing to it the same philosophies that they had in group practice. So I think the practice of law is becoming far more meaningful, just as a matter of protecting people's rights.

AFG: I think radical lawyers take a different approach to litigation than traditional lawyers, regardless of generations. We try to go on the offensive to defend the rights of the people and the Bill of Rights. One important technique was refined by Arthur Kinoy, who practices constitutional law and teaches at Rutgers. The U.S. Supreme Court bought his argument in *Dombrowski v. Pfister* in 1965 that a person should not have to wait around in fear of being prosecuted under a state or federal law if the law is clearly unconstitutional. He can sue and challenge the statute instead of getting arrested and tried and convicted and then hoping some appellate court will declare the law void. Dennis Roberts worked with Arthur in the Center for Constitutional Rights in New York, and he explained how widely this *Dombrowski* theory could be used against statutes whose very existence has a "chilling effect" on the exercise of free speech and other First Amendment rights by people seeking social change.

Student: Do you think the Court, with its new Nixon appointees, will continue to follow *Dombrowski?*

AFG: I think they certainly should. It is a clear statement of the spirit of the people who wrote the First Amendment after the American Revolution.

Shapiro: You see, minority people now, or so-called minority people—the blacks, the Chicanos, the women—are all conscious of the discrimination, social, political, and economic, that they have to fight. In fighting it they come in conflict with the law, which is the whole establishment. And the kids, the hippies or far-out kids, the ones who have their own life styles, are also challenging the establishment. So with all these challenges the establishment is becoming more and more repressive. The role of the lawyer in protecting these people is more important. And the role of the lawyer protecting the establishment has also become important. The district attorneys and U.S. attorneys have become better, too—don't fool yourself. They're hiring brighter guys who are more determined. They concentrate more on political issues. So the whole practice of law has become more meaningful.

As I said, it means enough to my family so that my wife and daughter want to do it now. It's a part of my life, a meaningful part and a full-time job. The more time you have, the better you can do. The really sad thing about getting older is that you lose your energy. I find that it's much more difficult. I can't work at night, as I used to. I work weekends. But when you're practicing law, if you're doing anything meaningful, you're not through at five o'clock, because then you have to see clients till eight o'clock or do a brief or something. You can't do a brief during the daytime. The research that is required to put together an appellate brief has to be done at night.

But you see very few lawyers quitting the practice of law for something else. It's meaningful if you want it to be meaningful. If it is to your liking you can do well. Over the years, you'll see some of your cases in the case books, and you'll cite your own cases. It's a very satisfying thing to be able to cite a case in which you persuaded the Supreme Court to decide and establish a principle of law.

When I was a carpenter I used to get a great deal of satisfaction driving around and seeing buildings I had built. It's the same thing for a lawyer when he reads a case book and says, "My God, that's my case!"

WHAT LIES AHEAD
Ann Fagan Ginger

The lawyers in this book concentrated on describing their present role in representing political clients and working on social questions. They spent some time analyzing their past experiences to give perspective. They spent less time analyzing the nature of their opposition today, and only a few minutes on problems and possibilities in the future.

The outlines of the politics of the 1970s are not yet entirely clear. It is obvious, however, that middle America will be chided and sweet-talked into forgetting democratic traditions in the name of saving the taxpayers' money. Liberal lawyers and professionals will be told to sacrifice tradition to gain "efficiency in the administration of justice." Americans will be Agnewed to fight the old "Communist menace" and the "new-left, hippie bombardiers." The unspoken fear of the poor, of the black, brown, red, and yellow—and of liberated women—will be brought into the open and made respectable if one section of the establishment has its way.

There is an effort to tighten the screws on labor, with the wage freeze added to the ninety-day cooling-off period during strikes. There is increased repression against blacks, students, and generally throughout the society in response to the rising chorus of demands for change in the face of an economic recession. There is increased monopolization of power in the Pentagon and the conglomerates, higher appropriations for the enforcement of "law and order," and growing opposition to spending for "social welfare."

Many lawyers and political clients talk about the danger of fascism in the United States. They define fascism as the takeover of government by powerful business interests who use open violence to suppress citizens and seek domination over other countries in order to insure their continued power and wealth. Mary Kaufman has described briefly how this system worked in Nazi Germany. People disagree on the likelihood of an open shift to fascism here, but everyone agrees that there are efforts to turn this country sharply to the right.

Certainly some leading establishment lawyers are busy attacking most of the specific *due-process* protections developed through English and American history, described in the introduction. Nixon, his Attorney General, his Chief Justice, congressional spokesmen, and leaders of the American Bar Association peck away at jury trial in civil cases. It should be replaced by arbitration, they say; twelve-member juries should be cut to six or eight; the lawyer should not be able to question jurors before they are accepted for duty to see whether they are biased; the jury should not have to reach a unanimous verdict so it can be "hung" by one dissenting vote. They maintain that some wiretapping and other forms of search and seizure should be permitted; that the right of privacy does not extend to welfare recipients; that preventive detention without trial is necessary for "dangerous criminals"; that the privilege against self-incrimination can be emasculated; that lawyers should be kept in line as officers of the court; and that their primary duty to their clients must be submerged when the clients disagree with the system. These forces in the establishment cannot accept a situation in which large numbers of people don't stay quietly in jail. Some get bailed out; others actually get acquitted by juries or win new trials from appellate courts. The ones sent to prison demand fair treatment there.

Powerful forces are attacking the broad concepts embodied in the First and Fourteenth Amendments. They say *freedom of expression* should be limited by the need for "law and order." The right of labor unions to achieve their goals through demonstrations and strikes should be replaced by appeals to administrative boards and compulsory arbitration. Federal funds should be used to bus children to private, religious schools but not to public, integrated schools. They say *equal protection* does not require federal funds for housing or employment when equality really requires integration. This segment of the establishment faces objections from its own class, from Congress, and from some parts of the business community and the legal profession.

It also faces objections from all parts of the movement the people have been building in the last decade. If this segment is successful in moving society backward, the people will have much more difficulty in making the steps forward they require: stopping the use of U.S. military force abroad, prohibiting racist and sexist practices, achieving full employment with an end to inflation and poverty, and improving the quality of life.

The people also demand continuation of the liberties now guaranteed but denied them, and expansion of their basic rights. They are talking about the right to eat, for example, and the right to live. Can these be read into law and enforced in the courts? The Universal Declaration of Human Rights of the United Nations pointed in this direction in 1948, but the U.S. has not yet followed its lead.

In the face of these conflicting forces, it would be very comforting to know what lies ahead, whether counterrevolution, revolution, or a long period of inconclusive struggle. The lawyer is lucky, however. He can do effective work without knowing what time it is politically. Even if Elson is right about his own inability to tell the time correctly, he and other lawyers can be relevant by just letting people know they will take significant cases. They will have an endless stream of clients seeking specific assistance on specific cases and causes, and they can get some satisfaction from helping them. A progressive lawyer's major problem is to avoid inundation. Somehow he must keep moving forward—in the face of firsthand knowledge of the enormity of the injustices in society and recognition of his finite resources to challenge them.

The lawyer has a role to play, whether we are moving forward or struggling not to move backward. In either event he must use the three big concepts of freedom, justice, and equality in the First, Fifth, and Fourteenth Amendments, and must hug close the people who are struggling with him.

Arthur Kinoy, professor and practitioner, deals with this question in Marxian terms in his chapter in *Law Against the People* (1971). He argues that the lawyer's classic role in maintaining the bourgeois-democratic rights won in the struggle between feudalism and capitalism gives a modern radical lawyer a specific role. At a time when some forces in the establishment seek to erase the system of bourgeois democracy as a form of domination by the governing circles, and to replace it with open terrorist dictatorship, he says that the lawyer and client who understand the dynamics of the period can become the masters, rather than the victims, of the contradictions.

One way to figure out, in specific terms, what lawyers should do in the future to be relevant to the movement for social change is to notice what the movement people ask of lawyers. They want lawyers to give accurate advice on the alternatives open to them as they plan their tactics, to represent them in court, to explain the law to organizations engaged in particular campaigns, and to explain their struggle to the public in terms of the Bill of Rights.

The job of the lawyer is to know all of the legal tools, to show clients and their organizations ways they can use these tools in various trials and hearings, and to act as their counsel. Lawyers should be sensitive to shifts in the political climate that require changes in legal tactics. When the President appoints judges who reject the protections of liberty in the Constitution and the Bill of Rights and pretend that these documents protect only property interests, the judicial arena will not answer the people's needs. When the Burger Court erodes the human-rights decisions of the Warren Court, lawyers may need to retrace their footsteps. They may do more for their clients by going to the legislative halls to lobby than by going to federal court to file suit. Of course, Congress will have to reassert its authority as the representative voice of the people before we will see any significant legislative action. Stender and Burnstein talked a little here about the legislative process, and George discussed what his campaign for Congress cost and accomplished. Margolis described the extent of change possible solely through changing the present tax laws, to a return to the democratic concept of taxing the income of the rich to support social progress, and lifting the weight of taxation from the rest of the people, which was the reason for adopting the income tax amendment in 1913.

There is also a need to work out a "radical" approach to political cases in general. For example, if a lawyer believes that the working class must move before the people can bring about any basic change in our society, should the lawyer represent unions, even if they exhibit racist and reactionary political attitudes? Are there radical ways to handle a draft case, as compared to liberal ways? Are there revolutionary, rather than reformist, ways to represent a prisoner? Can a struggle for reform lay the foundation for more basic change as people come to understand the need to get to the roots of a problem?

Maybe we need to list the traditional "public policy" rules now followed to see whether they still fit our commercial, industrial, mobile society, and whether they will help us build the society we need in the future. Do we really want to continue the rule that a person can be sued for damages if he gives the wrong kind of assistance to an injured person, but goes scot free if he leaves the victim unassisted? Or should we make first-aid instruction mandatory? Should we continue to justify the shooting to death of a person fleeing with stolen property? Should the buyer still have to beware except when Nader's Raiders or others push regulatory agencies into action? Should a corporation continue to be considered a "citizen" entitled to more due-process protections than a human being labeled "alien" or "Selective Service registrant" or "juvenile"? Is it time to require courts to scrutinize the economic factors in contracts between large corporations and individuals, such as leases and installment sales contracts?

There are also very practical questions: Should a lawyer charge different hourly rates to clients who are AWOL, sell dope, run porno movie houses, or are charged with ripping off crimes like embezzlement? Should a socially conscious woman lawyer become an expert on sexism and limit her practice to cases of discrimination, or combine such practice with broader work?

These questions sometimes come to the fore in the minds of movement lawyers in private practice, but busy lawyers have little time to ponder them fully or to reach final conclusions. This may be just as well, as any one of them is sufficiently complex to lead to endless pondering, inaction, or rejection of law practice.

Questions in the minds of the new breed of government and institutional lawyers are a little different. Do test cases really serve a useful purpose? Do lawyers for the poor and uneducated actually disarm the people they are trying to help? If a sound approach to social progress depends on building institutions run by the people struggling for greater power, how does the funding game fit in? Is there something basically unsound about federal and private groups funding new programs for two- or three-year periods and then shifting the funds to a new, hotter crisis area? Even if the lawyers and other professionals are shrewd enough to find berths in the new program, what happens to the clients left behind with an empty service office and unfulfilled plans? Can lawyers have any significant impact on poverty or its side effects on clients? Is poverty a permanent feature of capitalist America?

Brotsky and Van Bourg might ask a different question: Why was the establishment willing to fund legal-service programs for the poor after seeking to break up legal-service programs organized by unions? Van Bourg insists that the establishment knows that organizations of workers, however weak or corrupt, hold the key to constructive social change, and he hangs in there looking for a united front that will move society forward.

Each lawyer ultimately asks himself whether there are things he could do differently that would accomplish more for his clients, and society as a whole.

Just when the lawyer would like the time to ponder the answers to these questions, he finds himself confronted with several knotty, materialistic problems. His office income is going down as economic recession and automation hit more and more of his clients: a divorce action can be put off; it doesn't even pay to go through bankruptcy if one is broke enough; fewer workers are injured and entitled to workmen's compensation when the work force declines. His draft clients are dwindling and he doesn't know how to handle courts-martial at distant military bases. His paying dope clients may also evaporate if marijuana is legalized or possession is made into a minor offense. The lawyer's base in personal-injury work is threatened by proposals to change the system of compensation in automobile accident cases. If litigation is replaced by administrative procedures or arbitration to settle claims, clients will stop gambling on high recovery under the present system, and large attorney's fees will be out of order. The lawyer is also caught in the publication explosion, the impossibility of keeping up with developments in all of the fields of law necessary to handle a general practice. He is going to have to specialize more and learn to adapt some of the standardized forms to keep up with his clients' problems and meet his overhead. Somehow the people's lawyers have to gear up to conduct a fairly even struggle against the latest wiretapping, computerized, automatic-typewritered lawyers for the establishment.

While these problems have started to plague the conscientious progressive attorney, he can hear a rising demand for quality legal services at a workingman's price. The poor can go to OEO offices and sometimes get top-quality representation free. The well-to-do can go to Spring Street, Cadillac Tower, or midtown Manhattan. But when a workingman needs advice about a legal problem that involves a small amount of money, he has nowhere to go in the big city. (He can see a Carl Shapiro in some small towns.) He may be the decisive force in society according to Marxian theory, but he is the forgotten man in most law offices today. Meanwhile, his problems with the law have increased, and the inadequacy of preventive law is frightening. Lawyers spend days in court extricating clients from situations that would never have arisen if the clients had known their legal rights.

A worker can use "antilabor" laws to help a rank-and-file movement in his union, but when he goes on strike he faces the wage freeze and a Presidential back-to-work order for ninety days. When he wants to start a small business or cooperative to produce an item or provide a service, he must fill out a myriad of forms designed for large profit-making enterprises.

As individuals, working people need legal help just to get all their income-tax deductions, to mortgage their homes, to figure out child-support agreements, to write wills, and to help their children when they are arrested for dope or demonstrations. But they can't afford to pay $25 to $40 an hour for legal advice, and individual practitioners can't look up the answers and grind out the papers quickly enough to charge lower fees. Many employed people are willing to pay a regular monthly premium for advice on legal questions, just as they now pay for medical insurance, and they want the boss to pay a share, too. Political lawyers with practical experience in law-office administration should be able to set up good legal-service programs on a proper scale to avoid bureaucratic monstrosities that lose contact with the human beings who are clients. But such lawyers don't seem to be the people with entrée to foundation grants to study and plan such programs.

This group of problems is not probed in this book. Neither is the problem of training new political lawyers. The practitioners here, like their colleagues, just take a few pot shots at the inadequacy of legal education today. They have never found time to set up their own training programs for students and graduates. If Shapiro has his way, there will be an increase in apprenticeships. Others would like to establish schools in which the staff and the students represent real clients: the faculty consisting of experienced lawyers, legal secretaries, legal workers, investigators, law librarians, and bookkeepers; the students including everyone interested in becoming competent in any of these specialties; the clients bringing cases ranging across the legal spectrum.

Realistically, nothing can be done about legal education until the students discover that they are being short-changed by having inexperienced law graduates teach theoretical and clinical courses, and instead demand that seasoned political lawyers come out of their offices to become part-time professors. Together with professors like Thomas I. Emerson at Yale, these new law teachers and students can figure out how to reorganize part of law-school curriculum to focus on the legal problems most clients face today, while revamping establishment law courses to relate to contemporary Wall Street practice. A lawyer for the people can defeat a lawyer for the establishment only if he is fully aware of the law in its broadest sweep. He needs sharper tools than his opponent, because the burden of proof is always on the innovator. He needs a profound course in Social Interests instead of or in addition to Future Interests. The issues and conflicting claims of the parties are equally challenging in the two fields, but Social Interests touch the future ownership and development of the public sector, rather than the vesting of conflicting claims to Blackacre in the private sector.

Apparently lawyers are also going to have to address themselves to the need for a national political-legal defense organization, since they are most acutely aware of the present void. Fay Stender described a strong, single-purpose defense organization around a prisoner case; Ed Dawley explained why lawyers for another defense organization, the National Association for the Advancement of Colored People, would not join him in suits to desegregate the Norfolk courthouses in the early 1950s; while Carl Shapiro described the successful draft-counseling center established by lawyers in the more relaxed atmosphere of Marin County in the 1960s. Only Archie Brown could look back on the effective work of a national mass defense group, the International Labor Defense, in his trials in the 1930s.

These days it is as customary to write about the revolutionary overthrow of the government as it was forbidden to do so twenty years ago. The question in both periods is one of relevance. The lawyers in this book feel that something must be done about the flagrant violations of human rights they have observed in their own legal work, to say nothing of other inequities in society. But it has taken most of their waking hours for most of their professional lives just to do something about their individual clients' problems.

Practicing law helps a person deal with concrete facts and specific people in struggle situations. This frame of reference leads just this far at this time: no highly developed imperialist country has gone socialist so far. In other words, there has never been a basic change in the relations between the owners of the machinery and the people who work for a living in a country like ours. The last basic change in relations between the owners of property and the working people in this country occurred when the property known as slaves was freed. Before that, the Revolutionary War changed the property relations between American colonials and English imperialists. It seems worthwhile to study these events quite closely in order to understand why they occurred when they did and not sooner, who participated and who emigrated, how far they achieved their stated goals and why they did not go further, how long it took for the advances to touch everyone in the society. In other words, I disagree with Dawley's uncertainty about the value of studying history in order to participate in social change, and I recommend W. E. B. DuBois's *Black Reconstruction* (1935) to provoke deeper thinking on the nature of basic social change, and Loren Miller's *The Petitioners: The Story of the Supreme Court and the Negro* (1966).

It is enlightening to study the end of the capitalist system in Russia, China, and Cuba, and to watch the changes in Chile and Tanzania. Where the transfer of power has taken place, a new series of problems have come to the fore, including questions about how to achieve justice. Of course, Americans cannot look to others for a blueprint on making changes in the United States or on what changes to make.

All of the lawyers in this book allude to the inadequacies of the present system of operating this country. None of them explains exactly how to achieve a new society. That was not the subject matter of the Tom Paine School. Yet Mary Kaufman has tailored her professional work most closely and consciously to conform to her assessment of the political priorities in this country at each moment, and all of the lawyers seem to keep in close touch with the critical questions through their clients, when not through their own analysis.

Our present system is full of contradictions that are not yet obvious to many Americans. We have combined businesses run on the profit motive with charities run on moral principles. The human problems created by the former are supposed to be solved by the latter. As the population expands and the land mass remains the same size, this system is not meeting the needs of all the people. To see all the evils without seeing the cause or glimpsing a cure can lead to inaction and defeatism. Lawyers and others may have their hands full for some time just digging deeper into the contradictions between the present American way of making money and the necessary human way of living together.

Meanwhile Henry Elson suggests that we remember that the American legal system has some features of value in any society, and Ed Dawley thinks we should at least consider how to practice law now, since the revolution may not occur for some little time. (When activist Archie Brown was asked, "When's the revolution?" even he answered, "That's a question!")

These pages may not have sorted out all the multitude of forces constantly impinging on the lawyer seeking basic social change. I hope they do convey the sense of excitement of working in a political law office expressed by all of the speakers, the fun to be found in struggling for social change during working hours. This book is only a summary of where lawyers have gotten so far in their efforts to be relevant to the people's movements. It paints a realistic picture of many common problems and depicts solutions that worked sometimes. It raises some basic questions that it cannot answer. Its purpose is to help people who are already committed, and to encourage broader commitment, to building a legal system that is truly responsive to the needs of the people, while recognizing that any legal system is only a reflection of the fundamental relationships in a society.

Index of Cases and Statutes

441